GOING TO
THE WARS

ALSO BY MAX HASTINGS

Reportage
American 1968: The Fire this Time
Ulster 1969: The Struggle for Civil Rights
in Northern Ireland
The Battle for the Falklands (*with Simon Jenkins*)

Biography
Montrose: The King's Champion
Yoni: Hero of Entebbe

Military History
Bomber Command
The Battle of Britain (*with Len Deighton*)
Das Reich
Overlord
Victory in Europe
The Korean War

Countryside Writing
Outside Days
Scattered Shots

Anthology (edited)
The Oxford Book of Military Anecdotes

MAX HASTINGS

GOING to THE WARS

MACMILLAN

First published 2000 by Macmillan
an imprint of Macmillan Publishers Ltd
25 Eccleston Place, London SW1W 9NF
Basingstoke and Oxford
Associated companies throughout the world
www.macmillan.co.uk

ISBN 0 333 77104 4

Grateful acknowledgement is made to A. P. Watt on behalf of the
National Trust for Places of Historic Interest or Natural Beauty
for permission to quote an extract from Rudyard Kipling's
Arithmetic on the Frontier.

Extract from 'A Cock-Eyed Optimist', words and music by Richard
Rodgers and Oscar Hammerstein II, copyright © 1949, Williamson
Music International, USA, reproduced by permission of EMI Music
Publishing Ltd, London WC2H 0EA.

5 7 9 8 6

A CIP catalogue record for this book is available from
the British Library.

Typeset by SetSystems Ltd, Saffron Walden, Essex
Printed and bound in Great Britain by
Mackays of Chatham plc, Chatham, Kent

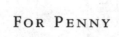

FOR PENNY

BARRY FANTONI

'Things must be bad, amigo. I think I just saw Max Hastings.'
The Times, 6 June 1983.

Contents

List of Maps and Illustrations

LIST OF MAPS AND ILLUSTRATIONS

Foreword

SOLDIERS AND JOURNALISTS make uneasy bedfellows. Members of any decent army, navy or air force are formed in a tradition of duty, discipline, honour, teamwork, sacrifice. Journalists are individualists, often even anarchists. Whoever heard of a successful reporter respectful of regulations and hierarchies? To the eye of your average regimental officer, correspondents are irresponsible, disloyal, undisciplined. Soldiers have to see things through to the end. Journalists almost never do. After the Falklands War, Captain Jeremy Black, RN, vented his disgust about the selfishness of the reporters he carried on his own ship, the carrier *Invincible*. Soldiers and sailors of all nationalities have echoed his sentiments through the ages. Kitchener's pithy remark about drunken swabs has passed into Fleet Street legend. The commanding officer of 2 Para, with whom I marched to the edge of Port Stanley in 1982 before the unit was ordered to halt and I went on alone in pursuit of a scoop, said afterwards that he would never take me on an operation again, because he thought my behaviour so irresponsible. I wasn't too impressed with him either.

Yet over the years, on battlefields all over the world, I have enjoyed encounters and made friendships with soldiers and sailors that I cherish, and which I think some of them, too, have gained pleasure from. My experiences among warriors have been among the most important of my life. On their side, it is compulsory to express disdain for publicity. Yet it is only natural for men who are risking their lives for their country to appreciate recognition. However much they dislike the media, commanders of Western armies have been obliged to acknowledge that soldiers in modern war want to know that their efforts and sacrifices are being reported at home. They need journalists to tell their story. I am one of those who has often been happy to do so, although this book also records plenty of occasions when I have caused trouble by wilfully disobeying or deceiving military authority in various parts of the world. That has been my job as a journalist and, to be honest, great fun too. Even when we admire soldiers, it is not our business to record their doings on their terms. Of course, I have often been frightened and run away. I have seen soldiers do some terrible things. I have also, however, seen them do fine and even great ones.

Until the last years of the twentieth century, warriors and heroes were almost synonymous. *Arma virumque cano* was a cliché. Young bloods in their hearts subscribed to Johnson's view, that 'every man thinks meanly of himself, for not having been a soldier'. Today, this is a wholly unfashionable view. I spent some of the most rewarding days of my young life not in being a soldier – or at least only briefly and without distinction, as I shall recount – but instead witnessing and recording the doings of soldiers, as a correspondent and later as a military historian. Few people in Britain today dislike soldiers, but most have never met any, creatures from another planet. I have known lots. Hollywood has created a myth of the modern soldier as psychopath, in silly films like *Platoon*. It is true that every army has its eager killers, and it is a matter of history that some of these served in Vietnam. But there are fewer than most movies suggest. I was among many fans of Spielberg's *Saving Private Ryan*, because for all that film's flaws its central character is exactly the sort of understated, decent officer struggling to do a tough job against the odds whom I have met on battlefields all over the world.

Some of my experiences with warriors have been droll, some dramatic, others merely absurd, which reflects more upon my trade than upon theirs. Over half a century after its publication, *Scoop* remains the definitive work on foreign correspondence. Schools of journalism might be taken more seriously by journalists if Evelyn Waugh was a set text. One of the limitations of the American newspaper business is that so few American journalists acknowledge our absurdities, or grasp the fact that reporters are only privileged spectators of the divine comedy. That does not mean we should not take our role seriously, but rather that we should never forget its huge, inherent shortcomings. So many American reporters, especially those who work for that vast suet pudding the *New York Times*, see their part in majestic, even heroic terms. British journalism remains rooted in a literary, rather than a political science, tradition, which helps to explain why it produces more and better jokes, if also more shameless fantasists.

Most soldiers – British ones, anyway – have a remarkably well-developed sense of comedy even on the battlefield, and are under few delusions about the follies which have made it necessary for them to fight. Every intelligent soldier goes to war knowing that the fact he must do so reflects political failure. Yet this does not prevent him from rejoicing in the chance of adventure, which is more often to be found at war than in peace. The very word 'adventure' sounds irresponsible and politically incorrect today, especially when coupled with conflict. I grew up believing adventure to be the proper purpose of any young man. My greatest fear as a boy was that

I would prove unequal to the chance, as indeed I often did. Nothing I have experienced can match the adventures of my parents' generation, who went through the Second World War. I recently read the war memoirs of a Scots Guards officer, Carol Mather. Mather joined the army from Cambridge at nineteen, in 1939. After a spell training with the French army's ski troops, he was posted to North Africa. He transferred to the fledgling SAS, and endured all manner of dramas in the desert before he was captured and imprisoned in Northern Italy. After escaping, he walked the length of the Apennines for two months with a fellow officer to reach the British lines. He spent the rest of the war as a liaison officer with Montgomery in North-West Europe. I quote his experience not because it was unique, but because it was not untypical. What are a few weeks in the Falklands or Vietnam or a Middle East war, to compare with years in the trenches in the First World War, or living as Mather did between 1939 and 1945?

Yet each generation must find adventures within its own compass. I feel wonderfully lucky that as a young man in my twenties, I was paid to travel the world and do exotic things in exotic places. It would be wrong to convey the impression that I was ever a full-time war correspondent, as were the great Alan Moorehead and many others in the Second World War, and their successors in Vietnam, Lebanon, Bosnia. As a roving 'fireman', I covered all sorts of assignments, most of which have no place in this tale – famines in Ethiopia, Yemen, Mauritania; crises in Greece, Egypt, South Africa, the United States; a coup in Grenada; tales from Brazil, Kenya, Sudan, the Seychelles, China and so on. I reported from more than sixty countries in all, for the London *Evening Standard* and BBC TV.

Yet this is a story only about my experience of conflict and armies. Observant readers will notice a slight lack of symmetry between my own behaviour and the fortitude and heroism –

often heroism – of the men whose doings I was reporting. It is almost impossible to write matter-of-factly about war, because it is the most moving of human experiences. Few reporters under fire fail to become emotionally engaged. Some find themselves identifying with the men whose trenches they share, as I did in the Falklands; the writing of others is dominated by their revulsion towards the excesses of their fellow men, like that of so many correspondents in Lebanon and Indochina. I have tried to check dates and events with my own files and with old colleagues. I am sure passages remain, however, in which memory has played me false – this is a bedside story, rather than a campaign history. It is not a narrative of what happened to Ulster, or Vietnam, or the Middle East, or even the Falklands, but merely a tale of what happened to me, as a journalist, in those places. It has been a delight to write, because few things are nicer than to recall in middle age, warmth and tranquillity, past moments of youth, discomfort and fear.

I owe a debt to my family, who put up with so much while I was on assignment abroad. On battlefields, I thought a lot about my wife and children, but it never occurred to me for a moment that my parents might be concerned about my fate, or even that they had any rights in the matter. It was my life, for heaven's sake. But now that I am a parent myself, forever worried to death about my offspring, I understand what my own parents went through, and how selfish I was, as all children are. Belated apologies are due, not least to my mother, Anne Scott-James, from whom I have probably inherited a good measure of whatever qualities have enabled me to bluff my way through the newspaper business all these years.

Charles Wintour, for so long the *Evening Standard*'s greatest editor, gave me marvellous opportunities as a very young reporter, for which I owe him more than I can say. I am also indebted to a host of old colleagues and soldiers of many countries who put up with me on the battlefield, and whose companionship warmed my heart more than any camp fire. I should mention especially Will Aaron, who directed many of my films for BBC TV's *24 Hours* and *Midweek*, together with fellow writing journalists such as Simon Winchester, Colin Smith, John Clare, Robert Fox, Richard Johns, Stewart Dalby, the late and great Nicholas Tomalin. I am indebted to far too many soldiers and sailors to name them here, but I must pay special tribute to Michael Rose, Nick Vaux and Jeremy Larken from the South Atlantic War. I love and revere them all – and cherish our shared memories.

MAX HASTINGS
HAYWARD HOUSE, BERKSHIRE
NOVEMBER 1999

CHAPTER ONE

Tarnished Wings

THIS IS A story about soldiers, and about my experiences reporting their doings. I had better begin by admitting as much of the truth as I can remember after all this time, about my first love affair with the British army, and its ignominious ending. I grew up steeped in the romance of soldiers. Nanny pushed my pram across Hyde Park in the days when clusters of Guardsmen sat on the grass with their rifles every summer morning practising the naming of parts, and as a child I leaned out eagerly to watch them, between annual pilgrimages to the Royal Tournament. In Coronation year, 1953, when the park became a vast tented encampment for the procession, at the age of seven I was thrilled to be taken around the horse lines by a glittering cavalry officer nanny and I met in Rotten Row. The nursery songs of the period were still much influenced by relatively recent military history.

> *Goodbye, Dolly, I must leave you,*
> *Though it breaks my heart to go,*

was among nanny's favourite ditties from the Boer War, which she remembered with some enthusiasm. We heard plenty of 'Come to the cookhouse door, boys,' and of course a rich assortment of First World War musical fare in the bath, or even sometimes, more eccentrically, on top of the bus:

> *Pack up your troubles in your old kitbag,*
> *And smile, boys, smile.*

Though my father had not been a soldier, like most of his generation his colloquialisms showed a marked military influence: 'Ease springs,' 'Reveille at seven,' 'Steady, the Buffs.' I must have read my first book about warriors when I was seven or eight, and after that I never looked back. G. A. Henty, C. S. Forester, Conan Doyle's Napoleonic romances, John Masters' *Bugles and a Tiger* – that most charming of all Gurkha memoirs – followed in their season, before I immersed myself in an endless succession of books about the Second World War which appeared in such profusion in my childhood: *Boldness be My Friend, Immortal Sergeant, Cockleshell Heroes, Escape or Die, The Cruel Sea, The Young Lions, The Naked Island, Bomber Pilot, Enemy Coast Ahead, Dawn of D-Day, The Colditz Story, The Last Enemy* – some were classics, many were rubbish, but I devoured them all, in my teens at the rate of one or two a week. In those pre-video days, I could not match the modern habit of Nicholas Soames, who claims never to go away for the weekend without copies of *Zulu* and *The Dam Busters* in his suitcase, in case he finds himself in a house so depraved as not to possess them, but I felt the same way. Like many boys of my generation, I could almost have flown a Lancaster, certainly have stripped a Bren gun or driven a Sherman tank, merely from a vast accumulation of second-hand knowledge.

I read Winston Churchill's *My Early Life* when I was thirteen. His wonderful tale of adventure in India, Sudan and South Africa has remained my favourite book ever since. The very names woven into his pages echo like trumpet calls – Sir

Bindon Blood, the Malakand Field Force, the Guards Camel Corps. Who could resist that peerless passage about his experience with the 21st Lancers at Omdurman? 'In one respect, a cavalry charge is very like ordinary life. So long as you are all right, firmly in your saddle, your horse in hand, and well armed, lots of enemies will give you a wide berth. But as soon as you have lost a stirrup, have a rein cut, have dropped your weapon, are wounded, or your horse is wounded, then is the moment when from all quarters enemies rush upon you.'

My father encouraged me to regard history as a glorious procession of agricultural advances in the English countryside matched by triumphs on the battlefield over lesser races such as the French. 'Turnip' Townsend and Coke of Norfolk vied for primacy in the Hastings family pantheon with Wolfe and Wellington: 'Up, Guards, and at 'em!' Like most of his generation, father possessed a large fund of war reminiscences, some possibly founded in fact. He liked to say that when captured Wehrmacht officers strutted extravagantly in prisoner-of-war cages, it proved efficacious to remove their jackboots. He recalled with relish the ruin of the German army in the Falaise Gap. He cherished the hotel room key from a night in the London Blitz when he returned to find the building flattened. Father was war correspondent of *Picture Post*, the legendary magazine of the period, of which my mother was women's editor. He published in 1941 a book of his dispatches based on experience with all three services, under the wry title *Passed as Censored*. It was dedicated 'To the Censor – in the hope that our association may soon be discontinued.' Reading the book in my teens, I put it to father that flying bomber operations against the *Scharnhorst* – for instance – must have been rather less of a boys' own adventure than his account for *Picture Post* made it sound. He answered, 'We were at war, for God's sake. What I was writing was part of the British war effort.'

In my childhood the house was littered with cherished detritus of that experience – military maps, webbing, German pistols, photographs of father in Normandy looking as if he was enjoying himself enormously. Years later, I was touched to receive a letter from an old Green Howard who had been his escort officer on the battlefield: 'your father always simply wanted to get as far forward as he could'. He tried a parachute jump in company with my great-uncle Lewis – Major Lewis Hastings MC, Military Correspondent of the BBC in the Second War – to whom he was devoted. Lewis was over sixty at the time, but quite untroubled by parachuting, which he regarded as a poor substitute for taking more active personal measures against the Germans, as he did during the Kaiser's War, in which he served as a trooper in the Imperial Light Horse in South-West Africa before taking a commission in the Royal Field Artillery, with whom he was badly gassed. Lewis was too cultured a figure to be entirely comparable with Nancy Mitford's Uncle Matthew, who preserved over his fireplace the entrenching tool, still matted with hair and blood, with which he had whacked eight Germans to death one by one as they came out of a dugout in 1916, but we are in entrenching-tool territory here. Lewis's son Stephen, my cousin, served in the Scots Guards and won an MC with the SAS in the desert, before joining the partisans in Northern Italy. My mother's father also gained an MC as a First War gunner in Flanders. For most of his life he was a literary critic. Yet it is in the uniform of a gunner officer that his framed photograph still sits in my house today. How I should love to have done anything in my life worthy of an MC! I am afraid that for years I undervalued the huge gifts of my stepfather, the artist Osbert Lancaster, partly because Osbert seemed not to have done anything very military between 1939 and 1945. I caught a glimpse of the bleaker reality of twentieth-century war, however, when browsing through the family archive one day. I came upon the sad letters from France written by Lewis's brother Aubrey, whose loathing and fear of his predicament in the trenches as a young subaltern with the East Surreys were scored through every line. He begged my grandfather, a well-known playwright at the time, to pull any string to help him wangle a transfer to the Royal Flying Corps, which Aubrey thought sounded a cushier billet. Poor unhappy man, he was killed at Loos in November 1915.

These experiences and connections mirror those of countless English middle-class families through the twentieth century. Most people possessed first- or second-hand knowledge of the soldier's life. Few veterans wished to repeat their own experience, or to see their children emulate it. In my childhood, there was evidence everywhere of the recent scars of war, from farm labourers driving their tractors in old battledress blouses and berets to decaying service buildings and tangles of barbed wire, yawning bomb-sites even alongside our home in Rutland Gate. Limbless ex-servicemen, victims of the First World War, remained familiar figures on the streets of most cities, with their accordions and banjos and collecting boxes. In Britain in the 1950s and 1960s, successful warriors were celebrities. I knew a big landowner who allowed his estate to be ruined by the management of a wartime comrade, whose stewardship he defended with the simple, if agriculturally irrelevant, assertion, 'I will trust to the grave any man who possesses three Military Crosses.' Most children, including me, collected toy soldiers avidly. The services were acknowledged as a perfectly respectable career choice. Every public school possessed its cadet force which almost every boy was compelled to join, to spend at least an afternoon a week engaged in military training. In the event of war, a former cadet's accent and his training certificates were supposed to ensure him a commission.

Yet it was one thing for boys to enjoy reading war stories, quite another to expect them in peace to endure the bull and drill and tedium of military training during precious school spare time. At Charterhouse in the early sixties, 'the corps' was almost universally detested. Anyone barmy enough to be keen was dismissed as a 'corps fiend'. My turn-out was never smart enough to qualify me as a corps fiend, and my lifelong inability to co-ordinate the movement of arms and feet handicapped me as a convincing marcher. But I compensated by devoting myself to the rougher side of the business. I adored map reading, bivouacking, weapon training, night exercises. Everybody had to attend a week-long camp in the Black Mountains once during their school careers. Most boys turned up reluctantly. Some resorted to fantastic expedients to get out of camp. I went four times, and loved every moment of those days on the hills, often lost with a section, almost invariably soaked to the skin, struggling to keep a solid-fuel cooker alight amid a half-gale in the bracken. One always felt so wonderful when it was over. I was perhaps the only human being in history to relish living on 'compo' – the British army's tinned composite rations. I even loved compo biscuit. I became addicted to the clash of breech-blocks, the scent of wood smoke from a camp fire, and have remained so all my life. The only distinction I achieved at Charterhouse was to become a sergeant-major in the corps, in my last term when our house also won the platoon tactical competition, to the chagrin of my fervently anti-militaristic housemaster. Crawling through the gorse of Hankley Common with a Sten gun – a perfectly normal fashion accessory for a schoolboy in the early 1960s – I rejoiced in fantasies of Norman hedges and Malayan jungles while every other cadet around me was thinking only about getting back to the house for tea and shedding those detested green drab denims.

My enthusiasm was tempered by occasional brushes with reality. Father took me as a fifteen-year-old to Jersey, where he was making a television film. In the pub with the crew one night, I was expounding loudly about military glory. The assistant cameraman lost his temper. 'You wouldn't talk such unspeakable balls if you'd gone out with a patrol in Korea which left the lines with thirty men and came back with seventeen. If you had the slightest, tiniest effing clue what a war is like, what utter bloody misery it is from day one to the bloody end, you'd never open your mouth again.' I was cowed by the authentic voice of experience, though in my heart I was not persuaded that it need be like that for everyone.

Yet as I wondered what to do with my life and, yes, whether I should try to become a professional soldier, I was conscious of a considerable obstacle in the path of glory. I was a coward. *The Anatomy of Courage* was among my early reading, and I have always accepted Lord Moran's view that courage is capital and not income, a quality of which each man possesses a varying and expendable amount. I knew how slender was my own balance. At school, I was not merely an incompetent and clumsy games player, but also a notoriously passive one: 'For God's sake, Hastings, get in there!' 'Go on, Hastings – go for the ball as if you mean it!' 'Don't just stand there as if you're frightened of the man!' But I did, because I was. At home I lingered for hours over the pages of my father's tales of his own assignments – riding the Cresta Run, being cast away on a desert island, making a submarine escape, crossing the Kalahari. I was horribly sure that I could never do these things. An attempt to escape an afternoon rest in my bedroom by leaping deftly from a first-floor window at the age of seven foundered in anticlimax when I merely twisted my ankle rather nastily and sobbed for hours. Faced with either moral or physical difficulties, my instinct was always to flee. Indeed, I achieved the worst of all worlds, by frequently threatening to run away from school, while never summoning the nerve actually to do so. I read Eric Linklater's droll novel about a wartime Italian soldier. I sensed that like Private Angelo, I lacked the *dono di coraggio*. Forget about leading men out of a trench. If my courage was tested, would I be capable even of following others over the top?

I had to find out. In the summer of 1963 as I was preparing to leave school, the Parachute Regiment came up with an unusual offer. Its supply of former National Service officers was drying up. The regiment invited volunteers from Charterhouse and Wellington to undergo basic training and take the parachute course at Abingdon, with a view to becoming possible regular soldiers, more likely officers in 10 Para, the London Territorial battalion. Privately, hardly any of the boys who came forward had any intention of making soldiering a career. Most were tempted merely by the glamour of a chance to win parachute wings. Seven recruits from Wellington, seven from Charterhouse were nominated.

Through our last summer term, an amiable staff-sergeant from regimental HQ at Aldershot drove over to the school each week to coach us on the usual platoon weapons to a standard that should enable us to qualify for the pre-para course. We sweated over parts of the 36 grenade, 3.5 inch rocket launcher, 2 inch mortar. We practised assembling musketry order, loading Sten magazines, stripping the 7.62 mm rifle, Immediate Actions on the Bren: 'Gun stops. Magazine off. Cock gun. Check magazine. Magazine on . . .' I loved all this. I was much less happy, however, when time came for a weekend at Aldershot undergoing the pre-para 'confidence course'. Every kind of test I feared and loathed was there: jumping from platforms to seize ropes and swing across chasms, dropping down free-fall pulley slides and edging over rope bridges. Then, in teams, we

8

were sent over the assault course, to carry great baulks of timber over walls, under wire, through water against the clock. We staggered mud-caked, bruised, spent to the finish, and departed to the showers before being told the results. I tasted a brief moment of distinction, as one of only two in our batch who passed immediately. All the other public-school trainees had failed the weapon-training tests, which bored them profoundly. They were required to waste a good many hours being crammed to retake them. With hindsight, my illusory moment of glory resembled that of Guy Crouchback, in the early pages of Waugh's *Men at Arms*. Nemesis awaited. My housemaster, a Victorian pedant in outlook, wit and prose style, wrote in my final school report: 'I shall not say of him, as was said of Kipling, that all the good fairies came to his christening, and they were all drunk. I will merely say that many came, and none were quite sober.'

Our teenage batch met again on a sunny day in August, at No. 1 Parachute Training School, Abingdon, in Oxfordshire. The Charterhouse group was squadded in a 'stick' with a middle-aged TA major and a lone private soldier. A slightly built, good-natured regular lieutenant, David Herberts, had been sent down from regimental HQ to keep an eye on the public-school trainees. He did his best to smarten us up in those two weeks, and advanced our training with an orgy of practice on the small-arms range, where we were allowed to fire more pistol and sub-machine-gun ammunition than I ever loosed again under para auspices. We slipped into the daily routine. The army woke us in the barrack rooms, marched us to and from breakfast amid a large contingent of trainees drawn from our regular brethren, and then surrendered us to the gentler mercies of the Royal Air Force, whose personnel were the objects of much soldierly mockery for their late rising and carelessness in matters of dress. The course reflected a leisurely, painstaking approach to parachute training, taking a fortnight to cover ground which civilian skydivers now master in a morning, though our business was made somewhat more complicated by having to learn to jump among forty men leaving an aircraft, each burdened with a bulky parachute weapons container.

Our RAF sergeant instructor, Pete Keymer, was in the timeless, fatherly, Janet-and-John mould of service teachers. 'Now this morning, we're going to practise exiting from the aircraft. You will all sit yourselves in the mock fuselage you see before you, number one at the rear, number eight nearest the front. On the command "stand up!" you will stand up. You will then turn to your right or left to face the rear of the aircraft. On the command "Check equipment!" you will check the equipment of the man in front of you . . .' My troubles started early. When others rolled as they practised landings, I fell into a heap. When they sprang, I hopped. When they pulled on their front rigging lines, I somehow became entangled with the rear ones.

'Come on now, Hastings – a big bugger like you ought to be able to fly out of that aircraft like a bird, not fall out like my old grandma tripping over her washing!'

'Where did you get the idea, Hastings, that landing after a parachute descent is like dropping a load of old bricks on the cat?'

'Wake up, Number Three – you in the glasses! Stop looking as if you're auditioning for the Fairy Queen!'

We practised landings from the fan exit trainer, which released a man on a cable from a 40-foot platform to the ground at the same speed as a parachute descent. We learned to pack and fit the parachute weapons container which carried each man's equipment in action. We were taught to steer during the descent, suspended in harness from a 60-foot gantry.

And on Saturday night, we went to *Rigoletto* in Oxford, swaggering in our red berets and battledress with the blue Pegasus flashes – not that any girls seemed to notice. Uniforms of all kinds were commonplace in those days, and to cut a dash one needed to have something more than seventeen callow years inside them.

The following Monday we started balloon jumps at Weston-on-the-Green. Most men find these a bleaker ordeal than jumping from an aircraft, because the process is so cold-blooded. Our masters employed balloons because they thus had their pupils under closer control. All morning we sat on the grass watching others jump. Each stick mustered in turn to file into the cage. The urgent whine of the winch receded as the balloon rose on its cable until it was swaying gently 600 feet above Weston. Then, after a brief pause, a body hurtled forth, checked as the static line broke the twine restraining the parachute packing and jerked open the great canopy. An instructor on the ground shouted corrections through a megaphone as the pupil descended. 'Pull down on your lift webs! Feet together now! Knees bent! Head down – watch the ground!' Then the man was crumpling on to the grass, pulling in his collapsed canopy hand over hand according to the book, and walking towards the rest of us, grinning exultantly. 'Gor, it's better than sex!' shouted a world-weary cockney, with all the confidence of nineteen years spent learning a lot more about the world than we knew. Most of us were in no position to make the comparison.

Then it was our turn. Six of us stood clinging to the outer rail of the enclosed cage as we rose above Oxfordshire, with Sergeant Keymer (who later enjoyed a long and not inappropriate second career as a prison officer) showing off his best bedside manner. 'This is the easy bit, lads, the one you can boast about to all the girls afterwards. Piece of cake for any bloke as tall as you, Hastings. You've only got to step out of the door, and you're on the ground.' (God, not that dreary line again.) The sergeant lifted aside the rail securing the opening. 'Right, you're first, Hastings. Arms folded across your reserve. Just remember – don't *fall* out – *jump*. Ready? Go!'

I departed with more of a hop than a leap, propelled by that timeless spur which drives most of us to overcome repugnance about doing the unnatural: fear of the mockery of others. There were two or three brief seconds of uncontrolled precipitation, when I was conscious of my stomach still lingering above me in the balloon cage. Then there was a jerk, and I found myself swaying beneath the nylon canopy, gazing down upon a lush stretch of English countryside which I have never since passed without remembering the moment. Faces peered pinkly up from the grass below. Somebody was shouting instructions through a bullhorn, of which I grasped nothing. I merely peered around in gratitude and exhilaration as the ground rushed up to meet me with unseemly haste. I collapsed on to the turf, twisted and banged the release box to free my harness, and rose, half-winded, to gather the billowing folds of parachute fabric. The RAF officer in command ran over, seething. 'That is the most idiotic performance I have ever seen here. Don't you remember anything? You came down with your arms on your reserve and never touched your lift webs. You do that in a wind, and you'll be maimed or dead. Do that again here and you're off the course.' Crestfallen, I retreated to the company of the comrades. We replaced helmets with red berets and got somebody to take a triumphant little group photograph.

An aside: the fittest and most athletic man in our stick, a good friend from school named Chris Pope ('You want to see how you should be doing it, Hastings? Just roll like Pope,') made a characteristically perfect jump, save that he landed with his feet slightly parted. He wrenched his ankle, had to drop out of the course and return to qualify later. The moral, I have always thought, is that there is less to parachute training than meets the eye – certainly less than meets the eye of the RAF. Parachutists risk injury often, death seldom. 'Roman candles' are rare, and unlikely to be fatal, given that every man nowadays wears a reserve parachute. Luck is the decisive factor about who gets hurt. My conviction was strengthened years later as I read about the French experience at Dien Bien Phu, the battle that cost them Vietnam, in 1954. When they ran out of trained parachutists with whom to reinforce the embattled garrison, they dropped soldiers with no jump training at all. The casualty rate was identical with that for any other massed parachute operation.

The bus took us back to Abingdon. In the days which followed, between waiting hours for the wind to drop to an acceptable speed, we made one more balloon jump, then completed the course with five aircraft drops in progressively larger numbers, until at last our 'sticks' were leaping out of the big Beverley transports simultaneously from both side doors and the hold, the sky over Weston filled with long columns of swaying parachutists, each man successively releasing his weapons container after jumping, to allow it to hang from his harness on twenty feet of rope. If balloon jumping was a disturbingly silent pastime, the ritual of a massed drop from an aircraft cargo hold crammed with men and equipment was never less than noisy and spectacular. On the first short flight, I read *Kenilworth* to take my mind off the matter in hand, a lifelong habit, somewhat to the bemusement of a journalist accompanying the flight to report on the schoolboy trainees.

We rose clumsily from the canvas benches on an order bellowed by the RAF dispatcher over the roar of the engines, each man's chin poised a few inches behind the parachute pack of the one in front, peering intently at two lights above the rear door. 'Prepare to jump!' The red light came on. 'Stand-in-the-door!' The densely bunched files of men edged astern, the half-light of the hold thrown into bold relief by the brilliance of the summer sky streaming through the two open doors. Green light. A slap for No. 1 from the dispatcher. 'Go! Go! Go! Go!' I only remember one man in our detail making the terrible last-minute decision to refuse to jump – a regular army trainee. I don't know what happened to him. The columns of men shuffled rearwards with the stamping feet of the Seven Dwarfs going to work in a hurry until, suddenly, it was my turn to meet the door, the sky, a brief blast of slipstream, and then a wonderful quiet broken only by the rapidly fading drone of the aircraft. Look up, check canopy. Peer around for other parachutes. Release container legstrap (and if you don't do that first, you'll break your ankle by landing with the bloody thing tied to you). Release container chest clips. Pull down on lift webs. Steer as necessary to check drift. Take up landing position, knees slightly bent and boots in tight embrace, touch the ground and roll – yes, well done, Sergeant Keymer, I remember the drill much better now than on the day you taught it to me thirty-six years ago.

It's over. I am a parachutist. I can keep my red beret. I swell with pride, thinking of myself as the newest member of that awesome fraternity which dropped into Normandy and Arnhem and Suez. The RAF and the Parachute Regiment are skilled in making each man feel a soaring sense of personal achievement, when the military jump course is over. We mustered in three ranks in front of a hangar to be presented with our wings by the RAF Training OC. 'Well done, Hastings – to be honest, there were times we didn't think you'd make it.' He gave us the time-honoured farewell to newly qualified jumpers: 'Don't forget – always go for the left-hand seat in the bus,' so that the world could see our newly adorned right shoulders. We were richer too, because by the convention of those days which treated military parachuting as an exalted and demanding skill, we received the princely sum of three pounds for our first jump, two pounds for the second, a pound for the third, and ten shillings for every jump we made thereafter. At seventeen in 1963, this felt like serious money.

I hitch-hiked home in battledress, kitbag over my shoulder – I thumbed everywhere, and it was easy for a uniform to get a ride in those days when the experience of military service was common to almost every man in the land. I had seen almost all my fellow-trainees for the last time. None of the others in our public-school group maintained any link with the Parachute Regiment after qualifying at Abingdon. They went their several civilian ways, though one later became a regular officer in a regiment of 'craphats' as the paras have always dismissed mere groundlings. My own love affair with soldiering, however, was in full bloom. I was still unsure what to do by way of a career. My father had wangled me a job as a researcher in BBC TV, working on a vast 26-part documentary series on the First World War. It was a marvellous opportunity, which taught me a lot of history and something about television. In every spare hour, however, I thumbed my way to Territorial training weekends at Aldershot and attended drill nights at 10 Para's HQ, which by a happy chance lay next door to Television Centre at White City. I was an officer cadet now, wearing a white disc behind my cap badge. I much respected the colonel, Adrian Lee, who was kind to me. He let me borrow a 7.62 mm rifle from the armoury when I wanted. I took it off to Bisley to practise, and found myself in seventh heaven a month or two later when I shot for a battalion team with Bren, rifle and Sten. We won Pegasus ashtrays at the Brigade musketry meeting; I still have mine somewhere. Remember, this was still only eighteen years after the Second World War ended. I looked with awe on such fellow team members as Company Sergeant-Major Boyling: leathery, impeccable, moustachioed (does memory deceive me when I recall that he may even have waxed it?), perfectly at ease with any manner of man or military tool, a veteran of Arnhem. Watching Sar-Major Boyling run a pull-through down the barrel of a bren with loving ease, it required no great feat of imagination to see him in a last-man, last-round defence. He was cast in the mould which has formed the British army's senior NCOs for three centuries and more – sceptical, unselfish, wholly to be counted upon. I was less comfortable with one of the officers under whom I served as a weapons instructor. A man of the world, shall we say, this character enlivened the instructional films that he showed recruits with pornographic sequences which, he told us carelessly, he shot himself on odd weekends in Brighton. This was a trifle outside my sheltered experience, and I blushed crimson in the darkness as the projector whirred.

That autumn, I took two days off from television to sit the Oxford entrance exam, and was given an exhibition to read history at University College. I loved working at the BBC. It was obviously absurd not to go to Oxford now I had the chance. Yet how far should I go to consummate my affair with the army? My father nursed a touching conviction from the moment of my birth that I would be a writer. He said as much in a long letter which he wrote when I was three days old at the end of 1945, and gave to me when I was twenty-one. Now, he believed I should simply stick with the part-time Territorials, and take a commission if I had the chance. He would have been appalled had I suggested that I should become a regular officer. And somewhere in my own heart, amid my deep love for the romance of soldiers, I harboured doubts about whether my life belonged with them, whether I possessed the gifts of fellowship, character, fortitude, the *dono di coraggio*, to make a success of a career as a warrior. Abingdon had been a small test, which I narrowly passed. I overcame fear sufficiently to perform the sort of feats which are nowadays a recreation for supermodels. But my physical awkwardness remained as conspicuous as my gaucheness in the mess. How long before one or the other found me out, an uneasy adolescent in this company of men?

Not long. I precipitated the climax – or if you will, anticlimax – of my brief military career one evening in October during an officers' mess dinner at 10 Para. The occasion reminded me of Waugh's evocation of army life: 'the vacuum, the spasm, the precipitation, and with it all the peculiar, impersonal, barely human geniality'. The star guest was the legendary Lieutenant-Colonel Tony Farrar-Hockley, CO of 3 Para. Short, clipped, ruthless and fluent, he had fought under age in Italy during the Second World War, then served as adjutant of the Glosters through their doomed stand on the Imjin during the Korean war in April 1951. After a series of failed escape attempts, in captivity he sustained guerrilla war so relentlessly that the Chinese frequently wondered whether Korea was worth the company of Farrar-Hockley. He was too abrasive, too ambitious, too clever to be a popular figure in the British army, but he was always an immensely respected one. That night, as I sat nervously in my best-pressed battledress among twenty-odd men in their dark-blue mess dress, many with decorations, Farrar-Hockley chatted to me. He was taking his battalion on exercise in Cyprus in a few weeks and some Territorials were to go on attachment. Would I like to be one of them? I accepted eagerly.

Our detachment took off from Lyneham on a November morning in a Hastings transport. In those residual days of empire, some aircraft staged through the big British base in Libya. Ours stopped overnight in Malta. I found myself sharing the Luqa officers' transit mess with a solitary regular major, civil but obviously a little puzzled by my status. I revelled in the attentions of the white-jacketed mess waiters under the gently turning fans. It seemed thrilling to be travelling abroad under such auspices, but it was a lonely evening. Like a half-trained gundog puppy, I was unsure what was expected of me. Next afternoon, unpacking my kit in the officers' mess of the vast tented Queen Elizabeth camp outside Nicosia, I felt more uncertain still. A tough young Glaswegian lieutenant accosted me almost immediately, on the orders of the second-in-command who had observed my turn-out without enthusiasm. 'I don't know what you think you look like, but it won't do. What's that disc behind your cap badge? You wear it at 10 Para? Well you don't wear it here. Get yourself some proper shoulder flashes. You will come *now* with me to the tailor and get some decent drill trousers. And for God's sake – do up your puttees properly.' The days that followed were worse. In the mess, I was foolish enough to talk too much, a lifelong vice which has got me into no end of trouble.

One night, everybody went to a strip club in Nicosia, a harmless enough diversion for any group of soldiers, but as a young prude, I recoiled from the seediness of it all. To this day I can remember the leering features of a moustachioed major, bawling encouragement at the stage. I wondered: what have this awful man, this awful place, to do with my romantic fantasies about the warrior's life? The answer, of course, was that the strip-club outing was of a piece with the world into which I had chosen to blunder, and for which I was ill-equipped. I have generally found soldiers on operations to be rather less interested in sex than they feel obliged to pretend, but in those days I thought myself lucky to get back to camp without being obliged to go on to a brothel. I remembered John Masters' description of his misery as a young subaltern, making himself priggishly unpopular in a pre-war officers' mess in India. If I could have found anywhere to do so unobserved, I should have cried that night, in frustration and loneliness because nobody appreciated me, though heaven knows why they should have done.

Next evening, we gathered in the failing light at the airfield, a thousand men clambering down from trucks, fitting parachutes among serried ranks of aircraft, Landrovers and trailers on their pallets, guns and mortars and heavy equipment assembled for the onset of Exercise Solinus II. I had been placed in command of a seven-man section, soldiers I had never seen in my life before, who did not seem impressed by their first glimpse of me. The senior officer of our aircraft, a young major, delivered the sober formal warning that refusal to jump was a court-martial offence for qualified parachutists. Then the Argosy took off into the deepening darkness, among a long procession of heavily laden transports, towards the dropping zone at Morphu. In the brightly lit fuselage, kindly RAF dispatchers handed out paper cups of coffee. Some men dozed a little. Those who knew each other – for ours was a motley company – chatted nervously. Many times since, when I have been apprehensive or outright frightened, I have been comforted not only by age and experience, but by comradeship, the most precious of all military assets. That night, I was merely basking in self-pity, least splendid of sentiments, yet most common among the young. Then the order came: 'Prepare to jump!'

A few minutes later, I was hanging in the night sky over Cyprus, seeing nothing save blackness. I released my weapons container. Almost immediately the world came to an end. I thought: This is the finish. I am dead. I have been killed. After a few stunned seconds, however, understanding and relief came. I had landed, oblivious, in a crumpled heap on the rocks of Morphu. Cautiously moving my limbs, I found them undamaged, and clambered to my feet. Men were hitting the ground on all sides, cursing considerably. A good many red lights were visible. Because we were dropping close to the sea, every man wore a Mae West, and had been instructed to switch on its light if he was injured. There were obviously plenty of injuries. That night taught me something at first hand about the limitations of mass parachute drops as operations of war. Whatever parachute enthusiasts may say, they are conducted on what fishermen call the 'chuck and chance it' principle.

I pulled off my harness, and set off on an unsteady course towards the rendezvous beacon, half a mile or so distant. Then I thought: everybody else seems to have something I don't – oh Christ, I've forgotten my PWC. In my mildly concussed condition, I had set off leaving Sten and equipment in its container with my parachute. It took me an hour to find them in the darkness, to exchange helmet for beret, pull on my webbing and pack. It was a relief to reach the beacon and discover that everybody else seemed to have had troubles of their own. I had kept no one waiting. At last, we set off in long files in search of whatever daylight might bring.

I did not know then, and I certainly don't recall now, what was the purpose of Exercise Solinus II. A battalion group had been dropped into the mountains with the usual equipment and heavy weapons to fight a battalion of the Glosters, who were acting as enemy. All that matters for the purpose of this tale is that we marched through the mountains of Cyprus for some days, during which my unfitness to serve among parachute soldiers, or even part-time ones, was brutally exposed. I remember being told to take my turn on 'stag' for a couple of hours that first night, to lie watchful with my weapon on the edge of the bivouac while others slept. Within minutes, a passing officer found me asleep. I was lucky his rebuke was so mild. My section quickly grasped that I had no leadership to offer them, that I was too preoccupied with my own weakness even to spell the man carrying the dead-weight of the Bren. The platoon commander, a competent Territorial, was irked by the heavy weather I made of the dust, the heat, the shortage of water. 'Come on, Hastings — somebody your size really should be able to hack it.' In those days, the British army still believed in the nonsense of 'water discipline' — that it was a right and proper part of men's training to seek to condition them to survive on a minimum liquid intake. In truth, of course, this is a fantasy. The Israeli army, recognizing that the body simply needs all the water it can get, has always allowed its soldiers to drink whenever the wherewithal is available. But in those days in the baking Cyprus heat, even the toughest British regulars suffered terribly from the meagreness of our water ration. I saw wireless-operators bent under their burdens, gasping and sweat-drenched, kept going only by a mate's supporting arm on each side of them. More than a few men succumbed to heat exhaustion. I pitied the heavy-weapons teams, as we watched them toiling up the hillsides with mortar baseplates or MMG barrels on their backs. As usual, however, I was chiefly busy pitying myself. My old tormentor, the Glaswegian lieutenant from the camp, encountered me one dawn in an orange grove, as soon as the light was strong enough to distinguish features. '*Mister* Hastings — *fall* out and *do* your puttees up properly!' Somewhere in the confusion of those days, we were briefly halted beside an armoured-car troop when we heard via their radio net that President Kennedy had been shot. Whatever we made of the news later, hardly a man at that moment had energy to spare for shock or alarm about a distant president. We simply wanted water. I saw David Herberts, our old mentor from Abingdon, standing by a Landrover in the white armband of an umpire. Had he got any water? He shook his head. A Hunter ploughed a leisurely con trail high across the sky overhead. I felt a stab of jealousy for its pilot in his cool cockpit, on the way home to breakfast in a fan-cooled mess.

In later years, I looked often upon the mountains of Cyprus and admired their beauty. But one of the first casualties of exhaustion is appreciation of externals. Today, I can recall the images that drifted past my eyes on that march in 1963, the sun-warmed olive groves and tranquil villages, steep hillsides and mellow valleys. But I perceive these only with the distance of years, looking back in watered and well-fed comfort. At the time, I had eyes solely for the boots of the man in front, the only markers by which I could keep my own feet moving. I set out with considerable faith in my own powers as a hill walker, founded upon all those cadet exercises in the Black Mountains – I had once marched fifty miles in twenty-four hours. Here, however, I was struggling against a depth of tiredness I had never known. At every brief halt I lay with my face against the rock, asking myself: is this the moment at which I say I cannot go on, or do I shuffle just one more stretch?

My experience in those hills provided a foretaste of the simple truth that almost all military operations are carried out in darkness, when one is very tired, very wet, very hot or very cold, as well as hungry and thirsty. Because I had read so much about soldiers at war, I knew that throughout history men not much older than me had persevered through far worse hardships, driven by an internal strength which owed nothing to size or physical prowess, and everything to will. On that Cypriot hillside, it was courage which was failing me, rather than any genuine bodily collapse. The knowledge made my condition no easier to bear. I understood, in the abstract, that the essence of military life is selflessness, a will towards a common cause, an acceptance of sacrifice. Yet I cared for none of these things. I was gnawed by a single-minded obsession with water; not water for everybody – I was quite indifferent to the sufferings of any other man in those long, dusty, over-burdened files – but water for *me*.

Disgrace followed swiftly. We were halted, supposedly in tactical defensive positions, near a Turkish village. Colonel Farrar-Hockley passed by, descending from his helicopter for a brief conversation with the company commander. He gave me a perfunctory glance as I lay among the rocks and prickling grass – 'You all right there, Max?' – then he was borne aloft once more in a whirlwind of dust, in search of higher things. A small, dark, unsmiling Cypriot boy in shorts wandered over. He gazed down at me with mild curiosity. The memory of EOKA's terrorists was very strong and very fresh for every British soldier on Cyprus, fuelling a hatred for the Greek 'Cyps' alongside a considerable sense of fellowship for the Turks. This boy was a Turk. I fished deep in my denim pocket for the only currency I carried – three crumpled English pound notes.

'You speak English?'

'Little.'

'You fill these' – I dragged the aluminium waterbottles out of my belt pouches – 'in five minutes' – I tapped my watch – 'and I give you these.' I palmed the notes. The enormous sum was a measure of my despair and greed. The boy nodded, took the bottles, and ran away. Men lying nearby eyed me narrowly. Hell, they were only jealous because they carried no money. Please, please, I begged the sky, let us not be ordered to move inside five minutes. It was the first successful prayer I had offered since landing in Cyprus. The boy returned, handed me the bottles, and took the thirty pieces of silver, price of my treachery to the caste to which I aspired. I drank, and drank.

Sir Philip Sidney would have been speechless. Minutes later we moved on, dust clogging our boots, hair, faces, smocks, weapons, mouths. I made no offer of water to anyone else, and I anyway doubt whether doing so would have saved me from the discreet denunciation which followed to the platoon subaltern, and thereafter to the company commander. Both these harassed but effective young men were already weary of me. After a few withering words, I was told to expect to hear more when we returned to England. A day or so later, the exercise ended. I was amazed that I had stayed on my feet. We clambered gratefully on to the waiting three-tonners, and bumped and dozed against our packs through the long miles to camp, and thence soon after by RAF Argosy back to Lyneham. I wanted only to find a hiding place from everything to do with this nightmare for which I had so idiotically enlisted. As our truck passed Newbury on the way from the airfield to London, I handed my Sten gun to a corporal with a plea that he should return it to the armoury, jumped down, and hitch-hiked home to Hampshire. I fell into bed at my father's house in the small hours of the morning, bitterly conscious of failure, consumed with the knowledge of inadequacy at this thing in which I had so much yearned to excel. I couldn't hack it.

Retribution came swiftly, with a telephoned request to present myself before the colonel at White City two evenings later. There was no equivocation about my predicament. I was marched into Colonel Lee's office by the RSM with all the harsh 'one-two-off-beret' formality of a military criminal facing sentence. Once we were alone, however, the colonel's manner relaxed a little. He had a report on me from Cyprus, he said gravely. It was not favourable. There was my general demeanour and behaviour among the officers, together with obvious lack of leadership skills in the field. I had incited the mess corporal to wangle me an extra ration of duty-free cigarettes, an imposition that worthy had immediately reported to higher authority. There was the business of my buying water in the field when nobody else could get a drink. I had failed even to return my personal weapon to the armoury after landing in England. The colonel glanced up from the sheet before him and asked if I had any comment. I shook my head. Obviously I could not remain an officer cadet in the battalion, he said. It seemed best if I simply wrote a brief note offering my resignation. I nodded. How old was I? A month short of eighteen? Perhaps I could try again when I was older. But I knew I should not try again. I sobbed then, in the colonel's office, not least for forfeiting the regard of a man I respected. When I had regained a measure of self-control, I slipped away into the night. Next day I returned my kit to the impassive quartermaster sergeant in the stores, paying only for the 'loss' of my red beret and jump smock. These, even now, I was determined not to forfeit. Then the Parachute Regiment parted with 23972379 Private Hastings, M – officer cadets do not carry officers' numbers.

If any writer who admits a fondness for Henty may quote Proust without seeming absurd, I think of a passage about adolescence: 'There is hardly a single action we perform in that phase which we would not give anything, in later life, to be able to annul.' Years later, when I published a brief account in *The Spectator* of this, the failure of my only personal experiment as a soldier, my old and dear friend the military historian John Keegan asked why I had done it, what possessed me to expose long-forgotten scars in such a fashion. I told him that it was because those distant days in Cyprus remained the skeleton in the cupboard of any celebrity I later achieved as a correspondent. I hated to think of men who remembered me in those barren Mediterranean hills, reading my dispatches in the years that followed from Israel or Vietnam or the Falklands, often projected on the front pages in heroic fashion, and thinking, 'But we knew him when he was trying to be a soldier, and we remember what a royal cock-up he made of it.' For some of us, confession of the failures of the past does something to lay ghosts.

In December 1963, only 10 Para, my family and myself knew about my failure in Cyprus. By a lucky chance, a bitter letter I wrote to the company commander who had compiled my report from Nicosia was returned 'address unknown'. I still went happily to the BBC each morning, with the promise of Oxford a few months ahead. My father observed wryly that it looked as though I would have to be a writer, whether I liked it or not. As time passed, I perceived that I was lucky to have learned very young, at no lasting cost, how ill-suited I was to become a soldier. I had acquired a knowledge of soldiers' ways, their language, their weapons, which later served me well on distant battlefields. I had learned the vernacular of the trade, the significance of 'buckshee' and 'take a shufti', 'say again' and 'as you were', together with all those innumerable military initials – SMG, RAOC, 2ic, SLR, GOC, AQMG. Perhaps a part of the respect I have preserved for warriors stems from the fact that I discovered at first hand, without hearing a live round fired, that I was not cast in the mould of the heroes of my childhood. I maintained an unfashionable belief – part of my bond with John Keegan, who has expressed the conviction so brilliantly in his writing – that the soldier's is an honourable calling. But I knew that thenceforward, if I was to play any part in the lives of armies, it would be as spectator and recorder, not as a member of the military fellowship.

Years later, I published a biography of Montrose, Charles I's lieutenant-general in Scotland during the Civil War – he who wrote:

He either fears his fate too much
Or his deserts are small
That puts It not unto the touch
To win or lose it all.

In the winter of 1644, with his motley little army of Irishes and Highlanders, Montrose made a winter march through the snows from Blair Atholl to fall upon the Marquis of Argyll and the Campbells. At Inverlochy one February morning in 1645, as the clansmen arrayed themselves for battle beneath the royal standard to conquer or perish, they were dismayed to see their resident bard, Ian Lom Macdonald, remove himself from the line and clamber away on to a rock overlooking the battlefield. His comrades cried after him, 'Ian Lom, wilt thou leave us?' 'If I go with thee today and fall in battle,' replied the bard with unanswerable logic, 'who will sing thy praises and thy prowess tomorrow?' All day, from his rock he watched the struggle below, until Argyll fled to his galley and the ruined Campbells broke and fled. Then he composed a great Gaelic ode describing the triumph of Montrose's army, which survives to this day. Ian Lom's excuse must be that of the war correspondent through the ages.

CHAPTER TWO

Street Apprentice

THE FIRST SHOTS I heard in anger were not fired on any great battlefield or even by soldiers, but by American policemen in the midst of Roosevelt Street, Chicago. When I had been reading history at Oxford for a year, the editor of the *Evening Standard*, to which I had been contributing since I was eighteen, offered me a job, a salary of thirty pounds a week, and a passage into journalism which I accepted at once, to the fury of my family. My first foreign assignment was to write about riding the Cresta Run. I loved the Fleet Street life, and gradually began to believe that I might make a living as a writer. In 1967, I went to spend a year studying in the United States as a fellow of the World Press Institute, and then lingered for several months to report for the *Standard* the succession of crises and disasters which beset America in the 1968 election year. I was twenty-two, still raw and awkward among my colleagues, as well as lonely in that vast continent. But I was given wonderful opportunities to practise the craft of reporting and to witness some of the greatest dramas of the decade. I interviewed Lyndon Johnson, Ronald Reagan, Richard Nixon, covered the Poor Peoples' March and Eugene McCarthy's campaign, the San Francisco flower children, and the disastrous Democratic Convention in Chicago. A delightful black reporter named Joe Strickland took me round Detroit, a few months after the disastrous race riots in the city. He said to me, 'Don't you believe all that crap blacks give to whites round here about how sorry they are about the riots. When one black man talks to another, he says: "It was a great fire, man."'

'What do you think, Joe?'

He shrugged and grinned. 'It was a great fire, man.'

When Martin Luther King was shot on 4 April 1968, I flew to Memphis the same evening. The story became my first front-page 'splash'. The following night, when the terrible anger of black America erupted into rioting and destruction in a string of ghettos across the nation, I caught another plane to Chicago. A taxi took me through the midnight darkness from O'Hare to dump my bag at a hotel, and then – for double fare – on to the nearest point of the freeway to the eye of violence on the West Side. I paid off the driver, then clambered up an embankment, scaled a fence, and began to walk fearfully up a street deserted save for a handful of looters and a patrolling police car. I hastened on, past wrecked stores and cars and occasional burning ones, unsure what I was seeking. 'SPRING HAS SPRUNG', proclaimed the sign above a furniture ware-house, where a handful of dim figures were picking over the wreckage for anything overlooked by the first wave of pillagers. I saw armed National Guardsmen – local reserve troops – in fatigues and helmets dropping from a truck at an intersection, beginning to deploy down the side streets. Suddenly a patrol car stopped with a shriek of rubber, and a shotgun poked from the window towards a black man scuttling for a corner carrying an unidentifiable box. 'Boom – boom-boom' – three quick shots from the car, so loud in the city street, only speeded the running fugitive. He disappeared down an alley. I hurried on, sensing that a man who looks as if he knows where he is going is less vulnerable to interference than one who seems lost.

Black figures running hither and thither, some carrying obviously stolen burdens, glanced at me curiously. Stopping at a cross street, I saw a line of National Guardsmen doubling towards a group of black men hurling bricks at a store window. I kept checking my watch, mindful that it was already 8 a.m. in London, almost time to file. It was the usual dilemma – how much to try and see before sending a story? The problem was taken out of my hands by a short, fat National Guard major wearing a helmet low over his eyes. He sprang from a jeep and ran towards me, clutching his pistol. He was hysterical, mostly with fear, I think. 'Who the hell are you, boy? Journalist? What you think you're doing here? Where the hell you get that funny accent? I don't like you, boy – follow my men now – you're going with them, and they'll have you if you make a move they don't like.' We walked in an absurd little procession for six or seven blocks, past buildings where National Guardsmen were covering fire-fighters hosing flames, over a million shards of broken glass and endless garbage, past riflemen herding small clusters of sullen black men along the sidewalk. I will not claim to have been shot at more than most reporters, but I do seem to have had guns pointed at me an awful lot over the years. It must be something about my face. The Guardsmen followed, rifles presented – 'Don't walk so fast, mac, this isn't a race' – until we arrived at the police station house. My escorts hustled me up to the desk. 'You see this guy – God knows where he's from – got an accent like you never heard – you take him in.' Then they departed, leaving me to a world-weary desk officer who kept me waiting while he booked four alleged snipers. Oddly enough, given the subsequent experience of their brutality in smashing the demonstrations during the Democratic Convention in the city a few months later, that night Chicago's police kept their cool very well. At the station house, they were friendly and apologetic about my detention by the Guard. 'Those guys lost their heads right at the beginning, and they haven't found them again yet.' We talked about the events of the night for a few minutes. Then they nodded in farewell, and I hurried down the steps alongside a young policeman reloading his revolver, and into a phone booth for one of the thousands of such connections every reporter makes: 'Is that Fleet Street – three zero zero zero? This is the international operator. Mr Hastings is calling you from Chicago, Illinois – will you pay for the call?' In those faraway days before mobile telephones, any journalist was absolutely dependent upon a vital umbilical cord, an unbroken landline. That night was the first of many in which I also learned what a formidable substitute ambition could become for courage. The raw urge to get a story, to make the front page, outstripped in my mind the fear of penetrating the black ghetto of Chicago in the midst of a near-insurrection. In those days, innocence protected me from understanding the full dangers of going alone, even in a great American city. I was thrilled simply to get my front-page story. I wanted to do it again.

I returned from New York in the autumn of 1968, and wrote an instant book about the events of the year in the United States of which the *Sunday Times* reviewer shrewdly and charitably observed that, 'This is the first book of a very young man. Most . . . of its merits derive from the author's youth and innocence.' I found myself back on the *Evening Standard*, covering the usual run of reporting assignments. They seemed pretty humdrum to my impatient soul after the events of the summer, but the editor remarked acidly that drama could not be conjured for me on demand. I had no thought of becoming a professional reporter of conflict. At that stage, I was merely trying to make a reputation. Yet like every ambitious young journalist in every generation, I grasped the simple truth that newspaper front pages were dominated by wars. There was Vietnam, where everybody wanted to go, but at twenty-two I was still too green for anyone to want to pay my fare to Saigon. There were the Middle East and various African conflicts, but the same applied. I was so desperate for promotion that when a glossy magazine wrote to the well-known writer and playwright Michael Hastings offering a commission and the letter was somehow misaddressed to me. I wrote back, asking: would I do instead? No, I would not. Instead, like many young British reporters at that time, I found myself dispatched by the *Standard* to cover the strange and violent events unfolding in Northern Ireland.

When the first English reporters went to Ulster to report the campaign for Catholic civil rights, we found ourselves in the condition of men and women precipitated into some lost valley isolated for decades from 'society as we know it'. Most of us were the products of conventional middle-class liberal education, men and women who had been borne along comfortably enough by the erratic currents of sixties Britain. We came to Northern Ireland ignorant of its history and briefly deceived by externals. The houses, the shops, the 'white goods', the scenery, even the inner-city streets were not much different from their counterparts across the Irish Sea. But the people, the political landscape, above all, the manner of the province's governance, stunned us. The cheap crack was coined early: 'You are now landing at Belfast Aldergrove airport. Put back your watches three hundred years.' As we began to learn what was being done by the Unionist Stormont government in the name of the Crown, we felt ashamed that we had lived so close, part of the same nation, yet oblivious of Ulster's dreadful injustices. We heard the story of Emily Beatty, the unmarried nineteen-year-old policeman's daughter, who was given a council house in Caledon when a family of homeless Catholic squatters was evicted, because she was a Protestant and secretary to the local Unionist councillor's solicitor. Early in 1968, this commonplace action by Ulster's Protestant rulers provoked one of the first peaceful protests by young Catholics. We saw for ourselves how the Royal Ulster Constabulary – the paramilitary arm of the Unionist government – ruthlessly crushed civil rights protests or, more sinister, held the ring while Paisleyite thugs did the job for them. The Cameron Commission on Northern Ireland's civil disorder reported in 1969 that it 'had as its background, on the one hand a widespread sense of political and social grievance for long unadmitted and therefore unredressed by successive Governments of Northern Ireland, and on the other, sentiments of fear and apprehension . . . of risks to the integrity and indeed continued existence of the state'.

Journalists cover many assignments ingloriously, and some which dissolve into self-indulgence. But the reporters who went to Belfast to record the political dramas of 1968 and 1969, that quickly degenerated into a crisis of civil order, brought some lasting honour upon our trade. Journalists such as Harold Jackson and John Cunningham of the *Guardian*, and later Simon Winchester; John Clare, Tim Jones and afterwards Robert Fisk of *The Times*; Fergus Pyle of the *Irish Times*; Mary Holland of the *Observer* (for all the unashamed Catholic partisanship which compromised her more than most of us), along with some able broadcasters, forced the British government as well as the British public to recognize what shameful things were being done in their name.

Throughout history, most of the British people have switched channels when the word Ireland is mentioned. They loathe the country. They find its quarrels and penchant for violence repugnant. Many English reporters and politicians who visited Ulster were appalled by the place and the people, and fled back across the water as swiftly as they could. Others, however, among whom I counted myself, developed a fascination for Ulster bordering on obsession, and returned again and again. This was not merely for the cynical reason that it was 'a good story', but because we came to care deeply about those involved. I later lived for two happy years in Co. Kilkenny, which increased my affection for Ireland's people on both sides of the sectarian divide. Much of our writing in 1969 and afterwards was driven by anger, which mounted as the months went by and folly succeeded bloody folly. English reporters were frequently accused by the Unionists of Catholic partisanship. As the situation on the streets deteriorated, many of us found ourselves at the wrong end of confrontations on the streets with Protestant mobs. Once later, when I was making films for BBC TV in Belfast, an anonymous caller telephoned Broadcasting House to announce that unless I apologized on the air for being a 'Catholic-lover', my father's house at Brown's Farm, Old Basing, Hampshire, would be bombed. The police were sufficiently bothered by the fact that the caller had troubled to discover Father's address, that they obliged him to live for some weeks surrounded by constables with an inexhaustible capacity for tea and biscuits.

Some right-wing Tories look back across three decades of bloodshed to our coverage of the events of 1968 and after and say today, 'You can see it now, can't you? "Civil rights" were always just a cover for the IRA. You were one of the silly buggers who wouldn't understand, who helped bring down the Stormont government, and got us into the mess we are now.' I cannot agree. What has befallen Ireland since 1968 is the fruit of British indifference for forty-seven years after the 1921 Partition Treaty. Having grudgingly allowed Ulster to remain part of the United Kingdom, successive Westminster administrations wanted only to hear as little as possible about the place. They left the Unionists to crow on their dunghill,

gerrymandering constituencies and local government bound-
aries, tolerating institutionalized discrimination against Catholics
in jobs and housing, employing an armed police to suppress
revolt or even dissent. It was a shameful story, which grew
worse in 1968 when the Stormont regime set about the
suppression of Catholic protest, apparently without any objec-
tion from Westminster.

It was the hatred which shocked us, wherever we went. No
one seemed ashamed or embarrassed to speak in the language
of bigotry. The pretty – invariably Protestant – waitresses in
the Royal Avenue Hotel mocked our sympathy for 'the Taigs'.
Whatever apologists claimed about the innocent folk tradition
of the annual marches of Orangemen and the Derry Apprentice
Boys, in 1969 we perceived that we were watching the tribal
war dances of a sect which, if not literally headhunters, were
proven headbreakers. At Westminster over the years, as a
Democratic Unionist MP, Ian Paisley has come to be perceived
merely as an eccentric figure. Thirty years ago, few of us
doubted that he was an entirely evil one.

Day after day, and often night after night, through the
summer, in Belfast reporters went out to cover marches and
demonstrations and riots in which sticks and stones and broken
paving were met by police water-cannon, batons, riot shields,
and the clubs of the Catholic and Protestant mobs. We were
scared many times, because the temper of mobs – and of
officers of the Royal Ulster Constabulary – was uncertain,
especially towards the media. But though matters seemed grim,
and the Stormont government's grip precarious, guns had
hardly ever been drawn, far less fired. Every great historic
drama has somewhere a beginning and a turning point. Ireland's troubles can be traced back to the Middle Ages and
beyond. But between the Second World War and 1968, they
had been in suspension. A brief IRA campaign in the North in

the 1950s swiftly petered out. So much violence has disfigured Ireland over the past thirty years that recent history has merged into an interminable catalogue of bombings, burnings and shootings. Yet the modern tragedy had a beginning, a moment at which a decisive threshold of pain and savagery was crossed, on a summer's day in 1969.

On the afternoon of 12 August, Catholics throwing stones at a Protestant Apprentice Boys' march making its usual triumphalist way past the Bogside, the great Catholic estate outside the walls of Londonderry, became engaged in a running battle with police. In an already explosive situation, the march was the last straw. Petrol bombs were hurled. Through the evening and into the night, the struggle escalated, with policemen thrust into the siege of the Bogside in ever-growing numbers, while young Bogsiders in their thousands became engaged in the struggle to frustrate them. Mounting hysteria prevailed on both sides. The Stormont government, the police and Protestant Ulster perceived a direct challenge to their lawful dominance from Derry's Catholic community. The Catholics, in their turn, believed the police were committed to the forcible suppression of their people. Alarm grew in the Irish Republic, where there were wild demands for the Irish army to intervene, to 'save our people'. Today, the world has had a generation and more in which to grow accustomed to crisis and bloodshed in Northern Ireland. That night of August 1969, increasingly feverish excitement ran through ghetto communities all over the province. It is hard to recapture the disbelief, shock and incomprehension which also echoed from Stormont to Westminster, down Whitehall, Fleet Street and the television studios, thence back across the Irish Sea to Dublin. The flames that lit up Derry as petrol bombs arched through the sky from the tower blocks towards the police lines were watched by stunned audiences all over the country. Here was an urban community of the United Kingdom, in a state close to insurrection. The notion that petrol bombs, such clumsy weapons by the standards of what followed, yet so awful in the context of 1969, should be hurled flaming at policemen astounded and appalled us all. The answering clouds of CS gas were unleashed upon the streets of Derry, yet their choking vapours dismayed a world as far distant as London and New York. Worse, much worse, was now to come.

In Belfast, through months of spasmodic rioting, reporters had established a routine. Trouble most often erupted in the evening. After an early dinner at the seedy old Royal Avenue Hotel in the heart of the city, each of us would set out for the area where trouble threatened, by taxi if conditions allowed, or on foot if matters were already out of hand – the Falls Road, heart of the Catholic ghetto, began only a few hundred yards from the hotel. Around seven o'clock on the night of 14 August, I found myself standing on a corner of the Falls – to be exact, where the lower Falls becomes Divis Street – watching some three hundred young Catholics attack Hastings Street police station. Bricks, rocks, broken paving stones hurtled through the air. Most landed with a dull thud, but occasional missiles struck glass or metal, and more alarming noises followed as debris crashed on to the street. The police response was unimaginative. At intervals, a grey RUC Landrover, windows protected with heavy grilles, roared up the street, momentarily scattering the rioters, but attracting a storm of missiles which did not do vehicles much good, even armoured ones. At this stage, while the situation looked nasty, no reporter saw anything to make matters look more threatening than many other Ulster disturbances we had watched for months past. Stone throwing was a familiar form of demonstration against authority by young Catholic hooligans. Scarcely a gunshot had thus far been heard in Ulster. Broken heads were still the chief currency of violence.

Matters began to worsen around ten thirty. I thought I heard a shot not far away, though not until next morning did we learn that a Protestant had fired a shotgun in Percy Street. I slipped up one of the rabbit warren of side streets that link the Falls with the Protestant Shankill Road, a few hundred yards distant – or at least, they did in those days, before Belfast's notorious sectarian dividing wall was built. Between the rows of decaying terraced houses in both Dover Street and Cupar Street, advancing mobs from the Shankill were locked in strife with the men from the Falls. Bottles, bricks, stones, steel bolts were raining between the rival crowds. All over the Falls area, perhaps a square mile in all, Catholic and Protestant crowds incited by news of events in Derry were coming out on to the streets, edging warily towards each other on the interface of the sectarian divide like so many beasts emerging from their cages – then joining battle at twenty, thirty separate points. The police launched baton charges to push back the mob attacking Hastings Street police station, but they seemed unwilling or unable to separate fighting Catholics and Protestants. Darkness was closing in, and with it grew a mood of hysteria. 'Ah, do you see them lads from the Shankill, come to murder us all?' demanded a furious housewife, snatching my sleeve as I passed the terraced doorway in which she stood watching, less frightened than excited. Belfast housewives have seen too much to give way to fear when only bricks and bottles are being thrown. Many of the Shankill men had armed themselves with staves and protective dustbin lids, and between skirmishes they banged their lids like men possessed, in unison like a Zulu impi. Petrol bombs flew between the two sides now – fevered young men were assembling crates of them in both the Protestant and Catholic lines. I saw two teenagers fighting each other for one bomb, vying for the honour of hurling it.

Where were the police? What were they going to do? Suddenly, a column of armoured vehicles accelerated up the Falls, some fifty policemen following on foot. The mob fell back in their path, until the police reached the huge modern high-rise, Divis Flats. A storm of missiles, lumps of paving, pieces of grating, petrol bombs showered down. A chain of residents was passing paving stones and other munitions from the ground to the roof. They believed themselves threatened by the same sort of police invasion as their tribe had suffered in Londonderry. The police, in their turn, in the later words of Lord Scarman's Tribunal of Inquiry, believed 'that they were dealing with an armed uprising engineered by the IRA'. They retreated to their station, defeated, and thereafter abandoned baton charges in the Falls. Young boys were throwing most of the petrol bombs, some not above eight or nine, their faces lit by unholy glee. What larks, Pip, what larks, Belfast style. One, perhaps two bombs, struck the Arkle Bar on the corner of Dover Street, which began to burn merrily. A police Humber armoured vehicle which was rash enough to roar up the street received a hail of Catholic petrol bombs, caught fire and crashed into a lamp post. Its crew narrowly survived. As battle was joined in the sectarian cross-streets higher and higher up the Falls, one of the decisive moments of the evening came. Soon after midnight, an unknown gunman fired a series of shots at a group of policemen and Shankill men standing on the opposite side of the road, in the mouth of Dover Street. A Protestant named Herbert Roy was killed. Three policemen were wounded. Though Protestants and police did most of the shooting that night, there is no doubt that a Catholic fired those first lethal rounds. From that moment on, Belfast learned the power of fear, rumour and gunfire in a crowded city area. Every shot, from whatever quarter, stirred counterfire and fed panic for a dozen streets around. The police and the Shankill men believed the bullet which killed Herbert Roy had come from Divis Flats opposite, though the later inquiry found otherwise. In response to the shooting, the RUC's senior officer on the spot, Head Constable Gray, summoned the heaviest reinforcement in the police armoury: three Shorland armoured cars, mounted with .30 calibre Browning heavy machine-guns.

By now it was plain that the ghetto area of Belfast faced rioting on a scale hitherto unknown – and indeed, never again surpassed in the Troubles. The city was to see many nights which cost more lives, but none which spread inter-communal violence so widely between Catholics and Protestants. In Dover Street, the Protestants were led by the veteran Shankill Union- ist MP, an iron-hard old man named Johnny McQuade. In Percy Street, a Catholic had seized control of a great yellow bulldozer that belonged to some nearby roadworks. We watched him struggle to start it up and master the controls, then lurch dangerously forwards with a great squealing of caterpillar tracks, and set about knocking down a telegraph pole. The driver fled when a group of RUC men made for him, batons swinging. But the police retreated in the face of the Catholic mob, their sergeant radioing hastily, 'in the absence of assistance, will have to withdraw'. Another Catholic boarded the bulldozer even as a Protestant petrol bomb sailed through the air and smashed against it, setting the vehicle on fire. It crawled forward a few more yards and was then abandoned to the flames.

I rounded a corner to see a large group of police and Shankill men. The RUC had drawn their revolvers. Some officers were also carrying rifles and Sterling sub-machine-guns. I asked their commander what Shankill men were doing, armed with sticks and dustbin lids, in among the RUC ranks. Anyone could tell what impact the sight must make on Catholic Belfast, always so ready to perceive a conspiracy between the RUC and the Protestant mob. The policeman answered with a shrug, 'After all, they've got to think about protecting their homes.' And now, here too were the 'B Specials', the police reservists whom Catholics hated and feared above all things, Protestants whom membership of 'the Specials' enabled to take the streets uniformed and armed on a night such as this, to wreak vengeance on 'the Taigs'. The cry echoed round the Falls, raising the temperature of fear and emotion past boiling point: 'The B men are out.' Catholics were knocking up the handful of old IRA men they could find, demanding that they get their guns to defend the people. Precious few were found. Next day, we heard that some men spent all night tearing up floorboards of houses in Cyprus Street near the Republicans' favourite watering hole The Long Bar, because an old man remembered there were guns buried under one of them and could not recall which.

Most of the street lights had been knocked out by now. The battlefield was in near darkness. Suddenly, some of the Specials convinced themselves that 'the Taigs' could spot them in the sodium glare from a handful which survived. I watched them destroy the nearest two or three with an erratic barrage of revolver fire. Intermittent shots echoed from other streets. Surges of flame lit the horizon from time to time, as petrol bombs exploded a few terraces away, or light flickered from buildings set on fire in the fighting. The lower Falls had emptied of people since shooting started. Several policemen stood peering cautiously around the corner towards Divis Flats on the opposite side of the street in the darkness, weapons poised. I heard them arguing about where the IRA snipers were: 'There he is – there he is – up on that roof.' 'No – look at that balcony – the man moving now.' Were there really snipers in the Flats? I thought I might go and see. Slipping away from the police line, I backtracked a couple of streets towards the city centre, then scuttled hastily across the Falls, empty of bystanders and even rioters at this end now, and of course bereft of traffic. Like every street for a square mile, it was carpeted with broken glass and shattered paving. I was walking under Divis Flats when a Shorland armoured car screeched up the street and halted. This machine of war, its crew invisible, looked implacably sinister in the midst of Belfast. Its turret traversed towards the building above me. Flame began to ripple from the muzzle as the gunner fired a series of long, careful bursts at the Flats. The measured hammer of the Browning seemed to go on and on. Then the turret and its short, black perforated barrel traversed back to fore and aft. With a lurch, the Shorland disappeared up the street. For a moment, absurdly, I believed it had been firing blanks. Whatever horrors I had seen in American street wars, I could not come to terms with the notion that the police were using heavy machine-guns in earnest in the midst of a city of the United Kingdom.

My delusions quickly collapsed. There was an uproar on a lower balcony of the flats above me, cries, moans. I ran up the concrete stairway and met a shocked man who gestured desperately at a doorway and said, 'There's a boy shot in there.' Inside – not in the front room, but in the back – lay a child with a ghastly headwound, and a man sitting beside him. His father. 'He needs help. He needs help. What can we do?' he asked hopelessly. There was blood everywhere. The child was still bleeding profusely, his fair hair matted crimson. In those pitiful, cardboard, system-built flats, Browning fire had torn contemptuously through two or three partition walls, to hit this nine-year-old where he lay. Yet no one cared to cross the street to the police line for aid, braving the Shankill mob.

The Protestants were unlikely to attack me. I said I would go. Downstairs from the shelter of the building I shouted to tell the police who I was, however, before crossing the street – this seemed no night to run suddenly towards frightened men with guns. When I reached the police riflemen, I told them about the boy.

'Get an ambulance – quick!'

'And how's he to get here through all this?' demanded the Head Constable, waving an arm towards the nearby streets where the sounds of battle echoed so audibly.

'There's a child dying in there.'

'You'll never get an ambulance to go to the Flats.'

'Then get it here, and we'll bring him across. Have you no one with medical knowledge?'

'What – to go into the Flats?'

'There's a child dying. They're hardly going to shoot your man with me watching.'

In the light of subsequent experience in Ulster, this was one of my sillier utterances. The RUC officer who agreed to return with me was a brave and decent young man. His comrades obligingly assured us that they would cover our passage. The constable took off his helmet and tunic so that he was less conspicuous a policeman, and followed me across the street in his blue shirtsleeves, clutching a vehicle first-aid kit, pitifully inadequate panacea. Instinctively ducking as we ran, we covered the few yards to the Flats. Behind the parapets of the balconies crouched men and boys with milk-bottle crates of petrol bombs, intent on watching for the enemy below. We passed on to that terrible scene in the back bedroom. The constable laid a dressing on the boy's gaping headwound. We persuaded his father that he must bring him down.

'Come on. They're getting an ambulance.'

The man picked up his ruined child, and carried him down the stairs. We could still hear spasmodic shots. Police riflemen on the roof of Hastings Street believed they were being fired upon from the top of Divis Flats, and loosed a succession of shots at the supposed IRA marksman. A soldier on leave, Hugh McCabe, fell dead from one of them. The constable and I waved white handkerchiefs in the air as we crossed the street back to the RUC lines ahead of the father and his boy. An ambulance carried little Patrick Rooney to hospital in time to be pronounced dead at 2 a.m.

I was stunned by the wicked folly of the policemen responsible. The boy's shooting highlighted more than any other event that night the collapse of the RUC's discipline in the face of a situation they could no longer control. The armoured-car crew who killed Patrick Rooney later lied to the Scarman Inquiry which investigated the night's events. They denied that they had ever fired on Divis Flats. I was among those who gave evidence of what had taken place. Lord Scarman concluded: 'We believe that, appalled at the human consequences of their shooting and frightened by the spectre of revenge, the Shorland crews have not made to the Tribunal a full disclosure of what happened.' Never an admirer of the Unionist government of Ulster, that night I became its committed foe. Nothing could justify the resurrection of the IRA and almost thirty years of terrorism which followed. But anyone who was there that August night in Belfast, who saw the Catholic community perceiving itself threatened with destruction by police and Protestants acting in accord, understood how the revival of the IRA became possible, and why the Royal Ulster Constabulary forfeited for ever the trust of Catholic Ireland.

There was plenty more shooting before dawn – indeed,

considering the amount of ammunition expended, it is remarkable that only four people died and fifty-five were admitted to hospital with gunshot wounds. When a Shankill mob attacked St Comgall's school with petrol bombs, members of one of the few old IRA cells in Belfast arrived with a Thompson gun and a couple of pistols, opened fire on the Protestants and wounded eight of them. A police Shorland roared up and responded with another barrage of Browning fire which left the school scarred and pitted with strike marks, and blood all over the chairs of the nearest classroom within. In Dover Street, I watched police fire a volley of aimed automatic-rifle shots at the roof of the great looming shape of Andrews' Mill a couple of streets distant, where they persuaded themselves there was a Catholic sniper. They lowered their weapons only when someone muttered that there were night watchmen up there.

Frightened but bewitched local people huddled in every doorway behind the front lines, watching disaster envelop their community. I chatted to a Shorland crew, drinking thick brown tea provided by Shankill housewives in a side street behind the police. They were convinced, like almost every RUC man in Belfast that night, that they faced a Republican insurrection. One of the armoured-car drivers said, 'Of course, Dr Paisley has been telling us this would happen these nine months, but none of us had the sense to listen.' In Conway Street, where there had been an exchange of fire between police and Catholic gunmen earlier in the night, frenzied Protestants were begging the RUC to hand over their guns if they would not use them for themselves. Though no RUC man is known to have done so, the weapons of B Specials did their share of mischief. In the early hours of the morning, Protestants broke through the Catholic defences in Conway Street and set it on fire. Forty-eight houses, two-thirds of all the Catholic dwellings in the street, were torched. Catholics claimed that the RUC kept them back so that the Protestants could fire the buildings. Lord Scarman later reported, 'No doubt the police concentrated their attention on the Catholic crowd because they saw them not only as a threat to themselves, but to the whole system of law and order in the city. Nevertheless, the police on duty in these streets were seriously at fault in that . . . they failed to control the Protestant mob, or to prevent the arson and the looting.' Barricades were going up everywhere, frenziedly assembled by both communities in every mixed street, to signal the limits of each tribe's territory. The barricade has a long and sorry tradition in Irish history. This was the first 1960s manifestation of what was to become a phenomenon of the new phase of the Troubles. Behind each rival barrier, combatants sheltered, defying their opponents.

Even as their society dissolved into sectarian warfare, the most chilling aspect of that night's work was the number of people who seemed to be enjoying themselves. Not the police, to be sure, but many of the inhabitants of the ghetto, both Protestant and Catholic. There was an awful glee about the manner in which people of all ages and both sexes exulted in conflict and destruction. It was as if they rejoiced in fulfilling historic destiny. Far from drawing back, seeking truce or compromise now that they saw the predicament into which strife had driven them, many seemed stirred to a kind of ecstasy. A few years later, making a film about the Catholic community in Belfast for the BBC, we were filming late one Saturday night in Anderstown Social Club. By then, there were many more corpses, a terrible debit of political failure and physical destruction on the ledger. Yet at 2 a.m. in that Republican stronghold, every man and woman in the place joined the local group, The Wolfhounds, singing the hit of the moment at the tops of their voices and with absolute conviction:

46

It's up along the Falls Road,
That's where I long to be,
Lying in the darkness with a Provo company,
One man on me left, another one on me right,
And a clip of ammunition for me little Armalite.

In 1969, we still had much to discover about the madness and depravity Northern Ireland was capable of. Yet Belfast's experience on that August night gave us a terrible foretaste. I wrote in my front-page dispatch for the *Evening Standard* on Friday morning, 15 August:

> The province of Ulster awoke today to face a crisis that has ceased to be moral, religious, or even political. It has become the brutally simple problem of dealing with thousands of inhabitants of all backgrounds and beliefs, who are thoroughly roused for battle . . . This has been a melodramatic night, because whatever one's feelings, it is a melodramatic experience to move through a British city at a running crouch, flattening into doorways and hurling oneself for cover as armoured cars roar past, blazing fire, and a column of smoke rises from a blazing building. The first light of dawn found the same groups on the same corners, begrimed and very dirty now, watching firemen quelling the last of the half-dozen major blazes that had sprung up, which for hours they had been unable to tackle in the face of the struggle around them. Houses and shops, pubs and businesses, have been wrecked in plenty. Falls Road is a blitzed area.

More than a hundred houses and a dozen factories had been destroyed. Almost every tree and telegraph pole in the Falls area had been felled at its base to make a barricade. Sixty buses had been pressed into service to barricade Catholic streets, along with bakery vans, upturned cars and trucks, creating obstacles ten, twelve feet high. Trucks were hastening through the streets laden with furniture and baggage, as Catholics on the edge of Protestant territory fled with whatever possessions they could gather. Both sides were too busy consolidating and fortifying their positions to fight. It was as if the combatants feared to face the daylight. Most retired from the front lines to eat, drink, proclaim their grievances to any reporter who passed by, and await the return of darkness. There was not a policeman to be seen in the Falls Road that morning. Local small boys were directing cars past the debris. Every traffic light had been destroyed. Law and order were in suspension. The normal processes of policing and government had crumbled as sectarian warfare gripped Belfast and a score of other Ulster towns and villages.

Then, with the afternoon, came the British army. The Stormont government had been obliged to acknowledge that its armed constabulary, even with the aid of 8,000 B Specials, could no longer control Ulster. Three battalions marched into Londonderry and Belfast. The soldiers brought an immediate pause in hostilities in Derry, where with rich irony – in the light of subsequent history – Catholic crowds cheered them through the streets. Only the fiery Bernadette Devlin stood atop a burnt-out car, berating her co-religionists for their folly in failing to recognize the real, British enemy. There were not nearly enough soldiers to protect the Catholic ghettos of Belfast. They knew next to nothing of the geography, never mind the politics, of the situation to which they had been summoned. A battalion of the Queen's and another of the Royal Regiment of Wales deployed in the Falls area with helmets and fixed bayonets, looking frankly bewildered. The Catholics of Ulster greeted them as deliverers. From every doorway came housewives offering tea and warm words. The Protestants stood watching behind their own barricades, chatting darkly to RUC men who were now deployed only in front of the Protestant lines. And as night fell, the two communities once more fell on each other's throats wherever they could engage without military interference.

Protestants attacked outlying Catholic streets wherever these were not protected, above all in the Ardoyne area. An army patrol found two Catholics holding off one Protestant mob with shotguns. The soldiers told the men to lose themselves fast. They themselves were under strict orders to fire only in desperate circumstances. That first night of 15 August, the troops still had much to learn about the ferocity of the struggle they had entered. We were all in an emotional mood after the events of the past twenty-four hours. I was not alone in finding myself deeply moved by the spectacle of files of British soldiers deploying to save the Catholic area, the Other Ranks making the resigned throwaway jokes men of the British army always make in action, officers calm and understated even as they reported into their wireless sets the burning buildings in their paths, the petrol bombs and screaming mobs. 'Thank God for the military!' shouted a woman as a platoon advanced up a wrecked street past a blazing truck. 'We can't be everywhere at once,' harassed young Lieutenant Adams of the Royal Regiment of Wales told a crowd of furious Catholic housewives, who reported the systematic Protestant destruction of whole terraces of houses off the Springfield Road. 'We asked for fire engines at six thirty,' he told me. 'It's now midnight, and there's no sign of them.' One of his men had already been wounded by a shotgun blast from the Protestant lines. His platoon fired the army's only two live rounds that night, to cover the wounded man's rescue.

I followed his platoon as they headed towards the mounting

conflagration in a place that became a byword for sectarian destruction: Bombay Street. He was radioing again. 'We have a reserve force, I think. This might seem a suitable moment to bring it up.' A police armoured car suddenly halted in front of us. Adams crisply told its crew to vanish. Their appearance here, now, among Catholics, would provoke hysteria. We turned into Bombay Street. Almost every house was burning. Flames licked forth from doors and window frames. Wreckage littered the street. Behind us, Catholic families were struggling to salvage what possessions they could. Ahead, on the corner of Kashmir Street behind a barricade lit by the terrible blaze, stood the mob from the Shankill which had done the night's work. The lieutenant advanced to parley with them. I lingered a few yards behind him. After a few moments' conversation, he turned back and told me wryly. 'They say they are in danger. They say the Catholics are about to attack them. You know there's a police inspector and two B Specials behind there with them?' A few yards further on, a crowd behind a Protestant barricade in Bellevue Street saw me scribbling in my pad. There was a howl of rage. 'It's a reporter! It's a newspaperman! Get the bastard!' I was terrified. The RRW officer held up his arm in their path. 'This man is with me,' he said decisively. That night, the mob was sufficiently frightened of the soldiers and their weapons to stand back. The subaltern turned to me. 'You'd better disappear, or it could get sticky round here.'

I turned, walking quickly back around the corner alone. A couple of cross-streets away, I came upon a fire engine manned by the craziest bunch of volunteers I have ever seen, addressing a blaze in Clonard Gardens. A ragtag of young men in jeans and windcheaters dragged out hoses and began to play them on the flames. 'Where did we learn to use it? We just tried it and found out,' said one. He was a Liverpool lad who had come over for a motorcycle race and ended up manning the engine after its regular crew abandoned it. Belfast's professional fire-men, too, were Protestants. An army officer said, 'I can't help thinking the blazes the volunteers are handling are just the ones the fire crews would have been happy to leave burning.' He was learning. Not a city fire engine took a hand in that night's events. The stiff breeze which persisted through the hours of darkness fanned every blaze, sending sparks and embers flying fiercely across the sky.

That Saturday morning of August all of us – rioters, housewives, soldiers, reporters – were blackened and filthy by dawn. Why had the army not fired in earnest, to turn back the Protestant arsonists? The troops could have been relied upon to use weapons in a far more disciplined fashion than the RUC the previous night. Yet respect for the sanctity of life and reluctance to use live ammunition were still very strong among the British army in those first days, and perhaps they were right. They were lucky enough to be out of practice in killing people – or in being shot at. I remembered John Masters' tale, when he was serving as a young officer with the Duke of Cornwall's between the wars, on an operation against the Pathans. As a bullet smacked against a rock alongside him, an outraged young soldier, more accustomed to Salisbury Plain than tribal warfare, protested furiously, ' 'Ere, Sir – them buggers is using ball!'

'Them buggers' was using ball in Belfast, too. But the soldiers were under orders to fire back only on the orders of an officer, when life was directly threatened. They covered every movement with their light machine-guns, but never fired them. They loosed an occasional gas cartridge to stem an attack, but gas was small change in Belfast that August. Behind the Protestant barricades, we could hear the men from the Shankill chanting their great war songs: 'No Surrender', 'The Sash My Father Wore', 'The Protestant Boys'. It was the year of Lee Marvin singing 'I was born under a wandering star'. In Protestant Belfast, they sang:

> *I was born under the Union Jack,*
> *I was born under the Union Jack,*
> *Heaven's up the Shankill, hell is up the Falls,*
> *If you see a Catholic, kick him in the balls.*

Only one civilian died that Friday night, a Catholic, shot presumably by a Protestant rifleman. But it was not for want of trying that there were no more fatal casualties. Lord Scarman later concluded that 'there was a considerable amount of shooting from both sides'. Most of the injured, both Protestant and Catholic, were hit by shotgun pellets only – neither community possessed much heavy hardware. The destruction of property was once again fearsome – thirty-eight houses in Bombay Street alone had to be condemned for demolition. A mass of property in Cupar Street, Kane Street, Kashmir Street and Clonard Gardens was burnt out, every Catholic house, all of them burnt by Protestants. Ian Paisley, as usual, fanned the Protestant hysteria of the night by claiming that Ardoyne Church had been used as a Catholic arsenal, where priests were serving out ammunition. Lord Scarman declared himself 'perfectly satisfied that the church was not used as an arsenal, and that the priests did not hand out bullets'. It is a measure of the untold evil wrought by Paisley in those days that authoritative denial should have been needed.

A day or so after the horrors which befell the Ardoyne area, there was a mass meeting of Catholic residents, at which there were emotional demands for arms, to defend themselves. A local priest, Father Gillespie, walked out of the meeting after he asserted that he himself 'did not agree with guns, and that they should not have guns'. He was denounced by his own people as 'a cheek-turning fool'. After those nights in Belfast, the locals called the IRA the 'I Ran Away'.

Walking the length of the battered, blackened Falls Road in the early morning light of Saturday 16 August, in my innocence I supposed we had seen the worst Ulster could do to itself. Soldiers lay sleeping the sleep of exhaustion in doorways, weapons cradled in their arms. Knife-rests, concertina wire and military checkpoints were being erected at intervals, army vehicles loaded with men, and stores were arriving and unloading. Landrovers festooned with aerials cruised the streets. From behind their barricades, Protestants and Catholics peered at each other, not in fear, but in bitter loathing. In the years that followed, I saw many more riots in Northern Ireland, some gun battles, plenty of bombings, all manner of scenes of horror. But it is the beginning of the story, in those August nights of 1969, which lingers so vividly in my memory. Neither sectarian camp possessed a monopoly of either folly or violence. The first acts of destruction in both Derry and Belfast that August were indisputably the work of Catholics. Yet the Catholics were victims not only of institutionalized injustice, but also of clumsy and brutal efforts by the Stormont government and the RUC to put them down. Henceforward, the bloody Irish story would be dominated by the revival of the IRA, and the resurgence of every old Nationalist and Republican creed and prejudice. I am one of those who believe that the Provisional IRA has set back the cause of Irish unity by a generation. Nothing could justify the terrorists' dreadful deeds over almost thirty years that followed, which tipped the balance of grievance so drastically away from Catholic Ulster. But those of us who witnessed the events of August 1969 understood, as many others did not, how and why the Catholic community spawned a new terrorist movement, and rejected for ever a body politic ruled by the Protestant majority. For the latter at least, I could never reproach them. It was part of Ulster's tragedy in 1969, to have to endure three more years of Unionist government, amid ever-growing Catholic alienation, before Westminster belatedly acknowledged the bankruptcy of Stormont and its Unionist rulers.

I learned a lot during 1969, about conflict and about reporting. What we saw left scars in the memories of most reporters who served in Ulster. But I also discovered what a privilege it can be to witness a great human drama. That winter, I wrote a reporter's book about the events of 1969 in Northern Ireland, in the optimistic belief that we had reached some kind of punctuation mark in the tragedy. History demonstrated otherwise. Most of those on this side of the water are bemused when I say today that I love Ulster and knew happy times there. It is a paradox that many Irish people, sincerely committed to the concept of peace, have also found a stimulus in the intensity of their experience, which contrasts with the bland prosperity and humdrum nature of most English people's lives on this side of the Irish Sea. For those on both sides of the sectarian divide in the Falls and the Shankill, it has been one of the chilling realities of the Troubles that a career among the IRA or the Loyalist paramilitaries offers far greater fulfilment and purpose than that of a barman or unemployed bricklayer. For a Belfast working man, facility with an assault rifle remains the most plausible passport to an audience with a British prime minister. I cling to the hope of living to see the Ulster story attain a tolerable, if not a happy, ending. The candle of peace has been lit, but still flickers uncertainly.

CHAPTER THREE

A Taxi to Biafra

AT THE END of 1969, the long and terrible Nigerian civil war approached a climax. In the first days of 1970, General Gowon's Federal army, armed and supplied by the British government in the face of passionate opposition from British liberal opinion, began its decisive drive into Biafra, to crush the Ibo rebellion led by Colonel Odumegwu Ojukwu. Few issues in British foreign policy had stirred more dissension at home than the Nigerian conflict, in which both sides possessed passionate advocates. As Biafra crumbled, I begged Charles Wintour, the *Standard*'s editor, to be allowed to go to Nigeria for the paper. He hesitated, considered for a few hours, and at last succumbed. Exulting, on 12 January, I caught the flight to Lagos.

My first glimpse of Africa was gained from the tarmac at Kano airport, while we refuelled. The heat was fierce, the flat wilderness beyond the runway unprepossessing. I was simply nursing the thrill of finding myself in the most exciting continent on earth, where my father and uncle Lewis had enjoyed so many adventures. I loved the brilliant fabrics in which the Nigerians clothed themselves, the palm trees, even my first glimpse of a huge African butterfly. Officialdom at Lagos airport was sullen – the country had not been flattered

in recent years by foreign journalists – but after the usual
weary bureaucratic paperchase, we made our way through the
darkness into the city. The main hotel was already crowded
with journalists, most of them British, all bitterly frustrated.
Nobody was being granted permission to go to the front, or
indeed anywhere near Biafra. Many of the assembled press
pack were legendary Fleet Street figures in the bar and out of
it, men like Cyril Aynsley of the *Daily Express* and Walter
Partington, whom Nicholas Tomalin rendered immortal by
recording his terse advice to a tyro reporter: 'Always take five
carbons, and never stuff a colleague.' I spent a frustrating day
in Lagos, filing routine copy about the situation alleged to
exist in the shattered province three hundred miles away. Even
the British officers of the official international observer team
would tell reporters nothing – the British government was
deeply compromised by its support for General Gowon, the
Nigerian dictator. We were driven back on the sort of leaden
clichés which were all that Lagos offered in profusion: 'In the
capital, while the bands play in the night-clubs and the
sandbags outside a handful of public buildings rot and break
apart, the answer to every question is always "tomorrow" . . .'

I knew this sort of thing would not satisfy Charles Wintour
on my return. If I was to make good on my promise to justify
the air fare, more drastic measures would be needed. Whatever
the rest of the hack pack was or was not doing, I had to make
a stab at getting to Biafra. What followed owes more to Evelyn
Waugh than to William Howard Russell. It added nothing to
the sum of human knowledge, not much even to useful
journalism. But there is a kind of reporting which exasperates
officialdom and pleases newspapers by creating a brief front-
page splash – literally so, in the jargon of the trade. A reporter
gets a story which is woven of gossamer fabric, but achieves

celebrity for a moment because it is the only news to be had. In the country of the blind, the one-eyed man achieves a scoop.

On the plane from London, I had met an old friend from Belfast, *Times* correspondent John Clare. John is a thoughtful, measured, absurdly good-looking man a few years older than me, who lived and worked in South Africa until he left one step ahead of the apartheid regime's security police in the mid-1960s. He and I were to share many adventures, and he was to become one of the most respected reporters of our generation. The only way to Biafra lay by road to the Niger River, and thence by ferry past a blown bridge to Onitsha, three hundred miles eastwards. John came to join me for an evening drink on the hotel verandah, where I was brooding over a large-scale map. At first, he thought I was crazy enough to be thinking of walking to Biafra. No way, I said. It would take too long. A vehicle was essential. We quickly agreed that together we would attempt an unauthorized dash to get across the river. Secretly, I was much relieved that he was game to join me, for on my own I knew that I should have been very nervous indeed. Before first light next morning, Wednesday 14 January, equipped only with water and sandwiches, we hailed a taxi outside the hotel. The first driver in the queue wanted nothing to do with us, or with any trip beyond the town limits. The second was more susceptible to persuasion, but it quickly became evident that he, too, would baulk at the notion of accepting a fare to the Niger. We set off out of the city, with an agreement merely to head for its outer limits, and see what happened. I had already filed a holding piece to the paper, so that something would appear under my byline from Lagos that day. Some other correspondents remained in the hotel, resigned to accepting the official ban on travel. Needless to say, however, we were not the only taxi-hirers that morning. A string of correspondents and TV camera crews were setting forth on the same mission as ourselves. It was a hot, intensely humid West African day. I was dressed for the part, or so I thought, in desert boots, an old bush jacket of my father's and a camouflage silk scarf ditto, which I prized because he cut it from a parachute at the Rhine Crossing. John and I knew next to nothing about Nigeria or – let us be frank – about the war. The permanent-staff foreign correspondent has become a rare species in recent years, and media reporting of many world events reflects this. We were representatives of that dubious breed of journalists 'firemen' – reporters sent into a country in search of sensational files for a few days' front pages, rather than to stay, learn, and provide an informed news service for months or years on end. Firemen are regarded with dismay by resident correspondents, because we care nothing about making trouble with the local government. When the BBC is in disgrace in India, for instance – as it often is – the uproar has almost invariably been created by a visiting camera team, rather than by residents like the great Mark Tully, in Delhi for so many years. I know. I was more than once among the visiting film crews who caused such grief.

In the back of our taxi, John and I chattered about our lives, jobs, fears and hopes. We knew we had a very long way to go, and that our troubles would start only when we encountered the first road blocks. We were soon out of Lagos, driving among palms and lush greenery by the roadside, interrupted by occasional small towns, villages, corrugated-roofed huts and those featureless, sunburned concrete buildings of indeterminate purpose which are the chief contribution of modern architecture to every society in Africa. John talked about his experiences in South Africa, where he worked for Alan Paton's Liberal Party until the apartheid regime drove him out. I told him some of my American stories, suitably

58

embroidered. Suddenly, we were past our first roadblock without having noticed that it was there. There had been a couple
of bored soldiers by an upraised knife-rest – and we were gone.
But we knew there were more obstacles to come. Our driver
was not a happy man – indeed, he was an extremely nervous
one. But by a happy chance, in those days when everybody
smoked obsessively, we were well equipped with cigarettes.
We fed him a few packs. He liked them. He drove on,
encouraged by bland and careless assurances from his passengers. From there on, drip fed with cash and cigarettes, this
hapless man bore us three hundred miles across Nigeria. With
every mile our hopes rose, and so did the tension. At the next
block, we were stopped. There was a brief exchange, we
flourished our press cards authoritatively – and were waved on.
It was a day of miracles. We cruised through Benin, a big
town which marked the halfway point between Lagos and the
Niger. Roadblocks we passed thereafter were deserted. Yet
every other correspondents' car which drove to Onitsha that
morning was apprehended and turned back. We learned later
that one guard detail was absent when we made our passage,
because they were escorting the CBS TV crew to jail.

We were very hot and dry and dusty, eaten up with tension
stirred by a growing belief that we might make it. It was mid-
afternoon when before us, suddenly, we saw the great brown
river. The road, which had been empty of traffic for many miles
save an occasional military vehicle and long-abandoned,
wrecked food-relief trucks, ended abruptly where the ruins of
the triple-arched bridge caved into the fast-flowing water.
Beyond, on the other bank, lay our own promised land, Biafra.
We persuaded the taxi-driver by suitable inducements to linger
for us, however long the wait might prove. Unsurprised by
almost anything, he settled himself to sleep behind the wheel.
Then we made our way down to the shore. The Nigerian officer

in charge was visibly horrified to see us. He might not know much, but he knew that two white journalists in his sector were likely to mean trouble. For some very nasty moments, it seemed that here, at the last hurdle, we might founder. But we were delivered by our insistence that we had no wish at all to cause him unhappiness. We wanted only to pass on, out of his life. He saw salvation. He decided that it did not matter which way we went, as long as we went. In the water lay an army assault boat with an outboard motor, presided over by a large Nigerian soldier with a steel helmet tipped back on his head with a nonchalance that would have won the admiration of John Wayne. One gesture from higher authority, and we had our passage. The coxswain nodded us aboard amid a motley crew of other passengers, military and civilian. We cruised smoothly across to the Biafran shore, in a state of euphoria worthy of Moses' lesser feats in this field. Waving thanks, we made our way a few hundred yards eastwards, into the town of Onitsha. This had once been one of the biggest textile centres in the country. Now, its buildings were battered and bullet-scarred. Desolation reigned. Fighting in Biafra had stopped only hours earlier, and Federal anti-aircraft crews were still training Bofors guns watchfully at the sky. The streets were crowded with Biafran soldiers – scarcely even prisoners, merely men still wearing the vestiges of uniform and camouflaged helmets, who had crossed into the Nigerian lines to surrender, desperate for food and medical attention for their wounds, knowing their war was lost. We had a story, now, whatever happened. We talked to them as best we could, photographed them in their bewildered columns.

Then a Nigerian soldier beckoned us, in a not unfriendly fashion. He took us to his officer. His officer was unsure what to think or what to do with us. But he played safe in the fashion of junior commanders all over the world – he passed us on to higher authority. We were led through the palm trees to an anonymous concrete building which, we discovered, was serving as headquarters and officers' mess for Five Sector of the Nigerian 1st Infantry Division. A sentry challenged us stridently, presenting a fixed bayonet, in one of those moments of military theatre which I would learn in the years to come are inseparable from African armies. Inside the mess, however, the mood was impeccably Sandhurst – clipped, perfect English – 'Good afternoon, gentlemen. And what can we do for you?' There was no question of allowing us to roam loose across the countryside, but nor did they detain us. We got exactly what we so desperately needed – the chance to talk to people.

It was an evening full of incident. We interviewed men in the long lines of prisoners queuing for food in the sweltering heat outside the Gaumont cinema in the midst of the town. While we were talking to the Federal commander, a local chief suddenly arrived. 'I am Chief Okoluji,' he said, presenting a neat visiting card to the Nigerian officer. 'I have just come in from the bush. Until July, I was detained by the Biafrans. Since they released me, I have had nowhere to go. Can you give me a pound for food and transport for my family?' With John and me looking on, the colonel didn't have much choice. He handed over his pound, and promised the new guest transport for the twenty-seven members of his family. Initially apprehensive, the Chief now started to swell somewhat and assert more ambitious claims. 'Before the war, I had four houses in this town,' he said wistfully. 'Now I have nothing, nothing at all.' The colonel shrugged: 'That is what happens in war.'

We were invited to spend the night in the officers' mess. We sat down to dinner at a table glittering with the candlesticks and regimental silver, in those days inseparable from the social life of any ex-imperial regiment. It was only as we ate that we discovered the identity of the short, handsome figure in civilian clothes, chatting animatedly to the Federal divisional commander. Until the previous day, Brigadier Conrad Naaou had been a senior officer of Ojukwu's Biafran army. He and the Federal officer had been at Sandhurst together. Now, he talked to us with the sophisticated resignation common to most of that highly educated elite. 'I regret very much that we did not negotiate earlier,' he said. 'Unfortunately, in a negotiation there must be a spirit of compromise, and this never existed on either side. There was a peculiarly African kind of righteous indignation on both sides.' He reminisced about thirty months of war, talking of the air shuttle to the legendary Uli airstrip thirty miles from where we sat, Biafra's lifeline to the outside world, and of the problems of learning to use weapons of a dozen nationalities without even instruction manuals. We sat with Naaou for hours into the night, listening intently to every detail of his tale. We also interrogated every Nigerian officer who would speak to us. They were savouring their victory, achieved in the face of bitter Western media hostility, and amid the scepticism which prevailed to the end in the outside world about the Federal army's ability to defeat the Biafrans in the field. The collapse of Ojukwu's forces had come very suddenly. 'They said they would fight to the death,' an impeccably dressed captain told us, 'and we believed them.' A signals officer said gleefully: 'These Ibos thought they were the greatest thing in Africa. It is good that they have learned better.'

John and I could now go back and confirm that it was all over with Biafra. The Federal forces had gained total control, they were merely struggling to handle thousands of prisoners, and a region in which almost every utility and essential for survival had been destroyed by the war. The threat of a great human disaster hung over the region, unless urgent steps were taken to feed tens of thousands of desperate people. The divisional commander acknowledged this to us. 'The Red Cross are still scratching their heads,' he said. 'They are planning to set up relief centres here, but so far they have not been able to.' John and I knew that these strands of anecdote and eyewitness report gave us a story, a front-page story, when no one else had crossed the river. Or had they? All night, we were racked by uncertainty: first, about whether others had done as we had done, or better; and second, whether we could get our tale out. By now, there must be a good chance that Nigerian officialdom was on our track. The sooner we could get free of our courteous military hosts, before any signal reached them ordering our arrest, the better for us.

Early next day we shook hands with the officers who had entertained us. We saw Brigadier Naaou standing patiently outside the mess with an aide, waiting for transport to captivity in Lagos – and a future of what? At best exile, at worst the firing squad. There had been plenty of those on both sides in this bloody civil war. We hastened back down to the river, past more desolate refugees. We passed a woman and her baby trudging through a small village. 'Hello,' she said. John asked, 'How are you?' She replied, 'Hungry.' Our last glimpse of the Biafran bank was of a woman walking empty-eyed down the road, clutching two children, an enormous basket and that universal, pitiful symbol of status throughout the Third World, an electric fan.

The assault boat was still there at the shore – and so, mercy of mercies, was our taxi-driver on the other side. Could we get back down the road unapprehended, to file the story and send the pictures before we were arrested? We were six hours from Lagos. I began making calculations as we rattled steadily westward. We could not reach the capital before the *Evening Standard*'s editions closed for the day. John would get the scoop for *The Times*. I loved him like a brother, then and later, but I could not endure the notion of being second, after such fantastic luck. Could I make an excuse to stop the car, and somehow abandon him by the roadside? Possible, but extreme. Could I somehow delay our return overnight, until we were back in *Standard* filing time? Hazardous and speculative. One gleam of hope remained. Three hours down the road, we would pass the city of Benin. It was possible, just vaguely, remotely possible, that from Benin I could get a telephone line through to London. I scribbled fiercely, putting together the story in my usual spidery handwriting, almost illegible even to myself. Somehow, in twenty years on the road, I never learned either shorthand or ten-fingered typing. I told John of my hopes for Benin, and with his customary generosity, he showed no inkling of resentment, nor even a hint of sharing my demented sense of rivalry. The miles flashed by. No roadblocks bothered us, travelling away from the front.

Then there was Benin, and the taxi-driver was leaning out of the window in a crowded marketplace, asking directions to the telephone exchange. I hurried in, to see before me a long row of girls clad in all the exotic primary colours of Nigerian womanhood, glancing up from their switchboards at the spectacle of an absurdly tall young white man in an old bush jacket, covered in dust and apparently verging on hysteria. I waved a wad of currency and promised the earth, or at least a princess's dowry, to anyone who could get me a line to London. They were untroubled by the request, happy to help, sure there would be no problem. I ran outside, and told John I thought I could make it. As we had agreed before we stopped, he set off for Lagos in our dust-caked taxi to send his own story, leaving me to hire another vehicle when I had filed. In Benin, heading west, I should have no problem. Five minutes later, I was dictating my story in time for the lunchtime editions: 'Biafra is a shambles. The roads are clogged with starving refugees searching for their families and food. Biafran soldiers are coming out of the bush in their hundreds to surrender to the Federal army ... the Nigerian Red Cross have as yet implemented pitifully few of their promises of relief for the civilians ...' I made my splash: 'STANDARD REPORTER GETS THE FIRST EYEWITNESS STORY OF BIAFRA'S LAST HOURS.'

Now, I cared nothing for anything the Nigerians had to say about our travels. I found a taxi, drove exulting into Lagos, and walked into the hotel to meet a gaggle of bemused, bitterly envious colleagues, who reported that Nigerian Special Branch had been looking everywhere for us. But the police were temporarily nowhere to be seen. Was there a chance of just one more miracle? John was already on the telex machine at the post office, filing his own story which made the front page of next day's *Times*, in appropriately more measured language than my own. I stood crouched over the developing tray of the film processor's office in the local Reuters' bureau, while they made a dozen prints from my precious film. Then I jumped back into our faithful taxi with the wet photographs and drove to the Cable and Wireless office. I stood over the Belinograph while the drum speeded round and round, and the scanner transmitted my cherished images one by one to London. Then I went back to the hotel. Cyril Aynsley said, 'I'd better buy you a drink, because nobody else round here feels like doing so.'

I was fast asleep when a courteous, tight-lipped Special Branch man in smartly pressed civilian clothes knocked on the door and told me to pack. In the corridor, I met John Clare with his own escort. We played the innocents and asked what it was all about. The officer declined to enter into a discussion. We were led downstairs with our suitcases and pushed into a

Landrover without further explanation. We were a little frightened, but not very. Too many people knew about our arrest,
and the Nigerian government needed its relationship with
Britain too badly for anything seriously unpleasant to be done
to us. That is how John and I reasoned to each other, anyway.
We shivered in the cold darkness as we were driven across the
city, and were eventually decanted into a plain, bare room in a
concrete building on the edge of the airport, which we found
already occupied by the formidably effective Tony Clifton of
the *Sunday Times* and his photographer John Bulmer. They,
too, had got into Biafra. They had found the same sort of story
as ourselves – but it wasn't Sunday yet. They were not best
pleased by our highly publicized antics, which were already on
the front pages in London, forcing Nigerian officialdom to act
forthwith against disobedient foreign journalists. The *ST* pair
had been hoping they could lie low in Lagos for a day or two
longer. Those hours in detention passed in acute boredom. We
speculated about our likely fate. We agreed that it was
overwhelmingly likely we would be 'PI'd' – declared prohibited
immigrants and deported, an occupational hazard of foreign
correspondents. To pass the time, we began to sing, though
whatever the Clifton-Clare-Bulmer trio contributed, I was
conscious that my voice was unlikely to be of much assistance
in auditioning for either employment or popularity. I paced
the room; relentlessly, maniacally, my restlessness threatening
the others with derangement (as they told me later) even if the
torturers of the Nigerian police stayed their hands.

Then our Special Branch friends returned. Monosyllabically,
they directed us back into the Landrover – and thence, ten
minutes' drive away and without further ado, up the steps of a
glorious, welcoming BOAC VC-10. One of our escort murmured a brief word as we left him. I turned to John.

'What did he say?'

'He particularly liked your rendering of "Oobla-di-oobla-da".'

We gorged ourselves on champagne in the air. Our triumph had been a very small one, indeed imperceptible to a public outside our own trade. If most journalism skates lightly across societies and situations, here we had barely achieved a nodding acquaintance with the rink. But I was just twenty-four, desperate to make a reputation. I knew that I had taken a small step. John Clare vanished to the lavatory. A splendidly upholstered, dazzlingly pretty blonde stewardess, who had scarcely been able to keep her hands off my colleague since we took off, leaned over the seat and seized my arm. Ah, my turn, I thought. Not before time. 'Where has that *divine* man gone?' I sighed deeply. This was the price one paid, and which I was to pay many times again over the years, for going anywhere with John Clare. Landing at Heathrow on Saturday night, we savoured the experience of our first television interviews, of flashbulb-length celebrity on the news bulletins, under the glow of the lights in the VIP Lounge. It *could* be done. I might make it as a reporter, a scoop hunter. This was my first glimpse of the manner in which all sensational newspaper foreign correspondence is conducted: by exploiting a willingness to forget the pack, ignore the conventional wisdom, get away from the colleagues – just go for it. 'Could you give us a line?' the *Telegraph* man pleaded with John Clare as he punched his telex tape in Lagos. It was all about making a line, rather than begging for one. Take a chance. Trust luck and the gods. I basked in that brief experience of Africa, a continent which was to mean much to me in the years ahead. I loved that glancing flirtation with the big story, the major league. I wanted to do it again and again. I once interviewed Desmond Wilcox, a BBC executive whom I disliked almost as much as he disliked me. He dismissed me afterwards to a colleague who

passed on the remark to me: 'typical Beaverbrook journalist'.
Golden words. In those days, I wanted to be nothing else.

I came home to an empty flat, because in many ways I was
a lonely creature. The headlines on my front-page story made
up for any lack of company with whom to celebrate. I sat
gazing at them until I fell asleep with the paper on the floor
beside my pillow. The *Evening Standard* gave me a bonus of
£100 for my scoop, with which I bought a coveted portable
television. The editor and our proprietor, Sir Max Aitken, sent
me flattering notes of the kind all young reporters stick in
their scrapbooks. But I would have preferred to be manhandled
by John Clare's stewardess.

CHAPTER FOUR

Shooting Vietnam

ONE EVENING EARLY in May 1970, four months after my adventure in Biafra, I was at my typewriter in the grimy old *Evening Standard* office in Shoe Lane when I had a call from Anthony Smith, editor of BBC TV's current affairs magazine programme, *24 Hours*. Tony was a former *Tonight* producer who had made a string of films with my father a decade earlier, a clever and pleasantly donnish figure in his early thirties, who later became president of Magdalen College, Oxford. We had last met when I was a teenager, and he was directing my father on the assignment in Jersey during which I was so savagely rebuked by the cameraman for saying that I wanted to go to the wars. 'Max,' said Tony, 'we've got a producer and camera crew lined up to leave tomorrow for Cambodia, but we have no reporter available. Would you like to go?' The American invasion of Cambodia had been launched a few days before. The country was plunged into warfare on a vast new front, or more accurately six or seven fronts. The Americans were attempting to purge the North Vietnamese sanctuaries in the east of the country, while the military government in Phnom Penh, having taken power in a coup, sought to assert control against both Hanoi's forces and its own communists, the Khmer Rouge. I was twenty-four. For any ambitious journalist,

Indochina remained the biggest story on earth. I knocked on Charles Wintour's door. Would he release me to go, if I promised to file for the *Standard*? He sniffed and pondered for a moment. Like most newspapermen of the day, Charles regarded television with some disdain. Through a quarter of a century as an editor, he affected a chill which frightened anyone who didn't know him well. I could find him pretty alarming myself. But over many years, he gave me marvellous opportunities. 'Okay,' he said in his clipped, nasal tones, with a sudden smile. 'I know how much you want to go.'

I was dazed with surprise and excitement. An hour later, I parked outside Lime Grove, the old Rank studio building behind Shepherd's Bush which was the lair of BBC Current Affairs. This was where I had worked as a researcher back in 1963, and where I spent so many lunches in the BBC Club, soaking up the incestuous gossip and dipping my fingers in stardust. I found my way through the rabbit warren of terrace houses alongside the studios, in which the programme makers worked in conditions of unremitting squalor. Tony Smith greeted me effusively, in his invariable schoolmaster's dark suit and V-neck pullover. 'Max! Welcome, welcome. You'll do it, then? Good. Good. It was your stuff from Ulster last year that made us think of you. How's your father?' He introduced me to a string of *24 Hours* staff – clever, noisy, bustling men and women, due to put a programme on the air in a couple of hours. In those days of television's relentless expansion, everybody seemed almost as young as me. Thirty was getting on a bit for a director or even a reporter at Lime Grove in 1970. I shook hands with Tony Summers. He would be my producer, one of the famous wild men of Current Affairs, with an amazing track record of acquiring both girlfriends and unlikely stories all over the world. Summers was in his late twenties, a figure of flowing locks and manic commitment, with a manner that suggested what Byron might have been like, had he been imbued with the spirit of the sixties flower children. He and I had met once before, on the plane from Washington to Memphis two years earlier, the night Martin Luther King was shot. I liked him, and respected his energy. I was nursing considerable secret apprehension, about how I could live up to the part for which they had cast me, as an on-screen reporter. I had appeared in a few television studio discussions, and many times watched my father performing on location, but I had never stood in front of a film camera in my life. What would it be like, to make a debut in the midst of a battlefield? But I was buoyed through the rush of getting jabs and paperwork by euphoria about this wonderful opportunity to report from Indochina. 'Don't worry about money,' said Tony carelessly, 'I've got lots.' In the years since, I have always believed that the BBC's chronic financial difficulties stem from those days when Summers and a few score more of us flew the world, lavishing largesse in all directions from an enormous, apparently inexhaustible wad of 'the Corp's' cash. Still, at least then we spent it on programmes rather than management consultants.

I drove home for a few hours sleep before take-off. Next morning, as I packed I rang Nicholas Tomalin of the *Sunday Times*, that great reporter who had added much to his own laurels in Vietnam. Nick, almost fifteen years older than me, had always been a very good friend to a very young colleague. Now, he gave some rapid practical advice, including the address of the Indian bookshop on Tudo Street in Saigon which offered the best rate for black-market money changing. 'Just remember,' he said in farewell, 'they lie. They lie. They lie.' He meant the Americans and the Saigon regime, of course. But his words represented pretty good advice for a reporter on any assignment. Tony Summers and I were reunited at Heathrow. I tried to avert my eyes while he played out a tearful scene with the woman of the moment, but experience taught me that for Summers, such occasions went with the turf. It was not he who did the crying. We flew to Paris to pick up the camera crew. *24 Hours* used a lot of freelances. They were much less encumbered by the ludicrous and expensive BBC union regulations about manning, overtime and use of lighting – especially on dangerous jobs. The Americans in Indochina did not possess a helicopter large enough to accommodate a full BBC union-approved camera crew. Instead, now, we were taking a two-man French one. Philippe Grosjean, the camera-man, proved to be a slightly built, impish figure in his early thirties who had worked all over the world, and used his boyish good looks and laughter to pursue women even more success-fully than Summers. He was still taking his medicine, literally, for a somewhat disagreeable social disease acquired on his last trip to Saigon. Georges Meaume was a huge, fatherly fellow some years older, who looked like the other half of a successful comedy double act. 'Philippe,' he told me later as I pondered what I could learn from the cameraman's fabulously successful career of sexual conquest, 'is always like a little boy with the girls. He just makes them laugh.' Both men were highly professional, effective operators who had worked with Tony before. No tripods for their cameras – they hand-held their way across the world. We dined lavishly. After years of penny-pinching at the *Standard*, I was impressed by the expansiveness with which Summers threw money about. Television produc-tion staff were not well paid, indeed they were significantly worse off than writing journalists. Crews compensated on assignment, notably by prolific use or abuse of MCOs, airline 'miscellaneous charges orders'. It was an ITN staffer who told me that he bought a wine bar with his proceeds from one Vietnamese campaign.

We flew to Cambodia on an Air France Caravelle, watching

the dubbed version of *Butch Cassidy and the Sundance Kid*. It seemed a long, long way. Eighteen hours and a couple of stops later, we stepped on to the tarmac at Phnom Penh to be met by that blast of clammy heat which remains inseparable from Indochina in the memory of every veteran of the region. We took a couple of rickety taxis to the Monorom Hotel, then reported to the press centre to collect accreditation papers, quaintly expressed in English and Khmer. The city was crowded with refugees – Vietnamese Cambodians seeking to flee the country, in the face of the wave of popular fury towards them following the country's descent into war with Hanoi. They filled churches, warehouses, even the British Embassy garage, as they waited for evacuation flights to Saigon. We gaped at the marzipan temples and monuments, the irresistible beauty of the women in the streets, to whom laughter seemed to come so easily. Indeed, everybody in Cambodia seemed to laugh in those days, almost all the time. We met Fred Emery of *The Times*. In the previous few weeks, Fred had become an honorary adviser to the Phnom Penh government of General Lon Nol, who deposed Prince Sihanouk with a group of fellow army officers. Fred's dispatches since the crisis broke had become required reading. He was one of a handful of foreign correspondents who seemed to have a real grasp of events. Cambodia had lived in its own eccentric time capsule for so long that even the leaders of the country possessed a pitifully unsophisticated world-view. They found themselves soliciting the views of Emery and his French counterpart about how to do business with the Americans and the Vietnamese, even about how to fight a war. Cambodia, far from having fallen into the hands of a determined and brutal military clique, seemed in those days merely to be drifting into an increasingly bloody nightmare, in the hands of a clumsy, confused leadership with no policy beyond that of clinging to power for themselves, and somehow resisting the Khmer Rouge and the forces of Hanoi. The CIA had played a decisive part in precipitating the coup which evicted the government of Prince Sihanouk. But the bewilderment and innocence of Khmer officers and officials about the future were manifest to every foreigner who met them. It was a source of boundless delight to journalists that the Cambodian army's senior intelligence officer responsible for briefing the foreign media was named Am Rong.

The morning after our arrival in Phnom Penh, we set off to find the war. A Cambodian column, we were told, was pushing down Highway One towards the Neuk Long ferry, thirty-odd miles from the capital, where Vietnamese communist troops were dug in. Most of the villages on the road seemed to have been abandoned, though water buffalo still grazed in the fields, the inseparable egrets on their backs. Great tall trees stood stark against the flat horizon of the paddies. We were lucky that we did not know enough to be as afraid as we should have been, given the fate of so many Western journalists on those roads in the weeks that followed. There was no clearly defined front line. The enemy was everywhere and nowhere. An hour out of Phnom Penh by Mercedes taxi, we came upon the Cambodian army. A ragtag of cheerful soldiers was pottering forward, some on foot, others mounted in a miscellany of battered buses, military and civilian trucks. The column, perhaps a battalion strong, was moving at walking pace. We got out of the taxis to march with them. We found Michael Clayton of BBC News, Michael Nicholson of ITN, that great war photographer and best of companions Don McCullin, and a handful of other journalists already among the convoy.

The heat was stultifying. The pace was slow, with constant pauses to steer trucks past or over craters blown by the communists, or to shift felled tree trunks. The road lay along a tree-lined embankment among paddy fields, which stretched

C H I N A

NORTH VIETNAM

Dien Bien
Phu

Hanoi

Nam Dinh

BURMA

N

Mekong River

L A O S

Vientiane

Demilitarized Zone

Cam Lô
Quang Tri
Khe Sanh
Hue
Phu Bài
An Hòa
Da Nang

Tam Ky
Chu Lai

My Lai

T H A I L A N D

Pakse

Dak To

Kontum

Pleiku

Qui
Nhon

An Khê

Central Highlands

SOUTH VIETNAM

CAMBODIA

Bangkok

Mekong River

Ban Me Thuôt
Gia Nghta

Nha
Trang
Dalat

Tuy Hòa

Cam
Ranh
Bay

Phudc Binh

Phan Rang

Phnom Penh

Tay Ninh
Bao Loc
Lai Khe
Xuân Lôc
Phan Thiet

Gulf

Ben Cat
Ben Suc
Biên Hòa
Saigon

Kâmpôt

Long Binh
My Tho

of

Vung Tou

Ha Tien

Thailand

South China

Rach Glê
Can Tho

Sea

Bac Lieu

0   100 miles

SOUTH EAST ASIA

to the horizon on both sides. Summers and the crew began to shoot footage. At this stage, as so often in television, the reporter was a mere supercargo. I chatted to Mike Clayton, mostly about his passion for fox-hunting. The morning wore on. We were very hot, very thirsty. The air of a dusty and uncomfortable holiday outing pervaded the occasion. Even in uniform, Cambodians seemed the most charming and easygoing people. They gave no hint of the capacity for mass murder their people were later to display to such terrifying effect under the communists. None of the soldiers seemed much troubled by their mission, or by any sense of danger. They giggled a lot. Officers shouted and gestured crossly as they struggled to keep the column moving.

The shooting began without warning. Bursts of fire began to sweep the road towards us, interspersed with occasional heavier explosions of mortars and shellfire. I glimpsed our taxi-driver, desperate for the safety of his precious Mercedes, reversing frenziedly towards the rear at thirty miles an hour. The BBC News car took a bullet in the windscreen. More alarming still, the three old tanks which had been leading the column clattered hastily back down the road, far too precious to risk, when the crews discovered that the enemy possessed rocket launchers. The rest of us stumbled down the embankment in search of cover and awaited events. When it became plain that the firefight was likely to persist for some time, Tony Summers said, 'Do a piece to camera.' What? Here, now? I had never done a filmed piece to camera in my life. My shirt was soaked with sweat and dust, my long hair falling over my forehead in lank strips. I squatted in the ditch, scribbled a few trite sentences in my notebook, and sought to memorize them. The crew crouched opposite me and Georges passed me the hand microphone. Tony told Philippe to roll, and I began mouthing my nervous phrases. '*This* is the war in Cambodia.

This column of Cambodian soldiers has been pinned down . . .'
There was another burst of fire over our heads. I lapsed into
a string of frightened curses. 'Cut,' said Tony, exasperated.
The shooting flagged. 'Camera running,' said Philippe. 'Sound
running,' said Georges. I started again. There was another
succession of loud crumps on the road. I collapsed once more.
'Cut,' said Tony. On the eighth take, I completed my little
piece.

In the years that followed, I learned some of the tricks of
doing successful front-line war reports for television. The object
is to convey a sense of the danger of the place – sometimes
spurious – without oneself appearing terminally rattled. This
was the first test I failed on the road to Neuk Long. The other
problem, which took me years to appreciate and begin to
remedy, is that however hostile the conditions, a reporter on
camera may look weather-beaten, but he should not appear
merely a mess. In most of my appearances on *24 Hours*, my
hair was untidily long, and lapsed into a greasy slick after a
few hours in sweat-stained sunshine. My thick spectacle frames
often hid my eyes. My lanky form and uneasy verbal delivery
lacked conviction. The general effect was eccentric rather than
romantic, and tended to make producers reluctant to show me
on camera more than they had to. Whicker I was not.

By the time the shooting stopped – both gunfire and
sixteen-millimetre – thirst as well as fear and dust had eaten
deep into our spirits. We picked ourselves up, retrieved our
taxi-driver, and drove wearily back to Phnom Penh. We had
been given a salutary glimpse of the limitations of Lon Nol's
army, which knew so little of tactics that it merely advanced
to contact in a straggling crocodile. Its guns were ancient and
various, its leadership utterly at a loss, its enemy ruthless and
effective. The communists broke off that action on Highway
One after five hours, withdrawing from their bunkers and

ambush positions with only negligible loss, against a numerically much stronger government force. 'Many Cambodian soldiers simply do not know how to fight,' I wrote in my file to the *Evening Standard*. 'They regard emptying machine-gun fire into the jungle as a substitute for direct assault, move into action painfully slowly, and are facing an enemy who holds every tactical initiative . . . Lacking a total change of mood and strategy, Cambodia remains perilously exposed.'

It was the unpredictable nature of the war, the impossibility of measuring risk or anticipating danger among a people who could not do so for themselves, which cost the lives of twenty-four Western journalists and cameramen in those first months. Almost all were lost not to fire on the battlefield, but through capture and execution by the Khmer Rouge or North Vietnamese army while travelling in search of the front. No correspondent ever knew, as he drove down a road or sought out the latest reported confrontation between government forces and the communists, when or where he might encounter guerrillas who would kill any Westerner without troubling to inspect his press card.

Next morning, Tony and the crew returned to the scene of the previous day's skirmish. At first light that morning, the enemy had staged a suicidal attack on the Cambodian positions, which cost them thirty dead and considerably revived the morale of the government troops. Philippe filmed Cambodian troops stripping the enemy dead of weapons and documents. Their paybooks showed them to be members of the North Vietnamese army's 472nd Regiment. Whatever the demerits of Lon Nol's cause in Cambodia in the eyes of Western liberals, nothing could alter the simple truth that the communists were indeed using the country as a sanctuary from which to wage war on South Vietnam. It was only later, as the war progressed, that Pol Pot's terrible Khmer Rouge of indigenous Cambodians became the chief communist force on the Cambodian battle-field. Later in the day, and through the day that followed, we shot on locations around the capital. We then spent most of a night in our baking hotel room, where I underwent my baptism of commentary recording. Painstakingly, and with constant retakes, Tony set about teaching me the tricks of pitch and emphasis which are essential to every successful broadcaster. When at last we were done, he marked up his notes of how to cut picture to words – 'wildtrack', in the jargon of the trade – for the film editors in London. Then we airfreighted our report, which emphasized the confusion sur-rounding the Cambodian war effort, for transmission on *24 Hours* three days later. In those years before instant satellite transmission became the norm, this was a quick turnaround for a film. All foreign correspondents live for 'herograms' and 'play messages' about their stories, and indeed require a constant drip-feed of hyperbole from their offices, to stave off paranoia in faraway places. Tony Smith cabled from Lime Grove: 'HOORAH YOURE A FILM REPORTER STOP THOR-OUGHLY SUCCESSFUL PIECE OF WAR REPORTING UNRAVELLING OF IGNORED COMPLEXITIES CLEAR WELL PHRASED AND READ STOP SIXTEEN MINUTES STOP REGARDS TONY. Er, yes, well, maybe. Of course I was thrilled by his kind words, but I also knew how wide was the gap between these and the reality of my performance. I had a long way to go to earn my spurs as a broadcaster.

I was captivated by the excitement and novelty of the business. I found the strain very great, however, of learning to be a television reporter in the midst of a great Asian war, rather than in some dozy English provincial setting. Summers never stopped. He was inexhaustible, always on the telephone or calling a taxi to another interview or meeting with a contact. He was a hard taskmaster, unequivocally the prime mover of our team. More than any foreign assignment I have experienced before or since, on that trip to Indochina I allowed myself to be led. Tony was the boss. I followed with the crew. We made one more Cambodian film report, in the beleaguered coastal town of Kampot, which was threatened by a communist encircling movement. 'This is a struggle,' I said in my commentary, 'in which the Cambodians cannot conceivably defeat the communists on their own.'

We received instructions from London to move to Saigon. Tony decided we must first ship our Kampot masterpiece from Hong Kong for 'safety in transit'. I was ecstatic. In those days 'Honkers' was where good foreign correspondents went instead of heaven. I caught my first glimpse of the glittering city by night, before the ferry wafted ourselves and the hotel Rolls-Royce across to the island. With his usual aplomb, Tony had checked us all into the Mandarin. I felt like a peasant storming the Winter Palace. I was twenty-four and had never known such blissful luxury. For thirty-six hours we ate, drank and shopped for toys. Then we flew to Saigon.

Vietnam was the greatest single influence on my generation of journalists. It was the destination to which every ambitious young reporter aspired. Throughout my time in the United States two years earlier, I had lived in a society obsessed with the war, its political implications and the protest against it. I had watched countless newscasts and documentaries from the battlefield. Now, at last, I had got there to see for myself. The bedrock of the war's reporting was a corps of resident staff correspondents for every great international news organization, some good and brave men and a few women, others frankly indolent. At any time, there was also a large floating population of visiting reporters or camera crews like ourselves. Finally, of course, there was a host of eager aspirants who had spent the last few hundred pounds in their own bank accounts to fund a one-way ticket to Saigon, to seek their fortunes as 'stringers' for anyone who would use their work. A few made their reputations that way. Rather more eked out a precarious living by hard work for small reward. A good many others abandoned any pretence of expecting to become stars or even to make careers. They slid effortlessly into the routine of Saigon – the beer, the bar girls, the dope, the Cercle Sportif, the black market, and occasional injections of danger. They fell in love with the infinitely seductive cocktail of Asia, war and an absence of responsibility for anything save ordering the next drink or girl. Some of the freelance photographers, in any other setting on earth, would have been confined as lunatics.

As we sat on the open verandah of the Continental Palace Hotel that first evening, sipping our drinks, gasping a little in the stifling humidity, and watching the lizards scuttle up the walls, at last I felt that I had joined the ranks of foreign correspondents. The relentless clamour of scooters, mopeds, cars, military vehicles dispelled any illusion of oriental tranquillity. Yet this was the bar Graham Greene had made famous, the setting for the greatest media story of modern times. I watched with discreet envy the comings and goings of the press-corps veterans, tanned men in US army fatigues or locally made safari jackets – the first act of every self-respecting journalist was to visit the tailor and order his short-sleeved 'TV suit'. The correspondents threw down cameras and packs beside their tables and sat swapping abuse of the day's US Command briefing, the 'five o'clock follies', or exchanging experiences of what had been going on upcountry, in the combat areas. We looked painfully white, as well as green, beside these men, and a few women, who lived the war.

I wandered for hours around the streets of Saigon, taking in the flower market and innumerable open-air workshops, the Catholic cathedral, the exotic food stalls – and the rubbish.

The thick heat made pollution inescapable. Almost every vehicle seemed to spew black fumes. Stolen military equipment was on sale everywhere. Roundeyes moved about the city in a succession of lurches between the clinging, clammy, almost choking warmth of the streets, and the icy islands formed by air-conditioned offices and hotels, which gave many of us permanent sniffles. The black market was not a place, but a ubiquitous reality whose tentacles were woven through the fabric of the whole city and reached out into the military suburbs of Long Binh and Tan Son Nhut. Saigon's population had grown vastly since the war escalated, swollen by refugees from the countryside. The city was said to contain seventy-seven orphanages, and it must have held at least thirty times that number of bars and whorehouses catering to the vast transient military population. Among all the Americans in the streets, there were more than a few Australians, both soldiers and correspondents. When one saw a body hurtling through a bar window, it was extraordinary how often either the victim or the thrower proved to be Australian – perhaps one of those talented and formidably drunken journalists who loathed Poms and were all called Bruce. I learned to avoid them after, say, 9 p.m. when their eyes reddened dangerously and I was the most conspicuous Pom in sight.

Our first morning was spent at the PX – the US army post exchange – equipping ourselves with American boots and jungle fatigues. A few correspondents wore civilian clothes in the field, but most accepted that they were safer, more likely to get flights and facilities, better clad for the bush, the boonies, the sticks, if they looked as if they belonged. Vietnam was the only war I knew, save for the Falklands, where most reporters dressed army in the field. At US headquarters, MACV – Military Assistance Command, Vietnam – we were issued with a prolix collection of identity cards, entitling us to a high seating priority on flights around the country, and access to American messing facilities. One card included a polite request to the enemy, if he captured the bearer, to treat him as if he held the rank of major. Very generous. The British, on their own military operations, gave correspondents the honorary rank of captain. There is no evidence that an enemy took the slightest notice of either flattering hint.

American generosity to the media in practical matters has become part of the legend of Vietnam. Most journalists, of whatever nationality, accepted it as no more than their due, and were frequently to be seen arguing ferociously at airfields if they found themselves displaced from a C-130 to make way for say, a Marine NCO trying to get home on compassionate leave. The more sensible reporters, such as Nick Tomalin, freely conceded, 'The Americans may not tell you the truth, but they provide the means for you to go and find out the truth for yourself, if you can be bothered.' This was the important reality about Vietnam, unlike so many war zones where journalists are entirely denied access to the front line – including the Gulf conflict as recently as 1990. A core of journalists, some of whom remained in the country for years, were perfectly happy to report from the briefings and comforts of Saigon. There was another faction of madmen, mostly photographers, who had no intellectual interest in the conflict, but obsessively pursued the 'bang-bang' wherever combat was to be found. More than a few paid with their lives. I was reading a book recently about photographers who died in Vietnam, which treated their contribution with reverence. Some indeed took extraordinary pictures, but it seems hard to dignify their loss. They exposed themselves relentlessly to danger because they fell in love with battle, and even with death. All journalists are guilty of voyeurism in some measure. The essential self-indulgence of the war correspondent seems to me to annul any claim to a martyr's status, if death suddenly touches one's own shoulder.

Most reporters of all nationalities worked between the barflies and the death freaks. That is to say, they strove diligently to explore the war and travelled a lot. They saw plenty of combat, but used the fine judgement every correspondent acquires, to avoid excessive risk. Few were foolish enough to travel unescorted by road in dangerous areas, or to land with an airborne spearhead in attack. It is possible to see a good deal of fighting, and to hear a good deal of shooting, without wilfully exposing oneself in the front line. Most television pieces to camera in a war zone – any war zone – are shot beside artillery positions, which convey the necessary sense of lethal activity, while being located beyond the risk of exposure to enemy small arms fire. I have done plenty of 'stand-uppers' in this category myself, although sometimes because the military commanders on the spot would not allow us further forward.

On our second day in Vietnam, clad in embarrassingly virgin-green fatigues, we set off in search of the action. We took off from the hotel in a couple of tiny old blue and cream Renault taxis for Hotel One, the Americans' principal Saigon helicopter pad. We checked in, as for any flight anywhere in the world, and were duly entered on the list for the first available ride to join the 1st Air Cavalry Division inside Cambodia. The sky was heavily overcast. As ever at that season, rain threatened. We spent much of the morning waiting and reading, waiting and talking, waiting and gazing on the relentless, fantastic American air activity all around us. A myth has grown up that in Vietnam a reporter could whistle up a chopper to the battlefield on demand. The truth was a little different. You could always get where you wanted to go – in the end. But among the memories of every Vietnam correspondent are those of endless hours, or even days, lingering in flyblown huts beside remote airstrips.

Many hours and many choppers after we arrived, the GI desk clerk at Hotel One waved us out to a UH1 – the legendary Huey – rotors churning dust on the tarmac. We ran forward in the usual helicopter-boarder's crouch, burdened with packs and camera gear, strapped ourselves into the canvas seats between the door gunners, and a few seconds later swirled into the air. That ascent into the upper atmosphere was one of the most delicious sensations Vietnam had to offer. We were lifted away from the sweat-soaked stifling heat below, into the coolness three hundred feet up. With the doors removed, the view of the ground was perfect. Between the paddy fields, truck convoys and mopeds beetled across the flat horizons. Villages and sandbagged military positions dotted the green landscape. The surrounding sky was rarely empty. Other Huey transports, 'Loach' observation and Cobra attack helicopters criss-crossed our path as they went about the warlike business that never stopped. High above us, there was an occasional glimpse of a pair of ground-attack aircraft, or a lumbering C-130 ploughing on its schedule. Below, even quite close to Saigon, the craters left by bombs and shells pocked the countryside like some fell territorial disease. A madman claimed to have counted them, and worked out that there were twenty-two million across Vietnam.

The Americans had created a vast military society from end to end of the country, with its own barbed-wire-encrusted towns and villages, messing routines, entertainments, transport facilities and daily life, wholly divorced from those of the Vietnamese people outside the perimeters. In 1970, there were 300,000 Americans 'in country', well down on the half-million peak in 1969, still a vast army. Yet the majority of GIs lived

in a wired-off American world, which owed its existence to the
war, but followed a pattern seldom interrupted by the sights
or even sounds of conflict. Only a much smaller number of
soldiers, 'the grunts', the 'poor bloody infantry', were out there
in the boonies, fighting the war for a medal no different from
that later worn by a filing clerk who spent his year in-country
amid the vast coastal base complex at Cam Ranh Bay.

The pitch of the helicopter engine changed sharply as we
began to descend, creating the usual whirlwind of dust, flying
rubbish and flapping groundsheets among the cluster of bivouacs, guns and vehicles on the ground beneath us. We shouted
our thanks to the crew and jumped out, humping our unwieldy
equipment. It was a miracle that any camera or recorder worked
at all amid the chronic red dirt that clung to every living or
inanimate object in the country. Within minutes of washing
in the morning, every man had acquired a second skin, a layer
of soaking grit beneath his fatigues.

At the 'firebase' where we landed on the Cambodian border
– a battalion-scale defensive ring of the kind the Americans
created everywhere they went in Vietnam – we were greeted
with the curiosity bored soldiers often show to correspondents,
especially foreigners. Graham Greene wrote of his experience
with the French on the same battlefield, almost twenty years
earlier: 'The further you get from headquarters, the looser
becomes the control until, when you come within range of the
enemy's fire, you are a welcome guest – what has been a
menace for the état-major in Hanoi, a worry for the full colonel
in Nam Dinh, to the lieutenant in the field is a joke, a
distraction, a mark of interest from the outer world.' Most war
correspondents anywhere in the world discover the truth of
Greene's observation in *The Quiet American*. Here, among the
bunkers and vast accumulation of military stores, the Americans talked to us about their brushes with the enemy, their

86

dislike of being in Cambodia, their passionate personal obsession – how many days 'short' of going home they were – with
the fluency and lack of inhibition common to almost every
American in any situation. We filmed all day around their
positions, and then spent a hellish night in a tiny tent, never
able to sleep more than an hour at a time, amid outgoing
artillery fire. A section of long-barrelled 155 mm guns was
dug in fifty yards behind us. In accordance with routine
American practice in Vietnam, at intervals throughout the
hours of darkness the gunners laid down 'harassing fire',
shooting blind at likely looking grid references in the hope of
discouraging enemy movement. 'H & I' – harassment and
interdiction – was among the most grotesque tactical practices
of the war. The thunderous explosions jarred our eardrums and
nerves as we strove to sleep, even though we knew 'outgoing'
fire posed no peril to ourselves. In that narrow perimeter, there
was no place else to go. We crawled out of the bivouac at
dawn, filthy and weary, to start work once more.

An hour later, a torrential monsoon downpour drenched
the camp. Scores of soaked and dirty GIs tore off their clothes
and scampered whooping and yelling under the sheets of warm
water. On the ground, streams of red rain swelled into torrents,
flooding foxholes and bivouacs, gathering sodden rubbish as
they ran between the gun positions. When the rain stopped,
the BBC contingent presented a sorry spectacle, matted hair
falling on to our mud-soaked fatigues, camera equipment only
feebly protected by polythene. When we had finished shooting,
we waited four hours for a chopper out. That evening, as we
approached Hotel One I dreamt of hot baths and cold drinks
just a taxi-ride away. Tony Summers shouted above the noise
of the chopper, 'Just time to get a flight up to Air Cav
headquarters and interview General Casey.'

'Fine,' I shouted back. 'First thing tomorrow.'

'*Not* first thing tomorrow,' corrected Tony. 'If we're to ship on Friday, we must get up there tonight.'

I pleaded, I begged, cajoled, argued the crew's even greater exhaustion, quite in vain. An hour after reaching Hotel One, filthy and exhausted as ever, we took off again for 1st Air Cav's divisional headquarters. We landed on the edge of a rubber plantation an hour north-westwards at Quan Loi, amid the routine concussions of the night's harassing fire, and a monsoon storm which had churned every track into red mud, and caked us even on the brief jeep ride from the airstrip to the head-quarters. An American officer told us they liked the place, because they always knew when a communist attack was imminent. The French plantation manager, who like most of his compatriots lived in comfortable concord with the local Viet Cong, disappeared to Saigon in his light aircraft twelve hours or so before shooting was due to start, returning when peace was restored. After a tolerable night in one of the Air Cav's huts, early next morning we interviewed the divisional commander, General George W. Casey, an affable officer who dismissed my questions about the growing vulnerability of helicopters to communist ground fire with the assurance: 'Max, the Hueys can handle it.' Casey himself was killed two months later, when his helicopter was shot down by North Vietnamese ground fire.

We finished the film after another all-night recording session in the hotel room, as always sweat pouring down our faces, because the air conditioning had to be switched off to prevent the noise intruding on the soundtrack. I may not much have liked Summers that week, but my respect for him was immense. His energy pushed us to work a timetable that I could never have sustained alone. He lobbied relentlessly for an interview with either President Thieu or Vice-President Ky, at a time when every official assured us that neither would talk to foreign media. On our last day in the country, both accepted simultaneously. We shot a long interview with Thieu. Tony brusquely informed Ky's staff that their man would not be needed.

We now moved on to cover the Vietnamese assault on Cambodia from the south, riding in from Chow Duc with General Dzu, the burly, ruthless, famously corrupt Vietnamese IV Corps commander who was killed a year or two later. We filmed with him in the captured Cambodian ghost town of Kampong Trac, and saw the sorry remnants of the Cambodian garrison there. There were helicopter trips to land with the Vietnamese – 'the Arvin' – weary plods across the paddy fields behind their infantry, filming those uneager warriors emptying their weapons into the jungle ahead to cover their advance – that awful American-inspired habit of 'reconnaissance by fire'; we were shown endless caches of captured communist weapons, but nothing which persuaded us that Saigon's drive into Cambodia was worth the terrible purchase price in both politics and blood. In the field, I found myself yearning for water as passionately as ever I had in Cyprus seven years earlier; and learning to spend days on end in fatigues beneath which one's entire upper body was sodden with sweat. Everyone smoked, all the time. Any Vietnamese would have been justified in laughing hysterically at the idea of being endangered by lung cancer. How strange it seems, looking back, that one grew accustomed to riding a Huey sitting on the floor at the open door, feet on the skids, arm locked carelessly around a stanchion as one gazed down on the patchwork of paddies a few hundred feet below. We took it for granted, because that is what everybody did. How I loved those choppers, thrashing through the cold upper air, and how I hated to march on foot in that terrain, especially in the rainy season.

We knew moments of intense beauty, such as when we flew up to the old French hill station of Dalat to shoot a sequence in one of the loveliest places in Indochina. When Summers found the airline schedule to get there unsatisfactory, he merely chartered a Dakota to take us. Dalat seemed a million miles from the war, with its stone walls and pine trees, the giggling high-school girls in their white ao dais, weekending couples boating on the lake in the cool breeze. The old Palace Hotel, a marvellous imperial relic, was panelled in wood, decked in antlers and other sporting trophies, and possessed a library of elderly French novels.

Those who know Vietnam only from Hollywood's perverted version, the idiocies of *The Deerhunter*, are often amazed when I say that I fell in love with the place. So did many Europeans, who were untroubled by the paucity of television channels, the unhygienic markets, the absence of freeways, and all the other shortcomings of the country which so distressed Americans. Those who know Vietnam from the terrible images of combat photographers think of the country only in terms of pain and suffering. There were plenty of them, to be sure. But there was also much that was lyrical and wonderful. Forget the war, ignore the armies for as many hours as you could, and Vietnam and its people seemed captivating. Dinners at the marvellous riverside restaurants which served some of the finest seafood in the world, hours gossiping in the cafés ogling the girls, or merely gazing entranced at the beauty of the Central Highlands in early morning, the water buffalo in the fields – stripped of its appalling alien vulgarities, of the awful dead weight of tawdriness flown in daily across the Pacific, this seemed one of the loveliest places on earth. Vietnam was once among the richest agricultural societies in Asia, but its economy had been tragically distorted by the import of consumer and luxury goods on a fantastic scale. I am not in the least anti-American, indeed I love and admire the United States and its people. I was never a Vietnam radical, committed to the victory of the communists. I was merely one of many Europeans who recoiled from the poisonous, crass, irredeemably materialist anti-culture America had imported to that marvellous society. People like me found ourselves in uneasy political limbo, despairing of Washington's unwinnable war, yet convinced that the Vietnamese deserved better than a life under Hanoi's commissars.

We pored over endless drafts of scripts on my Olivetti portable, Summers bent beside me in the mercifully air-conditioned room at the Caravelle, opposite the Continental Palace. Tony, Philippe and Georges were seasoned veterans of Asia. They found the best French restaurants, the cheapest tailors, the black market which so enriched every roundeye who came to Saigon with green money. My primitive school French was enhanced by acquiring a more practical vocabulary for the situation in which we found ourselves, from Philippe and Georges. *Je m'en fous* and *j'en ai marre* covered most Vietnamese predicaments admirably. And of course, there were the girls. I remember a restaurant run by a stunningly beautiful half-French, half-Vietnamese mother and daughter. As I recollect, Summers got the mother, Philippe the daughter, and Georges her daughter's friend. Me? I sulked in my room and read Frances Fitzgerald's modern history of the Vietnamese *Fire in the Lake*, the author of which commanded much respect in Saigon, because she was one of the very few US correspondents who had troubled to learn the language.

We made one film in an American base north of Saigon, about the intense hostility to the war which now prevailed among GIs. They talked to us outside their huts and bunkers with a fluency and indifference to disciplinary consequences that would have seemed extraordinary in any other army and place. 'Fragging', the terrorization or even killing of over-enthusiastic officers, was becoming a commonplace. We realized that we were witnessing a moral collapse unknown in any Western fighting force for generations. I saw no heroin, though we knew it was there in most barrack rooms, but every day we were meeting men visibly stoned on duty. It was disconcerting to notice chopper pilots smoking pot in the air. I have always been so frightened of my own weakness for excess in almost everything, that neither then nor since have I dared even to puff a joint, but I must have been almost the only living creature in Indochina not to do so. It was raining heavily most days now. When we could not get helicopter places, or flights were grounded, we travelled in jeeps with the road convoys, arriving caked in mud from head to foot.

One day, we were filming with an American airborne unit, alongside one of the captured communist rice caches inside Cambodia. I was interviewing their crew-cut commanding officer in deep shade beneath the jungle canopy, when several short bursts of incoming small arms fire flew over our heads. Everybody dived for cover. After a few seconds of panic, men crouching behind the rice sacks returned fire, and then set off into the thick vegetation in abortive pursuit of the attacker. After a few minutes, peace was restored. We all stood up and shook ourselves down.

'Did you get any of that on film?' Tony asked Philippe.

'*Non*,' said the cameraman, tossing his head. '*J'étais sous le camion.*'

Tony brooded for a moment. Then he turned to the American colonel. 'Do you think we could do that again?' he demanded.

The colonel looked astonished. 'How do you mean?'

'Oh, you know – get somebody to fire a couple of rounds, then take cover and return fire.'

It has been heavily on my conscience ever since, that the obliging Americans eventually did what was wanted. The sequence Philippe shot appeared in one of our films. This was a classic demonstration of the difficulties of shooting a war.

The solution adopted was – and remains – very common to television. In the heat of the moment, it proves too difficult to catch a dramatic episode on film. Thus, it must be reconstructed. In the mind of the director, the reconstruction is valid, because the incident really took place. Much of television's current affairs output, in the hands of any nation or any producer in war or peace, is created by these means. Yet, when they are extended to life and death situations, many of us who have worked in television are deeply troubled, because we are party to a deceit. I have no ready answer to the dilemma – over the years of making seventy or eighty television films, I have been party to the use of these techniques many times, though only once to simulate action in battle, on that day in Cambodia. But the necessity to employ them is one reason why I, like many journalists, was far happier recording war for a newspaper than for television. Some very brave television reporters shoot extraordinary sequences in battle, at mortal risk to their lives – I have seen Mike Nicholson of ITN, for instance, do remarkable things under fire. But I have also seen many, many camera crews incite artillery batteries to open fire on the enemy – frankly, to try to kill people – simply for 'the shot'. The overwhelming majority of alleged combat sequences shot on film in the twentieth century and screened and transmitted again and again as authentic are, in reality, fakes – or at least heavily embellish the nature of the experience they purport to show. Every knowledgeable and honest television documentary-maker knows this. Newspapers perpetrate their own deceits, but there are lies woven into the very nature of television which most of its creators ignore, because they take them for granted.

We flew home via Hong Kong, and another marvellous two nights at the Mandarin, laden with the duty-free toys that seem so wonderful when you are twenty-four, and so meaningless when you are thirty years older. Autocrat though he might be on location, Summers was meticulously egalitarian when it came to dividing the spoils of war, and dealt the balance of the production budget into four neat heaps of fifty dollar bills before we took off from Kai Tak. We had made five films in all, and back in London Tony Smith was charmingly complimentary about them – much more so than my work deserved. A few very young men prove themselves effective television presenters. But most are flawed in the eyes of the viewer by their immaturity. I was one of those, and I have blushed ever since to look back at the tapes of the first Vietnam reports I shot. How strange it seemed, too, to watch our films in the cool comfort of the Lime Grove viewing theatre. In vivid colour, our experiences looked lush, glossy, seductive. They captured little of the heat and exhaustion and sometimes fear in which they had been shot. I have always believed that war looks infinitely more real in black and white.

Yet Tony Smith was sufficiently pleased with our doings to send me on another tour a few weeks later to Yemen and the Trucial States, where, thanks to my very able producer Will Aaron, we prospered. A month or two after that, I was offered a full-time contract as a *24 Hours* reporter. I accepted. The novelty and glamour of television current affairs were irresistible. Television seemed to represent the future of journalism, and the hub of its power. No one would then have predicted the fashion in which, by the end of the century, the camera would so starkly have shown its limitations, nor would they have dared to anticipate the prosperity of so many British newspapers at the millennium. Charles Wintour responded kindly to my letter of resignation at the beginning of 1971, but wrote, 'You are wise to make the change. I did not wish to suggest it myself, as I value your work for the *Standard* very highly. But it is really not possible to work for two masters, and we cannot satisfy your wanderlust.' I felt a pang of guilt. I knew that the *Standard* had less than its moneysworth out of me after I began to film for the BBC. On the one big story to which I was dispatched for the paper, the mass aircraft hijackings to Jordan in September 1970, I behaved ingloriously. My copy included the memorably rash prophecy, 'It is plain that King Hussein's long honeymoon with survival is drawing inexorably to a conclusion.' A few days after arriving in Amman, I agitated to come home, because I had rented a Scottish shooting lodge for a holiday and was due to meet a dozen friends on Euston station to travel up there. By dint of frenzied intrigue, I got a place on what proved the last civilian flight out of Jordan for weeks, as the country erupted into civil war. I knew I had let down the paper by flying out just as the big story was breaking. I ran away from the Intercontinental Hotel in Amman hours before it embarked on weeks under siege, as some old colleagues still like to recall when they fancy I am getting above myself.

I would miss Charles Wintour and the *Standard* very much, and returned to the paper less than three years later. But meanwhile, I had to get television out of my system.

CHAPTER FIVE

Ticket to Firebase Six

SOON AFTER I moved to Lime Grove, *24 Hours* was wound up and replaced by a new late-night current affairs programme, *Midweek*. Like most of the editorial team, I simply transferred from the old show to the new one, and went on making the same kind of films, though under a much less sympathetic editor than Tony Smith. In the spring of 1971, I returned to Indochina with Will Aaron – a delightfully fey, witty and immensely talented Welshman who became a close friend – and a British camera crew, Alan Phillips and Freddy Downton. Fred was one of Lime Grove's longest-serving veterans, a skinny, fatalistic, bespectacled northerner in his early fifties, who would eat anything and go anywhere without complaint, as long as the producer signed his extravagant time sheets. There was no location in the world where Fred had not already seen the camera tripod erected, with Alan Whicker or Fyfe Robertson or Julian Pettifer, for the old *Tonight* programme, *24 Hours* or *Panorama*. His chirpy catchphrase, as he listened to interminable exchanges of Lime Grove gossip around the hotel dinner table was always: 'He speaks very well of you, y'know.' Will Aaron had not much wanted to go to war. He was a peaceful, reflective, highly creative man, happiest among his Welsh-speaking friends in the hills of Snowdonia. But we had done well together in the Gulf and later making a film in East Pakistan in the aftermath of a cyclone. There were never any of the tensions between us, of the kind which so often prevail in television between the front-camera presenter and chronically resentful and jealous production staff. I badgered and cajoled Will into accepting the Indochina assignment, because I wanted very much to travel with him again.

We landed once more in Phnom Penh, and drove off southwards in the same fashion as the previous year to find the war. Little had changed. The communists had gained ground. American influence and destructive power had become more pervasive, above all through their devastating heavy bomber campaign. The government forces seemed no more effective. The atmosphere in forward areas with the Cambodian forces remained untinged with any sense of purpose, far less bellicosity. The ambition of those gentle people seemed focused upon the struggle for daily existence, rather than any wish to move mountains – or, in the case of the soldiers, enemy positions. The profound tragedy of the situation was evident. As the country crumbled, its government became ever more despotic and corrupt. Beauty was still there – there was always beauty in Cambodia, the lush flowers and foliage, the fading colonial buildings, above all the people. But the worm of destruction was eating deeper and deeper into this society assaulted by forces guided by Hanoi and Washington, which it lacked the will, the ambition, the ruthlessness, and the means to defy successfully.

From Phnom Penh, we flew north to Vientiane, to make a film about the war in Laos, an even more confused and desultory affair than the Cambodian campaign. Journalistically, this trip was not a success. The Byzantine politics of Vientiane, where to fulfil some mad clause of a past treaty the communist Pathet Lao maintained an official diplomatic presence a few miles from the ministries of the anti-communist government with which they were alleged to be at war, defied rationality. The corruption and tangled loyalties of the Lao warlords, overlaid on the colossal, institutionalized inefficiency of the country, negated every American effort to pursue a strategy for military victory. From the heavily fortified American compound, Washington's ambassador 'Almighty' Godley – much derided for his bombast and belligerence, not least by the British ambassador – sought to arrange the flattening of the communist forces by air attack and sponsored client warfare. Perhaps it was our own immaturity which caused us to focus as much upon the black farce of the Laos situation, as upon its tragedy. But we were in good company. If this was not a comic-opera society, the struggle for its dominance was conducted by a gallery of comic-opera characters, albeit employing deadly weapons, and extracting a terrible price from the Lao people.

We spent a week playing miniature skittles beside the hotel swimming pool, before we could gain permission to leave Vientiane. Will Aaron was in his element, filming one of the annual, very drunken, Lao 'rocket festivals' that fell during our enforced stay, but we were in the country to report a war, not to bask in local folklore. After growing almost mad with frustration, at last we were given permits to travel. We went east into the hills, to film among the Meo tribesmen, who had suffered so desperately at the hands of both sides. The place and the people were enchanting, but it remained hard to get a grip on the context, the significance, of their predicament.

We flew on to the town of Pakse, where the communists were reported to be massing for an assault. On our arrival, we found apathy and lethargy, apparently indistinguishable from those which prevailed on so many other alleged battlefronts in

Laos and Cambodia. We shot a few hundred feet of film of such military activity as we could see. We were setting up in a street close to the centre of the town when a jeep drew up alongside, containing two Americans in civilian clothes. 'You people media?' they demanded. Yes, we said, BBC. 'Then get your asses out of here and up to the airfield as fast as you can. We have word that the communists are going to hit this town tonight with everything they've got, and we're evacuating all US personnel and TCNs.' TCNs were Third Country Nationals – citizens of Thailand or Korea or wherever – whom the Americans used in Indochina on jobs for which they were reluctant to pay American salaries or risk American lives. Our Paul Revere stand-in sounded far too plausible to doubt the truth of his message. As the jeep swung away, we looked hastily for our taxis and ordered them towards the big airfield. We arrived, bundled out with our equipment, paid off the drivers, and hastened over to the nearest hut to ask about the evacuation.

Three crew-cut Americans in slacks and civilian shirts were standing nearby, erect and unclubbable. Many of the spooky types in Indochina cultivated a conscious air of menace, and we did not need the M16s and heaps of equipment at their feet to know that they belonged to the CIA or one of the various American-sponsored private armies in Laos. ' 'Scuse me, guys, but please could you tell me where the evacuation's happening?' I asked. I was ignored. I repeated the question twice before one man muttered bleakly, 'We're not here. We don't exist.' He resumed his scan of the far horizon. I gave up. For twenty minutes, we straggled hot and nervous around the airfield asking for guidance, until a Lao officer apprehended us, perhaps at the instigation of those unsociable Americans. 'You are not supposed to be here. You come to my headquarters,' he said crossly. We were bundled into a truck, driven a couple of miles down the road to a cluster of barracks and huts, shown into a bare room, and left there with a sentry on the door for the next two hours.

We were not happy. The Lao made it plain they knew nothing about any evacuation. For all we knew, they might hold us in detention until every roundeye had bailed out of Pakse, leaving us to face the music when the communists stormed in. Afternoon dragged into evening. At last, the door opened to reveal the American who had first warned us of the evacuation, obviously embarrassed, and a Lao officer, obviously furious. 'Come on, quick,' said the American, bundling us into his jeep. We were driven back to the airfield, and shoehorned on to an old C-47 Dakota, already heavily laden with assorted Americans and TCNs. Sagging with relief as we lay on the floor among a mass of bodies and equipment, we dozed our way back to Vientiane, grateful to have escaped the impending bloodbath. In reality, the communists did not attack Pakse that night, nor for many months afterwards. But our absurd flight highlighted the cultural chasm between the Lao and the Americans. The Americans had evacuated Pakse without giving local government forces the smallest indication of what they were doing or why.

A few days later, we flew back into Saigon. We made three films in Vietnam on this trip, and I was far better pleased with them than with my novice efforts the previous spring. For the first, we travelled north to the port of Da Nang on a fixed-wing aircraft, and filmed the departure ceremony of the 1st Marine Division, which had been based at Da Nang since it waded ashore in 1965. Now, from the reviewing stand its commander proclaimed the triumph of the United States, another job well done by the Marine Corps, as the companies of big, stern young men marched past for the last time, so grateful to be going home. Every man on the tarmac knew that the division was packing up for the same reason every American was packing up. They had had enough. The patience of their nation was exhausted and Nixon was taking them away. US troop numbers had fallen to 160,000, and were now shrinking fast. We spent a strange night in the officers' club on the beach, eating lobster in what might have been a set for *South Pacific* to the strains of Hawaiian guitars on the sound system. The letdown was the lack of romance. In one corner of the club sat a cluster of American nurses, not all lacking in physical attraction, while in the other stood hunky Marines in crew-cuts and camouflaged fatigues, occasionally glancing at the women with expressions of naked fear. Those Marines and those nurses never spoke all evening.

Next morning, a Huey lifted us first to Firebase West, the usual wasted hilltop stripped of vegetation, disfigured with bunkers, equipment and a forest of radio and television aerials. From there we flew on to join a company of the US 23rd Infantry Division, to march and film with them while they conducted a sweep of the Hep Duc Valley. The Huey dropped us into a clearing in the midst of dense jungle, then swung away again, spinning round in its own length in the air, driven with the wonderful dexterity which almost every American chopper pilot in Indochina seemed to possess.

By 1971, the American army's disgust with its own role in the Vietnam War, which had been growing ever more bitter for three years past, was plumbing its nadir. The commander of A Company, 4/31st Regiment, an efficient and impressive career officer named David Borrison, was so weary with the struggle to guide his men, if only in the interests of their own survival, that he had applied for a transfer to the Vietnamese Rangers. 'Perhaps there was a time about a year or two back when we had to make a decision here,' he told me. 'It was obvious that discipline and morale were starting to crack right open. We had to choose between really jumping on the trouble and stamping it out – which would have been unpopular back in the States – or just letting things ride. We let it go. Now, it's too late. Most of the professionals have just stopped trying to make their boys do things they don't want to. Oh yes, they'll still do all the routine things like running supplies and working on maintenance and keeping the hot showers going. But what we've lost, and I don't see how we ever get back, is the will to engage and defeat the enemy. We've established a precedent of letting soldiers opt out of doing their fighting.'

In the midst of the jungle, we interviewed men who described on film their unwillingness to fight, who talked of the daily negotiation process with their own officers, about what they were or were not prepared to do on the battlefield. It was an extraordinary experience, to be allowed to talk freely to soldiers in a state of institutionalized mutiny. Any pretence at tactical discretion in the field had been abandoned. One of Borrison's platoon commanders had made a personal decision that he would fight only with small arms, and would not employ Claymore mines, Mickey Mouses or other lethal explosive devices, because he thought them 'unfair'. Fear of enemy booby traps, heightened by their own frequent casualties caused by men tripping so many in the bush, had eaten deep into morale. 'Maybe "higher-higher" has a plan,' shrugged a corporal, 'but we don't know what it is.' I lit a cigarette with a man's lighter inscribed wearily:

We are the unwilling,
Led by the unqualified,
Doing the impossible,
For the ungrateful.

Hueys dropped in daily to deliver hot food and goodies to a unit supposedly conducting a covert sweep through hostile territory. One evening, before we bivouacked, most of the company tore off their clothes, threw down their weapons, and ran whooping for a swim in the river, overlooked by miles of densely covered hillside on each side of the valley. Any enemy could have massacred them. Yet in those last years of the war, it was impossible to persuade these men that no combatant in any war can look for safety by abandoning the struggle all on his own. Many Americans paid with their lives for refusing to accept this. I said in one of my film commentaries: 'In war it takes two to decide that it's all over.' Was it Firebase Mary-Anne which was overrun while most of the garrison were stoned out of their minds?

When our company advanced, Borrison called down the usual artillery 'reccon by fire' across the line of march. 'Direction 5600. Proximity. First round Willie Pete . . .' We stood watching and filming the laconic fire orders for a deadly cocktail of White Phosphorus and high explosive, the salvos plastering the countryside a few hundred yards ahead. The previous night, the company had unleashed thirty rounds at a sampan passing on the river, for this was a 'Free Fire Zone', in which every living or moving thing not American was presumed to be hostile. It was hard to conceive that these operations fulfilled any useful military purpose. We plodded through the grasses, which reared a yard above our heads, the men looking like parodies of soldiers in their sun specs, plastic insecticide bottles taped to their helmets. Like tens of thousands of other American combat infantry in Vietnam at this stage of the war, they were going through the motions. Their chief ambition was to deter the enemy from making any rendezvous with them. They felt not the slightest shame about admitting as much on camera.

'What are you fighting for?'

'Survival. To get out of here.'

Maybe it is often like that for any army, especially a conscript one, but the matter is seldom made so brutally explicit.

The physical strain on a camera crew was considerable, of accompanying a force in the jungle even for a limited period. The cameraman, for obvious reasons, could hump only the Arriflex and battery belt; the sound recordist, likewise, only his big Nagra and tapes. In our packs, Will Aaron and I were carrying spare film and magazines, together with water, food and kit for us all. Before we boarded the Huey for Hep Duc, the Americans urged us to take M16 rifles, and were bemused when we declined. I told them truthfully that we had more than enough equipment on our backs. I never had moral scruples about carrying a weapon for self-defence, only practical ones. No enemy meeting a reporter in a firefight wearing American jungle greens was likely to look at his press card before pressing the trigger. Even Richard West, least bellicose of British reporters, carried a sub-machine-gun when he was writing about the American Special Forces elephant unit because he believed his own survival might depend on doing so. But only a couple of times in my own war corresponding days have I briefly picked up a weapon, both in the Falklands. I never fired it. In general, a gun is unlikely to save one's life. Self-preservation is the only justification for being armed. It is obviously not the business of journalists, even in their own nations' wars, to kill people. Some correspondents routinely carried arms, in Vietnam, Afghanistan and elsewhere, but these were almost invariably the 'war freaks' who did so to add to the excitement. They were by no means reluctant to find an excuse to shoot someone.

Filming in the boonies was punishingly hard work –

lugging the gear, setting up for shots, helping Alan and Freddy's constant struggle to keep their equipment serviceable. Emulsion sometimes began to peel off the tapes in the heat. In those days of mechanical rather than electronic cameras, it was not only possible, but often essential, for crews to spend hours dismantling their kit piece by piece to repair a fault, and faults there were plenty in the wilds of Indochina. Will Aaron was directing superbly, as always, but he loathed every contact with military life, from wearing fatigues to gunfire. He was rather less afraid than I was, but frankly furious that I had let him in for this bloody assignment. We ate the usual C-Rations without much enthusiasm and slept in hammocks, jabbing the insects in our sleep, listening to the incessant night noises of the jungle. We were vastly grateful when we could agree that we had enough film in the can. The grunts called up a Huey to pull us out. As the chopper approached, a GI tossed down a coloured smoke grenade to mark a landing place. The red cloud billowed forth, and that welcome chopper descended into it like a pantomime monster beckoned by the sorcerer. A few minutes later, we were on our way back to Firebase West, and thence on to Da Nang. It was characteristic of the unreality about so much of Vietnam that by evening, showered and changed, we were eating a lobster dinner in the officers' club on the surf-washed seashore.

A few days later, we flew up from Saigon to Pleiku in the Central Highlands, and thence onwards to Tan Kanh, the support base for a beleaguered South Vietnamese position named Firebase Six. We were filming a sequence for a report on the progress of Vietnamization – Nixon's attempt to rationalize the transfer of responsibility for the war from American to South Vietnamese forces. The wounded and the dead were coming in constantly. Firebase Six was a desolate, blackened ridge perhaps five hundred yards long, and almost shorn of vegetation by the time we arrived, as was the ground below it for hundreds of feet in all directions. It looked like the scene of a terrible forest fire, as indeed in many respects it was. It stood close to the border with Laos, and had been under siege by the North Vietnamese for many days. Its survival was considered a critical test of the ARVN's – the Army of the Republic of South Vietnam – will to fight.

We waited hours to catch a ride on a resupply chopper for the last few miles to the base, meanwhile filming wounded being brought in, ammunition rushed forward, and the guns firing support missions. Then, as at last we sat in a Huey on the strip with the rotors turning, waiting for take-off, a communist rocket slammed into the tarmac nearby. Shrapnel blew several holes in our chopper's windows, and did no good at all to our nerves. On the twenty minute run-in, our door gunners sprayed the ground beneath us to try to keep the enemy's heads down. None of the heavy fire from the ground seemed to come near us. Wrecked helicopters lay everywhere. We could see long convoys of ARVN trucks on the ground, stalled in the path of North Vietnamese interdiction fire. When we finally hit the ground at Firebase Six, we threw ourselves out and crawled into a nearby foxhole, before creeping warily out again as the sound of the Huey engine receded into the distance. We found ARVN Rangers standing in a long row on the skyline above us, laughing heartily at our grovelling figures. We had arrived during a pause in the North Vietnamese bombardment. Nobody had fired a round on this flank for some hours. The defenders took no 'incoming' throughout our visit, though artillery fire and Cobra gunship attacks continued to pound the countryside relentlessly a few hundred yards westward. There was never silence.

The ARVN here were among the best troops in Saigon's army, and looked far more professional and confident than most of their comrades in line units. But there was something inherently incongruous about the sight of those slightly built figures clad in the clothing and equipment provided by the Americans, the GI helmets which looked grotesquely huge on their modest heads. Even weapons looked oversized in Vietnamese hands. Most South Vietnamese soldiers affected skintight combat fatigues which emphasized the contrast. They always looked like men fighting a borrowed war, rather than one that was their own property. Herein lay the worm which gnawed Saigon's war effort from the first day to the last.

I did the inevitable piece to camera at Firebase Six, and we filmed in the ARVN positions for a few hours before catching a ride back to Pleiku. It was plain that the position was being held solely on the back of overwhelming American fire and air support. President Thieu had told me in an interview the previous spring that he was confident that within a year the ARVN could sustain its war with only the aid of American fire support and logistics, and that within two to three years he believed they would be able to manage without even these. This was fantasy. I wrote: 'If President Nixon is looking to the Vietnamese to save themselves, the heavy American hardware had better stay very, very close.' It would not do so, of course. There were only gestures. I have an odd memory of wandering into a hut on the American base at Pleiku and finding it crammed with small boxes. Curious, we opened a few, which proved to contain nothing but medals – thousands upon thousands of medals. As the Vietnam War crumbled around Washington's heads, the higher command's most significant response appeared to be to load every grunt, however humble, with baubles in such profusion that a GI in dress uniform jangled as he walked.

At the airstrip that night, looking for a lift to Saigon, we asked about the C-130 being loaded on the tarmac. 'You can't

ride that,' said the air-force desk clerk. 'It's carrying KIAs. Air-
force regulations say no passengers can travel with KIAs.' We
retired. The regulation about live bodies not travelling with
dead ones, men Killed In Action, seemed unbreakable. Then
an American CBS reporter hustled into the hut with his crew.
He had the same conversation with the clerk, with the same
result. The CBS man shouted a good deal and demanded a
telephone connection to MACV in Saigon. If I had tried the
same line of language on an RAF officer which our American
counterpart unleashed down the line on USAF headquarters,
we would never again have ridden on any RAF flight. But now
we saw a demonstration of the vast power of the media in
American society. A few minutes later, we were clambering
into the belly of the C-130.

It was a sombre flight. We were exhausted, and our little
group huddled dozing or reading at the forward end of the
almost empty hold. At the rear, under the stark, bright cargo
lights, as we droned through the darkness I gazed on the lonely
green body bag containing the remains of a US infantry
sergeant. He had been an adviser at Firebase Six. Around him
were stacked his pathetic personal possessions – a portable
stereo, guitar, suitcase, the usual crude local handicrafts. 'Crazy,
isn't it?' said the loadmaster, shaking his head. 'Getting
knocked off when we're giving up anyways.' Poor bastard.
There was no more glory to be won here, if there ever was any.
There was only the dud lottery ticket of being one of the last
victims of American failure. In Saigon, as an honour guard
received his body, I could not forget seeing it so carelessly
tossed down from the helicopter which had brought it back
from Firebase Six. In a day or two in his home town back in
the United States, the sergeant's coffin would be endowed with
all the ceremonial and sentiment in which Americans enfold
their war dead. The more remote this man became from the

battlefield, from reality, the more honoured would be his carcass. Back in the hotel room in Saigon that night, I wrote a piece for the *Evening Standard*, centred upon the lonely corpse on his way home, and what he seemed to symbolize for the United States in south-east Asia. There were all manner of things I wanted to say, which I knew would not fit into a television script.

Nothing distresses the American army more about the whole business of winding down this war than knowing that some American, somewhere, is going to have to be the last one to die in Vietnam. It's all as unfair as a boardroom row in which the director who's already agreed to resign finds himself not only hustled out of the door, but being kicked down the stairs as well. Yet it would be wrong to imagine the Americans in Vietnam as a defeated army – there is still enough of that seductive air of irresistible might to make one marvel that there is an enemy left. What has happened to this army is something subtler, and in the long-term perhaps far more devastating, than outright military defeat. It has simply quit. It has given up discipline, it has given up wanting to fight, it is past caring what it does. It has abandoned anything but the idea of staying alive long enough to catch the 'Freedom Bird' out of south-east Asia. Five years ago the British army fought out the last wretched months of the imperial presence in Aden, battling on until the final day in much the spirit as they went in. They were professional soldiers doing a job. A conscript army is not like that. Vietnam has exposed the greatest weakness of an army of the compelled. It can only be the mirror of the nation from which it is drawn. If the heart of the nation is not in the fight, nor is that of its soldiers.

If the American soldier here ever had any time for his

Vietnamese allies, the day is long past. If a Vietnamese is in uniform, he may be called an ARVN, but that has become almost as pejorative a term as those reserved for the enemy and Vietnamese civilians alike – 'gooks' or 'dinks'. Oddly enough, it is conscripts in the field who have most sympathy for the plight of America's newest martyr, Lieutenant William Calley of My Lai. 'I may hate this war, but I sure like killing dinks,' muttered a young conscript radio operator who a moment before had been bewailing his fate.

'Beware your aggressive instincts,' says the sign in a mess hut. 'Keep low and enemy fire MIGHT get you. Start asking for VC to kill and friendly fire WILL get you.' The Americans have not been sacked from this war, they are being allowed to resign. But what future that leaves an American army which, having always trained for war, is now ending a war in which battle has become a dirty word, seems deeply open to question. That sergeant with whom I rode back in the plane from Firebase Six must have known all this. It seems to make being dead here even less useful than it has ever been.

By this stage of the war, most correspondents of all nationalities had despaired of the American cause. They merely wanted to see the roundeyes leave. I was one of many who believed that the Americans had forgone any hope of military victory at least two years earlier, despite their military triumph over the Viet Cong when they defeated Hanoi's 1968 Tet offensive. Then as now, whatever success they gained on the battlefield, they were the absolute losers in the propaganda war with the communists. It was difficult to sustain any vestige of faith in Washington's tactics, or those of the Saigon regime. One day, when we were filming a Vietnamese fighter bomber squadron, I flew in the co-pilot's seat on a Skyraider ground-attack sortie. Our pair of aircraft circled for more than an hour above a rendezvous near the Lao border, waiting in vain for a target. Then the pilot radioed to the American Bird Dog spotter aircraft that his fuel was running low. 'Okay,' replied the Bird Dog, 'you see those hooches maybe one click east of the river? Bomb on my smoke.' We made three passes at the 'hooches' – huts – with bombs and cannon fire, to no visible effect, save that I came close to throwing up all over the cockpit as the old prop-driven aircraft dived, banked and soared upwards again. Any vestigial glamour attached to the trip had faded for me soon after take-off. I felt so ill in the oily, stifling grip of the cockpit atmosphere, that I yearned only for the sortie to be over. But, back on the ground, we asked the questions: what was the target? What was the point? Were there civilians in the huts? The truth was brutally simple. There had been no defined purpose or military objective – merely a requirement to record the unloading of a defined weight of ordnance somewhere within a defined region of that tragic country. This was the way the Vietnam War was by 1971.

That night, we slept in the huts of an American Cobra squadron. They were bidding a noisy farewell to one of their pilots in the mess. We ate and dozed as they performed the tribal rituals of strapping their departing comrade into an aircraft seat, flooding him with beer, burning candles over his head, singing their black comic songs. At dawn, one of those wonderful red Vietnamese dawns, we walked blearily towards a helicopter for yet another flight up country. The spectacle before us was awesome. Across the entire breadth of the airfield, Hueys and Cobras were starting up, lifting a few feet, then sweeping forward into the eastern sky in their familiar, effort-less, nose-down posture as they set off for the day's work of carriage and destruction. The display of power and technology, amid the extravagant beauty of the morning sky, took our breath away. We asked ourselves for the hundredth time: how could these people, these masters of the universe possessed of such stupendous resources, conceivably lose a war against men of rubber sandals and tunnel life? Yet lose they would, it was plain. Indeed, they already had. The absolute disengagement between the vast American war machine and the society it was alleged to be in Vietnam to defend was evident to the most casual observer. The Americans had laid their presence as an insulated web across the country, no strand of which achieved any but the crudest social contact with the Vietnamese people or their institutions. Even among the most experienced and sympathetic resident correspondents in Saigon, only a tiny handful knew more of the Vietnamese language than was necessary to sew the words *Bao Chi* – Press – on the breast of a field jacket. The vast machinery of the US military operation ground relentlessly day and night, amid thunderous noise and every appearance of industry. Yet its achievement was that of a model steam engine. A child delights in the spectacle of the racing flywheel, the surging steam. Yet even a child feels a growing disappointment when it becomes plain that this is the sum of the engine's genius, that it is coupled to no useful purpose. And no steam engine inflicted the dreadful 'collateral damage' of the American war machine in Vietnam.

The films I made with Will Aaron in Indochina in 1971 were better than those we shot in 1970, but none deserved a lasting place in the journalism of the war. Television is a medium for reporters – most of them older men – who can convincingly project their own personalities on camera, and for directors. Will was one of the best. He possessed a marvellous eye for the small visual human touches, cameos in peace or war, which I would often have missed completely. For those of us who are chiefly wordsmiths, however, television is much less

Above: Ancestor worship: my father, Macdonald Hastings, as war correspondent of *Picture Post* in a characteristic pose with an infantryman in Normandy, June 1944.

Left: Teenage parachutists: the author (bespectacled) at seventeen with my Parachute Regiment 'stick' after our first jump at RAF Weston-on-Green, August 1963. Instructor Sgt. Pete Keymer kneels at front with the borrowed beret.

Above: An early *Evening Standard* assignment: aboard a Royal Navy submarine in the Channel, aged twenty in 1966.

Below: Carnage in Ulster: the scene amid the blazing Falls Road, as the first soldiers of the British army deployed in Belfast in August 1969, watched by the author.

Right: Biafra, January 1970: the author photographed by colleague John Clare, with a welcome beer after reaching the Niger River.

Below: Some of the tragic victims of Biafra's agony, photographed by the author in Onitsha.

Above: Interviewing an American colonel for BBC TV beside a captured North Vietnamese rice cache in Cambodia, June 1970. Philippe Grosjean mans the camera, producer Tony Summers holds the clapper board.

Below: Seconds later, we found ourselves scuttling for cover amid bursts of incoming communist small arms. This was a shot I snatched as the Americans, taken by surprise, returned fire.

Above: Men of the 2/31st Infantry as we filmed them in Vietnam's Hep Duc Valley, June 1971. Producer Will Aaron, left, is talking to company commander Captain David Borrison, in the crewcut.

Below: The scene after most of the company abandoned their weapons and clothes and dashed into the river for a swim. We felt acutely nervous and vulnerable.

Above: Guest of a village chieftain on a visit to one of the remote corners of the Arabian Gulf with the Trucial Oman Scouts, 1971.

Below: With officers of one of the Indian army's most celebrated cavalry regiments, the Deccan Horse, outside their mess in north-west India.

Above: One of many such scenes as I sat in a hotel room recording a commentary tape for BBC TV's *24 Hours* directed by Will Aaron, while sound recordist Pete Smith adjusts the microphone.

Below: Yom Kippur: the Israeli advance across the plateau from the Golan Heights towards Damascus amid the carnage of the great armoured battle with the Syrians, October 1973.

Right: A dramatic scene during Israel's agony on the Golan Heights after the Arab assault in October 1973. One of scores of tank commanders who became casualties is lifted from his turret.

Below: The moment of Israel's triumph. Soldiers celebrate the ceasefire which retrieved their country's fortunes after weeks of anguish.

rewarding. The struggle to fit words to available film footage leads to chronic, often fatal distortion. Many words of commentary must be wasted, merely on describing the pictures. The most plausible and watchable 'talking heads' are frequently the least truthful. I remember interviewing an appalling old ham in the depths of east Bengal after a cyclone, a former policeman under the British raj who cried out incessantly as the camera rolled on him.

'Once I was a rich man! Now I am a street beggar!'

'Cut,' I said, throwing down the microphone in disgust. I turned to Will Aaron. 'We can't do much with this old phoney.'

'Carry on, carry on,' said Will enthusiastically. 'He looks terrific.'

And so he did, after the sixth take of his party piece. Our herogram from Lime Grove after that film said LOVED YOUR QUOTE STREET BEGGAR UNQUOTE ENDIT. The best interviewees, as well as television reporters, are part-actors: men and women who can achieve a personal sense of theatre on camera, not least in war zones.

Television requires endless effort to solve logistical and technical problems, above all to move heavy equipment in difficult country. Less time and energy are usually available to worry about content, if one is turning around a film in a few days, rather than making a set-piece documentary. It is sometimes possible for a writing journalist to be a fly on the wall, to observe without being noticed. This option never exists for a television crew. It is deceitful to pretend that it does. Whatever something is before the camera starts to turn, it becomes something subtly different thereafter. To add to these universal problems, I had a few personal ones as a presenter. My height rendered me an awkward spectacle in any full-length shot, and required almost any Asian interviewee to gaze steeply upwards to catch my eyeline, until I learned to avoid two-shots in which I stood talking down to some tiny Vietnamese figure, and to sit on a shooting stick to lower me to his horizon. Some colleagues who saw me carrying this piece of kit in the field thought it a silly affectation, but it was designed to solve a real problem. Then there was my voice, a nasal drawl which I have been striving to moderate all my life. It remains an imperfect tool for delivering commentary. I envied my father's perfectly modulated tones, characteristic of his generation of broadcasters — he always attributed his gift as a speaker to the fact he had been taught elocution as a school subject. I wish we all had. The words I wrote were, I think, better than those of many television scriptwriters. But words on a page are not what television is about.

Will Aaron was a fine programme maker, and we shot some great sequences under his direction. But I came home from that second tour in Vietnam convinced that I was far happier writing for newspapers about war than trying to convey its reality for television. The camera can see only what is before the lens at that moment. Especially when interpreting wars, this imposes huge limitations. It is true that Vietnam, as recorded by television, provided the most powerful images of violence and tragedy ever revealed to a mass audience. Television told the truth about one important fundamental: it showed that America's expenditure of blood and treasure was achieving little, and was imposing terrible suffering both upon the men doing the fighting, and upon millions of innocent civilians.

Yet it was not what the medium showed the world from Vietnam that troubled me and others, but what it did not show, because it could not. At no time in the war were the ruthlessness and brutality of the communists revealed to the public. The North Vietnamese won the propaganda battle by systematically denying information and access to the media. Only a handful of carefully chosen sympathizers such as James Cameron and Harrison Salisbury were allowed to catch meticulously framed glimpses of North Vietnamese civilians suffering and defending themselves under US air bombardment. American veterans are wrong to argue today that the media lost the war for the United States. The US government and military did that for themselves. But the communists won the propaganda struggle at home and abroad by cloaking their own military and political operations in obscurity, even invisibility, while the Americans bared their follies and misjudgements to the gaze of the world. The sorry lesson is similar to that revealed by modern perceptions of Hitler, Stalin and Mao Tse Tung. We know that Stalin and Mao killed more people than Hitler. Yet most people today unequivocally regard Hitler as more evil. We have all seen films of the Nazi death camps. Western audiences have seen no visual evidence of Stalin and Mao's butcheries.

By the time I returned to London from Saigon in 1971, like many other observers I doubted that America's client regime in Saigon could – or even should – survive. Yet nor could I bring myself to believe that the North Vietnamese communists deserved to rule South Vietnam. History will find Hanoi's apologists naive. Jimmy Cameron, for instance, was one of the greatest wordsmiths of his generation, a superb descriptive reporter and polemicist whose literary gifts I admired as much as anyone. But he proved wrong about almost every cause he espoused, from Korea in 1950 to Vietnam a generation later, because he refused to attempt to make relative judgements, which is what most of life – and grown-up journalism – are about. Whatever the Vietnamese people gained when Hanoi triumphed in 1975, it was not freedom.

I covered one more war for *Midweek*, so ingloriously that it merits scant attention here, save that it reinforced my own misgivings about the difficulties of covering conflict on the small screen at any level which transcends mere pictures of gunfire. In December 1971, much against my will, I was asked to go to India to report the worsening crisis with East Pakistan, which threatened to explode into all-out conflict. Will Aaron and I had worked in east Bengal only a few months earlier. This time, we were asked to take with us a cameraman who was known to be an aggressive racist. It would be unbearable to film in the subcontinent with such a character. After a bitter row with the camera department, who threatened us with union sanctions, it was agreed that we should take another crew, but Butch Calderwood, our new cameraman, made it plain that he wanted no part in filming a war. The whole feel of the assignment stank. Eventually, Will and I climbed crossly on to the plane for Calcutta. I have always enjoyed teasing lefties, who seldom fail to rise to the fly. On this occasion, my protest gesture towards the Lime Grove International Brigade was to order a huge hamper of supplies from Fortnum and Mason, to console us on our travels. The lefties were outraged all right, but the joke was on us, when we later tried to eat *pâté de foie gras* which had travelled in a temperature of 110 degrees.

We spent days stranded in Calcutta among a host of other reporters, denied permission to travel anywhere near East Pakistan, or to India's other borders. Eventually a despairing Will suggested that until there was some action, for a few days we should drive up to Simla, the great old hill station in Himachal Pradesh. It was an inspiration. In that wonderful place in the foothills of the Himalayas, we found a cluster of elderly English ladies, last survivors of the raj. Among them, we made one of the best and happiest films I ever scripted for BBC, guided by Will's brilliance. We arrived back at Delhi in time for me to go duck shooting with the BBC stringer, a self-consciously upmarket Indian. As we drove out to the lake before dawn, I suggested we might need dogs to retrieve our bag from the surrounding swamp. He glanced round in astonishment. 'Dogs? *Dogs?* Who needs dogs, when *men* are five rupees a day.'

Next day, war broke out between India and Pakistan, and we returned eastward. I have seldom suffered a more dispiriting experience than the weeks which followed. We languished in Calcutta while colleagues in Dhaka recorded the great and terrible drama. With a television crew, and a cameraman furious even to find himself working in a country at war, there was no scope for private initiative. Even working alone, a white face doing anything illegal or unauthorized is impossibly conspicuous anywhere in the subcontinent. India has always been one of the most security-obsessed nations in the world. Eventually we gained some access to the western front – glimpses of Pakistani bombers, of wounded being brought back, anti-aircraft guns that fired for a few seconds, then fell silent again before the camera was even out of its case. We were allowed to visit one sector in the Punjab the morning after a Pakistani attack and found an Indian regiment in the forward positions digging energetically among the corpses.

'Burying their dead?' I enquired conversationally.

'Actually no,' said the company commander with a friendly grin. 'Digging them up again. We buried this lot earlier – the heat, you know – but we thought you chaps would like something to see.'

Elsewhere in this book, I have told tales of conflicts in which I saw some action, wrote some words that may have contributed at least infinitesimally to readers' or viewers' understanding. When I want to remind myself that I did not always get that far, I think of our black comic dabbling in the

India-Pakistan war. At every turn, I found myself trumped by swifter or cleverer colleagues. One morning some fifty journalists were being briefed by an Indian general at a press camp behind the lines. He made a few vacuous remarks, then turned to his jeep. 'Well, it's been splendid meeting you boys, but now it's time for me to get back to the front.' Harold Jackson of the *Guardian* shot up his hand. 'Please sir, may I come and represent the foreign press?' The general was taken aback, but after a moment nodded. 'Don't see why not.' Harold disappeared triumphantly down the road frontwards. The other forty-nine of us sat regretting the absence of firearms with which to demonstrate our feelings.

I returned to London frustrated and disappointed, having added nothing to my laurels and feeling a growing sense of doubt both about my fitness to be a successful television reporter and my desire to do so. I was weary of the fantastic union restrictions which afflicted film work even in a war zone. No journalist who has ever filled in an expenses claim can boast about his conscience, but the sheer scale of racketeering by Lime Grove film crews in those days would have commanded the admiration of Al Capone. I stayed with *Midweek* for another eighteen months, enjoying a few foreign adventures and some longer home assignments such as making the first big film on Robert Maxwell with Tom Bower. I also shot one of the most delightful military films of my career in Hong Kong, about the last surviving mule unit in the British army. Indeed, I seemed to spend a lot of time in those days recording the last flourishes of Empire, shooting with the Trucial Oman Scouts in the Gulf and directing several films myself with the British army in Cyprus. I did some good work, I believe, in Ulster as the terrorist campaign escalated. But by the summer of 1973 I was keen to return to writing journalism. Charles Wintour asked me to lunch. He made a handsome offer by the standards of the day, which brought me back to my old paper at a higher salary than I was getting at Lime Grove. I never regretted those television years. I learned a lot. I enjoyed the company of some of the crews, and above all the pleasure of working with Will Aaron and Tom Bower. But I believed by now that I was cut out to be a loner and a wordsmith, rather than to present a public face for the camera. Television also involves the carriage of too much baggage. It was time to get back on the road, on the war path, alone.

CHAPTER SIX

Yom Kippur

AT 1.58 P.M. on the afternoon of Saturday, 6 October 1973, five Syrian MiG-17s streaked across the old 1967 ceasefire line to launch the first strikes of a new Middle East war against Israeli positions on the Golan Heights. A few minutes later, 250 miles south-westwards, Egyptian commandos launched their rubber boats to begin an assault across the Suez Canal. In Israel, it was the feast and holiday of Yom Kippur, which had prompted the Arab choice of date. The timing reflected the fact that, remarkably, even in the age of missile-led warfare it is still perceived as a useful advantage to make the enemy fight with the sun in his eyes. Thus the Syrians in the east would have preferred to attack at dawn, the Egyptians in the west at sunset. The outcome was a compromise.

The secret of the Arabs' assault plan had been brilliantly kept. Although their armies were training and exercising behind the fronts for months beforehand, unit commanders were told only on the morning of 6 October that this, indeed, would be the day. The result was that for the first time, Israel had to start fighting a war unprepared, with most of her own forces unmobilized. Never before or since has the nation paid such a price for hubris. Only six years before, in the Six-Day War of June 1967, she had inflicted upon the armies of Egypt,

Syria and Jordan the most devastating military defeat of modern times. The capture of Jerusalem and the West Bank, the Golan Heights, and the entire Sinai peninsula to the banks of the Suez Canal gave Israelis what they had never possessed since the foundation of their state: space. Between 1967 and 1973, they experienced the luxuries of room to live free from the threat of direct enemy fire, room to farm and room to fight. Since 1947, large parts of Israel had lived and worked under intermittent Arab artillery fire. Now, they knew they could not be faced with an enemy assault launched from their doorstep. They had shown the world the flimsy nature of Arab armies, however impressive the equipment the Russians lavished upon them. Three times, they had crushed far superior Arab forces. Since 1967, there had been long and fruitless negotiations about the exchange of peace for some of Israel's huge territorial gains. Even in the face of military humiliation, however, the Arabs remained defiant about conceding Israel's right to exist. And even in those first years after the 1967 war, doubts existed about Israel's real willingness to make any exchange which involved surrendering the most sensitive of her conquests, the Golan Heights, the West Bank and the old city of Jerusalem. Modesty has never been among Israeli virtues. The nation's pride in its military achievements was reflected in an arrogance within the government and the military command which, in October 1973, almost precipitated disaster.

The Israeli bank of the Suez Canal had been fortified with deep-dug bunkers and a thirty-foot high rampart of sand, apparently impassable by tanks or vehicles, even if these succeeded in crossing the water. For many months, however, the Bar-Lev line, like the Golan front, had been thinly held. The garrison numbered a mere 450 men, facing five assaulting Egyptian divisions. Israel's armed forces depend overwhelmingly upon reservists for their ability to fight. To keep her

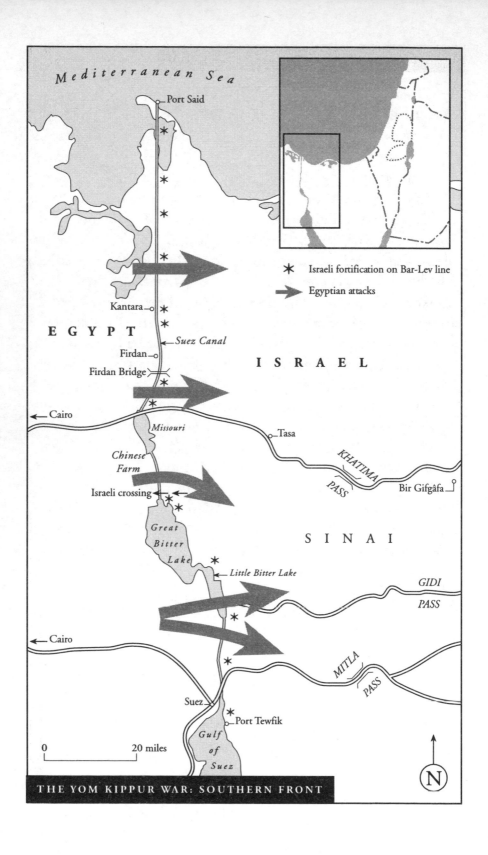

Mediterranean Sea

Port Said

Israeli fortification on Bar-Lev line

Egyptian attacks

Kantara

E G Y P T

Suez Canal

Firdan

Firdan Bridge

Cairo

Missouri

I S R A E L

Tasa

KHATIMA PASS

Chinese Farm

Bir Gifgâfa

Israeli crossing

Great Bitter Lake

S I N A I

Little Bitter Lake

GIDI PASS

Cairo

MITLA PASS

Suez

Port Tewfik

Gulf of Suez

0   20 miles

THE YOM KIPPUR WAR: SOUTHERN FRONT

N

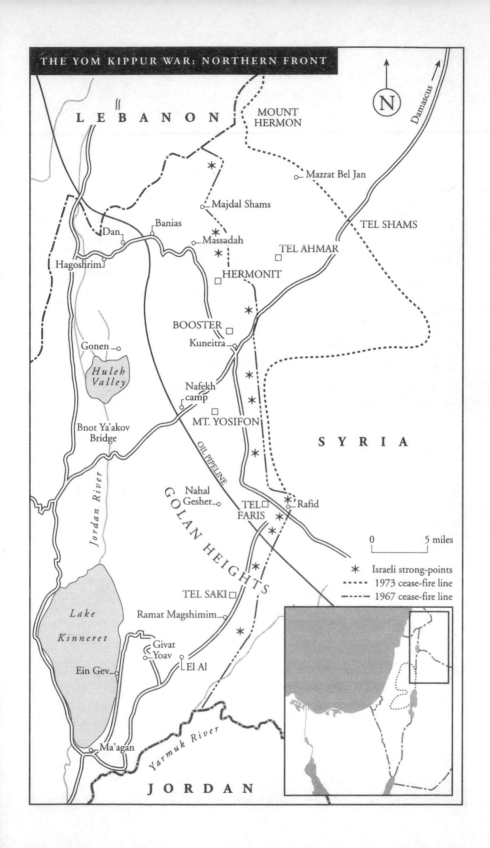

THE YOM KIPPUR WAR: NORTHERN FRONT

N

LEBANON

MOUNT
HERMON

Damascus

* Mazrat Bel Jan

Majdal Shams

TEL SHAMS

Banias
Dan

Massadah

TEL AHMAR

Hagoshrim

HERMONIT

*

BOOSTER
Kuneitra

Gonen

Huleh
Valley

Nafekh
camp

*

MT. YOSIFON

*

SYRIA

Bnot Ya'akov
Bridge

OIL PIPELINE

*

Jordan River

Nahal
Gesher

GOLAN

TEL
FARIS

* Rafid

*

0   5 miles

HEIGHTS

Lake
Kinneret

TEL SAKI

* Israeli strong-points

Ramat Magshimim

.... 1973 cease-fire line

*

Givat
Yoav

—·—·— 1967 cease-fire line

Ein Gev

El Al

Ma'agan

Yarmuk River

JORDAN

armies on a war footing would be an intolerable drain upon the national economy and manpower. In 1973, most of Israel's tanks, artillery and armoured vehicles for war were garaged or leaguered miles behind the fronts, to be manned and deployed at a few days' notice. Granted the brilliance of Israel's intelligence services and the warnings the Arab armies must surely give of their own mobilization, it seemed unthinkable that the nation would not be granted those days before any new war began.

But the successful use of intelligence depends upon possessing the will to heed it. All the world's intelligence services, and the governments which employ them, must contend with the problem of distinguishing 'signals' – relevant information – from 'noise' – the constant barrage of irrelevant, misleading data. It is hard for governments to avoid being deluded by seeing what they want to see, believing what they want to believe. They are seduced by logic, their own logic, the tendency to reject any possible course of action by an enemy which seems foolish or implausible to oneself. Stalin would not believe Germany intended to invade Russia in June 1941 until the Wehrmacht's tanks smashed into the Red army. The United States was astonished by the North Korean assault on South Korea in June 1950. The British were amazed by the Argentine invasion of the Falklands in 1982. The Argentines in their turn were equally bewildered when the British went to war to reverse the seizure of the islands. And the Israelis were utterly confounded when, after so many months of military posturing and manoeuvring on the Suez and Golan fronts, the Egyptians and Syrians launched their assault in earnest at Yom Kippur 1973.

Evidence of an Arab shift to a war footing mounted through the preceding week. But deployments and redeployments had played their part in Arab drum-beating for years. It was not enough to believe that the Arabs were militarily ready to fight. Did they also possess the political intention to do so? As late as Friday 5 October, Israeli doubts on this score persisted. When David Elazar, the army Chief of Staff, pressed for immediate mobilization, he was overruled by Moshe Dayan, the legendary Defence Minister. Dayan argued strongly to the Prime Minister, Golda Meir, that if Israel mobilized prematurely, the Arabs could still launch an attack, bolstered in the eyes of the world by being able to claim that they went to war only in the face of an Israeli threat. Western opinion, which for twenty years after 1947 had favoured Israel's struggle for existence against Arab encirclement, had shifted substantially since the Six-Day War. Unease and outright hostility towards Israel's expansionism had been growing. At all costs, argued Dayan, Israel must not give the Arabs a ready hostage in the battle for international support. And anyway – even if the Arabs did attack, could not Israel repel them, as she had repelled them so often before? Israel's air force was summoned to a war footing, a relatively easy and discreet move. Selected military personnel were called up by telephone. But the code words for broadcasting to the entire population, the signals for general mobilization, were withheld. When the Arabs struck, Israel's defensive positions were held only by the screening forces which had manned the 1967 ceasefire lines through many months of what passed for peace in the Middle East.

The Egyptians broke through the Bar-Lev line on the Suez Canal within a few hours, bypassing many of the Israeli bunkers, breaching the great sand wall with ingenious use of high-pressure hoses. Egyptian units had rehearsed every detail of the operation again and again. The Israeli oil pipelines with which they intended to set the canal ablaze under attack were blocked with cement by frogmen. The first Israeli armoured counter-attacks suffered a bitterly unwelcome surprise from wire-guided Sagger anti-tank missiles, with which the Russians had lavishly equipped their Arab allies. Egyptian commandos caused serious dislocation by landing well behind the Suez front. Worse, when Israeli Phantoms and Skyhawks began attacking the Egyptian bridgehead, they met a formidable screen of Russian-supplied ZSU-23 radar-controlled guns, SAM-3, SAM-6 and SAM-7 anti-aircraft missiles. Between them, the four systems could engage aircraft attacking at any height, in any fashion. In the first week of war, the Israelis lost seventy-eight aircraft, as they threw their air force headlong into the struggle to stem the Arab onslaught at all costs. The drain of pilots alone represented a bitter blow for a small nation's most highly trained manpower. On the Golan Heights, the Syrian assault easily overran the Israeli forward bunkers and swept forward towards the edge of the escarpment that looks down upon the lush fields and kibbutzes of northern Israel.

Israel's defensive strategy was incoherent, because its generals had failed to decide whether their static defences were intended as a mere tripwire or as a serious impediment to the enemy. Yet when the Syrians encountered Israeli Centurion tanks, dug hull-down in carefully prepared positions, they began to take formidable losses. The Israelis were overwhelmingly outnumbered. But they possessed some of the finest and most determined tank crews in the world. 'One tank in a good position is worth a hundred rambling across the countryside,' is a maxim of the Israeli armoured corps, vindicated many times on the Golan. In those first hours and days, while Israel struggled to mobilize and rush units to both threatened fronts, a handful of armoured defenders on the northern heights fought one of the most impressive battles of modern times, to buy time for their nation to recover from the devastating shock of war.

And of all this, of Israel's extreme peril in the first days, the outside world knew next to nothing. The military prowess of the Jewish state had become a legend since 1967, as had the incompetence of the Arabs. When news broke on Saturday afternoon of the outbreak of a new war, triumphant statements from Arab radio about the crossing of the canal and deep penetrations on the Golan front were widely dismissed as vainglory. Few people had forgotten similar bulletins coming out of Cairo and Damascus in 1967, even as the Arab armies were collapsing in rout. If Egypt and Syria had been foolish enough to embark upon a trial of military strength, surely they would be humiliated once more. The fog of war enshrouded not only the battlefield, but the world's news organizations and most of its chancelleries.

Civilian flights into Israel were halted that Saturday. Hundreds of journalists all over the world spent the night on their telephones, pleading with airlines and offices, arranging money and equipment, exchanging news with colleagues, striving as we always strove at these moments to find some means of getting to where this unique story had broken. My bag was packed, money and ticket in my pocket. I roamed relentlessly about our little house in Barnes, dashing for the phone each time it rang, breaking off in an agony of frustration when I found myself speaking only to friends. I remembered my frustration before the Six-Day War broke out in 1967, and I begged the Editor to send me.

Dear Max, [replied Charles Wintour, in one of his most acid communications]

You are the fifth (and least qualified) person who has today asked to go to the Middle East. James Cameron is airborne, and I am delaying further action until the situation has clarified. Frankly, I do not believe there is going to be a war there. Unless some shooting seems imminent, it is insane to dispatch correspondents to inconvenient corners of the globe when (1) our bread and butter lies in London and (2) the round-up of a developing situation can best be done from agency copy.

Exciting assignments do not grow on trees ready to pluck for hungry young mouths.

My chagrin was not diminished two weeks later, after the end of the war. As Charles Wintour passed my desk one morning, to the envy of my colleagues he enquired, 'Are you free at lunchtime?' Yes, yes, I said. 'Then you can go out to Heathrow and meet James Cameron on his return from the Middle East.' I was beyond speech, and the colleagues beyond laughter.

Six years on, my own claims to go to Israel for the *Evening Standard* were not disputed, but the difficulties of getting there seemed great, when fighting had already started. Sunday morning dragged interminably on. Tel Aviv was still not taking civilian flights. It could stay closed for days. I might miss the story altogether. It would be unbearable. I sat down to lunch at home with my wife Tricia, whom I had married in the spring of 1972, and our baby son. The phone rang. El Al was sending a flight to Tel Aviv that afternoon. I was on it, if I could get to Heathrow in time. Lunch was abandoned. We packed six-month-old Charlie hastily into the car. I drove headlong for the airport, and one of many abrupt and emotional partings from Tricia. There is not much to be said in favour of being a foreign correspondent's wife on these occasions, denied even the comfort of feeling that one's husband is off to do his bit for his country. I was off to 'do my bit' only for the strange, compulsive trade to which I belonged.

After the desperate dash down the motorway, at the airport there were more hours of waiting, among a small crowd of familiar Fleet Street faces, all of us terrified that Lod airport might be closed again before we could get in. At last we boarded, and took off. The rest of the 707 was full of anxious, emotional or coldly determined Israelis, set upon returning to their homeland to share its fate in a new hour of trial. Yet still no one feared or imagined how bad matters might be, because Israelis and foreigners alike shared boundless respect for Israel's military ability and, yes, a disdain for that of the Arabs.

I had visited Israel during the so-called War of Attrition in 1970, and again in 1971. I hated the food, the arrogance, the architecture and Tel Aviv, but I admired the people and what they had made of the country. I have always loved and believed in the Jewish genius. Israel in those days was still culturally and politically dominated by European Jews. It may have been naive of me to see the matter in such terms, but the country seemed to represent a bastion of the values of European civilization and culture in the Middle East. Much later, around 1980, when I had grown deeply disillusioned with what Israel had become, I said as much one day to that wonderful kibbutznik and novelist Amos Oz. 'People like you, who want Israel to be a European country, are going to be very disappointed in Israel in the years to come,' he responded. 'Israel is becoming a Middle Eastern country. In the future, I hope it will behave no worse than other Middle Eastern countries. But you would be rash to expect it to behave any better.'

All that still lay in the future – as did any sense of Israel's vulnerability. In 1970, I had been down to Suez to visit the Israeli positions on the canal and to catch a glimpse of the War of Attrition, the artillery and air duel around Suez which, for many months, represented Egypt's ineffectual attempt to impose some price on the enemy for its occupation of thousands of square miles of Egyptian territory. Two of us, British correspondents, drove down through Sinai with an Israeli escorting officer, past Gaza and the ruined train still lying beside the railway line at El Arish where it was caught by Israeli aircraft in 1967, and on deep into the desert. I dismantled our escort's Uzi machine-pistol to pass the time in the passenger seat – Israeli weapons, like their owners, attracted much admiration in those days, though the Uzi was nothing much to shout about. The heat was oppressive, the sand was soon everywhere about our throats and the car, but I loved to be in the desert, talking and arguing all the way about the future – Israel's future, for few Israelis showed much interest in anyone else's. Our escort, a reserve captain, was a sophisticated man full of unsophisticated cynicism about the Arabs. They would never beat Israel now. Israel would never give up the Golan or Jerusalem. Why should she? We halted behind a vast sand emplacement, where we met a local officer who equipped us with old Egyptian helmets, whether we fancied them or not. We clambered up wooden steps to a sandbagged observation platform. There before us lay the still, glittering water of the canal. It seemed very narrow, very slight, a modest obstacle to man or boat. There were no inviting palm trees on our own bank, only the long sand 'berm' raised by the Israelis and the occasional vehicle moving swiftly across the horizon, shimmering in the haze. There was a distant, intermittent crump of guns, but no firing in our sector. We chattered for a while to the few men of the garrison who were on duty, then set off back to the car, and Tel Aviv. The Israelis seemed invincible. I thought they would hold the canal bank for decades.

I learned one more lesson about journalism on that trip. The resident *Daily Express* correspondent, Robin Stafford, casually asked if I would deliver a letter to the office for him – as sister papers, the *Standard* and *Express* were in neighbouring buildings. I stuffed the envelope in my pocket without a thought, and dropped it at his office back in London the following morning. Next day, I saw screaming headlines on the front page of the *Express* about a secret raid by Israeli commandos, who had snatched an entire Soviet-built radar station from deep inside Egypt. This was the rich fruit of the 'letter' I had so innocently 'pigeoned' for Robin, which would have finished me for years in Israel had I been caught with it. Departing Tel Aviv passengers are searched. I have since found myself in trouble at Lod merely for carrying marked maps. Censorship is rigid, and the radar station snatch story had been kept tightly under wraps by the Israeli army. Robin knew that he could never have filed it himself – or rather, that if he did so he could not work in Israel again. So he found his 'pigeon'. Although I was pretty cross when I found out, not least about missing the story myself, I bore no grudge. I had merely played the greenhorn in a style worthy of William Boot, and been lucky enough not to get caught with the evidence. Of course, Robin would have been rash to cross the road in front of any bus I was driving for a while.

Now, three years later, the Israeli reservists on our 707 sang exultantly – and very movingly – as the plane touched down at Lod. We found ourselves groping amid darkness, sober faces and incessant military movements in all directions. We got taxis to hotels, made some urgent calls which revealed almost nothing. I checked in with the *Standard*'s veteran stringer, Teddy Levite. We snatched a few hours sleep, then started the usual round of business that goes with every story of this kind, for almost every foreign correspondent. Wake, listen to BBC World Service on short wave over breakfast, somehow find a few words to file so that the paper had something to run in its first edition under my byline. I wrote: 'There is some evidence to suggest that the fighting both in Sinai and on the Golan Heights is more severe than that of

1967, although Israel is releasing no details of her casualties
. . . However much one may share the Israeli conviction about
the final outcome of this campaign, it is difficult to accept
their current assurances that the Egyptians have been allowed
to build up their bridgehead east of Suez to 400 tanks and
supporting artillery, merely to provide the juiciest possible bait
for the closing of a trap.' I suggested that this time the war
seemed likely to last two or three weeks, rather than six days.

> While there is complete confidence about the outcome of
> what Israelis are calling the Yom Kippur War, there is also
> concern that this time, fighting a defensive action in contrast
> to their June 1967 blitzkreig, a costly struggle of attrition
> could develop unless they move swiftly. Israel's permanent
> fear, with her tiny population, is of becoming engaged in a
> slogging match that would involve heavy casualties. And
> they themselves are fully aware how much Egypt and Syria
> have staked on their desperate gamble in men and prestige.

Reading that first dispatch again almost thirty years later,
those were not bad guesses, given that they were filed a few
hours after landing at Lod. As soon as I had dictated, I set off
to get accreditation, and to submit a string of requests for a
string of facilities, knowing that none would be granted. There
were vague and equally futile briefings to be attended, equally
ignorant colleagues to be quizzed, endless coffees to be drunk
in the ground floor café of Bet Sokolov, the drab building that
passed for a press headquarters in Tel Aviv, where even at this
supreme crisis there were clusters of civilians and uniforms
chattering animatedly, fiercely, incessantly across the tables in
the usual Israeli manner.

That was how most of my first day in Tel Aviv passed – in
ignorance and frustration. It was the same for all the foreign

media. That Monday, even as the nation's embattled tank crews were striving to turn the tide against the Syrians on the Golan, and repeated armoured counter-attacks in Sinai were being broken by Egyptian Saggers, we were pleading and begging at desks in the city, exchanging exclamations of professional despair. Alan Hart of BBC's *Panorama* announced that he was sending Golda Meir huge bouquets of flowers twice a day until the prime minister agreed to be interviewed by him. We still had no notion that Mrs Meir's nation stood with its back to the wall, its northern defences close to exhaustion and collapse, while the Egyptians poured men and tanks into their bulging bridgehead on the east bank of the Suez Canal.

That evening, Chief of Staff David Elazar conducted a briefing for the world's media which few of us present ever forgot. A stocky, craggy figure who seemed in the conventional model of effective Israeli generals, he radiated assurance, even conceit. 'This morning we embarked on a counter-attack simultaneously on both fronts . . . We have begun to destroy the Egyptian army. In some places we have returned to the canal . . . We are advancing on all fronts . . . We shall strike them, we shall beat them, we shall break their bones.' As we got up and shuffled out, earnestly comparing notes, we agreed that the Chief of Staff seemed not merely confident, but ebullient. The Israelis obviously thought they were on top again – if, indeed, they had ever not been. Now that they were getting down to it in earnest, the war could scarcely last for long. We had no inkling that Elazar's brash performance was provoked only by the knowledge that his own army would hear his words, that in a desperate hour of trial, he believed his first duty was to hearten the soldiers of Israel. Even as he climbed on to the platform, he knew that the situation on the battlefield was as grave as ever in his country's history. And even as he stepped down after his speech, a staff officer murmured to him that the latest counter-attack in Sinai had been broken by the Egyptians with heavy Israeli armoured losses.

The Israelis obviously had no intention of taking many, if any, foreign journalists to the front. For the time being, only their own reporters and cameramen would be authorized to see the action. Even when Tel Aviv did offer any facilities, the American networks and agencies would be top of the queue. Anybody like me who was going anywhere would have to travel on his own. Very early the following morning, in the time-honoured fashion of foreign correspondents in Israel, I hailed a taxi and told the driver I wanted to go to the Golan Heights. Like most Israeli taxi-drivers, this one did not find my proposal unusual or daunting, if there was enough money in the trip. We set off northwards out of Tel Aviv. I knew we would be aided by the fact that Israelis of all kinds and conditions, in all manner and condition of vehicles, were doing likewise in order to join their military units. As the driver chattered away relentlessly – for no more than the rest of the world did he know how bad things were – I pored over the map. Once we were close to the Golan, I was sure we must leave the main roads, where there would be a succession of army checkpoints. The Bnot Ya'akov Bridge across the Jordan was certain to be closed to the likes of me. Our only chance of making it on to the Heights seemed to depend upon driving a few miles further north, then slipping up through the kib- butzes, by way of little by-roads which, with luck, would not be guarded – or anyway not against journalists coming from the south. 'No problem,' said the driver. 'I know those roads like my own mother.' Two hours on, we duly turned east off the main route, into the Huleh Valley. We passed through the miles of irrigated fields, kibbutz entrances where men stood with shouldered rifles and Uzis, murmuring earnestly to each other amid the extravagant waving of hands and shrugging of shoulders inseparable from any conversation in this nation. They seemed indifferent to our passage. We began to climb. I was taut with excitement, clenching my palms, murmuring to myself. We could make it. We might just make it. On and on we went. It was too easy. By taking the kibbutz tracks, we had sidestepped all the activity and hubbub at the rear of a front – especially this front. We passed no gun lines or tank parks, heard no growing thump of gunfire or scream of aircraft. There were only peaceful tillage, acre upon acre of greenness and the occasional civilian truck until suddenly, we breasted the hill and saw before us the Golan Heights.

We were stunned by what we found. Without warning, we were translated from the rural morning peace of northern Israel, on to a battlefield where the nation was fighting for its life. We saw blackened earth, several burning vehicles a few hundred yards in front, a troop of tanks lumbering in column towards the horizon, wrecked buildings and debris of all kinds littering the flat, barren landscape. In the distance – the not very remote distance – we could hear gunfire very clearly – only artillery, not small arms. If we were out of earshot of small arms, we were unlikely to be in great personal danger. But then we glimpsed a wrecked bus, a human arm dangling limp out of its window. Craters around it were still smoking from air attack. My driver looked panic-stricken. He swung right on to a lateral road running southwards along the ridge and drove wildly, jabbering to himself, until I hammered his shoulder to stop by a couple of half-tracks tilted on the verge of the tarmac. Men stood sorting kit beside their hulls. I climbed out and began to ask questions, which they answered monosyllabically. They had too much on their minds to bother with me. Then we did hear small arms. My driver exploded, 'You wanna stay here, you give me money. I go home.' I pushed a wad of the *Evening Standard*'s currency into his fist.

He accelerated away down the road up which we had come, shaking his head. Now I had my binoculars, a waterbottle, money and a notebook – but no wheels. I had deliberately come without a camera, because nothing can ring alarm bells so swiftly in a security-conscious soldier. I was uneasy, because somehow and some time I would need to get back to file a story. But for now, I was only thrilled that I had got to where the war was happening. I might have looked incongruously unmilitary, but some reservists were still dressed in fragments of civilian clothes in which they had been summoned from their homes. I called to the half-track crew, 'Anybody speak English?' A foggy Liverpool accent answered from beneath a helmet and three days' beard. 'I s'pose I do, a bit.' He had emigrated from England four years earlier. 'It's not so bad now,' he said. 'The Syrians seem to be getting fed up. But it wasn't much fun the first two days.' Even in those first few minutes of conversation, it became plain that a bitter and terrible battle was taking place. Within the first half-hour, while I had no means of grasping the big picture of what was happening, I had heard enough to be sure that the Israelis were fighting desperately against fearsome odds. I walked a few hundred yards to where a group of tanks was rearming, blackened and exhausted crews passing ammunition from civilian trucks into the hulls of their Centurions. It was hard to get them to talk at all to this strange, tall English beast in a clean blue shirt and cords, a man from another world. It was not security that inhibited them, I think, but stupefied tiredness. Like so many men I met that day, these talked in brief, staccato mutters. 'It is very hard ... Too many Syrians ... We've lost a lot of people ... Those bastards just kept coming. What kind of leaders do they have who will make them do this? We shell them, we bomb them, we kill them in hundreds, but still they're sent against us. Their commanders don't seem to care how many die. Each time, now, when they attack, we think, "This must be the last time they can do it." But somewhere, they find more still.' Men looked up and cursed as a column of half-tracks roared past, infantrymen spilling over their hulls, because the vehicles threw dust high into the sky, and dust attracts artillery fire.

I did not know it then, but we were standing close to the limit the Arab onslaught had reached. Here, the Syrian 3rd and 7th armoured divisions had smashed forward, trading scores of their own tanks for every mile, until at last their offensive was checked and pushed back the previous night – Monday 8 October. The tank crews to whom I spoke had been in action continuously for three days and three nights. Even now, Tuesday, in front of us the Israeli 7th Brigade under the famous 'Yanosh' – thirty-eight-year-old Colonel Avigdor Ben-Gal – was fighting furiously as the Syrians launched a new attack, covered by a devastating bombardment of artillery and katushya rockets. We could not only hear those guns now, but also see the smoke palls rising from their aiming points. The battle the Israeli 7th and Barak brigades were fighting ranks among the most extraordinary in the history of their nation. In the words of Josephus, 'Nothing is so productive of heroism as despair.' Some men crewed their tanks for weeks in the jeans and sweatshirts in which they had left home on the sabbath. Repair teams were labouring under fire to salvage damaged Centurions. Tanks were being sent into action as fast as their commanders could muster a driver, loader, gunner who had never met before. Squadrons reduced to one or two fighting vehicles destroyed Syrian T-62s in columns of ten and twenty by sheer gunnery and resolution. They inflicted staggering losses on the enemy – more than 260 wrecked Syrian tanks and hundreds more APCs and vehicles lay in 'the Valley of Tears', where the fiercest fighting took place. Very fortunately for the

Israelis, the Syrians neither exploited their Soviet night-vision equipment effectively, nor used smoke to cover their own advance, which could have been fatal for the defenders, who relied overwhelmingly on the eyes of their gunners to destroy the Arab tank columns. But now the Israeli weapons and ammunition were all but spent. Ninety per cent of the Barak Brigade's tank commanders had become casualties. Every few hours, a new detachment of Centurions arrived manned by reservists racing to the front not merely from every corner of Israel, but from every corner of the world. That Tuesday, Yossi Ben Hanan, who took command of the surviving armoured battalion of the Barak Brigade, arrived on the Golan direct from honeymoon in Nepal. He was a famous man in Israel, because six years earlier he had been photographed on the cover of *Life* magazine, wallowing exultant in the waters of the Suez Canal after his nation's triumph in the Six-Day War. Now, he had driven north from the airport, straight to the front, pausing only at headquarters before he took over a tank. In the first hour that he and his hastily assembled group were in action, they destroyed thirty Syrian tanks. The thin trickle of reinforcements, thrown into the battle as fast as they reached the Golan, sufficed by the barest of margins to hold the ridge and throw back the last great Syrian offensive. When that battle was over their commander, the legendary 'Raful' Eytan, spoke to the survivors of 7th Brigade over the radio net: 'You have saved the people of Israel.'

I spent that Tuesday talking to any man on the Heights who possessed the will and the time and the energy to help me. 'What prize can we give the men who held out on that first day?' asked a middle-aged ordnance officer passionately. 'What medal, what reward that would mean anything?' He spoke with possessive pride. 'This is a bad war. In 1967 we had much to gain. But now hundreds of men have died, for what? Because we have to stop the Arabs, yet again, from trying to take what is ours.' One of the revelations of Israel is the fluency of its citizens. Even in those days, in that predicament, they could talk, as well as fight, like no other nation. As dusk fell, the artillery flashes lit up the sky. 'God, we so much want to finish the Arabs this time,' said an unshaven teenager making coffee in his half-track. 'Why should we have to go through this every few years? Today, they have used their rockets on the kibbutzim. We know that if they had the atomic bomb, they would use that too.'

In the early hours of Wednesday morning, I shuffled back into my hotel. I had hitch-hiked in military vehicles down to the Jordan valley, then found a taxi to take me to Tel Aviv. I hated to leave the Golan, because I knew how hard it could be to get up there again, and how lucky I had been to make it the first time. But for every correspondent in every war, before the coming of portable satellite telephones, the issue has been the same. There is no point in having the greatest story on earth, if you have no means to file it. I led my dispatch that day with what I had learned from the tankers – that Israeli advanced forces had again crossed the 1967 ceasefire line in several places. But I added, 'The fighting on Golan and at Suez is still very heavy . . . The Syrians are still hurling themselves at the Israeli lines with men, tanks, artillery and aircraft . . . The situation on Golan is by no means as peaceful as Israel's army Chief of Staff implied at his press conference on Monday night.'

Some years ago the journalist Philip Knightley wrote a history of war corresponding, entitled *The First Casualty*. His principal theme was that journalists in battle have generally got it wrong, often contemptibly so. The author sought to make a virtue of the fact that he himself had never reported a war. Yet I have always thought his book profoundly flawed, because it ignores the fundamental problem of writing about conflict. One is seeking to assemble a jigsaw, from which most of the pieces are missing. The choice for the war correspondent is not between retailing truth and falsehood, but between reporting a fragment of the reality or nothing at all. All journalists must compete with official deceit, in war and peace. In war, not only do commanders tell reporters lies, often they themselves do not know the truth. I have always been conscious, never more so than during the Yom Kippur War, that I was transmitting to London news of mere fractions of the great events unfolding around me, some accurate, some misleading, together with snapshots, cameos of scenes I had been able to observe at particular times and places. I have never doubted that journalists in wars should doggedly pursue those fragments, as long as we – and our readers – perceive them for what they are. The historians must fill the great blank spaces in the story we tell. If war correspondents contrive to catch some glimpses of the battlefield, to interpret these, and to recount honestly what they have seen, then they are doing the only job that can be expected of them. That is what some of us were trying to do, groping on the Golan in October 1973.

CHAPTER SEVEN

Israel's Victory

IT WAS TIME to shift to the Sinai front. Once again, there was no point in harassing the Israeli press department for assistance – none would be forthcoming. Richard Johns of the *Financial Times* agreed to team up with me. He possessed a jewel: a yellow Hertz Ford Cortina. Wheels. On Wednesday morning, a few hours after I returned from the Golan, we set off with sandwiches, water, sleeping bags, a few camp cooking tools I bought in Tel Aviv, a spare can of petrol and a pretty basic map of Sinai. Once again, we were lucky. Israel was still too busy fighting a war to have spare men to stop people like us. We sailed past the checkpoints, waving our accreditation brusquely at the sentries without stopping, the Cortina just one among a procession of civilian vehicles taking reservists to their units. Six hours of sand after leaving Tel Aviv, we dropped down through the Mitla Pass, and found ourselves in the rear areas of the Israeli army, once again interrogating exhausted, intolerably strained tank crews. 'It's not good,' said one officer. 'They are not making ground, but nor are we. However many of their tanks we knock out, they have more. They are so many.' I wrote in the dispatch I filed next day: 'The Israeli army's will to fight is if anything stronger than ever. But the officers on the ground are talking of anything from a week to a month to break through.'

Soldiers described the barrages of ground-to-air missiles they watched rise from behind the Egyptian front whenever an Israeli aircraft overflew it, and which we soon saw for ourselves. The men among whom we talked had been rocketed by Egyptian aircraft the previous day, an unwelcome and wholly unfamiliar experience for Israeli soldiers. 'They were cowards, because they made only one pass and then ran away across the canal,' said an earnest young sergeant. 'But never, never will I forget those rockets coming at us.'

An Israeli hutted camp nearby had been wrecked by shellfire and abandoned. We met a half-track crew emerging from its ruins. They had armed themselves to the teeth with weapons from its armoury. 'If nobody else is doing anything with them, we'll make good use of them.' They grinned. Men murmured to each other in the gathering gloom of evening. One prayed, standing head bowed against the hull of his tank. 'Our movement is very slow,' said another of his crew. 'We know the high-ups have a plan, but we don't know when we will have the reserves to attack again.' The intense night movement, of troops retiring from the front to rest and others moving forward, began on the road beside us. Artillery fired spasmodically close at hand. Further north we could hear the guns booming continuously. The battery beside whom we had stopped suddenly received an order to redeploy. They moved off into the night with the roaring, squeaking clatter of caterpillars which echoed all over Sinai that week. We climbed back into the Cortina.

The trouble with reporting a war without authorization or escort is that you do not dare to ask for directions from senior officers on the battlefield, in case they arrest you and send you packing. One must grope from encounter to encounter, never

sure where the front line is, or – more important – how far
distant is the enemy. As dusk fell, we were edging the little
Ford along a road without much idea where we were. The
moon rose rapidly, enabling us to glimpse vehicles and men on
the sand with extraordinary clarity. Somebody shouted at us
for having been fools enough to put on our lights, a ludicrous
civilian reflex when driving in darkness. Then the crew of a
half-track bawled even louder and waved their weapons as we
passed. Reluctantly, we reversed a few yards back to them.
They shouted in Hebrew. We looked baffled. Did anyone speak
English? Yes, of course. 'Are you crazy? There's nothing but
the Egyptians in front of you down that road.'

We put the car into gear, provoking another shout of anger
as our reversing lights came on. Before they would let us drive
further, they made me get out and smash the offending lights
with the jack. Mopping our brows, we headed south-east.
Within a few yards, we had to swerve off the road to avoid an
approaching tank column – and promptly bogged in the sand.
When the tanks had passed, we found ourselves alone in the
desert. After half an hour's bad-tempered digging, we got the
car back on the road and retreated another couple of miles, to
bivouac beside an infantry unit among the hills of the Mitla
Pass. We brewed coffee on our little gas stove, and made
ourselves as comfortable as we could among the rocks. Richard,
a few years older than me and cast in the classic mould of
literate, thoughtful *FT* journalists, was the most delightful
companion, unversed in war, but up for almost anything. A
sentry wandered over to us from the nearby leaguer. He was
another middle-aged reservist, a widely travelled businessman
who spoke impeccable English, full of sophisticated thoughts
about the battle and about life in general.

'You are from the *Financial Times*? Ah yes, the pink one.'

'Whisky?' We proffered the bottle.

'Thank you, no. Only water – until we reach the canal.'

It seemed a marvellous romance, camping under the stars with the army of Israel at this great moment of her national crisis. I loved these people, the manner in which they talked and lived and fought. Now that we grasped how close to disaster the Arab attack had brought this country, I was filled with admiration for the manner in which Israel responded – and I felt very moved. For the rest of the war, we did little enough sleeping, but I was borne along on a wave of adrenalin and euphoria, gripped by the privilege of seeing this great society at a unique moment in its history. These were soldiers very different from those of the United States, or of Britain, or of India, or any other nation I had ever known – always civilians first, amateur soldiers second. But they made such soldiers as the world rarely sees, and in those days on the Golan and in Sinai, I loved them. Even today, though I have long since lost sympathy with the policies of Israel, I revere the men of her army.

The night sky was pierced at regular intervals by parachute flares and the distant flash of artillery. We slept uneasily for a few hours in our clothes beside the vehicle, often woken by cries and sudden vehicle movements. At first light, we stretched uncomfortably, brewed coffee and ate a couple of biscuits, then set off west once again. Back in the forward line into which we had blundered the previous night, they told us that Egyptian patrols had been probing during the hours of darkness. An abandoned Egyptian armoured car stood just in front of the position, its crew taken prisoner. Through my glasses, I gazed on the enemy positions five or six hundred yards forward. There was no hint of movement, but we knew they were there, with their Saggers and RPGs and all the other tools of the Russian arsenal which had caused Israel such grief in the past five days. The impetus of the Egyptian attack had

144

been broken. They had created and executed a brilliant plan for crossing the canal and establishing a bridgehead on the east bank. But they lacked the initiative and flexibility to exploit this and push on across Sinai. The contrast between the performance and attitude of Egyptian and Israeli commanders could not have been more marked. The Egyptians were deeply reluctant to advance beyond the protection of their powerful anti-aircraft missile screen, which effectively covered only the canal area. On the Israeli side, however, the men on the ground were paying a high price for their commanders' decision to build an army after the 1967 war which was based overwhelmingly upon armour, and upon the doctrine that tanks fighting alone could dominate the battlefield. Now, they needed infantry, mortars and armoured personnel carriers in close support to combat the Egyptian infantry with their missiles. They were desperately short of all these things. Ammunition expenditure was proving prodigious, and the Israelis had stockpiled far too little within reach of the front. Only the huge American airlift that now began, and of which we glimpsed the first fruits a day or two later when we passed brand-new American tanks being transported towards Sinai, provided the means to keep Israel fighting.

A line of half-tracks halted beyond the low ridge behind us. Their cargoes of infantry doubled clumsily forward through the sand to take up position around where we stood. Clouds of dust to our right marked the day's first movement by Israeli armour, advancing to contact. Suddenly an officer who had arrived with the half-tracks began to shout and gesticulate fiercely at our car. He did not know who we were, but he found it intolerably unwarlike to have a yellow Cortina on his battlefield. Richard and I consulted hastily and decided to go. I was anyway desperate to file a dispatch. We knew we would find no telephone in Sinai. For some miles Richard drove, while I scribbled in my notebook, searching for the sentences that would tell a story without causing the censors who monitored every call to pull the plug. Then I took over the wheel, and we raced eastward across Sinai. At Gaza, three hours later, I found a mobile telephone truck where Israeli soldiers were queuing to ring their families. After an anguished wait, I got through to London. I filed and then sagged, as every journalist sags with relief and gratitude when, for that day and that edition, he knows he has done the business. We headed back to Tel Aviv to attend the daily briefing and exchange tense gossip with colleagues – some of whom had been hanging around the city since Sunday, pleading for an official facility to visit the front. We ate, and even slept a little.

To my delight, I ran into Nick Tomalin of the *Sunday Times*. I had always adored Nick, the icon of my generation of journalists, though he was fifteen years older than me. He had been a brilliant gossip columnist, investigative reporter and then foreign correspondent. In London when he was already famous and I was nobody, he was kind, hospitable, generous. When I was barely twenty-three, he invited me to a dinner party at the trendy Tomalin house in Gloucester Crescent, where I found myself among Harold Evans, S. J. Perelman, Jonathan Miller, Karl Miller. I never forgot my gratitude. Abroad, I had met Nick's irresistible lopsided grin in Vietnam, and two years earlier in Calcutta during the Indo-Pakistan war. I am prone to show, as well as to feel, the strain of exhaustion and fear on the battlefield. I never saw Nick look troubled. He nursed the memory of choice moments of battlefield drollery until he found an audience to appreciate them. In Calcutta, he had just returned from the front, where the Indian advance was stalled before a demolished river crossing. Nick described the scene, as one of those superbly British Indian officers contemplated the wrecked bridge. 'I'll say this for your Paki,' remarked the colonel. 'He certainly does a sensational blow job.' Now, in the hotel in Tel Aviv, I had a hasty lunch with Nick before we went our separate ways towards the Golan. I teased him. 'What's an old man like you doing in a place like this? I've got to be here because I'm twenty-seven years old and trying to make a reputation. You're forty-two. You've been everywhere, you've won all the prizes. Why go through it again?' Nick didn't answer, because he didn't need to. He was there because, like so many journalists who continue to go to wars far too long, he could not resist being where the big story was.

Richard Johns and I climbed back into the battered Cortina, rather better provisioned than before, and equipped with winter clothing of the type the Israeli army wears. We had bought this partly for warmth at night, and also to fend off casual investigation at road blocks. We had abandoned any hope of being given official facilities to go to the front – as expected, these were being granted only to the biggest and most important foreign news organizations. We found ourselves spending the weekend in Syria. The Israeli army's counter-attack in the north had now driven far past the 1967 ceasefire line. Fighting was still intense. We simply drove hither and thither across the battlefield wherever we could, talking to anyone who would talk, seeing whatever we could see without being chased away. On the first night, near Kuneitra, we had an encounter with a tearful Israeli captain, who described how he and his men, retaking positions which had fallen in the first Syrian assault a week earlier, found the bodies of Israeli prisoners bound, mutilated and shot. I was profoundly shaken by his tale. I already felt emotional about the war, and about the cause of Israel. Now, to hear first-hand evidence of the enemy's barbarism came as a shock. When I sought to file this story, the Israeli censor deleted it from my copy, on the grounds that such tales would cause distress to the families of men who died on the Golan. But as soon as the war ended, I did report the episode. My story provoked a fierce exchange of claims and denials. The Israelis subsequently produced formal evidence and photographs to show that, in four places on the Golan, twenty-eight of their men had been murdered in Syrian hands. This news provoked riots in Israel by the families of 113 men still listed as missing on the Golan front.

Yet I must enter a postscript here. Four years after Yom Kippur, I was writing about the Sayeret Matkal, the General Staff Reconnaissance Unit, Israel's equivalent of Britain's Special Air Service. In the course of researching the book, I learned a lot about Israel's special forces, a tale I shall recount later. Much was to their credit. Other things were not. In June 1972, for instance, the Sayeret mounted an operation to snatch a group of Syrian generals visiting the Lebanese border, to claim as hostages for exchange against three Israeli pilots held by Damascus. The snatch worked. One veteran described to me how the generals' entire Lebanese escort was shot on the spot by the raiders, so there should be no witnesses to the fact that the operation had been carried out inside Lebanon rather than – as Israel officially claimed – after the Syrians had 'strayed across the border'. The ruthlessness of the Sayeret can be matched on occasion by other special forces units, such as the SAS during the disgracefully handled Gibraltar shootings of four IRA terrorists in 1987. But back in 1977, what I learned seemed a brutal corrective to my own emotionalism about Arab behaviour during Yom Kippur. Nothing can excuse Syrian brutality to some Israeli prisoners in those days, and indeed the Syrians have a long and documented record of cruelty to captives. But today all of us, and especially myself, know far more than we did then about the stains on Israel's record.

Almost all men are morally compromised by the experience of war. Israel's record on human rights remains far better than that of most Middle Eastern countries. But I blush to recall how, on the Golan Heights in my green twenties, I was still willing to believe in a world of moral absolutes, and in the untarnished virtue of Israel.

That October weekend – how ludicrous the word seems in the context of war, but it was important to me, because I had no need to file again before Monday – we were moving constantly among the debris of battle, bodies already starting to stink in the autumn sun, wrecked tanks, vehicles and buildings. We watched the crazy zigzag vapour trails of SAM-6 missiles pursuing Israeli Mirages across the sky. I prided myself on possessing a good working knowledge of military hardware. But in this first great missile war of the twentieth century, I realized that I knew nothing about missile technology and must learn fast.

On Saturday, we watched an Israeli fighter swoop down upon a Syrian MiG, which dissolved in a brilliant flash of light. Next morning by a ruined Syrian village – the Israelis were well across the border by now – we encountered the splendid Brigadier Sheriff Thompson, military correspondent of the *Daily Telegraph*. Sheriff, a man in his sixties who did not allow severe lameness to keep him away from the front, briskly harangued young Johns and me about the unnecessary discomfort of our bivouac, and ordered us to bring out a table and some chairs from a wrecked Syrian government office to eat luncheon in more appropriate fashion. We trotted off to do his bidding. I became briefly excited by discovering among the debris a brand-new Olivetti typewriter, a useful-looking candidate for liberation. Richard gently pointed out to me that the keys were in Arabic. Sheriff was delivering a superb assessment of Israel's military predicament when two Syrian

MiGs streaked overhead, firing and rocketing. Small arms and vehicle-mounted machine-guns opened up from the ground in all directions. Richard and I hastily sought cover. Sheriff did not budge. He resumed his discourse when the firing stopped, with the merest lift of an eyebrow to hint at his surprise that two young British journalists should scuttle about in such an unseemly fashion. Twenty-nine years before, Sheriff had commanded the guns of 1st Airborne Division at Arnhem. 'I suppose after that experience, anything else is just an anticlimax,' I muttered to Richard.

We drove on, stopping at intervals to scan the landscape through my binoculars and to talk to anyone who looked junior enough not to question us about our presence. Nights were hardest, because we never knew for sure where, amid the shelling, we could safely fall asleep in the car. In a war of movement, shooting is seldom continuous in any one place. The focus of fire can shift abruptly, without warning or explanation. Suddenly, there was the whizz and crump of an explosion a few hundred yards away, then another – then silence for hours. We passed a truck unloading ammunition by the roadside, which vanished seconds later into a heap of flame and twisted steel, victim of a direct hit. One night when the car on the road amid that featureless plateau looked horribly visible and vulnerable, and there was firing of all kinds from threats we could not pinpoint, we took to a roadside ditch and lay in it, unable to sleep. Fear attacks different people in different ways. Some become mute. Some shake. Some – like me – are driven to chatter incessantly. I wanted to live to see my small son grow up, I said. Crump, from a shell somewhere in the darkness. What were we doing here? Crump. What did it all mean? Crump. How could it possibly be worth risking our necks for this? Crump. It was all terrible rubbish – my words, I mean. Even the exceptionally good-natured Richard remarked in a London pub after the war that he minded the shelling much less than my babbling that night.

Next evening, we stopped to sleep in the car in the midst of an Israeli battery, seeking security from the gunners' presence. We sat for a time, watching the rippling flashes of Syrian Katyusha rockets being fired across the darkness on the horizon. Then we dozed off. We had been unconscious for only an hour or two when the Cortina door was torn open by a gunner shouting at us. 'Wake up! Wake up! Drive! The Syrians – they find us! We all go, quick, quick. They register on us.' All around in the darkness, men and vehicles were hastening away as artillery fire began to bracket the position. The guns moved only a few hundred metres. We were frightened enough to pull back four or five miles for the remainder of the night.

Israeli soldiers are the most politically conscious in the world. Every hour of the war, they listened obsessively to their radios – Voice of Israel, Voice of America, BBC. Everywhere we went, we met men still raging at the manner in which their nation had been allowed to be taken by surprise. They vented their disgust against their own government, against the UN, against the nations of the West, and even by name against Britain's Foreign Secretary, Sir Alec Douglas-Home. 'For the sake of *world opinion*' – this, in tones of infinite scorn – 'we let the Arabs attack first,' said an officer who had fought in Sinai in 1967. 'What is the result? We lose so much in the first days. Now we see that *world opinion* is not worth one Israeli soldier's life. You say you give us your *sympathy*. But where is your *help* now that we, the victims, need it most?'

I met a soldier who had been hitch-hiking near Braemar in Scotland, of all places, when the war started. He at once began a journey home which had now brought him by half-track ten miles into Syria. He spoke of a friend who had emigrated from England only two years earlier, and had been in one of the

Israeli positions on the Golan overrun when the first Syrian onslaught was launched. 'Many of his comrades were killed. When he escaped, he walked for three days until he was found by the Sea of Galilee. Now, he is in hospital with "shock". How could all this have been allowed to happen?' 'Shell shock' or 'battle fatigue' accounted for an extraordinarily high proportion of Israel's casualties in this war, a reflection of the trauma it inflicted on the whole country.

One could never forget that this was a conscript army, reflecting the nation's extraordinary diversity of character. I was struck by a story I heard afterwards, about a moment when men of the crack Sayeret Matkal lay in ambush during the retaking of Mount Hermon. A group of Syrians was suddenly flushed out in front of them. The commander ordered his MAG gunner to fire. There was a pause, and then the man said in a strangled voice, 'I can't do it. I can't shoot. I've never killed a man before.' To any outsider who knew the reputation of Zahal, as Israelis call their army, this would have seemed a moment of pure fantasy, but another soldier had to take over the gun and open fire.

In the early hours of Monday morning, 15 October, we drove back down into the peaceful valleys of northern Israel, to find a telephone from which we could tell our tale to London. 'The pace of Israel's advance into Syria has now slackened so greatly that the Israeli army may be planning to halt on a line within a few miles of where it now stands, holding all the heights commanding the Syrian plain below, and within artillery range of Damascus,' I began my dispatch, which led the front page of that day's *Evening Standard*. There was only one flaw in what appeared. 'Artillery range of Damascus', which we had correctly grasped as the key element of the situation, was printed by a mad copytaker's error as 'within the Idauiicoyy Range' – presumably interpreted as some non-existent mountain feature. That is a hazard of foreign communication in war, but a maddening one. Rather to my surprise, the censor also allowed me to say that 'in theory at least, this could very soon release tanks and aircraft for the Sinai battle'. Israel's key secret decision, within hours of the outbreak of war, had been to launch everything into throwing back the Syrians on the Golan – who represented by far the most urgent threat to the country – before shifting forces to deal with the Egyptians. We knew nothing of the General Staff's strategy, but we sensed that a moment had now come at which the hub of the war would shift to the Suez front. And although of course we were not allowed to report it, our hunches were confirmed within hours, as we saw vehicles and tanks on their transporters moving south – away from Syria, away from the Golan. They could have only one possible destination.

'It is very difficult to accept the Israeli claim that their casualties are still below those of the Six-Day War,' I wrote. 'The road to Damascus may be victorious for Israel, but it is also a *via dolorosa* for a nation to whom every plane, every tank, and most especially every life is so important.' I said above that we could not have been expected to be allowed to report Israeli troop movements. There is a powerful faction in the media today which argues that no self-respecting journalist should ever accept censorship of his dispatches. Most journalists, at one time or another, go to great lengths to avoid or circumvent censorship – I describe in this book some of those occasions in my own experience. But in a war of national survival, it seems hard to argue against any nation's right to preserve its military secrets, if it can. Many colleagues disagreed then, however, and disagree now. They perceive a media interest, a 'responsibility to our profession', which supersedes any mere national or public interest. This seems to me to reflect an almost insane collective conceit. In war or peace, the media can only justify itself by reference to the public interest, however wide is the scope for debate about what this means. It is not necessary to believe that war correspondents should file what governments want us to file, or broadcast opinions to suit the General Staff – I have never done that in my life – but merely that we should not wantonly pass on operational secrets which could cost lives. In a war, when issues of life and death are at stake, if journalists perceive themselves as mere spectators in the galleries of the Colosseum, turning a thumb up or down with absolute indifference towards those struggling for survival in the arena, they cannot expect much public respect.

A few minutes after we got back to Tel Aviv on Monday morning, I heard the stunning news that Nick Tomalin was dead. A Syrian rocket had hit his Volvo on the Golan Heights, killing him instantly. His colleague, the fearless Don Mc-Cullin, crawled forward at great personal risk to check that Nick was beyond help and to retrieve his identity documents. I remembered a conversation about death Nick and I had, some years earlier, sailing his tiny dinghy on a reservoir outside London. 'Did you never think of killing yourself, Nick,' I asked, 'when you were a hopeless teenager?' As a gloomy adolescent, like many adolescents I spent many hours toying with death. Nick looked at me in amazement. 'Of course not,' he said. It was not that Nick's existence was without its troubles, but merely that few men loved life more. And now, what had he died for? Not for his country, nor for some higher cause – simply because, as a reporter, he loved to be where the action was. After his death, there was a maudlin 'memorial meeting' in London in place of any religious service, on the grounds that Nick was not a believer. I didn't go. In an uncertain world, I thought Nick would have wanted a traditional, sentimental church funeral. He loved traditional, sentimental English occasions – he had written charmingly a year before about my own village wedding. But he received a characteristic NWI send-off, and I grieved for that as well as for him. I loved Nick as much as any man in my life, above all for his generosity of spirit. His lopsided posture, his voice, his laughter still echo across time to me as vividly as they did all those years ago in Fleet Street's wine bars.

On Monday, 15 October, I took my only 'official' trip of the war down to Sinai, in a bus with a group of fellow correspondents. The strain of working on our own had begun to tell on Richard and me – and yes, on that poor yellow Cortina. When I heard that a facility was on offer, I took it. Forty or so strong, our party ground its way across the desert in dusty charabanc, spared from the fear of running out of petrol or being stopped at checkpoints – but also without the chance of talking to men on their own, of probing and exploring away from official eyes. At front headquarters, five miles or so behind the lines, we were briefed by a couple of senior officers. We were told, entirely accurately, that Egypt's bridgehead at Suez was contained. Egypt's 100,000 men on the east bank of the canal were going nowhere. Israel would deal with them in due course. By now, we were all acutely aware of the scale of Israel's surprise ten days earlier, and of how heavily she had paid in blood to stem the Arab assault. We knew in outline, if not in detail, how grave had been her losses of tanks and aircraft. We were no longer naive, indeed we were downright sceptical, about Israeli official claims of impending victory. Little did we know that, at 5 p.m. on the same afternoon, General 'Arik' Sharon had launched one of the most daring strokes in the history of warfare, the offensive that was to cut a path across the canal for Israeli paratroopers and infantry in the early hours of next morning, smash deep into the Egyptian rear, and transform the face of the war.

The general who had been briefing us that afternoon in

Sinai mounted his half-track and drove away in a cloud of dust, standing erect and irredeemably cocky behind the windscreen, tank goggles pushed back over his soft cap. 'He thinks he's Rommel.' I laughed. One is not allowed to make remarks like that in Israel. Eric Silver of the *Guardian*, a fine journalist who identified without embarrassment with his own people, interjected crossly, 'You'll be saying we all look like concentration camp guards next.' But the revival of Israeli self-assurance, tipping over into arrogance, became more conspicuous as that week went on, from top to bottom of her army. The soldiers knew that the spectre of Arab victory had been removed. It remained only to discover how overwhelming a triumph Israel could now contrive, from her own counter-offensives.

The censor allowed me to file a story about the build-up of Israeli reserves in Sinai for a big push. 'The Israelis' greatest needs at the moment are more and better ground-to-ground and ground-to-air missiles,' I reported. 'Their own Hawks compare unfavourably with the Egyptian SAMs, and they have been staggered by the sheer quantity of portable anti-tank missiles that have been issued to Egyptian infantry.' 'Perhaps now the Americans are sending us equipment, they will decide to let us have something new they want testing,' remarked one soldier somewhat cynically. 'They know we are the best testers of military equipment in the world.' America had launched its huge airlift to ship tanks, missiles, ammunition into Israel – some of the equipment was being rushed straight from the airfields to the front. That Monday night, we watched in the darkness as the business of war gathered momentum around us: repair crews labouring under arc-lights on damaged tanks; helicopters clattering to and fro on casevac missions; shadowy figures clutching stretchers running with their bleeding loads to the emergency tents, drips suspended precariously above the litters. We garnered no hint of the huge drama unfolding along the canal bank a few miles away, but maybe we should have done, if we had listened more carefully to the nuances of the staff officers' conversation. 'The sooner it is over, the sooner we go home,' one said to me jovially. 'But perhaps we have lunch in Cairo first, ha?'

On Tuesday 16 October, when the Israeli spearhead was fighting fiercely to hold and reinforce its frail bridgehead on the West bank of the Suez Canal, we went back to Tel Aviv. Even as word trickled through that Israeli forces had crossed the canal, their commanders maintained the fiction that this was a mere 'commando raid'. Amazingly, for some days most of the world believed them. Yet some of us began to guess the real nature, and huge ambition, of the Israelis' attack under Sharon. They had launched their assault at the boundary between the Egyptian 2nd and 3rd armies, a chronic weak point in every army's deployments. The enemy had failed to counter-attack either quickly or effectively. I wrote for Friday's *Evening Standard*: 'The Israeli army appears committed to some form of envelopment movement on the west bank of the Suez Canal, and the Egyptians must know that unless they pull some rabbit out of the hat, their position is looking precarious in the extreme.' To my surprise, the censor did not interfere. Next day, I speculated: 'The Israeli army now appears embarked on one of its strategic master strokes. I would surmise that their aim is to checkmate the whole Egyptian force on the east bank of the canal without having to engage them in a costly head-on battle.' I have so often misread stories and military situations that I exulted then, and I look back with pleasure now, to know that I got this one right.

There remained a glittering prize for any reporter of the war: the first eye-witness view of Israel's bridgehead on the west bank of Suez. In Tel Aviv, I was devastated to hear on Saturday afternoon that the Israelis were taking an official party of journalists under escort to the bridgehead. Needless to say, I was not grand enough to feature on the list. What to do? We knew that security at the approaches to Sinai had been much tightened since the early days of the war. There was little chance of getting down to the canal again without authorization. I consulted Richard Johns. How about one more trip with the Cortina? He agreed. I told him I had a plan. When we got past Gaza, instead of heading straight for the canal, I could see on the map a road that ran for miles southwards, and then crossed Sinai westward again. If we came at the canal from the most unexpected direction, I thought we could avoid the roadblocks.

We stocked the car with petrol, water, Coca-Cola, a little food, and set off in the early hours of the morning down the familiar road through southern Israel. The first part of my scheme was to hit the entrance to Sinai at first light, when the guards would be least watchful. It worked. We were wearing Israeli army winter jackets. We belted past the checkpoint in the half-light, waving cheerfully at the sentries. Then we reached the key road junction, and turned left for southern Sinai, instead of right for Suez. This was where matters began to look less promising. The desert was entirely empty, of people or buildings. Mile after mile we ground on amid the heat. Sand had long ago crept into every interstice of the car and our clothing. The loneliness began to unnerve me. We passed occasional parties of Bedouin on their camels. We had always been warned that their friendliness could not be relied upon, and of course we were unarmed. Then we passed long-abandoned army encampments, old Egyptian barracks, and the wreckage of war from 1956 and 1967, derelict vehicles stripped of paint by years of wind and sand. On and on we went, into nothingness. I was increasingly nervous now, fearful of the consequences of bogging down or suffering a breakdown in the

empty desert, cursing the insouciance with which I had persuaded Richard to try this foolish scheme, which suddenly
seemed dangerous as well as barren of promise. I had already
lost faith in my own plan by the time we rounded a dune and
saw before us a small, heavily fenced army camp set amid a
cluster of palm trees – an obvious oasis – bristling with huge
aerials. Immediately beyond its gate stood a half-track full of
soldiers, engine running.

I was immediately sure of this much: if anybody there got
to talk to us, we would only leave under guard, and probably
find ourselves thrown out of the country as well as Sinai.
Sweating with fear and uncertainty, in the middle of that utter
emptiness I executed a three-point turn, and set off northwards
again. By a miracle which bemuses me to this day, we were
neither stopped nor pursued. Were those soldiers so completely
incurious about the presence of a solitary yellow Cortina in
the midst of the desert? Hours later, low-spirited, we found
ourselves back at the junction in north Sinai. 'Let's give it a go
to get through to the canal road,' I said. Instead of turning
back to Tel Aviv, we swung left for Suez. Ten minutes onward,
we were flagged down at a knife-rest checkpoint. The guards
refused to let us go further. Only by some fast talking did we
persuade them not to detain us. Utterly disconsolate, we began
to drive slowly back towards Gaza.

Then we had a marvellous break. Heading the other way
across the empty plain from the east came a column of
Mercedes, Volvos, Fords. Media cars. 'It's the official party!' I
said. 'We've just got to join them.' It was too easy. Once again
I swung the car round in the road and raced after the rear
vehicle. We sailed behind it through the roadblock and deep
onwards into Sinai. A hour further on, we reached another
moment of decision. At the huge camp at Bir Gifgâfa, the
media party's cars turned into the gates. I remembered what I

had heard in Tel Aviv. The authorized correspondents and their escort were spending the night there, before they went down to the canal.

Richard and I sped on. We agreed there was little or no chance of getting to the Israeli pontoons across the canal in daylight, or indeed by taking the direct route. Instead, we headed south, for the familiar Mitla Pass, scene of the famous Israeli paratroop action in 1956. Once we were winding upwards among its rocky defiles, we waited until there was no sign of another vehicle in any direction. Then we swung the Cortina behind a huge boulder and clambered wearily out. We had both brought books for this eventuality. I lay down with *Middlemarch*, to await the darkness. It was a hot afternoon, and the barren Mitla felt like a grill plate. After so many days of almost relentless activity, we were both desperately tired, yet we could not sleep amid the heat and apprehension about what the night might bring. It would be unbearable to have come so far and to be thwarted now. I, at least, had found our ordeal in southern Sinai that morning pretty unnerving. Only the last scrapings of professional ambition were driving me on.

At last light, we turned cautiously back on to the road. As we descended the western side of the Mitla, we glimpsed the vital right turn on to the lateral road north along the canal, which should eventually bring us to the bridgehead by the 'Chinese Farm' where Sharon had led his men into Egypt. The road was thronged with convoys, some moving, some stationary. Sometimes we had to edge along behind trundling tanks, lunging abruptly right and left on their tracks, sometimes to swerve dangerously along the sand, praying not to get bogged, to avoid a halted column of half-tracks or trucks. At last I said to Richard, 'I'm so tired I've got to ask you to drive. Otherwise I'm just going to crash us.' I shifted across into the passenger seat, and immediately fell asleep. A few minutes later, there was a thunderous jolt and impact. I awoke to find that Richard, as tired as I was, had locked the Cortina in metallic embrace with a tank. We clambered out. Its commander seemed amused by our presumption in venturing to lock horns with his beast. He spoke English perfectly, of course. 'You chaps *have* got yourselves into a mess,' he said indulgently. Then his monster lurched forward, leaving the Cortina somewhat dented, but still drivable. I took over the wheel again. We crawled on through the darkness, peering through the windscreen for hints of vehicles or obstacles ahead. Suddenly, there was a left fork ahead. I ignored a gesturing soldier, probably a military policeman, and accelerated desperately forward. We must be so close now. Our pace was reduced to that of the heavy west-bound stream of transport heading towards the three bridges which now sustained the huge Israeli operation on the far side. Then I glimpsed the girders of a pontoon only yards ahead. I swung off the road and stopped. I knew we could never bluff the Cortina past the sentries on the canal itself. We would have to do the last bit on foot. We climbed out. Exulting in the moment, we walked unchallenged among the vehicles and men crossing that frail, vital link between Sinai and Israeli-occupied Egypt. We found ourselves among palm trees and wrecked houses and vehicles, on the western shore in the early light of day.

Two or three hours later, we walked back across the canal without incident, and began to drive as fast as that poor, abused Cortina could take us towards Gaza with our scoop. Glee redoubled when we passed the officially escorted convoy of journalists advancing towards the canal from Bir Gifgâfa. We had done it.

*

'Poor Egyptians,' I wrote, in the dispatch I sent that morning, under the precious dateline 'Israeli-occupied Egypt':

'They chose the time, the place, the force with which to start this war. Now, the wreckage of their hopes is littered for miles around the west bank of the Suez Canal – tanks, jeeps, trucks and aircraft, destroyed in all their attacks, counter-attacks, and counter-counter-attacks. As Israeli forces widen their corridor north and south, the Egyptians already appear unable to make any effective counter-move except to lob spasmodic and wildly aimed artillery fire in the general direction of the bridgehead. Egyptian armoured attacks are beaten off with heavy loss, and at last the Israeli air force seems to have gained complete command of the sky. The last MiG that attempted to strafe the canal position was not even shot down, it merely mistimed its approach and crashed straight into the water.

Talking to some of the men who made the initial canal crossing on Monday night, it is clear that for the first two days the Israelis had to fight very hard indeed to maintain a foothold. The area around the canal on the Egyptian side is a shambles of blasted palm trees, broken vehicles and incinerated corpses. Poor old Suez Canal. No one who remembered the view from so many P&O steamer chairs would recognize the mouth of the Great Bitter Lake. It is littered with debris, the occasional body, and – a few miles out – the hulks of the ships trapped there since the Six-Day War, still rusting where they float.

Stray dogs wander through the Egyptian army camp, its parade square empty, its huts wrecked. Israeli bulldozers are carving innumerable sand roads through the palm groves. An Israeli officer was searching through the back of an Egyptian army truck. Souvenirs of Arab invasions are as indispensable to a Tel Aviv sitting room, as flying ducks on the walls in Epping. What are the Egyptians doing? 'Sitting on their arses. There's not much else they can do,' said one man when I asked if the Arabs' northern bridgehead had been able to intervene effectively.

The Israelis' spearhead troops have had a hard battle, and have not yet recovered their sense of humour. But the mass of this army now seems totally self-assured, eager only to be let loose on the Egyptian bridgehead remaining on the east bank. Fate and America's Dr Kissinger permitting, it seems only a matter of time before the Arabs' arterial roads to the rear are cut.

All this may seem small beer almost thirty years later, but in that place and at that time, it felt a precious achievement to have got far enough to glimpse at first-hand the Israeli triumph across Suez. When I had finished dictating, in the usual fashion of reporters I asked to be transferred to the news desk, and waited like a spaniel for my bowl of biscuits. ''Fraid everybody's at lunch right now,' said a laconic voice at the other end. 'But I'll see they look at your copy as soon as they're back.' God, after all that. A few weeks later, Richard Johns and I were drinking in a London pub with Johnny Moorehead, a mutual friend who is the son of the great war correspondent Alan. We were telling the tale of our doings, with suitable embellishments. Johnny recoiled in genuine bewilderment as well as laughter. 'You're both mad. Absolutely mad. You put yourselves through all this for some front page that nobody outside the trade will even notice, and was wrapping next day's fish and chips.' Rationally, of course, we knew that he was right. But journalism in general and war corresponding in particular demand a suspension of logic, an absolute belief in the value of what you are doing, which may help to explain why so many journalists are more or less unhinged. A state of mental equilibrium is a fatal barrier to getting a great story. Simon Hoggart once asked the ex-wife of a colleague of ours, who later made himself famous in the Middle East, why she gave up on her husband. 'He cared about nothing, absolutely nothing, except his work,' she answered wearily. 'The moment at which I finally decided I must go came one night when the telephone rang while we were making love. He picked up the phone and did an interview down the line with Radio New Zealand without even getting off me.'

Exhausted, Richard and I somehow summoned the energy to push that poor, long-suffering car back to Tel Aviv – for the last time, as it proved. That night, Israel signed a ceasefire. Although there were intermittent artillery duels and local clashes thereafter, essentially the war was over. At bitter cost, the nation had retrieved its fortunes on the battlefield in the most spectacular fashion. In the first days of war, the Arab assault took the Jewish state to the brink of disaster, above all on the Golan Heights. Yet in the weeks that followed, Israeli military genius reasserted itself. On the Golan, it was the dogged courage and skill of the tank crews which saved their country. In Sinai, however, strategic as well as tactical brilliance turned the tables on the attackers. The envelopment of the Egyptian bridgehead on the east bank of the Suez Canal was a masterstroke for which Ariel Sharon deserved huge credit, whatever the horrors of his subsequent career as a politician. The Arabs lacked the initiative, the flexibility and the tactical skill to exploit their early gains, and Israel had once more shown itself the greatest military force in the Middle East. The politics, of course, were another story.

In Tel Aviv, I slept and slept, leaving the agencies to

provide the paper with most of the developing news of par-
leys, ceasefire breaches and negotiations. When at last I found
myself on the plane bound for London, I leaned back in the
seat, asking myself: why am *I* flying home in one piece, rather
than Nick Tomalin, rather than any one of thousands of
young men who have died in the past three weeks? 2,523
Israelis and something like 16,000 Arabs had forfeited their
lives in those short days. Israel had lost around 800 tanks and
115 aircraft, the Arabs some 2,000 tanks and 480 aircraft, an
awesome rate of attrition. I felt the pang of mingled guilt and
exultation that comes to many men at these moments, that
they survive while others do not. I had found the Yom Kippur
War one of the most powerful experiences of my career. It
was also, of course, by far the biggest conventional campaign
I had ever witnessed. While I was still on the crest of my
emotion, I wrote an impassioned piece for the *Evening Standard*'s leader page, in praise of the country among whose
soldiers I had seen so much. I wrote:

Until this war, I have never much liked Israel. But to see
this society gathered in arms to save itself has been impossibly emotive. Down in Sinai under the stars, we sat and
talked for hours to sentries who are agricultural engineers,
tank commanders who are university dons, students who
drove amphibious assault craft in the murderous first crossing
of the canal. Israel at war is a family at war, perhaps the
most highly motivated family in history. Even in Syria, I
have seen Israelis treat their prisoners with nothing worse
than amused pity, embarrassed by a terrified Arab grovelling
for mercy to which he is quite unaccustomed, and thus does
not expect. This is why it has felt so shameful to be a
Western European in Israel; because we have been watching

the Israelis displaying all the qualities for which we look in our civilization – military genius not least – while on the other side stood an enemy of whom there could be no doubt that, armed with an atomic weapon, he would hurl it like a hysterical child ... I shall never go on holiday to Israel because the waiters are rude, the food is terrible, the architecture drab. But these last three weeks, I am proud to have shared the Israelis' camp fires in Sinai. For the only time in my life anywhere in the world, I wish that I had been carrying a rifle beside them. They are a very great people who three weeks ago came closer to destruction than blind Europe seems willing or able to recognize.

That piece made me briefly better known – or more notorious – than anything I had ever written for a newspaper before. It was scribbled in my notebook on the plane flying back from Israel, overwhelmed by the destruction and bloodshed I had seen, far beyond any previous experience I had known of war or peace. David English, the late and great editor of the *Daily Mail*, once said to me, 'All the best journalists are obsessives.' It is probably true, and sobering, to reflect that almost all the most memorable reporting is intemperate. Robert Fisk of the *Independent*, a superb journalist, has always been impelled by a deep passion for the Arab cause, and a matching distaste for the United States and Israel. Many American reporters made reputations in Vietnam denouncing the follies of their own nation with withering scorn. Most of the celebrated Western correspondents in the Balkans have been shameless partisans of one camp or another, or at least passionate exponents of the 'something must be done' persuasion. Looking back over my own writing, I must concede that the balanced, objective dispatches I filed have often been quickly forgotten. It was pieces like that one about Israel, written in the white heat of anger and emotional exhaustion, which lasted a little longer. A host of admiring letters from British Jews descended upon me. Some of my own colleagues, by contrast, were appalled by my remarks. There was a correspondence in *The Times*, in which the Syrian chargé d'affaires drew favourable attention to a British journalist who had denounced me as 'a blatant propagandist for the Israelis'. Among his other counter-blasts, the chargé flatly denied that Syria had been guilty of maltreatment of Israeli prisoners. I wrote in response:

Allegations of 'one-sided reporting', such as are often made by Syria and the Arab states in general, will continue as long as it is journalistically impossible to accomplish anything on the Arab side. My own reporting may have reflected the fact that I was in the Israeli lines, but at least I was able to attempt to judge the situation on the ground at the front. Any reporter in Damascus found himself in the invidious role of sitting in his hotel room, filing demonstrably untruthful official statements. The foreign press there had no opportunity to see anything for themselves but Israeli air attacks. Neither side in any war has a monopoly of either lies or brutality, and this latest is no exception. But it is the information policy of the Syrian government which creates the credibility gap. Any journalist at any time would welcome the opportunity to visit a Syrian-run prisoner-of-war camp to see captured Israelis being properly fed and watered. It would be an unprecedented scoop.

The comment following Yom Kippur which made me most thoughtful came from James Cameron. He wrote on 26 October, after the publication of my impassioned postscript upon the war:

Dear Max,

Forgive an impulsive note. I greatly admired your piece on Israel this evening. I know so precisely the emotions behind it, having experienced them almost identically there three times before, although I think you expressed them rather better than I did. It is quite impossible to work in combat with the Israeli army without this response, if you have any sense of history and drama.

I have sometimes wondered over the past few years whether this irresistible military mesmerism hasn't clouded for us some of the political falsities? I just don't know; I think I was marginally led up the garden in 1967. I suppose the truth is that what goes on in Sinai or the Golan has so little to do with what goes on in the Knesset. Anyway, you did a piece in this evening's paper that I would have tried to emulate if I had been there.

Yours, James

Jimmy had always been a Zionist, so his instinctive sympathies lay anyway with Israel. I valued his words of praise. I have often reflected since, however, upon his shrewd observation, about the manner in which love and admiration for Zahal, the army of Israel, blinded some of us, for a time at least, to the shortcomings of Israeli policy and strategy, which have been founded overwhelmingly upon the crude assumption of military superiority since 1967 at least. I do not regret my coverage of Yom Kippur. Those days represented one of the most vivid experiences of my life. I told the story of Israel's war as I saw it. Like most Europeans, I support Israel's right to exist as unswervingly now as I did in 1973. But after that war was over, in the cool light of peace, I thought more and learned more about the tangled nature of justice in the Middle East. Never again would I feel able to throw myself with such unbridled passion behind the Israeli cause, in the fashion that I did in October 1973. Israel's 1982 invasion of Lebanon caused me, like many others, radically to change my view about the balance of grievance in the region. Yet I came home from Israel that autumn day in 1973 feeling a great love for the country and the people. Today I still cherish the memory of the love, even if a bitter parting lay ahead.

When your own nation is at war, all those around you share a common understanding of the stress, emotion and trauma of the experience. But part of the strangeness of reporting conflict while England remained at peace was one's return from huge and violent drama to a society whose emotional temperature had been raised not a millimetre on the gauge by tragedy in faraway places. Sometimes, the gulf between the intensity of one's own experience and the indifference of those back at home made homecoming painful. When I got off the plane at Heathrow after Yom Kippur, Tricia and I drove to her family's house in Leicestershire for the weekend. I got out of the car on a beautiful autumn afternoon, scarcely able to comprehend the tranquillity of the countryside, to come to terms with a place utterly untouched by the things I had seen over the weeks that had passed. A farming acquaintance passed by in his Landrover. His beefy red face leaned cheerfully out of the window and called to me as I reached for a suitcase, 'Hello, Max! Finished with the Yids, then?' I have seldom felt so utterly remote from my own people.

CHAPTER EIGHT

Bush War

BY THE SUMMER of 1973, eight years after Ian Smith's Unilateral Declaration of Independence, white-ruled Rhodesia was facing an escalating guerrilla offensive. The ZANU movement, based in Zambia and operating through Portuguese Mozambique, was mounting increasingly bold forays to attack white farms and settlements. But how much trouble were they causing? How serious a threat did they present to the Smith regime? Reporting out of the capital, Salisbury, was tightly controlled. There was a blanket government prohibition on journalists visiting the Zambesi Valley, where much of the action was taking place. Charles Wintour sent me a note, suggesting that I should go and do a series of articles about the progress of the war, and enquiring how best I thought I could set about them. After asking some questions – for I had never been to Rhodesia – I felt sure I would learn nothing worth the ticket if I simply turned up in Salisbury as a visiting correspondent. A more circumspect approach was needed. I decided to exploit my private enthusiasm for shooting and fishing. At that period, many upmarket rural Englishmen still openly supported the Smith regime, and were certainly not regarded by Salisbury as the sort of soggy, long-haired liberals who might be hostile to white supremacy. I contributed occasional articles about country sports to *The Field*. I have sometimes been accused by fellow journalists of possessing 'a patrician manner', a notion which causes much laughter among patricians, but on this occasion might be useful. The Rhodesians, who were wildly unlikely to have heard of me, expected journalists to wear dirty raincoats and to carry half-empty whisky bottles. I believed that if I turned up in the country looking like some approximation of a would-be white hunter, I could get out to the farms in the sticks, where the story was to be found. I wrote to Charles:

> I am using a passport describing me as an author rather than journalist. My story (if questioned) is that I am on holiday after leaving the BBC. Through a safari company, I have arranged to go shooting sandgrouse in the prohibited area in the north-east, also tiger-fishing on the Zambesi. I have an introduction to several people from *The Field*, on the basis that I am writing about sport out there. I have told colleagues and friends here that I am going to E. Africa on holiday. I think my cover should hold up. I am not planning to approach any of the local correspondents or 'usual journalistic channels'. I shall just get on the local social circuit as a right-wing English sporting fanatic. Some of this may sound absurd, but if it comes off I think it offers the best chance of persuading people to talk to me. If not, I'll write to you from jail.

On 24 July, I flew from London to Salisbury, clutching my shotgun and cartridges (ammunition was short in Rhodesia, except for human targets). It was one of the odder ironies of United Nations sanctions that direct flights from Britain continued undisturbed. I was chiefly apprehensive not about whether I would be unmasked by the authorities as one of the detested hostile liberal journalists – I did not plan to do anything blatantly provocative – but about whether I could get a good enough story to justify the trip from the *Evening Standard*'s viewpoint. From the air, the first striking image of Salisbury was of rectangle upon rectangle of brilliant blue water beside every house. I was met at the airport by my safari guide, a charming and very English Rhodesian a decade or so older than myself. I spent a night in that bastion of colonialism Meikle's Hotel, the dining room of which was full of the sort of old English buffers who had become extinct in England a generation ago, and which also possessed a wine list that by some quirk of sanctions offered great French vintages for a fraction of what one paid in London. Alan Coren once memorably described Salisbury as 'a suburb without an urb'. Its citizens still detested his memory, as the man who touched their raw nerve. It was Surbiton, Woking, Tunbridge Wells – impeccably clean, manicured, sunny, genteel, uncultured, with the political and social values of Mr Pooter *circa* 1890. The city variety of white Rhodesian was the ugliest. Many were people who had come out from Britain since the Second World War with their little moustaches and blazers with RAF crests, searching for a world ruled by the code of an Epsom golf club, in which servants were easier to come by than at home, greens were properly maintained and blacks knew their place. Incredibly, between 1965 and 1973, the white population of Rhodesia increased, as migrants came out to make a life in a place of sun, low living costs, lots of staff, and who cared about democracy anyway? The weakest link in their society's extravagant claims for white Rhodesia's 'patriotism', however, was the simple fact that so many were first or at most second-generation immigrants, with no historic stake in the country at all. Urban whites basked in the comforts and unearned authority they could exercise, and which persisted for years after UDI. But they were widely despised by rural Rhodesians for their alleged

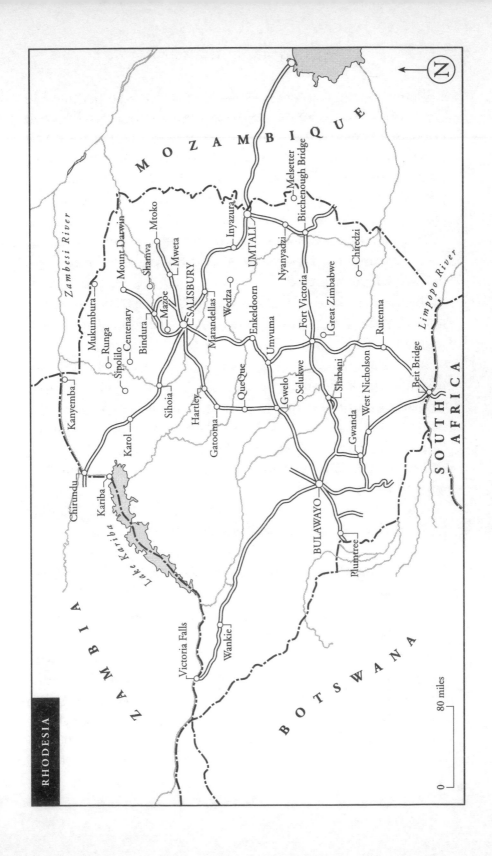

N

MOZAMBIQUE

Melsetter
Birchenough Bridge

Inyazura
UMTALI
Nyanyadzi
Chiredzi

Mtoko
Shamva
Mweta
Wedza
Fort Victoria
Great Zimbabwe
Rutenna

Mount Darwin
Mukumbura
Runga
Centenary
Bindura
Mazoe
SALISBURY
Marandellas
Enkeldoorn
Umvuma
Selukwe
Shabani
West Nicholson

Sipolilo

Zambesi River

Kanyemba
Sihoia
Hartley
Gatooma
QueQue
Gwelo
Gwanda

Beit Bridge

Limpopo River

SOUTH

AFRICA

Karol

Chirundu
Kariba

Lake Kariba

BULAWAYO

Plumtree

ZAMBIA

Victoria Falls
Wankie

BOTSWANA

RHODESIA

0   80 miles

willingness to avoid anti-terrorist duty in the bush if they could. The bombast of Salisbury residents towards pinkoes, liberals, commies, Harold Wilson, the media, the United Nations was impressive. But many of those armchair warriors were conspicuous by their absence from the rough stuff if they could find any excuse to stay at home – and as the 1970s advanced, there was more and more fighting to be done.

I felt not the smallest sympathy for the Salisbury regime. Ian Smith and his cohorts were near-fascists, committed to the permanent maintenance of white rule, and suppression of the black majority by ruthless use of force, backed by some ridiculous rhetoric about the justice of their own cause. 'If Churchill was alive today, I believe he would probably emigrate to Rhodesia,' said 'good old Smithy'. The Prime Minister enlivened an election meeting in 1970, at which he was heckled by African students, by singing an Afrikaans song entitled '*Bobbejaan, klim die berg*' – 'Baboon, climb the hill'. Smith and such colleagues as the Defence Minister, P. K. van der Byl, remain among the ugliest figures in the history of the struggle for Africa.

The government's iniquitous Land Tenure Act allotted half the country's land to the whites, who represented only 5 per cent of the population. The white farmers who tilled the land amid growing danger, who maintained their remote homesteads in an atmosphere of tightening siege, who uncomplaining sent their sons into the bush to fight the guerrilla war and bear the brunt of the casualties, seemed entitled to a respect for their courage which their leaders never merited. They were ruthless people, however. 'What do you do about the landmine problem, Mrs Smith?' I asked over tea after a guinea fowl shoot. 'Oh, first thing every morning we just pile the farm boys into the truck and send them to drive up and down the track until we can see they haven't blown up.' In those days, the farmers still believed that sooner or later, white middle-class opinion in Britain and America would force those countries' wretched governments to come to their aid. 'Uncle Johnny wrote from Cheltenham only last week to say that everybody in his part of the world is right behind us.' I cautiously suggested that Uncle Johnny and his friends had not the slightest intention of doing anything practical to assist the survival of white Rhodesia, but nobody was listening. I have always thought that some thousands of 'Uncle Johnnies' back in Britain had much to answer for. Their insouciant messages of support for a doomed cause helped keep alive the spirit to sustain Smith's blood-soaked sandcastle for years after it was plain that the tide must overwhelm it.

I rented a car and drove from farm to farm, covering many miles of red-dusted, unmetalled tracks through some of the most wonderful country in the world. I adored the bush, and revelled in the opportunity to walk for hours among the rocky kopjes in pursuit of francolin partridges or guinea fowl, to shoot spring hares from the back of a speeding truck in the cool of darkness. And between these forays, by their flickering firesides in sitting rooms so little different from any rural firesides in England, I listened to farmers talking about their war. At that period, the Pretoria government maintained South African police units in Rhodesia to assist Smith's security forces. I stayed at one farm near a South African base, and learned how little the Rhodesians respected their allies. 'They're just a lot of overweight city boys who like their beer too much. They haven't a clue how to fight a bush war.' There was no shortage of loose talk about the ruthlessness of the struggle, the accidental death of terrorist suspects under interrogation. 'Don't people in England realize that the Chinese want to colonize Africa?' demanded one farmer, to whom I gave the pseudonym Peter Holmes. 'Every terrorist who's been captured here is Chinese trained . . . All we've ever asked of the world is to be left in peace to get on with making a living. Have you read Desmond Morris's *The Naked Ape*? I wish more people in England would. They might talk less rubbish about the rights of the African.'

Sally Holmes, his wife, a formidably tough proposition, said, 'I think we're more British than the English nowadays. Are you really all so frightened of what a bunch of independent African states say that you jump whenever they want? General Gowon of Nigeria going to lunch at Buckingham Palace, indeed!' Even almost thirty years ago, the conversation seemed grotesque. Yet the courage of those families lent an edge of pathos to their predicament. The Holmes's had come to their farm a decade before, in their mid-twenties, carved their tillage and pasturage out of raw bush when UDI was not even thought of. If they abandoned it now, they would lose everything. They worked very hard. Peter Holmes rose at five thirty every morning, changed the cylinder head on the tractor because there was no one else to do it, supervised the loading of the supply truck, checked the cotton baling, and drove endlessly round the farm like every Rhodesian farmer, because only by relentless supervision did his African workers do the business. 'Have you read Robert Ardrey's *Territorial Imperative?*' Sally demanded. 'That's how we feel about our land. We made all this, in spite of the Africans rather than because of them. They're great fun, but they are children. We'll stay here because there is nowhere else for us to go. That's how everyone feels. We don't want to go to South Africa. And what is there for us in England?'

At that time, only some four hundred guerrillas were operating into Rhodesia, behaving as savagely as the government towards the local population – as is usually the case in a guerrilla war. The Holmes's told me about the cache of terrorist mines they had found on their farm a few weeks earlier, which they left booby-trapped, and about the rising unease among their workers, being aggressively interrogated by army patrols. They lived behind a ten-foot security fence, the windows of the house covered with anti-grenade mesh, Alsatians patrolling inside the perimeter after dark. Once a week, Sally Holmes took her turn manning the local police radio. Her husband was required to spend an ever-growing quota of days on police reserve patrols. Manpower, always the shortage of manpower, was white Rhodesia's crippling problem, in a country where Smith's people were outnumbered by blacks twenty to one. In the school holidays, almost all the farming local families left the high-risk rural areas such as Mount Darwin and Centenary, because mothers were reluctant to have their children at home. My hosts described recent army and police operations against local terrorists. They talked with such contempt for their own blacks that I asked why they did not invest more effort in winning local 'hearts and minds'. Peter Holmes shrugged. 'What can we offer them? Our only hold is that they look to us, as their bosses, to pay and feed them. But once you start talking about equality – well, what would they need us for?'

I felt pity for both Rhodesian races, as I journeyed among the whites and their doomed society and glimpsed the circumstances in which the blacks strove to sustain an existence between the hammer of Smith's security forces and the anvil of the growing guerrilla movement. A century before, the white farmers' pioneer spirit would have made them role models, even heroes. Now, they were living on stolen time – Africa's time. My father and my great-uncle Lewis – who himself used to grow tobacco in Rhodesia between the wars – nodded sagely to each other in the early 1960s and asserted that Africa south of the Zambesi would remain white-dominated. A decade later, that notion seemed absurd. The only point at issue was how many people, black and white, must yet suffer and die before Smith's Rhodesia conceded defeat. Already the government had imposed draconian punishments on the black tribal populations, mass expulsions from their lands for villagers thought to be assisting the guerrillas. And already it was black civilians, not white farmers, who were bearing the brunt of the war's casualties. The Rhodesians treated the 'terrs' with open contempt – 'Half the time they even plant the bloody landmines upside down. They'll never make "the indigenous" any real threat to us.' They brushed aside my suggestions that the terrorists would learn, would get better and more dangerous. But this was partly at least because they lived themselves in such utter cultural isolation, oblivious of the context of the outside world and its overwhelming hostility to the white struggle.

As a journalist, my best break of that first trip in 1973 came one night during a long drive between farms in the north-east. I caught sight of a heavily laden white hitch-hiker in the headlights. I was alone. I stopped. My passenger was grateful, and chatty. He was a corporal in the Rhodesian Light Infantry, returning to duty in 'the Valley' after weekend leave. He talked for two hours, almost without interruption and with no need of encouragement, about the war and his part in it. I was a white. I was on his side. What need for holding back? He described clashes with 'terrs' who were showing signs of growing sophistication. Sure, some threw down their arms at the first sight of a helicopter. But there was a hard core willing and able to fight tenaciously. The most important revelation I gained that night was about the scale of the Rhodesians' military commitment across the border in Mozambique. There had been reports for months about Rhodesian patrols crossing into Portuguese territory in 'hot pursuit' to seek out terrorist bases, but little hard evidence of how far they were going.

Now, my passenger described how he spent most of his operational time on 'search and destroy' over the border, often following spearheads of their Special Air Service and Selous Scouts.

I knew I had my front-page splash – 'SMITH'S CROSS-BORDER WAR' – and a highly detailed picture of how the anti-terrorist campaign was being waged by the Rhodesians, what it was like for the whites 'at the sharp end'. I had not myself heard a shot fired, but on an assignment of this kind one could not expect to. Throughout the Rhodesian war, only a handful of journalists committed to the Smith government were allowed to report alongside military units in action. I harboured mixed feelings as I caught the plane from Salisbury for London. I loved Rhodesia as a country, yet loathed the bloody and futile battle that was being waged to preserve white rule. I enjoyed my days among those farmers, yet recoiled from their views about almost everything. I felt a distaste for my own role, exploring their secrets under false colours. I was glad I had paid my bills to stay in those peoples' homes, rather than rely upon their hospitality. Subterfuge had been the only way I could gain the information I sought about the war. Whatever consideration and sympathy my hosts deserved, the Smith regime was fighting a dirty and brutal war, to preserve a system that was morally indefensible as well as illegal. That was how I reassured my conscience, anyway.

I visited Rhodesia twice more during the guerrilla war. I flew next to Salisbury three years later in the summer of 1976, this time as an avowed journalist. The struggle, as many of us had anticipated, was turning decisively against the whites. The South Africans, with plenty of problems of their own, had withdrawn their police units as Pretoria's apartheid government strove for détente with black Africa. Petrol rationing had been introduced two years earlier. In 1976, 15,000 whites quit

Rhodesia, a net white population loss of 7,000. The Portuguese had abandoned Mozambique and Angola, whose new black governments were sympathetic to Rhodesia's guerrillas. Sanctions were squeezing Smith's government ever more tightly. In a moment of folly, Ian Smith had himself closed Rhodesia's border with Mozambique, cutting off her vital link to the eastern seaboard. Yet still, many of the whites whom I met retained hopes of salvation by Britain or the United States, because they themselves were denied access to free information about world opinion by the Smith-controlled Rhodesian media. It is so often this way. Censorship is introduced by a government, to prevent the enemy from gaining sensitive military information. This is not merely legitimate, but essential for any regime fighting a war. Then, as the struggle worsens, embattled ministers face a huge temptation: to abuse their powers of censorship to conceal from their own people just how badly matters are going. I once visited an Israeli military training school, where an instructor said to me, 'You know what we mark most highly for here? Telling the truth. We find that so many disasters happen in war because somebody meant to be at point A is really lost ten kilometres away, or someone who is supposed to have reached objective B has lost half his company because he mistook one escarpment for another. We tell our students: "We'll forgive you anything if when you report by radio on the battlefield, you tell us the exact facts about where you are and what you are doing."'

This is a fundamental lesson for any army, any government, in any war. Do not lie to yourselves. In the early phase of the illegal Rhodesian regime, it is possible to argue that Ian Smith and his colleagues were merely foolish. But in the later years, their hands became steeped in the blood of their own people, both black and white, because they could not bring themselves to admit the inevitability of defeat – nor to allow their own

people to perceive it. To the very end, the *Rhodesia Herald*
painted a grotesquely sunny picture of white Rhodesia and its
struggle. Among the most conspicuous victims of the Smith
government's lies and betrayals as the war situation worsened
inexorably were their own people. Ian Smith, P. K. van der
Byl and the other sorry creatures who made up the Salisbury
regime could have made a far better deal with Bishop Muzorewa and the black moderates years, and a great many corpses,
before the final capitulation came at Lancaster House at the
end of 1979, in the face of the whites' obvious military and
economic defeat. In June 1976, I wrote a piece in which I tried
to paint a word picture of the paradoxes of the country as I had
known it. With a full and heavy heart, I sought to explain the
mood and thought processes of white Rhodesia, as I contrasted
the experience of visiting black African states with that of
being in Rhodesia, even as it stood on the brink of collapse.

> It is when one is tired that one becomes a racist in Africa.
> Clean, rested and well fed, it is no hardship to be patient
> and tolerant through the usual daily procession of black
> airport incompetence, black hotel stupidity and black
> government corruption. But as the day wears on, after
> crossing three frontiers and changing aircraft in a couple of
> black states, so many baser thoughts crowd in upon each
> other: here is Africa, the most fabulous continent in the
> world, and what a perfectly bloody mess most of it seems to
> be, and what a terrible waste, and how much better *we* could
> run it. You see? That is how one begins to think like a
> white Rhodesian.
>
> Then, late at night at Johannesburg airport, one sinks
> into a seat on the Rhodesia Airways Boeing 727 to Salisbury.
> Most international flights are silent affairs, gatherings of
> bored strangers. But as this plane fills with people, it also

fills with chatter and laughter and hellos, because almost all these passengers are going home, back to a village of a quarter of a million like-minded souls who know all their neighbours and believe with happy, absolute, conviction that – in the words tattooed on the bags they sell in so many Salisbury shops nowadays – 'Rhodesia is SUPER'.

Salisbury airport is full of noisy reunions and men in shorts and long stockings. The housekeeper at Meikle's Hotel reminds me irresistibly of my old nanny, who after half a lifetime in Kenya used to declare that black boys are very useful for chasing zebras out of the garden. The streets are clean and fresh as ever, the shops still astonishingly well supplied. The wives bustle to and fro, hailing each other between purchases. At lunchtime the restaurants are crowded with Rhodesians stuffing themselves with the enormous quantities of English school food on which the white tribes of Africa have traditionally sustained themselves. There are quite a number of Africans in evidence, the sort who look as if they have done well out of the race war.

How rich everybody seems, even after twelve years of sanctions. Shall we tackle that enormous buffet, or nip downstairs for a steak? How was London? Oh, England is *ruined* nowadays. Rhodesians are the only Englishmen left. *South Pacific* is being performed every night at the theatre down the road:

> *I'm only a cock-eyed optimist,*
> *immature and incurably green,*

Rhodesians know a good tune when they hear one. At dinner, somebody is saying what a glorious day it was out at the racecourse last week, with the grass and the horses and the Turf Club and the crowd looking at their best. Ian Smith was there, and made the sort of remark that quickly goes the rounds: 'Isn't this a wonderful sight? Isn't this what we're all fighting for?'

There is a report in the paper that a local store which unearthed a huge supply of 1953 Coronation paper napkins put them on sale, and got rid of the lot in a week. Everybody looks so *clean* in white Africa. There are so many pairs of black hands to wash and iron. Everybody is so delightfully hospitable. There are so many pairs of black hands to cook and serve.

And now, at last, out on the empty road, eating up mile after mile of gold and green bush, there is that heavenly feeling of liberation, allied to the certainty that there will be soft beds and fat steaks at the end of the journey. Every few miles there are knots of Africans squatting or standing by the roadside, mysteriously waiting for heaven knows what. By a gate, a white farmer sits on his horse, beautifully dressed in jodhpurs and glittering riding boots. Listen to the music of the towns: Marandellas, Quolque, Gatooma, Inyanda, Macheke. To the east, there is the glorious deep blue of the hills in the distance. The great rock *kopjes* rear out of the grass beside the road. The vivid purples and reds of the shrubs and flowers light up the bush for miles around them.

Rhodesia *is* super. This is one of the most beautiful countries in the world, which still provides the sort of comfort and happiness the English middle classes dream of as they lie in their mortgaged beds at night. To understand what is happening here today, it is essential to feel this country's magic as white Rhodesians feel it, to grasp the beauty of the prize they are being asked to give up. Then it is possible to begin to despair that they will ever see the reason of history, or perceive the vast injustice upon which their own edifice is founded. 'But why don't you sympathize with us? Why do you hate us,' they ask, when they know that one is a journalist. 'Oh, you just don't understand.'

The garden party never ends. One is reminded irresistibly of a little boy, in tears, refusing to go home at the end of the outing, insisting that somehow the music plays on. Yes, dear, we all think that it has been marvellous, but it's finished now. You don't believe me? You won't come home? There is a curfew south of Umtali, and the railway to the border is under constant attack. Mr Charles Holloway and his wife are in their late sixties. They took an outing last Sunday afternoon. They went home with multiple gunshot wounds. 'Oh yes, my son was involved in a great rev-up with the "terrs" a few days ago,' said the farmer from Fort Victoria gaily, describing an action in which there had been a shoot-out with terrorists. 'Six-love to us,' he said.

Ha, ha. We can take it. But Rifleman Niall Campbell, aged 33, died from his wounds in the Andrew Fleming Hospital on Sunday night, and he was the 23rd member of the Rhodesian security forces killed this month. Was it one of Conan Doyle's medieval heroes who said that 'no man save a blockhead ever fought odds of twenty to one'? I came down in a Salisbury lift with two Africans, one a local journalist. 'What's the news today?' the other asked him. 'Is Smith still saying he's got the support of every black in Africa?' The lift dissolved in laughter.

'Life was going on as normal yesterday in the Kezi area, where Mr Johannes van Vuuren (45) and his 14-year-old son Mark were killed by terrorists on Saturday,' reported the *Rhodesia Herald* on Tuesday. 'Mrs Kay van Vuuren, a sister of the dead man, said: "All is quiet here, and there has never been any panic."'

It is necessary to be very insensitive or very left-wing not to feel deeply moved by the tragedy of white Rhodesia, by its mad, grim battle to move back the time machine half a century. Who's for polo? They are still pretending marvellously. But, like the Spartan boy, they know the fox is gnawing deep into their vitals.

A dispatch of this kind represents a strange kind of war reporting. It was a strange kind of war, the last stand of English suburban values in the midst of the African continent. The following year, 1977, when I returned to Rhodesia to write another series of reports, the cracks were showing much more visibly in the defiant façade. More and more Rhodesians were slipping away out of the country, never to return, often leaving all their possessions behind them. In Rhodesia, former Kenyan settlers had been wearily categorized as the 'when we's', because they were forever beginning their sentences with the wistful words, 'When we were in Kenya . . .' Now, a growing stream of Rhodesians were becoming 'when we's' in South Africa. The bleak terraces of Cheltenham or Leamington loomed beyond, as the last white enclaves in Africa receded into history. The souvenir shops were selling biros 'made from cartridge cases used in the actual operational area'. More than 5,000 blacks and 448 members of the white security forces were dead. Rhodesian intelligence estimated that around 3,600 guerrillas were operating in the country, with a further 18,000 training over the borders.

Within hours of my arrival I was summoned by the seedy little Greek who ran Ian Smith's Information Department. He showed me a deportation order with my name on it signed by the Defence Minister, that grotesque parody of a Dornford Yates English gentleman, P. K. van der Byl. It was van der Byl, a right-wing fanatic with huge estates in South Africa, who responded wittily to a journalist who asked why the

Salisbury government had ceased to disclose the names of people hanged for terrorist or criminal offences: 'Why should we? Anyway it's academic, because they are normally dead after it.' His flippancy and open contempt for Africans – all Africans – embarrassed even some of his own people. The Rhodesian government still professed to allow free access for journalists to their country, but they had had enough of me. The *Standard*'s editor, Simon Jenkins, who had succeeded Charles Wintour a few months earlier, remonstrated by telex with the government, to no avail. 'REGRET UNABLE TO ASSIST YOU REGARDING HASTINGS STOP' telexed back the Defence Minister. I suppose I should have been flattered.

As I came out of the lift on the way to Salisbury airport to meet my deportation deadline, striding into the hotel lobby came the living embodiment of Smith's Rhodesia: a short, squat white man half-buried in his moustache, a great beer gut sagging from his shorts, his voice booming to a porter, one of the last group of blacks in Africa who still answered the likes of us with those musically docile words 'Yes, boss.' Across the chest of the T-shirt of this implausible representative of the master race were emblazoned the words: 'We made Rhodesia great.'

By a pleasant irony, on the aircraft to Johannesburg, I found myself sitting opposite the appalling van der Byl, presumably on his way to visit his South African counterpart in Pretoria. I hummed the fantastic government propaganda jingle which was assaulting Rhodesian radio listeners that year, designed to deter the growing number of white 'road runners':

> *Just think for a moment of all you gave up,*
> *When you made up your mind to leave:*
> *The sunshine, the women, the songs round the camp fire,*
> *The fishing, the life and the beer . . .*

Peering in undisguised horror at me across the aisle, van der Byl fled to the cockpit for the duration of the flight, returning only momentarily to seize his briefcase before I attempted to rifle it. The South Africans also deported me later that week, on van der Byl's advice, I have always suspected. It galls me today that until his death in 1999 this dreadful man, who as defence minister occasionally amused himself by potting at blacks from his helicopter with a hunting rifle, travelled freely in and out of Blair's Britain, to hobnob with his cronies at – appropriately enough – White's.

I returned to Rhodesia only in January 1980, when the Lancaster House settlement brought down the curtain on the Smith regime. Lord Soames flew to Salisbury, to act as interim Governor for the extraordinarily melodramatic transition to black majority rule. Once more, like other correspondents, I found myself renting a car to drive far out into the bush to witness the last act of the guerrilla war. Once more, I set off through the endless red dust of some of the most beautiful country in the continent. I drove with Simon Hoggart of the *Guardian* and another correspondent, a trifle nervous because a car full of journalists had been somewhat shot up in the same area a day or two before, by guerrillas unaware that a close season had been declared on white men. In the middle of the bush, we were less than amused to find ourselves punctured, even less so to discover that while we had a spare wheel, there was no jack. Fortunately, however, there was a police station not far distant. We walked in, to be greeted by a large white Rhodesian officer who listened to our tale of distress. It was not difficult to follow his thought process. If one event would have made that man's day, it would have been to find three English reporters riddled with holes in the middle of the bush by a gang of 'terrs'. What an opportunity. What a perfectly appropriate end for three of the reptiles who had helped bring

Rhodesia to this miserable pass. We thought we were pretty lucky to get our jack.

Remember, scarcely a reporter in Rhodesia had even glimpsed the 'enemy' through all those years of bloody conflict. Now, suddenly, there they were – a dozen of them – marching ragtag along the road carrying their motley assembly of weapons, AK47s, RPGs, even a rucksack of mines. They were headed, as we were, for one of the assembly points established all over Rhodesia, where Robert Mugabe and Joshua Nkomo's armies were to marshal under the supervision of British army ceasefire supervision teams. All those years, we had wondered about them: what they looked like, how many there were. We had glimpsed only the deadly fruits of their endeavours. Three years earlier, I sat in Salisbury speculating in print how it would be 'when those men at last come in from the bush, clutching their Kalashnikovs and memories of so much death, when they reach the white man's paradise of Salisbury with its loaded shops and gaily-umbrellaed patios and garden gnomes'. Now, at last, this was reality, and we saw them before us in hundreds, in their camouflage fatigues and wary looks. They were still deeply suspicious of the ceasefire – scarcely daring to believe in their own triumph. They had suffered so much. Many can have understood little of the struggle in which they were engaged. For years, they had seen white men only at the point of a gun. The resident SIS man with Mugabe's people in Mozambique had worked undercover as a cultural attaché. He told me, 'I began to think there might be a glimmer of hope for the future when Mugabe's staff ordered twenty copies of George Orwell's *Animal Farm.*' The Royal Air Force was parachuting Tampax and boot polish to the assembly points, to help convince the guerrillas of the whites' benign intentions. An Irish Guards officer told us that the guerrilla commanders were morbidly suspicious of proposals to hold film shows to prevent them from becoming bored. They said, 'No Muzorewa films here!' The doughty major explained, 'No, no – not political films – you can have James Bond.' As ever, tragedy and high drama merged into farce.

Over 16,000 people had died for this moment – more than 8,000 guerrillas, almost a thousand members of Smith's security forces, 6,000 black civilians, some 400 white civilians. White Rhodesia had purchased with these lives an extension of its own suzerainty for just fifteen years. Whatever tribulations have since befallen black Zimbabwe, its transition to majority rule in 1980 was a notable achievement for British diplomacy, albeit belated. It was the modest consolation for a tragedy whose white promoters, such as Smith and van der Byl, would have seemed ludicrous figures, had they not possessed the power of life and death over millions of people for so long after their lease from history had rightfully expired. Africa granted them comfortable, even pampered retirements. They deserved much less.

CHAPTER NINE

Goodbye to Da Nang

HEADING TOWARDS THE ripe age of thirty, I found familiar self-doubts reasserting themselves about my nerve, bottle, courage. Unlike some of the freelance photographers in Vietnam, I was not in love with death. I adored journalism and the company of soldiers, but now I had a son whom I wanted to see grow up, a home life and all sorts of humdrum domestic enthusiasms – digging the garden, building cupboards in the kitchen, fishing a dry fly. The ambition was still there, and the love for the big story. But the memory of Nick Tomalin's death persisted. Whatever I was doing by the time I was his age, forty-two, I was determined no longer to be going to the wars. My feelings were reinforced by an experience which befell me in the summer of 1974. At the end of July, I went to Greece for the *Evening Standard*, to report the fall of the colonels' dictatorship. Then I flew on to Cyprus, where Greek Cypriots committed to union with Greece had attempted a coup, which plainly threatened to provoke intervention from the Turkish mainland. I reached Nicosia just in time to cover the Turkish invasion, though I had no luck as spectacular as Mike Nicholson, who found himself interviewing Turkish paratroopers for ITN as they dropped out of the sky around him. I drove east, to report the invaders' armoured ground push across the island towards the large modern coastal town of Famagusta. It was a nerve-racking business, because once again I was driving alone, looking for the front in the midst of sporadic fighting, though the Greeks were incapable of mounting serious resistance. As an *Evening Standard* reporter, it was seldom possible for me to share a car with morning paper journalists with drastically different deadlines.

The entire Greek population fled Famagusta as the Turks approached. It was an eerie experience to drive through empty streets littered with personal possessions of all kinds, furniture, children's bicycles, toys. The traffic lights were dead. Twelve thousand refugees crowded the nearby British Sovereign Base at Dhekélia, which I knew well after making a series of films for the BBC about the island a couple of years earlier. I drove to the lovely port of Kyrenia on the north coast, former home to so many British expats and now evacuated. Here, too, was a ghost town. God, what an opportunity for a looter: the entire harbour was packed wall to wall with glittering yachts, and not a human figure remained for miles! What a chance to get into the sailing business!

I turned back, and headed once again towards Famagusta. Early on the morning of 15 August, I joined a handful of other Western reporters and cameramen, watching the Turkish crowd cheer their hearts out as the first armoured vehicles clattered into the old Venetian citadel. Twelve thousand Turkish Cypriots had been besieged there since 20 July without supplies, and towards the end without mains water. Greek artillery and mortar fire had killed twenty-nine people. There was no pity to spare for Greeks that day among the Turks of Famagusta, nor doubts about Turkey's commitment to a ruthless partition of the island; only joy in relief from mortal peril and persecution. I climbed back into my rented Escort for the easy half-hour drive to Dhekélia, to telephone my story to the paper. I saw not another vehicle or human traveller on the road, until I was two miles outside Fama-G, as the British army always knew the place. I halted abruptly. Two hundred yards ahead, a column of Turkish tanks was engaging an unseen enemy with cannon and machine-gun fire. Shots from the other side were zipping overhead. I did one of my hastiest U-turns, and began to weave through the side streets of Famagusta's suburbs, searching for another path to Dhekélia. Suddenly I saw three Turkish soldiers standing by the roadside among the little villas. They unslung their rifles and waved me down. I stopped and casually passed my Turkish papers through the window to one of the soldiers. I saw an unshaven, empty-eyed, brutally hostile face. The man tossed the documents contemptuously aside, yanked open the door of the car and dragged me out. I was searched, stripped of money, passport and watch, rammed against the nearest house, to stand feet straddled, hands on the wall, a rifle in my ear. The three began to argue fiercely. They spoke no English, but plainly they were debating what to do with me. I began to understand that they were not acting on the orders of the Turkish army. They were merely Anatolian peasants, pursuing their traditional view of warfare as a matter of rape, pillage and destruction. There was a sudden noise from a nearby house. One soldier doubled across and burst inside. We heard an uproar. He emerged dragging a small, moustached Greek Cypriot civilian in his forties, somewhat battered. His captor lunged casually at his head with a rifle butt, before pushing him against the wall beside me.

'Tell them I am British! Tell them I am British!' the Cypriot cried desperately, blood pouring down his face.

'So am I, but it's not doing me a lot of good,' I muttered.

The soldiers continued to dispute angrily. I was more frightened than I have ever been, before or since. I sincerely believed these men would shoot us. Logic demanded it. Kill us now, and they could keep a couple of hundred pounds from my wallet, throw our bodies in the rubble with no chance they would be discovered for months, if ever. But if these men let us live, they would be in bad trouble when I reached the Turkish Command. The deepest instincts of the English middle class kept saying that they could not shoot *me* – Charterhouse and Oxford, youngest member of the Beefsteak, only two convictions for speeding, standing just five miles from that bastion of residual British power, the Sovereign Base bristling with Royal Scots, armoured cars and mortars. But this nonsense was overridden by my experience of wars. I knew that these Turks, drawn from one of the cruellest societies on earth, now reduced by opportunity to brutes, could press the trigger at the slightest provocation. Like most foreign correspondents, I have often known the same sensation, the same acute awareness of life hanging by a thread, looking down the barrels of guns held by teenage Africans or Arabs. Absolute passivity is the only possible response. The power of the gun is absolute, against a man without one. In the Third World, or even the First one, this knowledge can make a soldier with no control or rights over anything else drunk with his own ability to destroy life. In these places, I have often thought of Kipling's wry lines, a century before:

> *A scrimmage in a Border Station, a canter down some dark defile–*
> *Two thousand pounds of education drops to a ten-rupee jezail–*
> *the crammer's boast, the squadron's pride, shot like a rabbit in a ride!*

I have always respected soldiering as an honourable profession. This was the reverse of the medal. For half an hour the Greek and I stood side by side with our faces against that wall, sweating even in the early morning chill, striving to comprehend every nuance of the spasms of dialogue between the Turks behind us, which seldom fell below shouting pitch. Then, glancing under my left arm, I glimpsed a wonderful sight. A car was coming. As it approached, I recognized the Volvo of ITN. One of the soldiers waved it down, presenting his rifle. Ignoring the Turks, whose attention it had diverted, I dashed into the road and threw myself down at the open window, before the astonished face of reporter Keith Hatfield.

'Keith! For Christ's sake don't leave me! These bastards are going to shoot us!'

Hatfield looked down in bewilderment at my grovelling, panic-stricken figure.

'Max, we've got Turkish papers. If you've got a problem and want a ride, you can come with us.'

'You don't understand. They don't give a damn about Turkish papers – they're on the rampage.'

Keith spoke to me again, with the studied patience of one hoping that repetition will get the obvious message across.

'Max, they can't do anything to *us*.'

Events cut short this manic conversation. The cameraman at the wheel casually put the car back into gear. A rifle slammed into his ear. The crew were yanked out. We were all led into an empty villa, gestured on to the floor, and sat down, still at gunpoint. The Turks began shouting at each other with renewed energy, gesturing with hands and rifles at us and each other. Attitudes among the British delegation were now reversed. The ITN crew was ashen, as terrified as I had been thirty minutes earlier. By contrast, I felt a rising glow of hope. It was much harder even for these three barbarians to swallow the notion of shooting four Englishmen and a Greek, than to dispose of just one of us. The odds were growing in our favour with every minute the Turks dallied and hesitated. That morning in Famagusta remains, however, one of the grimmest ordeals of my life. At last, at very long last, the Turks reached a decision. They gestured us to our feet, pushed and prodded us back out to the cars. I took the wheel of one, the ITN cameraman the other, each with a soldier beside us. Everybody else crammed in the back. Then we drove down to the Turkish citadel. Keith and I sprang out the moment we saw an officer, a major I think, and unleashed a torrent of denunciations. Our captors adopted the sullen air of whipped beasts. 'They will be court martialled!' the major thundered, unleashing a fine, theatrical flood of Turkish abuse at them. They disappeared under escort. I got back my watch and papers, but somehow my cash could not be found. Still shocked, we drove in slow convoy back to Dhekélia, to file and start looking for the next story. Our Greek companion in terror became yet another refugee.

That episode had a lasting effect on me. Reading back what I have written a quarter of a century later, I find myself wondering: did those Turks ever really think of shooting us? If their intentions were malign, why did they eventually commit such a fantastic act of folly, from their own point of view, as to take us to their headquarters? Yet it is sufficient to say that on that Cyprus morning, in the ghost town of Famagusta, I believed I was going to be shot, and so did Keith Hatfield. I realized how much I wanted to survive, how little I wanted the sort of Fleet Street martyrdom Nick Tomalin had achieved. One of the least attractive aspects of our trade is that journalists wallow in the death of a colleague on the job, not because they do not regret him, but because his killing makes the business of us all seem more dangerous, more glamorous, more honourable. I wanted to continue to roam the world, to tell the big stories. After Cyprus, however, I was more sure than ever that I was no candidate for a last man, last round defence. Unease about my dwindling nerve was soon put to the test, when I returned to Vietnam for what proved to be the last campaign of the war.

I made several trips to Saigon in the years between 1971 and the last, climactic phase four years later. For the *Standard*, always short of cash, the cost of air tickets was a serious matter. These days, when travel is very cheap, everybody has forgotten that thirty years ago flight costs represented a big drain on media budgets. But Charles Wintour knew how much I valued the opportunity to keep in touch with events in Indochina, and he felt that I had done some useful work there. Somehow, he found the money when it seemed important.

In February 1973, Dr Henry Kissinger as American Secretary of State signed the Paris Peace Accord with North Vietnam, that shameful document which allowed the United States to pull its troops out of South Vietnam, leaving its rickety government, demoralized army and people, to fend for themselves as best they could. The last American aircraft went home in February 1973, leaving only a few advisers and contract personnel. On paper, South Vietnam was still a formidable military power, with a million men under arms, 11 infantry divisions, 385 tanks, 370 jet aircraft, 560 helicopters to deal with 200,000 North Vietnamese troops ensconced in the South, and now with the sanction of the Paris Accords for their presence. Yet corruption and sloth had eaten deeply into every institution in the country. There was a chronic and worsening shortage of fuel and spare parts for all Saigon's expensive American equipment. If the US military withdrawal from Vietnam was understandable, it seemed incorrigibly cynical for Congress also to squeeze financial aid, so that the South Vietnamese found themselves facing a rapidly worsening ammunition situation. For years, only weight of firepower had held back the North Vietnamese. The ARVN infantry never possessed much stomach for the fight, among an army in which a private was paid £10 a month, a general a notional £40, and every able-bodied man who could not buy his way out was expected to serve until death or wounds released him. The cynics said that it was kinder to the people of Vietnam to release them from their long agony, to allow the triumph of Hanoi as swiftly as possible, since one day this must come anyway. I had no good answer, because it was indeed plain Saigon was losing, and that its government was incapable of motivating its own people anything like as effectively as Hanoi. Like many others, however, I found it unbearably painful to witness the descent of the South Vietnamese people into communist bondage.

They were in little doubt about the fate that awaited them. In the spring of 1974, I wrote a series of articles for the *Standard* from Indochina. The once vast American press corps in Saigon had shrunk dramatically, now that America's soldiers had gone home. 'What are you doing here, now *the story* is over?' a Vietnamese major asked bitterly, soon after I landed in Saigon. 'Where are all the other journalists now? They say that in America people do not want to hear about us any more. Yesterday, we had fifty-six killed. Last week, it was almost four hundred. Next week, it will be the same. Now everybody has gone home – except the Vietnamese. They will only take notice of us on the day the communists march into Saigon.' He was prescient. It was evident that unless the US Congress relented in its determination to cut off military aid to Saigon – and probably even if it did so – the war was lost. Month by month, the communists gained ground, steadily expanding the ugly pockets and bulges of South Vietnamese territory within their control in the north, west and centre of the country under the Paris Accords. Saigon's counter-offensives won breathing spaces. But the strategic dominance of Hanoi was indisputable.

Most military transport facilities for correspondents had vanished with the American evacuation. To visit a South Vietnamese Ranger unit in the Central Highlands, I had to catch a civilian flight to Pleiku, then take a taxi to the local ARVN headquarters, then plead for a place on a Huey riding into one of the firebases in the Central Highlands. The experience was worth it. The unit I joined was being harassed by a North Vietnamese regiment, which had been closing its grip upon the Ranger positions week by week. Rockets were coming in, mortar rounds going out, almost every day. I found myself captivated by the beauty of the setting for this small piece of Indochina's tragedy, among rolling green hills shrouded in delicate wisps of mist at dawn. Colonel Nhu, the impressively professional commanding officer of the 23rd Ranger Group, spent hours talking to me about Vietnam, and about his own part of the struggle. I declined a kind invitation to take a trip as his guest to shoot a tiger, and instead got him to send me out for a couple of nights to one of his companies in the deep jungle, to gossip with gentle, pleasantly pudgy Major Xuan and his fifty men in their hilltop post. I found them delightful. We talked endlessly about the war, and about their country which – like most Europeans – I had learned to love. His second-in-command, a young lieutenant who spoke good English, said, 'I used to think a lot about the end of the war. But now I find it is better just to live one day at a time, not think about next week or the one after.' I watched the ARVN soldiers labouring for hours, not on digging deeper foxholes, but on creating a perfectly crafted timber and straw-thatched mess hut in the midst of their positions. Yes, they were lobbing intermittent mortar rounds over our heads at the communists during tea, the men manning the tube grinning and bending aside to stick fingers in their ears at every concussion; but their hearts were in making a work of art of that mess hut. The Rangers were among the best units in Saigon's army, yet one perceived here the familiar picture of an army which, however desperate its strategic predicament, could not inject purpose or aggression into its units. The ARVN had learned to regard the war as a way of life which they somehow endured, but hated and resented. They were willing to wear the uniform, but they had no desire to fight. This attitude allowed for a little light patrolling, the regular discharge of artillery, but no head-to-head confrontation with the enemy's infantry if such a misfortune could possibly be avoided.

Colonel Nhu drove me one day to a certain place on Route 19 from which we looked down into a deep valley, where the vivid greenery was littered with stripped and rusted carcasses of tanks and vehicles on the track along which the old, pre-American road used to run. We were gazing upon the ruins of *Groupe Mobile Cent*. This was the place where, in June 1954, the communist Viet Minh's 803rd Regiment had destroyed a French column withdrawing from the Central Highlands piece by bloody piece. 'I was here,' said the colonel. As a young conscript, he fought in those battles, and was one of the few to survive them. *Groupe Mobile Cent* never reached the safety of the coast. In a superb, characteristic national gesture, the French buried their dead standing upright, facing France. I thought: not again. Let it not happen again. I wrote for the *Standard*:

Perhaps it sounds paradoxical to condemn what the Americans did here, while believing that it is vital to continue to support the regime that they created. But I think that in the past I was one of many Western correspondents who, in our dismay at American military incompetence and disregard for Vietnamese life, lost sight of the fundamental issue of South Vietnam's right to exist as a non-communist state. Now that the lumbering leviathan has departed, one sees here a society corrupted by American extravagance, yet still full of attractive, industrious, fatalistic people. The Thieu regime is a dictatorship under which many of its opponents languish in jail . . . yet there is no evidence of any act by the South Vietnamese government to compare with, say, the massacre of thousands of anti-communists by the Viet Cong when they took Hue in 1968. It has somehow become part of liberal mythology to equate the countless maimed and orphaned and dead solely with the doings of Saigon. Yet now, one feels, when this has become a Vietnamese war, the South deserves the chance to survive if it can take it.

I drove up to watch the battle for Ben Cat, one of the usual destructive, bloody, apparently inconclusive actions that went on for weeks. Ben Cat, at one corner of the old communist sanctuary known as the Iron Triangle, was just twenty-three miles from Saigon. My experience of Vietnam was far less risky than that of many resident correspondents, who attended the great set piece battles of the war. I saw the communist enemy only a handful of times during all my trips to Indochina, tiny figures glimpsed through binoculars. I never saw North Vietnamese soldiers close enough to read their faces. I interviewed some Chieu Hois, former Viet Cong prisoners who claimed to have 'rallied' – defected to Saigon. And once, driving out of Saigon, I stopped my jeep while some ARVN soldiers dragged a group of dead black-pyjamaed Viet Cong out of a paddy field beside the road, in which they had fallen during a night of skirmishing. I gazed in curiosity and revulsion at the dusty, half-naked corpses. The entrails of one man hung out of his body. Like a million men before me on battlefields throughout history, I thought: this could be my body. My entrails would look just like that, if a string of bullets struck me where they struck this man. And I put the jeep into gear with a shudder. If one is to be any use to anybody as a war correspondent, never mind as a soldier, one must learn to view corpses as butchers' sacks, which have nothing to do with one's own body, one's own reality. For a moment, I had been rash enough to let my imagination work.

One of the familiar sights of those days, almost every morning when we drove to the battlefield, was that of an Austin Maxi parked by the roadside, with a Union Jack on its numberplate. An impeccably attired British officer, adorned with red tabs and stable belt, leaned across the roof, map spread before him, binoculars in hand. This was Colonel Geoffrey Strong, the defence attaché from the Embassy, having the time of his life. His appreciation of the military situation was shrewd, penetrating and pessimistic. Until the last days of Saigon, the colonel's private briefings for British correspondents were of immense value to us all – far better than any of the US Embassy assessments. He was convinced the game was almost up for South Vietnam. He told us how and why, with a wealth of detail.

Yet even as logic told us that the country must fall to the forces of Hanoi, we found our imaginations faltered in grasping this reality. The pendulum had swung so often to and fro, while the scene amidst which we lived in Vietnam, the lizards on the wall of the bar at the Continental Palace, the dreadful 'buggery statue' war memorial in front of the National Assembly, the bar girls and the long lunches and circling gunships, had remained unchanged for decades. When the North Vietnamese launched their spring offensive of 1975 this seemed, at first, no more and no less significant than all the others which had preceded it in previous years. On 13 March, Hanoi's army struck at Ban Me Thuot, a town of 150,000 people in the Central Highlands, which promptly fell. South Vietnamese senior officers fled by helicopter, leaving their men to their fate. The communists pushed on. Within days Pleiku and Kontum had also gone. 250,000 refugees began fleeing eastwards towards the coast, amid a rabble of wrecked ARVN units. President Thieu made the decision to abandon the entire Central Highlands of his country to the enemy. The ARVN 2nd Armoured Brigade met exactly the same fate on its terrible retreat towards the coast as the French *Groupe Mobile Cent* twenty years earlier. How often I wondered what happened to my friends of the 23rd Ranger Group. The unit was never heard of again, after that first catastrophe. On 20 March, the North Vietnamese struck Quang Tri in the north, which Saigon's army had defended fiercely under assault back in 1972. This time, the city fell immediately. Hanoi, which began its offensive tentatively, exploiting opportunities as they developed, began to perceive the glimmer of an extraordinary breakthrough. Led by T-54 tanks, the communist divisions advanced upon Vietnam's old capital, Hue. Surely, surely, Thieu's divisions would fight for Hue.

I landed back in Saigon on Sunday 23 March. The north was obviously the place to be. I walked to the Air Vietnam office, where the usual stunningly beautiful girl made my booking. As she spelt my name down the telephone, she did not say in our harsh Western manner, '. . . India, Nuts, Golf, Sugar'. She said, 'Irene, Nicole, Georgette, Simone,' which in her lovely voice would have melted a stonier heart than mine. She reminded me of all the reasons why I did not want those cold, grey, ruthless men from Hanoi to win this war. I boarded an almost empty flight to Da Nang, the great port city, second largest in the country, once among the greatest American bases, which I remembered so well from 1971. There were no more officers' clubs or American compounds to feed and house us. I checked into a dusty hotel in the midst of the city, and found a dozen or so American and British correspondents already ensconced, searching for news of the battle further north. It was being suggested that communist forces had already cut the road between Hue and Da Nang, as they had earlier enveloped Quang Tri. Rumour was everywhere, but this one sounded extravagant, unreal, although spasmodic communist rockets were already landing in the city. I sat down for lunch with a cluster of correspondents at the harbourside, in one of the string of pleasant little seafood restaurants. Under the awning of matting, looking out at the sea and sipping white wine, we gossiped through some delicious shellfish.

Then, out on the water, we saw approaching the harbour a big, grey naval landing ship. Routine. As it closed in, however, we perceived that the ship's upperworks, as well as the decks, were crammed, bulging, spilling over with soldiers. When it came alongside, and the bow doors clanked open, a great throng of visibly uncontrolled, leaderless men poured ashore. They scuttled away empty-eyed into the city, losing themselves among the civilian crowds. I saw an elderly soldier coming ashore with his wife behind him, bent under the weight of his kitbag. A little girl, presumably his daughter, who looked no more than ten, carried his rifle. We briefly halted one of the fugitives.

'Where have you come from?'

'Hue'

'What goes on?'

'All finish. All finish. VC come.'

He scurried on, lost among so many other men with only helmets, sometimes webbing, very occasionally a weapon. Their coming could have only one significance. Disaster. Some, at least, of the Vietnamese units had broken. Yet there were 17,000 men in Hue. How could a force of that magnitude simply have dissolved within days? As the afternoon went on, more and yet more ships and small craft appeared. Some were naval, some civilian. All were crammed with men, most without weapons or equipment. We sought to talk to them, often in vain, for they wished only to slip away in anonymity and silence. This was obviously not a retreat, it was a collapse involving many thousands of troops. We scoured the city in pursuit of reliable information from the US Consulate, CIA and Air America contacts, South Vietnamese headquarters. All we could learn was what we could see for ourselves: the situation further north was terrible. Rumour, then at last reliable first-hand report, told us that Hue had fallen. The legion of beaten men pouring into Da Nang had straggled the five miles between the city and the sea, and the boats. What began as an organized evacuation by the government army, with tanks, guns and equipment being taken off, degenerated within hours into a rout. Men abandoned everything – packs, weapons, families, hope. Saigon seemed incapable even of providing effective air support, with much of its air force grounded by shortage of fuel and spares and maintenance, under the pressure of Congress's squeeze on South Vietnam. If this was the way it was, the North Vietnamese could be heading for Da Nang pretty soon. We were fascinated and excited by the story – and increasingly uneasy about our own necks. Here were these great teeming crowds in the street, civilians and soldiers infecting each other with a rising tide of fear. No reporter, just then, wanted to be on hand to write the eyewitness story of North Vietnamese tanks rolling down the harbour road. None of us had ever shared the experience of a great military defeat. This was the beginning of the collapse of all that had been familiar about Vietnam for so many years.

My file to London that Tuesday began, 'A turning point of the Vietnam War was reached today, with the South Vietnamese abandonment of the ancient capital of Hue ... It is now impossible to see how a retreat and collapse of this magnitude without any serious resistance can be easily arrested, and new lines drawn for defence.'

I experienced one moment of farce worthy of Waugh. Approaching down the teeming street, I saw a burly red-faced civilian in a bush hat and shorts, grenades in his belt and an M16 over his shoulder. He looked neither Vietnamese nor American. What the hell was he doing here?

'Are you CIA?'

'No – I'm from the Save the Children Fund.'

I laughed my first real, honest, funny laugh since reaching Da Nang. I have been hoping ever since that he was really CIA.

That night, we had been asleep in the hotel for a couple of hours when we were abruptly awakened by a couple of armed civilians from the US Consulate. 'The Consul wants to see all of you – now,' said one. Blearily, we pulled on clothes, climbed into vehicles, and drove the few hundred yards to the consulate building through the steamy darkness. We were perhaps twenty strong, almost all American and British. In the court-yard, US Marines were burning documents on a huge bonfire. We filed into the office of the consul, a tall, grave figure in his forties, wearing a safari suit. Do I remember that he was bearded? 'Right,' he said. 'I got you here because I want to tell you what we know about the situation. Our understanding is that the North Vietnamese are advancing rapidly. The South Vietnamese are not holding them. We believe the communists could be here within a matter of hours. Our advice to you is that all foreigners should leave this city as fast as you can get out – and I mean fast.'

We were stunned. This was Da Nang, one of the biggest cities in South Vietnam. It had often been harassed or rocketed by the communists, but it was a vast place, with a powerful garrison. Never in the course of the entire war had Saigon's hold been seriously threatened. If Da Nang was crumbling, anything was possible. Yet it is remarkable how far exhaustion – the exhaustion of tension and fear – can overcome even the astonishment of tidings on this scale. I failed to hear the last part of the consul's briefing. To my eternal embarrassment, I lapsed into unconsciousness in my chair in his office. I was nudged awake again by one of my colleagues, as everybody got up to leave. The consul was peering down at me. 'I have sometimes been accused of holding boring briefings,' he said crossly, 'but I scarcely expected to lose any of my audience tonight.' We drove back to the hotel, thinking and talking fast. Mike Nicholson of ITN said, 'The Saigon plane's not due till eleven, even if we can get on it. I'm going to take a jeep out first thing, and have a look round outside town.' I fixed to take a ride with him. Soon after first light, we set off with his camera crew, cruising through streets in which activity still seemed very normal, save for the great throngs of milling soldiers. We could hear artillery fire, but we had little notion of the targets. In Vietnam, neither a target nor a direct threat had ever been necessary to provoke a barrage. Outside the city, Mike filmed a piece to camera behind a South Vietnamese gun line, where the howitzers were firing desultorily towards heaven knows what. Mile after mile as we drove, bizarrely even within earshot of distant small arms fire, there were farmers bent over their paddy fields, winnowing their harvest by the roadside, beating their buffalo onwards, winding the handles of their pumps. Vietnamese soldiers often seemed to lack fortitude in battle, but how I admired the fortitude of these people, struggling to preserve their livelihoods and families while the world dissolved around them.

Mike and I could find out very little. But we did not doubt the US consul's warning. We were acutely nervous, wary of driving too far, of being cut off. We turned back to the airfield. We had to get that Saigon plane. While Mike hammered out a script on a portable typewriter in the terminal's café, I fought my way through a great heaving, panic-stricken mob of Vietnamese to get all of us boarding cards for the flight. It was one of those rare occasions when my huge size was an advantage. I exploited it ruthlessly, trampling Vietnamese underfoot as I forced a path to the desk. The minutes ebbed away. I was appalled by the notion of being stranded here to face the chaos that was growing visibly every hour. At last, at very long last, after hurling wads of piastres at the desk staff, and sobbing with relief, I grabbed our boarding cards. I ran for the café. Not a sign of Mike and the crew. I ran for the plane, on the tarmac, ignoring shouts and armed soldiers, and bolted up the steps. The ITN team were all in seats. 'We never thought for a second you'd get bloody boarding cards,' Mike shrugged. We were scared, all right. I shut my eyes with relief when at last the plane turned to taxi, and we took off out of Da Nang for ever.

This was no false alarm, like the afternoon at Pakse in Laos four years earlier. Ours was the last scheduled flight to leave Da Nang for Saigon. After our departure, there were only a handful of special evacuation aircraft. Within hours, panic and chaos overtook the city. Little more than a day later, the communists streamed in, triumphant pith-helmeted figures clutching their AK-47s, riding the tanks through the streets, as they were to ride through so many Vietnamese city streets in the weeks to come.

I remember a postscript to Da Nang. A day or two after our escape, I met a New Zealand Visnews cameraman in Saigon, who told me he had flown into the city on the last, notorious refugee mercy lift by a World Airways plane. He was filming from the aircraft's doorway as a panic-stricken mob stormed the steps. As its pilot turned to taxi and take off before the plane was overwhelmed by the seething bodies, with Vietnamese hanging onto the wings and undercarriage in one of the most terrible images of those days, the cameraman was swept off on to the tarmac. He was still there when this last link to safety was broken, as the aircraft disappeared into the sky. The pictures of terror and defeat evoked by that plane, with the fugitives clinging to the wheels as it left the ground, filled the front pages of the world and passed into history. The cameraman, a cool, tough operator experienced in playing a lone hand, picked himself up and walked to the control tower, where he explained his predicament to the Vietnamese controller. The controller listened sympathetically. There would be no more fixed-wing flights into Da Nang, he said, gazing out on the runway crowded with people and now bereft of aircraft. But he would try to raise Air America – the CIA's private airline – on the radio, and see if they still had helicopter assets in the area.

A few minutes later, the controller gained contact. He reported the presence of a roundeye straggler in his tower. After some uneasy haggling, Air America said, 'Okay, we will send a Huey to get your man out, if he can walk to the edge of the strip, well away from the mob. If there are people round him when the chopper comes in – no rescue.' Cameraman and controller hastened below. The controller jabbered urgently to a woman and children on the ground floor of the building. 'My family,' he explained, 'I want them to go.' With elaborate lack of haste, as a throng of Vietnamese surged hither and thither across the tarmac propelled by their despair, the little group sauntered as casually as they could contrive to the edge of the apron. A few moments afterwards, the grey and blue Air America Huey swept down. The Vietnamese pushed in his family. The New Zealander yanked himself up over the skids as the pilot began to lift off. He turned in astonishment to see the controller still motionless on the tarmac. 'Aren't you coming?' he yelled. 'No,' shouted the Vietnamese. 'I must stay, in case they get another plane in.' The Huey swirled away into the sky, carrying the New Zealander on his way to safety in Saigon, leaving the little Vietnamese controller to the mercy of the communists an hour or two later.

Amid the trauma of those days, that story seemed intolerably moving. In all the ugliness, fear, the ruthless struggle for personal survival which was rapidly overwhelming Vietnam, here was a Vietnamese who committed a brave and coolly selfless act. Yet, because he was on the losing side, a member of a doomed society, the world would never know. History is written by the victors. The deeds of men who would have been heroes if their side had won – and there were more than a few in Indochina that spring – are, to paraphrase Kipling's line for the gravestones of 1914–18, 'known only unto God'.

CHAPTER TEN

The Fall of Saigon

THROUGH THE DAYS that followed, we reported to the world a lengthening roll of ill tidings. We learned that the ARVN forces in the Central Highlands had collapsed and were being cut to pieces along their line of retreat east to the coast. The North Vietnamese possessed a great strategic advantage. While Saigon was still seeking to defend much of the country, with units strung out across thousands of square miles, Hanoi could concentrate its forces to strike as it chose, picking the objectives where it could outnumber and overwhelm President Thieu's dwindling forces.

Yet no military mitigation could alter the fundamental truth, that the will of Saigon's army to fight had collapsed. Even those of us who recoiled from the notion that there was any justice in Hanoi's impending triumph could not dispute the fact that the communist army possessed a motivation wholly lacking in the forces of South Vietnam. Thieu's soldiers were weary of war. They were led by politicians and generals who could no longer stir them to resist effectively. A few South Vietnamese soldiers fought hard and bravely until the last day. With the huge, clumsy, devastatingly destructive armoury of American support and firepower removed, however, there were not nearly enough of these to sustain the struggle.

We drove out to gaze upon battlefields that came closer to Saigon each day. Nha Trang, 200 miles north-east of the capital, had fallen without serious resistance. Yet still there was intense speculation that the North Vietnamese must halt for weeks or months to rebuild their logistics, grapple with their vastly lengthened supply lines, negotiate a deal from their new position of dominance. Saigon must get a breathing space. Washington, seeing this disaster unfold, would surely intervene. The United States could hardly stand and watch while South Vietnam crumbled into dust before the eyes of the world. 'Do they want us to lose?' demanded a South Vietnamese officer, gripping my arm fiercely. 'It is so easy for them. If they just threaten the North Vietnamese with more bombing . . .' Yet Washington, in the wake of Watergate and under the hand of an enfeebled Ford Presidency, seemed paralysed.

In Saigon, the sense of unreality, of disbelief that at last the entire shape of twenty years of war was being altered for ever, was heightened by the delicious dinners that we ate each night. President Thieu's most conspicuous response to the nightmare was a government order decreeing the closure of all massage parlours. The piastre was collapsing as a currency, trading on the black market for a fifth of its nominal value. Anybody with a few US dollars could buy cameras, watches, stereos for peanuts. Many of us did, to the disgust of those correspondents who found naked consumerism unbearable amid a collapsing society. 'I hope,' said Phil Jacobson of the *Sunday Times* one day, reviewing with deep disfavour a cluster of reporters staggering up the hotel steps laden with stereo equipment, 'that like King John in the Wash, you sink under the weight of your treasure.' The standard reply to that one was, 'If we don't get it, the communists will.' I found myself drinking in a café with a Vietnamese officer who had escaped from Da Nang by swimming out to a ship offshore. His account of the city's last hours was horrific. Soldiers were roaming the streets firing at will, shooting civilians for food or money. 'The army was like a snake without a head,' he said. 'I went to corps headquarters, and found just one man there, a colonel. I asked, "What shall I do?" He said, "Do what you like." So I swam.' I asked if he planned to rejoin his unit. He laughed. 'I am much more worried where to find rice for my family. In a few weeks there will be no more war and it will not matter. I only wish we could leave Vietnam before that.'

Fear, personal fear for our own safety, was a growing force among almost all the journalists now. What would it be like in Saigon, if we were there when the North Vietnamese came, and the scenes of Da Nang were repeated a hundredfold? Even before that, when it became clear that America would not act to save South Vietnam, how might its people behave towards any roundeye, in the rage of their betrayal? Nerves lent an increasingly frenzied air to the nightly correspondents' drinking parties, the wretched conversations with the bar girls who pleaded so desperately with us for an introduction to anybody who could get them on a flight out. It became a commonplace for the phone to ring in the hotel room of any roundeye, to find a frightened voice on the other end promising dollars for help with the US Embassy to get out, out, out of Vietnam. The Westerners' drunken teasing of the bar girls was sometimes very brutal. 'Back to the paddy fields for you lot, in a week or two!' somebody said cheerfully. The girls' eyes widened with fear. One of them asked, 'You think communists shoot us?' 'Never!' came the confident reply. 'You'll just be planting rice for the next couple of years.' That was indeed to be the fate of many. But more than a few bar girls got out, because they possessed green money. The ugliest aspect of those days was the manner in which bribery or interest dictated who found a seat on a plane out of Saigon. A reporter was astonished one day to see the entire canteen staff of the American Embassy boarding a plane — waiters, kitchen cleaners and all. There were the revolting, futile 'orphan lifts', launched because the West found it pleasing to 'save' pretty Vietnamese children. Yet no one in his right mind supposed the North Vietnamese would shoot orphans or even Embassy canteen staff when they came. It was the ugly, unromantic, pot-bellied South Vietnamese colonels, the servants of the regime and their families, whose lives were in deadly peril. Cynics would say that such people deserved their fates. I never agreed. The Americans did little, far too little to save the people who had been closest to them all through the years of war now the crunch had come.

The Americans' old five o'clock follies, the daily correspondents' briefing, had been replaced by a similar function held by the ARVN at three thirty. In a large, featureless white room fleshy Colonel Hien solemnly recounted in Vietnamese the loss of towns, the cutting of roads, the rocketing of villages. Captain An, his slight sad, boyishly handsome sidekick, then translated into English in a flat monotone. I wrote:

No one could conceivably find them funny, or wicked, or absurd now. They are simply tragic. Colonel Hien and Captain An know, and we know, and they know that we know, that we are watching the curtain fall on Vietnam ... We sit in Saigon, watching messenger after messenger enter from off, bearing fresh tidings of gloom ... It is the tragedy of South Vietnam that its continued survival has become an embarrassment to everyone except itself. Most American correspondents here now argue that, since the game is up, it would be cruel for the United States to give Saigon's army any more ammunition, because it would merely prolong the agony ... So many people in Europe and America have a picture in their minds of Vietnam as a hell of impenetrable jungle and exploding shells. It is difficult to convey how much beauty, charm and gentleness the communists are now within an ace of seizing.

Even as left-wing correspondents in Saigon openly exulted about the day of liberation at hand, I was among those who felt bitter and despondent. Every story I wrote now was filling the front page, as were those of my colleagues. Yet this experience was so dreadful, and embraced the misery of so many people, that no correspondent could rejoice about personal glory. On 3 April, I reported from Vung Tou, the port city sixty-five miles from Saigon, where tens of thousands of refugees from every coastal city in South Vietnam were flooding ashore, bringing only their grief and fear, and overwhelming the pitiful resources available to handle them. There were children with broken limbs dangling, families carrying their dead wrapped in blankets, and a desperate struggle for water by almost every fugitive after days aboard ships on which supplies were exhausted. Sickness and wounds went untended. Some vessels were scarred by communist shellfire. What would happen to this vast array of ruined people? No one knew, no one seemed to care. From beginning to end, the special horror of war in Indochina stemmed from the fact that its chief burden fell upon the civilian population. Here, at Vung Tou, in these last days, the plight of the innocent lay before us in its starkest colours. For the first time I found myself joining those who muttered, 'Oh God, let it be over.'

I drove north once more to Ben Cat, where I had seen so much shelling the previous year, and sat on the bridge there talking to the village secretary. 'The end will not be long now, *m'sieu*,' he said. '*Le jour n'est pas loin.*' Was he frightened, I asked? Yes, he said, but not so frightened as he had been thirty years ago, when he was a young man. He had grown used to

war. It was a nerve-racking business for all of us, waiting to
see where the North Vietnamese would show their hand, where
across a 150-mile breadth of front they would launch their
next onslaught. Now, it was Hanoi which held overwhelming
superiority, ten divisions poised to attack, and only 70,000
government troops to meet them. 'The battle for Vietnam is
over,' I wrote. 'The battle for Saigon is about to begin.'

I spent a wonderful evening with a Frenchman named
Claude Baquier, an engineer who had first come to Vietnam as
a handsome young army sergeant in 1947, fell in love with the
place, married Dédé, a beautiful Vietnamese, and had lived
happily ever since. He talked shrewdly about where the United
States had got it so disastrously wrong. 'The Americans tried
to change the Vietnamese, to make them be like themselves
and think like themselves. They did not understand that, to a
Vietnamese, patriotism goes no further than his own family.
He feels Vietnamese, yes, but he does not feel for the concept
of South Vietnam as a state in a political sense, as we do for
our countries in the West. The Americans always treated the
Vietnamese with scorn, however much they tried to hide it.'
He grieved for what he would lose when he and his family left.
'Let's face it,' he said, echoing the delight of many Englishmen
in our own colonial experience, 'where else could a man like
me have had as much as we have had here? What will we have
in France? A job. An apartment, yes. But nothing to compare
with what we have here.' Dédé, much more visibly frightened
than Claude, asked me, 'Do you think there is any hope?' No,
I said. None.

Just at the moment when it seemed impossible that matters
could grow worse, one of the appalling 'Operation Babylift'
flights, a giant C5A Galaxy, crashed on take-off from Saigon,
killing 140 of the 243 children on board. The wreckage was
still burning as we hastened to the flooded paddies in which

the aircraft had fallen. It was too wet to get closer. Vietnamese army helicopters were circling the scene. A Huey rattled down to where I stood marooned and alone. 'You wanna see?' shouted one of the pilots. I did not wanna see, but I gotta see. I pushed a wad of piastres into his hand, and he lifted me the few hundred yards to where Vietnam's latest horror had unfolded. Other pilots were chartering their services to other reporters for the same purpose, amid the carnage. Bodies and toys, wreckage and baggage were everywhere. I wrote: 'In a terrible spring for Vietnam, it seems as if this was merely the latest in a catalogue of biblical plagues.'

On Tuesday 8 April, I was sitting in the Reuters' office, cutting a telex tape ready for transmission – Reuters was the usual channel for scores of British correspondents' dispatches – when there was the roar of a low-flying aircraft overhead, and a heavy explosion nearby, which frightened most of us very much indeed, given the condition of our nerves already. The culprit was an aircraft captured by the North Vietnamese, bombing the presidential palace nearby. There was a belated barrage of machine-gun fire from the ground in response, which merely heightened the fears of everyone on the streets around the centre of the city. A curfew was proclaimed. Loudspeakers mounted on jeeps toured Saigon, playing martial music and ordering everyone indoors. The order was widely ignored, and it was easy for correspondents to bribe any difficult policeman to leave them alone as they travelled around the city.

It still seemed extraordinary to behold the routines of daily life continuing in Saigon, while we waited for the communists to launch their next offensive. One morning, I stood watching a worker at one of the dozens of cane workshops around the middle of the city, weaving hour after hour the sort of furniture Liberty's sell for hundreds of pounds. I wanted a basket and, like the boy tending the shop, I had time on my hands. We argued for forty minutes about a sum of something like thirty pence, both pleading poverty and agreeing that times were hard, finding flaws in the wretched basket and taking it in turns to walk offstage in a huff. Then, of course, we split the difference and I bought the basket, as we knew I would. We both laughed, and for a moment we were happy.

On 9 April, the communists launched a major new offensive at Xuan Loc, a town of 100,000 people set among rubber plantations forty-five miles north-east of Saigon. This time, they met much tougher South Vietnamese resistance. The Airborne Division, best remaining formation in Thieu's army, was thrown forward into the battle. The Americans provided the South Vietnamese with the latest and most deadly weapon in their non-nuclear armoury, the CBU 'Cluster Bomb', which killed by draining the oxygen from the surrounding atmosphere, to aid the fight to hold Xuan Loc. Reporters commuted daily to the town, to watch the progress of the battle in increasingly alarming conditions. I have never forgotten the spectacle of a stunningly beautiful, very upmarket English girl who had attached herself to one of the British television reporters, setting off for Xuan Loc and photographing the communist dead with her little tourist camera, for all the world as if she was on an Asian adventure package holiday. Some of us shuddered, not merely with jealousy of her boyfriend.

It was about now that I found myself facing a personal dilemma. I had always assured my family that whatever the temptations or demands of 'the story' I would never miss a big event at home. On 14 April, my son was having his second birthday party. Did I dare fulfil my promise to be home for it? I sat at the telex keyboard in Reuters, messaging Charles Wintour:

HOPE OKAY I COME BACK FOR SONS BIRTHDAY REGARDS MAX.

HOW LONG CAN SAIGON, HOLD??? REGARDS CHARLES, clattered back the machine.

FALL OF CITY UNLIKELY TO BE IMMINENT. SHOULD BE OKAY FOR SEVERAL WEEKS, I messaged back.

OKAY YOU CAN COME BACK CHARLES.

My colleagues thought I was mad, or that my nerve had broken, or both. I probably was, and it probably had. But I caught the Air Vietnam Boeing to Bangkok, and a flight thence on to London, just in time to help Charlie blow out his candles, and to watch a dozen sticky children immerse themselves in chocolate cake and crisps in our little terrace house in Barnes. Barnes. The very name sounded fantastic after the events of the month past. After all I had seen, all I had done, I found myself looking in disbelief on the middle-class housewives shopping in the High Street, the boats cruising past on the river, the commuters catching the 8.05 to the City. And another thing. I had got it badly wrong. Within hours of those West London mothers taking home their spoilt offspring from our party, it was plain that I had wildly miscalculated the timeframe for Saigon's survival. The battle for Xuan Loc was being lost. The town was going to fall within days. Saigon would then lie at the mercy of Hanoi.

I walked into Charles Wintour's office in Shoe Lane, deeply apprehensive. I had blown it. A return ticket to Vietnam was a significant item in the paper's budget. The *Standard* had been uncovered in Saigon for three vital days already, because of my return. In recent years, as an editor myself, under the same circumstances I would have sent another correspondent to finish the job, to rub in the lesson to the man who let me down.

'I'm sorry, Charles. I got it wrong. But I can't bear to miss the end. Please may I go back?'

He paused for a moment in thought, then grinned frostily. 'All right. You'd better go and book a flight.'

'Thanks more than I can say, Charles. You know how much this means to me.'

The Boeing 727 which took me from Bangkok to Saigon was almost empty, save for a few correspondents on the same business as myself. I found myself sitting next to a pleasant young Vietnamese. I told him I was surprised to meet him going in rather than coming out. In some embarrassment, but with remarkable frankness, he explained that he was a nephew of President Thieu, and that he had been in Bangkok starting to make arrangements for the family's future.

An hour or two later, I threw down my bag back in my old room at the Caravelle. To outward appearances, little had changed in the streets of Saigon. The frenzy to get a seat out had intensified. Flights were shuttling Americans, their dependants, and anyone who could bribe their way aboard an aircraft, every few hours to Guam. Outside the gates of the American compound at Tan Son Nhut airport, a heaving mass of desperate people fought for access, the chance to fight a way past the stony-faced guards, to plead their case for a boarding card with the American desk clerks. There were ugly stories about how rich some roundeyes became in those days. Incoming American pilots reported that they were seeing small arms fire from the ground. The enemy was that close. Hanoi wanted to finish this now, before the rains came in May. President Thieu resigned, but his passing seemed meaningless. The fate of Saigon would be determined between Washington, Hanoi, and the men on the battlefield. No one else. Phnom Penh fell to the Khmer Rouge on 17 April, though nobody yet possessed an inkling of the victors' terrible intentions towards their own people. Jon Swain was there for the *Sunday Times*, a splendidly laid-back figure who had immersed himself happily and exotically in the life of Indochina since he first made his way there as a freelance in 1973. His company had enlivened many of my evenings in Saigon the previous year. We wondered what had befallen him. Later, Swain produced one of the first, most vivid and terrible dispatches about the birth of Cambodia's Killing Fields. There was an atmosphere of deathbed embarrassment about conversation in Saigon now, with the fit and healthy – the ones who possessed the money and the passports to leave when they chose – conducting conversations in hushed tones, in corners out of earshot of those who perceived themselves doomed and damned. The fighting was growing audibly closer to Saigon. One morning a huge explosion reverberated across the city. Communist shelling had touched off a big ammunition dump at Bien Hoa. Bien Hoa was only fifteen miles away. Still we drove out of the city most mornings to gaze at the latest firefight, to check the situation at the front.

One morning in the street, I met my old friend Tom Bower, who had arrived in town with a BBC crew. Implausibly, they were all draped in M16 rifles and pistols.

'What in God's name do you think you are doing, Thomas?' I demanded.

He and his colleagues looked sheepish. 'We've been filming the evacuation of the British Embassy. Colonel Strong gave us the hardware. He said, "You chaps are going to need these more than I do. I'll give you the chocolates for them later."'

We parted. I was shaking my head a good deal. Many days later, out on the American carriers, I asked Tom what on earth he and the others had done with their weaponry. He looked sheepish again: 'Well, it seemed irresponsible just to leave guns lying on our beds in the hotel, so we unscrewed the side panel of the bath, and left them hidden in there.' I have always wondered whether the wherewithal to start a modest counterrevolution is still secreted in the bathroom of Room 209 at the Caravelle Hotel in what is now Ho Chi Minh City.

On Sunday 27 April, with half a dozen colleagues I was having lunch – one of the most delicious I have ever eaten in my life – at a marvellous French-Vietnamese restaurant. A friend from one of the news agencies stopped by our table. 'They say there's a huge refugee movement out on the road to Vung Tou, and quite a battle down there,' he said. 'I'm going to look. You want to come?' I thought for a moment. It was Sunday. I was exhausted, emotionally and physically. I had no paper to file for that day. But what the hell – I ought to go and look. We drove smoothly out of the city on an almost empty road, and within a few miles began to see refugees, thousands of them. They were walking fast, desperately fast, clutching bags and cooking pots and fans and sacks and boxes and bicycles and screaming children, all scurrying towards Saigon like some vast, compulsive African animal migration – for what? We drove on, and on. We met a column of South Vietnamese tanks, heavily draped in branches and foliage. They waved us down. 'Plenty fighting up there. You better stop.' We stopped. Two French journalists who received no such warning drove on that afternoon, and died. We pulled the car into the side, and got out. There was incessant artillery and machine-gun fire in the trees a mile or so ahead. Columns of black smoke reached high into the sky in a dozen places around the village of Long Thanh. And all the way down the straight road southward, refugees were still pouring towards us as far as the eye could see. Hundreds of soldiers, most without weapons, trudged sullenly among them. The tide of humanity was kicking up a vast cloud of dust. As many refugees as were physically capable trotted or ran rather than walked. These were people who had come from Vung Tou, and before that from Quang Tri, Da Nang, Cam Ranh Bay, Nha Trang, the whole tragic roll-call of Vietnam's fallen cities. They had fled again and again, and now they were fleeing for the last time, to the last place: Saigon. We stood watching in silence. They hardly seemed to notice us. I thought: is it not strange that at this, the last hour of a stricken society, the mere fact that we are roundeyes is still protecting us. How ridiculous. We are their betrayers. We are unarmed. There are thousands of them. Are there not two, or ten, or twenty of these people angry or ambitious enough to attack us, kill us, take our car? No, thank God. To the last, the extraordinary passivity of the South Vietnamese towards Westerners persisted. We climbed into the vehicle and drove soberly back into the city. The end was obviously very close. I met a friend from one of the US TV networks. He told me he was on his way to Tan Son Nhut, where a joint network charter aircraft from Hong Kong was on the ground to pick up their vastly expensive satellite trans-mission equipment. Would he take my baggage, I asked? If it was ready in five minutes. I threw into a case everything I possessed bar my typewriter, one camera, a shirt and a razor, and dashed downstairs to push it into his jeep. That was how, ten days later, I reached Hong Kong and found myself one of the very few correspondents to salvage my kit from the ruin of Vietnam.

We woke on Monday morning to hear that the war was now inside the city. During the night, some fifty Viet Cong had dug themselves into positions around the Newport Bridge, a big modern girder structure on the route to Bien Hoa. They had closed the road, and South Vietnamese Airborne and Ranger elements were fighting fiercely to reopen it. A vast traffic jam of vehicles and refugees had built up outside the city, their entry blocked by the VC. A group of us arrived nearby to find a significant part of the remaining Saigon media corps scuttling hither and thither around the surrounding streets in search of a view. Bursts of fire resounded among the buildings. TV cameramen were playing a terrifying game of grandmother's footsteps, leapfrogging past each other to shoot the action. I have written earlier about some of the war sequences made for television, which look much more dangerous than they are. On the Newport Bridge that Monday morning, the TV men took fantastic risks. They were a hundred, two hundred yards ahead of the rest of us. I watched a communist mortar round erupt on to the tarmac fifty feet from one crew. It was a good day to be a writing journalist, not a picture one. Almost for the first time in the war, some TV teams captured the faces of VC on camera, in a firefight. And miraculously, they lived to talk about it. The battle went on for most of the day before the last Viet Cong were killed and the Newport Bridge was reopened. South Vietnam's third president in a week was inaugurated in his palace amid a sudden monsoon storm, lightning flashing across the sky, and a continual rumble of artillery in the distance. Many correspondents muttered words about a setting worthy of *Götterdämmerung*. That evening, exhausted, we sat, silent and frightened, eating an apology for supper in the hotel dining room. The radio was continually tuned to the American news channel. Several diners nursed walkie-talkies, alert for the moment when the Americans gave the signal for evacuation. A middle-aged woman was entertaining two pickpockets and three child street beggars whom she had invited to join her. Poor souls, it seemed a sad sort of kindness to be trying to teach them to use knives and forks at such a moment, in such a setting. In the hotel lobby, a dozen Vietnamese of all ages and both sexes had been camping for days, hoping against hope to find a roundeye who would help them to escape. And a few hundred yards away, bricklayers worked into the night on a new perimeter wall for the French Embassy, where the cocky little ambassador, Jean-Marie Morillon, believed that he could provide sanctuary for his own colony and play the leading role in a last and decisive act of diplomacy to end the war. The conceit of the French, confident of their special relationship with Hanoi and the protection of French interests, had been one of the more vexing aspects of the drama for weeks past. The ridiculous Morillon had just replanted the Embassy flower beds in a gesture of pigeon-chested assurance that he would remain in permanency, even as the foolish Americans were ejected from Indochina. It was a source of infinite glee to us all afterwards, that the North Vietnamese bundled the ambassador and the French contingent out of Saigon as abruptly as everybody else.

I slept for a couple of hours that night before being awoken by a thunderous explosion. It was followed by another, which sounded pretty close. Go back to sleep, Hastings. We know your nerves are in pieces. We know you are wishing to God you had stayed in Barnes. But don't make it obvious. Sleep. Sleep. The shelling continued, and I shook between my blankets at each explosion. Why not get up and get dressed? What, admit defeat? Find myself wandering alone around the hotel while everybody else is sensibly getting a few hours in bed before the morrow? I lay there and lay there, listening to the relentless crumping and concussions. At last, I could bear no more. I would go out and see what there was to see. I dressed and made my way up to the roof. Arrayed along the parapet in the darkness was almost every inhabitant of the Caravelle. A long row of television cameras stood on their tripods, crews shooting the flashes of flame and explosions out towards Tan Son Nhut. I felt so much better. I was not alone in my sleeplessness and fear. I watched the fireworks among a few friends with something near equanimity through the rest of the night.

This sensation was short-lived. It was 29 April. At breakfast, not a meal that would have commended itself to Egon Ronay, I was gazing out of the window at a fixed-wing gunship, circling a mile or two distant. Suddenly, a lazy streak of light began to bore upwards towards it. The missile struck one of the twin tailbooms of the aircraft. The gunship spun slowly towards the earth, until it disappeared out of sight behind a line of trees, to be replaced by a shooting pillar of fire and smoke. SAM-7. If the communists were using shoulder-fired missiles, they were very near indeed. Now, we had to assume, they commanded the sky through which any fugitives from Saigon must escape. I walked down to the empty Reuters' office, tapped out my dispatch and handed it to the telex girl, whom we had bribed hugely to keep our lines open at just this moment. As I walked back to the hotel, a man on a moped suddenly swerved past a soldier, who shouted and emptied his rifle after him. Occasional shots were now audible very close at hand. I was among those less frightened of being shot in cold blood by the arriving communists than of being killed by maddened South Vietnamese in the last hours of anarchy. They were armed, they were despairing, the whole fabric of their society and armed forces was collapsing before their eyes. Anything could happen.

Back at the hotel, I returned to the roof, to find a strange spectacle. It was empty, save for a long row of camera tripods, abandoned for ever. The lobby was strewn with large boxes of electronic equipment, bought for a song in recent days, now jettisoned. The radio had played *White Christmas*. It was the signal for the White House's 'Option 4' – the final evacuation of Saigon. I found most of my colleagues clambering into buses, filming and photographing each other as they did so, 150 in all. They were ordered to abandon almost everything save the most portable personal kit. I said goodbye to a lot of friends including Tom Bower. Then the convoy departed under heavy American Marine escort for Tan Son Nhut, and a helicopter flight out to the Seventh Fleet in the South China Sea.

Who was left? People like Martin Woollacott of the *Guardian*, Stewart Dalby of the *FT*, the inimitable Sandy Gall of ITN – a much older man than the rest of us, yet determined to stay and report the arrival of the North Vietnamese – Peter Arnett of AP, Julian Manyon of IRN and a handful of others. No Americans remained, for obvious reasons. And me? Yes, I had told Charles Wintour I would report the fall of Saigon. Only the previous day I had telexed my expectation the city would fall in 48 to 72 hours: HOPE TO GIVE YOU SOMETHING REALLY WORTH HAVING BEFORE THE PLUGS ARE PULLED. The editor telexed back: YOUR STORY MAKES FINE LEAD THIS MORNING GLAD TO HEAR YOUR PLANS AND WILL KEEP IN TOUCH WITH WIFE AS NECESSARY STOP ACT SENSIBLY IF SERIOUS TROUBLE DEVELOPS BEST WISHES CHARLES.

The hotel seemed echoing and empty, with almost all the journalists gone. We were in a curious limbo. I had filed my front-page splash, which the *Standard* published under the heroic heading 'MAX HASTINGS stays on in Saigon to report the last dying hours of South Vietnam, and the dramatic exodus of the Americans.' Distant explosions continued to echo through almost empty streets. I walked to a nearby shoemaker to pick up some mended shoes, simply to have something to do. 'You help us get out,' they begged. 'You have dollars? You change money?' I suggested that dollars would be little use to them in a few hours. They should be safe if they stayed at home. The North Vietnamese were unlikely to shoot shoemakers. That is what I said, anyway. I was unsure whether I believed it myself. We ate some sort of lunch in the hotel, and then I went back to the deserted Reuters' office to file again.

Martin Woollacott came in, an exceptionally cool and steady correspondent, as well as a superb wordsmith. As I went out, he said, 'I suspect the next twenty-four hours in this place are going to be extremely unpleasant.' I thought: if Martin, of all people, is feeling apprehensive, then I am bloody terrified. I can't do this. I cannot stay with just a handful of colleagues, the only roundeyes left in a vast city on the verge of collapse, simply for a story. I want out. I want to live. I want to go home.

And so I ran away. I conceded to myself that I was not as brave as Martin Woollacott or Sandy Gall or Peter Arnett. I walked, and then trotted, the half mile or so to the American Embassy. There was a crowd seething outside its high walls, Vietnamese desperate to get in. Passing the big Brinks building, I saw looters already at work in the American offices, staggering out loaded with champagne, television sets, even refrigerators. South Vietnamese police, amazingly, were still holding back the mob round the Embassy, while the helmets of US Marines were visible over the parapet. Cobra gunships from the fleet were circling overhead, covering this last evacuation against any North Vietnamese intervention. A communist-inspired A-37 air strike on Tan Son Nhut had already killed two Americans – the last to die in the Indochina war. I forced my way through the shouting, shoving, increasingly hysterical crowd, calling to the Marines, 'Hey guys – how do I get in?' Long arms reached down and took my hands. They hauled me over the wall. I found myself inside the Embassy compound along with some 2,000 others, perhaps 500 of us roundeyes, the remainder Vietnamese, waiting to be pulled out of Vietnam.

The roundeyes and Vietnamese, now as ever, stood apart. Having made it thus far, I and my kind knew that we were almost safe. Whatever the Americans did or did not do, they were not about to abandon this last perimeter until every white face had been lifted out. But the Vietnamese – ah, that was another matter. There they stood and squatted, with their families and some fragments of baggage, a few impassive, most visibly terrified. Only the highest risk category of Washington's former allies had been admitted to the compound: senior police, army and intelligence people, civilians who had worked closely with the Americans. If they stayed, they would almost certainly die.

The evacuation moved painfully slowly. It was already late afternoon. Yet only one helicopter at a time could get into the compound, and there were long intervals between them. In the distance, we could hear the steady rumble of artillery from Bien Hoa or even nearer at hand, together with occasional small arms fire in the city, involving heaven knew who. We chatted nervously to each other. A lot of the roundeyes were American contractors, diplomats or spooks. The bulk of the correspondents had gone that morning, via Tan Son Nhut. To my amazement, however, I saw John Pilger, the Australian leftist. Pilger, whose views I disagreed with as passionately as he despised mine, had heaped more scorn and contempt upon the South Vietnamese regime and the American engagement than almost any other journalist. Here was a delectable irony: instead of waiting to throw his arms around Hanoi's liberators on their arrival, he was cadging a ride to safety with the capitalist running dogs and their Vietnamese stooges. At least I could offer the excuse that I never wanted Hanoi to win.

Like a good many men in the compound, I was still wearing my flak jacket. Who knew what the rest of the day might bring? A colleague took a picture of me standing incongruously by the Embassy swimming pool, gazing up at the sky. If one looked at that photo today without knowing the circumstances in which it was taken, one would merely ask: why is he wearing a flak jacket for an afternoon by the pool? It did not seem incongruous at the time. Two Vietnamese in civilian clothes sidled nervously over to me. 'You remember us? An and Hien.' Of course — the officers who had run the ARVN's daily press briefings. 'Will you tell the Americans we *must* — *must* get out?' They were grey with fear. I did not blame them. At this rate, it would be many hours before everybody was lifted out of the Compound. And how many hours would the North Vietnamese give us? Now, each time a helo clattered in, there was a surge forward of frightened people, restrained by the Marines with increasing difficulty.

A short, chubby figure in camouflage fatigues, helmet, grenades and all the usual accoutrements of war stepped forward, at his side a Vietnamese interpreter with a bullhorn — Major Keane, commanding the Marine contingent. He addressed the crowd in steely, emphatic phrases, measuring every word. 'Now, listen everybody. I know that there are a lot of very uneasy and uncomfortable people here in this compound today. This evacuation is a long, slow business. It's very frustrating for all of us. But I want to tell you people this: my Marines and I have been sent here from the Seventh Fleet to cover the evacuation, and that is what we are going to do. Not one of us is going to leave this place until every one of you has done so.'

It was an intensely moving moment. As his interpreter finished translating, every Vietnamese in his audience leapt to his feet and clapped in devout gratitude. I thought: good old Americans. They may have screwed up this war, but they're going to leave in style. At around 8 p.m., worn out with fear, my own turn came to scramble up the tail ramp into the big hold of a Jolly Green Giant, among a host of Vietnamese and the inevitable Pilger. For the last time, we flew out across all the familiar sights of Saigon, then over green paddy and buildings where columns of smoke were sometimes visible, and at last across the coast, knowing that we were safe. Others were not. This war had cost the lives of 57,483 Americans, over a million communist combatants, approaching half a million Vietnamese civilians. The ARVN had lost at least 110,000. It was characteristic that we should know so exactly the United States loss, so approximately the cost to the people the conflict was allegedly about.

We landed on the vast aircraft carrier USS *Midway* – a lucky choice, had we known it. The ship was one of the few which did not subject every arrival, roundeye or Vietnamese, to body searches, which included anal examinations for drugs. For many correspondents, those were the final indignity. In our exhaustion, we fell asleep as soon as we found a bunkspace below decks. At first light, I woke and climbed up to the flight deck. I saw a cluster of Marines who had defended the evacuation, clutching the crest they had taken from the Embassy portal before they flew off the roof, covering their retreat up the last stairway with gas grenades. I asked what time they bailed out. I said I was amazed they had managed to clear all the Vietnamese out of the compound so swiftly. One of them shrugged. 'We had to leave some. Things got to where we could only keep holding the perimeter if we opened fire, and Washington kayoed that idea.' So. There had been one last betrayal. I felt sick.

The day that followed was as unforgettable as that which preceded it. The sea was filled with ships of every size, small craft and even sampans bringing out refugees, civilian and military, pleading and fighting for a place with the American Fleet. Closer at hand, Huey and Jet Ranger helicopters were constantly landing on the flight decks, bringing Vietnamese pilots and their families, senior officers, officials, anyone who had been able to seize this one last privilege of skill or rank. As fast as the choppers were emptied, the American flight-deck crews manhandled them bodily to the side – and tipped them overboard into the sea. The carriers needed every foot of deckspace. There was no room for these countless millions of dollarsworth of high technology, the very symbol of America's war for Vietnam. An order came through to transfer correspondents to the command ship *Blue Ridge*. I found myself cross-decking in a helicopter with a party of Vietnamese officers. Three generals sat side by side in their fatigues directly opposite me. They were lost in silence. Suddenly when I glanced at them, I perceived that all were crying, tears rolling down their cheeks. They were crying for failure, humiliation, the loss of an entire society. Yesterday, they were near the summit of their own nation. Today, and for the rest of their lives, they were merely three more refugees among hundreds of thousands. Pilger might have said that they deserved it, but I felt only pity. For an instant, my hand strayed instinctively to my Nikon, to catch this unforgettable image of men in defeat. But I knew I could not do it, that I could not subject these people to yet another gratuitous indignity.

On the *Blue Ridge*, we were told Saigon had fallen that morning. The North Vietnamese were in the city. A few hours later, every correspondent on the ship was summoned to the briefing room. When we were assembled, a US Navy Commander faced us grimly. 'I am deeply sorry to have to inform all of you of this, because I know these people were your colleagues and friends. But I have to say that our information is that all the correspondents who remained in Saigon after your departure have been shot.' There was a stunned moment. The Commander proffered further commiserations, and then we broke up. We talked urgently and earnestly among ourselves. The story was not only terrible, it sounded fantastically implausible. Why should the North Vietnamese do anything so futile, so certain to gain the censure of the world? Most of us dismissed what we had been told, and of course we were right to do so. This was merely the last grotesque piece of misinformation peddled by the hierarchy of the American armed forces at the funeral of South Vietnam.

Soon afterwards, many of us were transferred once more to the helicopter carrier *Okinawa*, for the dreary four-day voyage to the Philippines. We were unable to file dispatches. There was nothing to drink save fruit juice, and nothing to do save gossip interminably while we sat watching the flying fish diving under the bow, and the ship ploughed through the deep blue of the China Sea. For all of us, Tom Bower and I agreed, the collapse of South Vietnam had been the most traumatic experience of our careers. Second World War veterans told me that they vastly preferred fighting in North Africa to fighting in North-West Europe, because in the desert there were only armies – no civilians, no villages, hardly a town. In Europe, by contrast, it was a source of daily misery to witness and undertake the destruction of homes and streets which looked so like one's own home or street, to see the destitution and often deaths of innocent people of all ages and both sexes. This was what we had now witnessed in South Vietnam, and the memories remained with us for ever. The flight of hundreds of thousands of Vietnamese boat people from their 'liberated' country in the years which followed, at appalling hazard, gave the final lie to those 'useful idiots' in the West who welcomed the North Vietnamese victory.

I caught a flight within hours from Manila to Hong Kong. I checked into the Mandarin, and then thought: why I am doing this? All I want is to go home, back to Barnes, as far away as possible from Asia and all I have just seen. I checked out again within an hour, and caught the evening flight to

London. I had done just enough for the *Standard* to justify myself to Charles Wintour, even if he knew that I had flinched from the last big story. I did not regret my premature departure from Saigon. I doffed my cap to the correspondents who stayed, but was glad to have admitted my own limits. Later, I was consoled by the fact that after two days of filing wonderful stories about the North Vietnamese arrival, the Saigon journalists found their communications cut off by the communists. They were obliged to linger idle for several weeks, before being flown out of the country.

I landed at Heathrow and passed into Customs, where I was liable for an extravagant amount of excise duty on assorted cameras and other artefacts I had obtained in Saigon. Back on the carriers, every other correspondent had thrown over the side his flak jacket and helmet as soon as he boarded. There was no more war. But, to the puzzlement of colleagues, I kept mine with me all the way to London, props for one last little piece of theatre, which now took place just as I had scripted it. The Customs officer looked at these warry symbols hung over my arm.

'Where have you come from?'

'Saigon.'

'Get on with you.' He waved an arm in dismissal. 'If you've come from there, I reckon you're entitled to anything you managed to bring out.'

There would be two opinions about that.

CHAPTER ELEVEN

Savimbi's Angola

MORE THAN TWENTY years after Saigon fell, when I became editor of the London *Evening Standard*, my predecessor left on the office desk for my amusement my own personal file with the paper, stretching back to 1964. Inevitably, most of its contents were petulant demands for more money penned by me, together with accompanying notes of rejection from the editor. There was one document, however, of which I was previously quite ignorant: a letter from my mother to Charles Wintour, whom she had known as a Fleet Street colleague for many years. It was written while I was bobbing about in the China Sea on the US carrier *Okinawa*, after fleeing from Saigon.

12 Eaton Square, 1 May 1975

Dear Charles,

I think the time has come when some rethinking has got to be done about Max. This constant danger cannot go on – for a start, his marriage will break up for a cert, and I cannot blame Tricia. He has done it now for some ten years, riot after riot, war after war, and I think it's enough. Somebody younger should take on a stint. After all, if your country is at war, you do it for your country. But this is almost non-stop, not for self-preservation or patriotism, but for a scoop and a byline. If you go on doing it for ever, you become an old warhorse like Jimmy Cameron – highly respected, but pretty dotty all the same. I think it's high time Max got on to the executive circuit. I know that Max himself thinks he could not be happy without the constant stimulus of excitement and danger, but one cannot be a schoolboy for ever. And I do think that a busy and important Fleet Street job produces more excitement than Max himself realizes. Anyway, do think hard about this. My point is that ten years is enough, and I honestly think he will get killed next time or the time after, because he has become careless in his enthusiasm.

Love, Anne

Well. There is no record of Charles's reply on the file, perhaps because he did not make one. He must have thought it a bit thick for an employee's mother to write demanding an executive role for her son, even if she is a friend, and even if she is motivated by a natural maternal concern about her offspring. I had not the slightest interest in taking a desk-bound job. More to the point, neither Charles nor anyone else considered me remotely suitable executive material – it would be another decade before Conrad Black showed himself brave enough to make me responsible for running the *Daily Telegraph*.

But I blushed to read my mother's letter for other reasons, also. It was especially ironic that she wrote it even as I was running away from the fall of Saigon. I was very aware, in Vietnam and on other battlefields, how many correspondents exposed themselves to danger far more often than I did. Don McCullin, for instance, took incomparably greater risks. I believed that I possessed more energy and ambition than most. I had seen my share of troubles. No correspondent of my generation, however, making a list of the bold and brave, would have included me on it. Eccentric, yes. Assertive, certainly. Noisy, maybe. Brave? No.

Many readers and viewers outside our trade misjudge relative risk when they think about war reporting. Covering a battle with professional soldiers of a serious army is seldom terribly hazardous. With the notable exceptions of Vietnam and the Falklands, correspondents have rarely been called upon, or indeed allowed, to march or fight among front-line infantry. The journalists are much more often to be found a step back, at a battalion headquarters or artillery position. That does not make them safe, but it does make them safer, in the obvious hierarchy of danger that starts at the point of a lead infantry platoon, and works down and back from there. Statistically, a journalist's chances of being killed in a firefight with a competent regular army are small – significantly less than those of the average infantryman. Reporters are at much greater risk among guerrillas and frankly incompetent armies, as we have been reminded recently in the Balkans, and thirty years ago in Cambodia. But they face the greatest hazards when they are on the move in a war zone, especially in Third World countries. More often than not, they are unescorted, do not know the territory, and have no means of assessing local risk. In the Third World, they are also imperilled by the chronically low standard of vehicle and aircraft maintenance, and of driving. Very few journalists I knew were killed by gunfire on the battlefield. A depressing number, however, died on assignment in crashes – of planes, helicopters, cars, even trains. At one time and another in my foreign corresponding days, I have found myself in all manner of travellers' disasters, including a string of car pile-ups. In Ethiopia, on my way to report a famine, I once fell asleep in the passenger seat of a hire car, and awoke to find myself upside down in a ravine, solely through the Ethiopian driver's absolute ignorance of how to steer the vehicle. He had bought his driving licence. In the middle of nowhere, with the help of a local village, we eventually retrieved and righted the car. It had lost all its windows and the roof had been crushed several inches, but it still ran. At the insistence of two Oxfam nurses, who were also passengers, I took over the wheel myself. Driving 200 miles on a dust road without a windscreen was a memorable experience. I have also seen some terrible crashes in wartime blackouts at night – it is sometimes forgotten that more British civilians died in traffic accidents in the Second World War than the Luftwaffe killed.

Not only was my mother, in her letter to Charles Wintour, optimistic about my credentials for being given other employment, therefore, she also wildly overstated my claims to heroic status in the eyes of my colleagues, the only people who really know. In general, because war correspondents are seldom backward in retailing their own deeds to the world – and if they are shy, their employers will certainly write deeds large on their behalf – the world is absurdly ready to think them brave, especially if they appear on television, and especially if they are women. Most war correspondents are at risk only for relatively short periods. Any soldier who went through, say, the North-West Europe campaign, eleven months of almost continuous heavy fighting in 1944–45, must laugh at what passes for battlefield experience in someone like myself, or even some of the more immodest television war reporters.

And yet, by the time I left Saigon, I was beginning to look for another life. I was very aware that my slender capital of nerve was overdrawn, and I was not yet thirty. My love for soldiers, together with my taste for foreign assignments, were as strong as ever. I wanted to write more books about war, because I thought I was good at this. But I did not feel that I wanted to see many more battlefields for myself, nor did I want to be as frightened again as I had been in Vietnam.

My mother gained part of her wish in the years that followed – the life that I led was little more dangerous than that of a travelling businessman. I covered the American Bicentennial, plenty of European politics, more Ulster, various African assignments. I presented a film profile of Pakistan's dictator, General Zia ul-Haq, for BBC TV's *Panorama*. But I did not hear a shot fired in anger. Only once did I even work in a war zone. In 1976, *Panorama* asked me to fly into southern Angola, to make a film about the UNITA guerrillas who were fighting it out with the Marxist MPLA regime for possession of the country, only two months after the Portuguese abandoned it to a chaotic independence. Robin Denselow, the producer, was a contemporary whom I liked, the best of company for a trip of this kind. We flew to Zambia, at that time plumbing the lowest ebb of Kaunda-sponsored national poverty. In Lusaka we were unable to buy more than a few of the most basic items of food and bush kit before we took off for Angola. The smart HS-125 executive jet that landed us on a bush strip near Silvaporto was owned, it transpired, by Tiny Rowland of Lonrho. We should have expected as much. It was part of Rowland's stock-in-trade to keep a finger in every pie in Africa, and he obliged UNITA by keeping open their vital link to the outside world. If they won the war, Rowland's company would no doubt benefit accordingly. This was how he achieved his well-deserved reputation as the cynical and rapacious tycoon, plotting war and peace across Africa for personal gain, whom Frederick Forsyth fictionalized in *The Dogs of War*.

Once we descended from the Rowland flying carpet, however, standards of comfort and safety declined steeply. At that period, UNITA maintained a tenuous grasp on the southern part of Angola with weapons supplied in part by the Americans

– who gave the movement some $32 million worth of arms through the CIA – and with rather more from the South African apartheid regime. Just two months earlier, Fred Bridgland of Reuters had exposed white South Africa's military presence in Angola to the world. The disastrous political impact on UNITA's fortunes of this revelation was already apparent. The MPLA were, of course, armed by the Russians. Between 1974 and 1976, Moscow poured some $400 million of arms into its client's forces in Angola and – more important – sponsored an 11,000 strong Cuban expeditionary force to provide weapons training, military advice, and strike jet pilots. There were also, of course, assorted mercenaries in the country. Many died. Four who were captured by the Cubans, three British and one American, died before an MPLA firing squad.

The ragged army which fought beneath UNITA's crowing cockerel banner was deployed in scattered battalions in the bush and various small towns created by the Portuguese colonial power. It was a flat, unlovely expanse of Africa, almost barren of creature comforts, in which the electricity only worked spasmodically, and the hapless population could hardly work at all. There was no beer, for instance, because while UNITA controlled the brewery, the bottling plant was in MPLA territory. Hunger, if not famine, was endemic. We travelled with difficulty in ailing vehicles on broken roads – at one point the camera crew was involved in a nasty Landrover crash. We filmed UNITA trainees in their jungle camp. I can't say that I took their military skills very seriously, although I was impressed by their willingness to crawl through the mud while their instructors fired live rounds a few feet short of them. I would not care to trust my own survival to the ability of a UNITA NCO to be accurate within a yard with an AK-47. As so often in the Third World, one gained an impression of a war that could take a very long time to reach any decision, chiefly because neither side possessed the means nor military competence to force an outcome on the battlefield. Stalemate is almost endemic in many African wars, because the combatants compete effectively only in their willingness to expend the lives of their own people. They lack the transport and logistics to exploit success, and their soldiers' training seldom advances beyond the ability to fire a weapon. They are dependent on mercenaries or foreign sponsors for any sort of fire or air support. What pass for battles in Africa seldom owe much to any engagement a European staff college would recognize.

It was hard not to be moved by the extraordinary African experience in which we found ourselves, which bore scant resemblance to conventional soldiering. UNITA's commanders paraded their men, perhaps a battalion strong, in a huge dirt square bordered by thick, lush tropical vegetation. The rain was sheeting down around us. And while we filmed, and the soldiers stood with water pouring off their heads and weapons, they sang songs – what Africans call praise-songs, some of the greatest songs I have ever heard in the continent. Urged on by their political officer, they chanted as our cameraman panned down the lines, and we asked ourselves what drove them: compulsion? Tribal loyalties? The better likelihood of food? All these things played their part in every African war. We interviewed Cuban prisoners, as apologetic about their presence in Angola as are almost all prisoners about the circumstances which have brought them to confinement. The Cubans seemed to be well enough treated, but we were a visiting television team. Poor wretches, who knows what was done to them when they were not on show? I doubt that they survived to go home.

There were several farcical moments of the trip. Once we drove around a corner and found ourselves confronted by white soldiers in bush kit – obviously South African. As soon as they glimpsed our own white faces – and also our camera – they dashed into the undergrowth. South Africa's forces were not even officially deployed inside Angola, and they had stringent instructions not to be filmed there. When we questioned senior UNITA figures on camera about the South African presence, they cheerfully denied that there was an Afrikaner in their territory, though it seemed unlikely that Angolans were flying the Pumas and Alouettes we saw overhead almost daily. We passed – and filmed – South African army trucks on the road. We ate and slept in various empty, echoing small hotels, factories, office buildings abandoned by the Portuguese. God knows how the local population ate at all – work and industry of any kind was at a standstill. Only the barest subsistence farming continued – along with the war, of course. You were a farmer or a soldier, or a mere victim. One lunch, I was sitting next to two impressively smart, well-turned-out young Zambian-trained UNITA officers. They quizzed us closely about life in Europe. How tall were the buildings? Had we ever seen snow? What were our houses like in London? Suddenly, one of them glanced at the book by my plate. Whenever I am abroad, I read about people and things utterly disconnected from the job in hand – *Mansfield Park* in Vietnam, Gibbon in Cyprus, Trollope in the Middle East, and C. V. Wedgwood's *The King's War* in Angola. Our lieutenant peered fascinated at the picture on the cover of the Wedgwood, depicting Oliver Cromwell in full armour. 'What is this?' he demanded. 'Is it a robot?' I was overwhelmed by the cultural chasm which suddenly opened up between us. His question was neither foolish nor ill-educated, it merely reflected the fact that men in armour have no place in the history and experience of Africa.

General Samuel Chiwale, UNITA's enormous senior field commander, took us on a tour of his area attended by his Chief of Staff, a charming man who had acquired fluent English at mission school and embraced the irresistible name of Colonel Smart Chata. Officers and men wore a hotchpotch of old Portuguese army uniform and equipment, and carried weapons from a dozen countries. At each village, crowds of school-children had been assembled to sing for us – or for the general – with that wonderful African rhythmic cadence which made irrelevant the propaganda lyrics extolling Savimbi's powers vertical and horizontal, as the intrepid traverser of the bush and sexual superman. The village elders came solemnly forth to greet the general, each in his aged solar topee, the headman wearing a yachting cap and an old wing collar and tie. A tyre fell off one of the Landrover wheels on the way back, but nobody seemed to mind. We watched a soldier who had run out of matches lighting his cigarette with a magnifying glass against the sun.

We were working close to the Benguela Railway, once the vital link between Zambia's copper mines and the sea, now severed by war and high explosive in several places. UNITA announced that they would take us to view a bridge recently blown across a river by the MPLA. Our mode of transport, it emerged, was to be a small diesel rail trolley, into the cab of which were crammed the driver, a couple of soldiers, the *Panorama* crew, and three other Western correspondents. We bucketed along the track in fine style for some miles, grateful for the breeze of our motion to assuage the heat, even if we were too cramped for any comfort. Then our escort grunted, and pointed down the track. Ahead of us lay a visibly tangled and twisted sculpture of rails and girders bent upwards into the sky – our destination. The driver applied the brake. How droll, I thought, if like every other form of transport in Angola, this one proved uncontrollable. We bucketed on. The driver pulled the brake again, and again. Nothing happened. We had time only for a few moments of sheer terror, before the trolley rushed briskly at the twisted steel of the bridge. We were stopped dead by collision with a bridge section bent across what was left of the line, and thrown into a hopeless jumble of black and white bodies in the trolley cab, gazing horrified at the river below us. It was a scene that would have enchanted Buster Keaton, or indeed any maker of early silent comedy. It seemed a fine moment for a display of cool good sense. 'Nobody move,' I said authoritatively, appalled by the notion that one lurch would precipitate us into the torrent. I have seldom been so comprehensively ignored. There was a brutal rush for the doors and windows, and a few seconds later our shaken group was standing by the bridge, laughing uneasily at the trolley, poised at a steep upward angle on the broken rails, as if on a ski jump. With the help of some bewildered passers-by – in Africa you are seldom alone for long – the trolley was eventually righted. Our pictures were taken. We rattled in subdued spirits back to the station. Farce is inseparable from much of foreign corresponding, and these moments are rendered no less comic for their proximity to disaster.

The Benguela Railway also, however, provided the most vivid and marvellous experience of that trip. We travelled along its intact reaches for many miles through UNITA territory in a long, slow freight train, pulled by a huge old steam locomotive. The trucks were laden with carelessly armed UNITA soldiers. A special passenger coach was coupled to the rear for us, such as we had never seen outside old American Wild West films. It was the sort of carriage Butch Cassidy might have run along the roof of. We were entranced. We sat in the station while the engine hissed and puffed and wheezed magnificently for three hours before finally breaking into motion. The train travelled at snail's pace through the bush, far into the night, its fifteen-hour passage to Luso interrupted by frequent stops and mysterious shouted conversations between soldiers and unseen voices by the track. We halted at a succession of tiny stations where soldiers stood smoking in the darkness, stirring mealie meal over their little fires, laughing and joking because everybody on the train seemed to know everyone at every station. Robin and I decided to make ourselves comfortable on the woodstack in the tender of the great locomotive. Hour after hour we lay there into the night, talking, listening to the sounds of Africa and the engine, sniffing the scents, gazing on the sights, enthralled by the experience.

'Are you thinking what I'm thinking?' I asked Robin, many hours down the line.

'Yes,' he said.

'It's incredible that anyone is paying us money to voyage across Africa in the middle of the night on the back of one of the last great wood-burning locomotives in the world.'

For both of us, this was the most wonderful railway journey of our lives, perhaps of anyone's. We were filthy dirty – deep down dirty in the way everyone becomes in Africa, when there are no baths to be had and red dust has rubbed into every pore of one's skin and hair, never mind clothing. I was grateful that I had given up smoking cigarettes three years earlier, and was not suffering the sort of deprivation which gnawed every hour at some of our colleagues. We were eating pretty horrible food, and we had finished our whisky. To be embarrassingly personal for a moment, I was suffering from piles, that most debilitating and humiliating of conditions, which had been worsening for years, and now caused me to bleed constantly, not much to the benefit of my strength. All this receded into insignificance, however, amid such a glorious moment as that which Robin and I shared on the Benguela Railway, where we savoured a sense of Africa of the kind that makes foreign correspondents go on and on with our curious and sometimes dispiriting trade.

I loved Angola and the Angolans then, and felt a surge of deep pity for their plight, prisoners of a war that can have meant so little to so many of them, save privation and death at the hands of alien forces.

I have written in the context of Vietnam about the massive limitation of television journalism – that an event can play little part in a broadcast story unless it has been recorded on film, which is often very hard to do, especially in a war zone. In Angola, we suffered a frustrating experience of this. We waited days for the opportunity to interview UNITA's leader, Dr Jonas Savimbi. One night in Silvaporto, we were quartered in the old Portuguese governor's palace. It was hard to decide whether to be captivated by the sheer incongruity of this monstrously decorated edifice in the middle of Africa, heavy with gilt and plush, or merely to be dismayed by the olympic tastelessness of it. The building was almost unique in the region, in that it had not been looted. It survived as a museum piece, perhaps because no sane person could have coveted its contents. We wondered at the ornate furniture, the cabinets full of cut glass, the European miniatures on the wall, the heavy curtains in the bedrooms, the hideous plush and velvet with which the late Portuguese ruler had sought to impose European culture, as he understood it, upon the millions of square miles of violent green bush beyond his walls. We sat eating the usual mess of rice at a massive oak table in a dining room that would have graced the lower end of the French brothel trade *circa* 1880, by the light of hurricane lanterns. People who eat in Chinese restaurants tend not to think much about their rice. But in Angola, there was soggy rice and long rice and short rice. One savoured the distinction, because there wasn't much else. We were offered fish. We were 500 miles inland, however, and after a sniff on the train a day or so earlier at the piscine delicacies we were now being offered, we found it prudent to plead vegetarianism. It was almost midnight. Suddenly the door rattled heavily. It was thrown open to reveal the bearded and green-bereted figure of Savimbi, clad in a black leather jacket, heavily ornamented with bangles and bracelets, and escorted by a huge bodyguard. I have seen bodyguards armed with pistols, sub-machine-guns, rifles, even swords, but never before a man boasting as his personal weapon a rocket propelled grenade launcher, which he laid carelessly beside our dinner. I found myself fascinated by the vision of what might happen to an assassin who threw himself at UNITA's President and encountered the bodyguard's terrible instrument. The malefactor would presumably disappear in a thunderous explosion and sheet of flame which would take with it most of the presidential staff.

'Good evening, gentlemen,' said Savimbi, seating himself beside us. 'I am sorry it has taken so long for us to meet, but as you may have seen for yourselves, travelling is not altogether easy.' His English was perfect, his manners would have equipped him for any university common room or, for that matter, drawing room. He was the most fluent, persuasive, magnetic African leader I have ever met. He glanced around. 'Do you want to get ready to do your interview?' We looked blank.

'We've got no lights. Can we do it first thing in the morning?'

'Alas, gentlemen, I must be gone before morning. Shall we just talk, then?'

We talked. Far into the night we sat at our table in the flickering glare of the lanterns and discussed Angola and Africa and the world's attitude to them, while his bodyguard sat in impassive silence, contemplating his enormous weapon. Savimbi, the grandson of a chief and son of a Protestant pastor, now in his early forties, reminisced about his days fighting the

Portuguese, about the heavy-handedness of the Russians and his time studying political science in Lausanne. Surely he must be embarrassed by the support of the white South African government? He shrugged. 'Sadly, gentlemen, one must make war as one can, not as one would.' All of us were captivated by this compelling man. He preached so-called peasant socialism and professed to despise the Christianity in which he had been reared. Bibles were burned in his territory. In the intervening generation since our meeting, Savimbi has become a discredited figure. His association with the South Africans made him a pariah in Africa. When Pretoria's white government fell, his chief prop was gone. He has continued to command enough local support to go on fighting his war against the Luanda government, but he has been tarnished by too many betrayals and acts of duplicity, too long a naked grapple for power at the expense of the people to whom he professes to want to bring peace. Like so many of his kind all over the world, victory and diamonds rather than peace now seem to dominate his objectives. The world long ago became disillusioned with Savimbi. But the power of his presence and his personality was real enough, that night in Silvaporto almost a quarter of a century ago. When he suddenly stood up to go, vanishing into the darkness with his lumbering human shadow at his heels, we were left with the image and the memory of a remarkable man, whose fall from grace I lamented for many years, as Angola's civil war dragged inconclusively onward – and persists to this day.

We flew out of the country a day or two later, by courtesy of Mr Rowland's aircraft once more. We were all pretty hungry, as dirty as I have ever been, and I was almost doubled up by my damnable piles and their consequences. As we edited the footage in London, I had to stand clutching a wall of the cutting room for support, in my agony. Our film was transmitted under the title *With a Little Help from their Friends*, and we were proud of it – justly so, I think. We explored the extraordinary intricacies of all the nations entangled in Angola – Zambians, Zairians, Americans, Russians, Cubans and of course South Africans. 'Only a foreigner,' I said in my commentary, 'would dare to perceive absolute virtue in any of the factions fighting this war.' What we had seen owed more to warlordism and tribalism than to any ideological contest for the soul of Africa. But those were the days when the Cold War was still booming, when the United States and the Soviets were competing across much of Africa through their rival clients, at terrible cost to the continent's people. I looked at our film again a few months ago, and was gripped anew by the long camera pans down the ranks of that guerrilla army, singing their songs for us on the parade ground in the bush. What we had been doing was not strictly war reporting, because we saw no shots fired in anger – not for want of trying. But it was an extraordinary tale of an extraordinary time and place.

CHAPTER TWELVE

Yoni

MOST JOURNALISTS VALUE what passes for integrity in our trade, but almost all of us have sometime tarnished it in one fashion or another. I have had a very happy life, and I have written here about some successes and some marvellous experiences. But if this story is to be an honest one, I must now describe one of the sorriest episodes of my own career.

On the afternoon of 27 June 1976, Air France flight 139 from Tel Aviv to Paris was hijacked by Arab terrorists with 246 passengers and 10 crew, and diverted to Entebbe, Uganda, in the midst of Africa. Uganda was then ruled by one of the continent's bloodiest and most unpredictable tyrants, Idi Amin. Most of the passengers were Jewish. Within hours of AF 139's landing, the terrorists began to issue extravagant demands for the release of the hostages they held at Entebbe airport. It became plain that President Amin would not intervene. If the Ugandans were not colluding with the terrorists, they were certainly not impeding them. The world waited apprehensively to see what would come next. Surrender or mass murder − either seemed equally plausible and repugnant. For five days, the passengers lay under guard in the Old Terminal at Entebbe airport, and people of many nations hung hour by hour upon the outcome of the drama.

On the morning of 4 July, American Bicentennial Day, the world awoke to hear news of a miracle. In the middle of the previous night, Israeli C-130 transport aircraft had landed covertly at Entebbe to disgorge a storming party disguised in Landrovers and a Mercedes. Israeli commandos assaulted the Old Terminal, killed all the terrorists, and rescued every passenger of AF 139, save an elderly Jewish woman who had been removed sick to hospital in the city, and was then never seen again. The assault force suffered only one fatal casualty. In a world of tragedies and frustrations, few people old enough to notice the event have forgotten the great uplift that day gave us. Terror was not invincible. Outrage could be fought and conquered. But only the Israelis, the world acknowledged, could have displayed the boldness and brilliance to launch and execute such an operation, half a continent from home. I was in New York to report the Bicentennial. I saw the euphoria which reigned on every television network that morning, as the news from Entebbe spilled joy into the exhilaration of America's national celebration. 'For this one day,' said the great Walter Cronkite on CBS, 'we have earned the right to be "sunshine patriots".' With hindsight, that day might also be perceived as the high-water mark of Israel's standing in the world, as a bastion of Western values in the Middle East, and a force for the pursuit of justice and freedom. Thereafter, amid the growing rancour of failed diplomacy, the brutal suppression of Palestinian dissent and the invasion of Lebanon, world sentiment drifted steadily away from support for Israel's policies. But the memory of 4 July 1976 deserves to be preserved, for one of the greatest feats of arms in a humanitarian cause since the Second World War.

Six months after Entebbe the publisher George Weidenfeld, most passionate of Israel's British sympathizers, asked to see me. I had met George before. Two or three years earlier he asked me, as he has asked almost every literate person in Britain at one time or another, to write a book for him – I think he suggested a biography of Rufus Isaacs. Not one for me, I said. This time, in the flat on the Embankment where he has entertained so many politicians and authors, actual and aspiring, he asked how much I knew about Entebbe. As much as the rest of the world, I said. He told me that the officer who commanded the assault force in the raid, Israel's only fatal casualty that night, was named Colonel Yoni Netanyahu. Yoni had been one of Israel's most successful and experienced soldiers, a man a few months younger than myself, thirty-one. Now, the Israelis wanted a book written about the colonel and the secret unit he led. They liked the idea that this should be done by a non-Jew, whose work would command more credibility outside Israel. They had been impressed by what I had done in the Yom Kippur War. Would I be interested? I was immediately keen, but I asked the obvious question: 'Are the Israelis really prepared to open up? If they are, it would be a wonderful story. But I know what their censors can be like.'

'For this, they are prepared to give all the access you need. The Prime Minister, Shimon Peres, is personally committed. With him behind you, you would be able to talk to anybody.'

I had never concealed my admiration for the Israeli army. The chance to spend months studying its operations and its people at close quarters seemed unmissable. George said that in the next few days, Yoni Netanyahu's father was coming to London. His approval was obviously essential to the project. I must meet him.

I shook hands with Benzion Netanyahu, a short, chubby figure in his sixties, in the coffee shop of the Royal Garden Hotel in Kensington. He had spent much of his life in the United States, where he now taught at a Jewish college in upstate New York, though he maintained a family house in

Jerusalem. He was immensely proud of his own intellectual credentials, as a lifelong student of Jewish history and thought. His family had emigrated from Poland to Palestine in 1920. He became a close associate of Vladimir Jabotinsky, leader of the so-called Revisionist movement, right-wingers who sponsored the Irgun terrorist group. Benzion himself had taken no part in the terrorist campaign, and went to New York to raise funds for the movement just before the Second World War. Thereafter, he divided his life between Israel and the United States, with the emphasis on the latter. At George's suggestion he had read my biography of Charles I's lieutenant-general in Scotland during the Civil War, *Montrose*, which was newly published in Britain. He sought to explain to me that his son had been both a soldier and an intellectual, an important thinker as well as a man of action. 'You are very young to understand these things . . . I ask myself – do you know enough about Jews, about Israel? . . . Yet perhaps the man who has written about the hero Montrose can also write about the hero my son. You would have to read everything he wrote. You would have to understand what being a Jew, what being a soldier of Israel means . . .'

Much of this drifted past my head. I wanted only to convince this emotional old man that I could do justice to his son, to win this project which offered so much to me – not least, a large cash advance. We parted amicably enough. A few days later, I heard from George: 'Benzion is happy that you should do the book. We only need to arrange the contract.' I signed with an exuberant flourish. A few weeks earlier, I had agreed another book contract with another publisher, to write a big study on a subject that had always fascinated me – the Allied bomber offensive against Germany in the Second World War. I decided to make a career change. For the next two years, I would abandon journalism. We would sell our house in London, and move to rural Ireland to write these two books which, I believed, could transform my life. My wife Tricia, five months pregnant with our second child, was understandably dismayed, but I cajoled her into uneasy acquiescence. We sold up in London, found a charming house in County Kilkenny and at the end of March 1977 our little family transported ourselves there, not without apprehension and some heartache. Then I set about exploring Yoni Netanyahu and the Israeli army, for the book, the epic, which I believed could make my fortune as a writer on war.

I went first to America, to see the Netanyahu family. I spent several days in Boston, talking to Yoni's younger brother, who was studying at MIT, living in a university apartment building with his wife, Micky. A tough, assured, young man who had also served in Yoni's old unit the Sayeret Matkal, Ben Nitay — for Binyamin Netanyahu had assumed a more manageable name for his American life — possessed the fluency and efficiency of a superior marketing man, which is how I imagined he planned to end up. While he grinned a lot, he was not strong on humour, but I was not in Boston in search of a soulmate. His grasp of the English language was perfect, of course, since he had spent more of his own life in America than in Israel. He heaped documents and photocopies upon me, both about his brother and about Israel.

Although several years younger than me, Binyamin was a man of overbearing force of personality and self-confidence. He and his family had achieved nationwide fame in Israel since his brother's death. Already, streets were being named after Yoni, who was hailed as a national hero. Looking back, I think Binyamin was already reviewing his career options in the light of his new status as the brother of a martyr of Israel. Before Entebbe, many people had expected him to make a career in the United States, but in Jerusalem later, I met several family friends who said wryly that they thought Bibi – as he was known there – was rooting to become a future prime minister of Israel.

Yoni's parents talked about their son with all the fervour one might expect from an elderly couple who had lost their first-born in such circumstances. Cela, his mother, was somewhat appalled by my ignorance of Jewish life. 'He does not know what a bar mitzvah is, this boy!' she cried. Benzion was more concerned that I should grasp the historic position of Israel, as he perceived it. I was bombarded by books with titles such as *The Plot to Destroy Israel, The Jewish Revolution, The Case for Israel*. Much as I admired the country, most of this stuff seemed well off the board. But I said nothing, and settled down to read Yoni's school essays, and some of the pieces he had written during a semester he spent at Harvard studying philosophy, physics and maths in the autumn of 1967, after serving with a paratroop unit in the Six-Day War. His parents had passionately wanted him to leave the army behind, to gain the credentials to become an academic. They were thrilled to have a son at Harvard, and deeply dismayed early in 1968 when Yoni had announced that he proposed to return to Israel, and to a career in the army. This grave young man found himself utterly out of sympathy with life in the United States of the late 1960s, amid the hippies and draft dodgers and political anarchy of a country rent by Vietnam, race, and strife on the streets.

I flew on to Tel Aviv, to start weeks of meetings and interviews with a long procession of serving and former Israeli soldiers. It was one of the most fascinating experiences of my life. I thought I knew Israel quite well, but now I found myself exploring it in a new fashion. I forget who said to me, 'This is not a country – it is an experiment,' but it seemed profoundly true. I spent hours with men who had taken part in some of Israel's greatest campaigns – as did Yoni – and who were also among the most distinguished veterans of her special forces. Hour after hour and day after day, I drove through Galilee, Judea, Samaria, exploring scenes from Israel's military past. I sat in austere little lounges in kibbutzes, and anonymous apartment blocks in towns up and down the country, listening to extraordinary stories of Israel's wars and anti-terrorist campaigns. In most Western societies today, the army is a side street, even a cul-de-sac. In Israel, it is a reality that pervades every aspect of work, thought, talk. One of Yoni's friends said to me, 'In this country, if you want to see creative brilliance, look for it in the army. Thirty years of fighting for survival have focused the finest imaginative minds in the country in Zahal.' Israelis like to say that there is no military caste in their country, yet their army is a fact of life that weaves itself into every strand of national life, to prepare for and argue about, to train with and love and hate with unique passion. National service in Israel is not as it was in America or even France, where the rich and clever could always readily escape. It is a badge of shame for any young Israeli not to do his part for his country at eighteen or nineteen, and as a reservist thereafter. Every general's reputation is grist for a family Friday night debate. Most Israeli girls can tell a T-72 from an M-60. I wrote later: 'Israelis have always been unhappily conscious of the corruption and dirtiness of their own politics. They loved Zahal, because it seemed to them to represent something clean, something pure that they could look out upon from their grey, jerry-built apartment blocks in Tel Aviv, Eilat, Jerusalem. Yoni loved the sense of virtue and purpose that he found in the army.' I learned about the Kelet where recruits are trained, about the manner in which men call officers by their first

names, and about the sense of precariousness which is fundamental to all that Israelis say and do, at home or upon the
battlefield.

I went on an exercise with one of the border units,
marching across the hills of Judea to get the feel of a hike with
a crack Zahal battalion. On the Golan Heights, Shaul, former
second-in-command of the tank battalion Yoni commanded
after the 1973 war, took me out in a Centurion, bucking and
twisting over the rocky ground, to understand what it was like
to fight a tank, learning the fire-direction sequence that sent a
105 mm shell tearing through the still air: *'Totah-Hash-Tank-
Alpayim-Al-Esh!'* followed by the fierce back blast that swept
over the turret as the gun fired. A tall beanpole of a man with
big, sad, dark eyes, Shaul's smile enchanted every girl in Tel
Aviv. He was a Brazilian from an Orthodox family who had
come to Israel at the age of thirteen, and still possessed all the
grace and charm of Latin America. 'Yoni is very serious,' he
said to me. 'When Yoni is going into battle, he makes a speech
to the men about the glory of Israel and the memory of the
Maccabees. I am not so serious. When I hear war has started
again, I say, "Men, I have great news for you. Your second-in-
command has a chance of making colonel."' Shaul did not
enjoy the Six-Day War. 'The first time I saw dead Egyptians
by Um Katef, I found I think about their mothers and feel
sad . . .'

Shaul told me not to believe any nonsense about the
supposedly professional relationships between men and girl
soldiers in Zahal. There were plenty of affairs in uniform,
whenever soldiers had the chance. Even when Shaul's tank
battalion was deployed for operations on the Golan, two of his
officers came to see him, to demand formal permission to sleep
with their soldier girlfriends in camp. Shaul brooded and then
sighed. 'Since every time we've needed you for the last month

we've had to turn out the whole camp to find you, yes, I think on the whole I prefer to know where you are . . .' Yoni himself, when he commanded the battalion, was sleeping with one of the girl soldiers under his command, Bruria, who followed him to his next posting and lived with him until his death.

I met officers and men who had taken part in the storming of the hijacked Sabena Boeing at Lod in May 1972 – including Bibi Netanyahu – and those responsible for the kidnapping of the Syrian generals in Lebanon the following month, and the landing from the sea to attack the PLO leadership in Beirut in April 1973. Even by the standards of armies, they were extraordinarily young. At the time of Entebbe, the average age of the Sayeret's specialist staff officers was twenty-three. Some were professional special forces officers and men, who never questioned the need for absolute ruthlessness in serving the interests of Israel. Others, I found, had been much less comfortable about some of their missions. One man in particular, who served as a conscript in the Sayeret Matkal, said, 'They were too tough for me. I didn't like some of the things we had to do. I remember when we were being briefed for the Beirut attack, and our team under Yoni was to take out Abu Youssef, Arafat's deputy, in his apartment among his family. When the briefing was over and the CO asked if there were any questions, Arik – a pseudonym – shot up his hand and asked like a wolf, "Yeah – who shoots the children?"' It is worth emphasizing that no one did shoot the children. But naively, I was shocked by the story, and the attitude of mind it revealed. From other stories I heard, there was no doubt Arik was indeed a ruthless and committed killer, who disliked taking prisoners. The curtain of Israel's security had been lifted in an extraordinary fashion, to show me how the country made war. I saw and heard many things that filled me with admiration – but others which made me flinch.

The day after the Beirut raid in which Abu Youssef had been killed, Yoni was driving through Bethlehem with Yael, an old girlfriend who worked for Israeli television. She prised out of him the admission of his own part in the raid, and asked why Zahal had to kill people in such a way. Her own husband had died with Israel's paratroops in Jerusalem in 1967. She said, 'I always used to worry about Zvi, about what he would have been like after he had killed someone. In the end it wasn't necessary, because someone else killed him, but I still wondered.'

'It's the easiest thing in the world,' Yoni replied, 'if you can shoot it out at long range, lying behind a sand dune and firing at a man. You don't relate to him. You needn't have worried about Zvi. He'd have come home the same man. But the sort of thing we did last night? It's disgusting. It has to be done, but don't kid yourself for one moment that one doesn't feel it.' He braked among one of those crowds of Arab children who dart dangerously around every car as it moves through every village. 'I won't drive any faster,' he said with a grin to the boys, 'because as Yael will tell you, you kids are the future of this country.'

I was conscious of the irony of old Benzion Netanyahu's position, as a sponsor of Irgun's terrorism thirty years earlier. He was outraged by any comparison. He affirmed with the same assurance as Menachem Begin that Irgun never committed atrocities against women and children, killed only Arab fighters and servants of the British government, and would have hurt no one in the 1947 destruction of the King David Hotel in Jerusalem if the British had heeded Irgun's warning. Like so many Israelis, the Netanyahus simply demanded: 'What can Palestinians know of this green land, when it is we who have made it green?' Benzion Netanyahu said to me, 'Under

Arafat, the Russian and Arab traditions of total annihilation and terror meet. Name me the Arab state where a minority is treated with justice or mercy. I was educated to believe that under tyranny, resistance by force is justifiable.'

I met Iddo, Yoni's second brother, who seemed a gentler and frankly less effectual figure than the others, though thus in some respects a more sympathetic one. He, too, had felt compelled to do his military service not merely in a line infantry unit, but in the Sayeret Matkal. At Bibi Netanyahu's dinner table in Jerusalem, I listened with crawling dismay to Bibi talking about the future of his country. 'In the next war, if we do it right we'll have a chance to get all the Arabs out,' he said. 'We can clear the West Bank, sort out Jerusalem.' He joked about the Golani Brigade, the Israeli infantry force in which so many men were North African or Yemenite Jews. 'They're okay as long as they're led by white officers.' He grinned. He and his kin despised what they perceived as the decadence of the West and of Europe, such feeble friends to Israel in her hours of need. I saw revealed at tables of that sort in those days a scorn for weakness, an exaggerated respect for strength and toughness, which made me deeply uneasy because it possessed a historical resonance of the most baneful kind. Jimmy Cameron's words after Yom Kippur came back to my mind. I was among those who had too readily conceded an exaggerated respect for Israel's military virtues.

Menachem Begin, Benzion Netanyahu's old comrade among the Revisionists, had just become Israel's prime minister. The Israeli Right were exulting in the conviction that under his leadership there would be no more 'weakness', no more 'surrenders' by Israel at the negotiating table. In private arguments, it was dismaying to hear how often the 'Holocaust card' was played, if the going got rough: 'You've got to let us do this – because of the Holocaust.' I was in Jerusalem, working on the book, when President Sadat of Egypt made his ground-breaking state visit, offered his extraordinary olive branch to Israel. I wrote for the *Evening Standard*, 'For thirty years Israel has been compelled to live as a beleaguered fortress. It is now in Mr Begin's hands to show that he is capable of leading a great sortie to civilization. The omens yesterday seemed inauspicious.' I was ever more deeply troubled by the gap, the yawning chasm, between my own view of the Middle East, and that of the Netanyahus.

One man in Israel was from the outset profoundly hostile to my assignment – ironically, of them all, the one I admired most. Ehud Barak was a stocky little kibbutznik with deep, piercing eyes, immense charm, and also a fine pianist. His grandfather had been murdered in a pogrom in 1913, his grandmother gassed in Auschwitz. As a boy, one of his first memories was of asking his mother why an old woman in the kibbutz eating place secreted a piece of bread under her arm every day before she left, though there was plenty of bread. His mother told him about the experience of the concentration camp. Ehud had been commander – *ha mefaked* – of the Sayeret and led many of Israel's most brilliant commando operations. He went on to become army Chief of Staff, leader of the Labour Party – and at last in 1999, Prime Minister. I found him captivating: shrewd, sharp, witty, the embodiment of Israel's genius and of its ruthlessness. At our first meeting, he sat coiled like a steel spring, staring intently at me. 'I am going to talk to you,' he said, 'because I have been ordered to do so. But I want to make it clear that I believe this whole project is madness. Madness. The idea of admitting a foreigner, not even a Jew, to our secrets seems to me very foolish indeed.' Then he did talk, brilliantly, about Yoni and about the Israeli army and about *ha yehida* – 'the unit', as everyone referred to the Sayeret Matkal – and its battles and operations.

Then I flew back to Ireland to write. During the routine search of departing passengers, the Lod security men explored my baggage with mounting suspicion, astonishment and horror. There were marked military maps, documents, notes, photographs, all containing references to people and organizations whose very existence was never avowed aloud in Israel. For once, I was wholly relaxed. 'You'd better call the Sayeret Matkal,' I told the glowering security men. I was held for half an hour, through a flurry of urgent telephoning. Then I was reluctantly told I could go. I knew I had the makings of a marvellous story. As I sat at my typewriter, gazing out of the window upon the lush green fields of Kilkenny, more and more strongly I became aware that the tale I was putting together was not the tale the Netanyahu family – or the government of Israel – wanted. I wrote it anyway.

I perceived Yoni Netanyahu as a tragic figure. He had been reared and indoctrinated all his youth to become the intellectual soldier, the embodiment of Benzion Netanyahu's ideal of militant Zionism. Yet from my own reading of his youthful writing, I detected no spark of the genius the family professed to see – rather, I saw a troubled young man of moderate intelligence, striving to come to terms with intellectual concepts beyond his grasp. I believed his flight from Harvard reflected less a sense of duty to Israel – though heaven knows, there was no lack of that – and more the fact that Yoni found being a soldier less difficult than being anything else. He was neither universally loved nor universally admired, in the army or out of it. Indeed, he was actively disliked by more than a few of his men. It seemed to me that his family had placed a huge burden upon his shoulders – not least the burden of being what his father had not been. Benzion Netanyahu, for all his extravagant commitment to Zionism, to the cause of 'Greater Israel', had spent much of his life in the United States, and had been almost invariably absent from the country whenever it was at war. Benzion was never one of those many Israelis who rushed for the airport to return to their own country, to be with their own people, when war came, as in his lifetime it so often did. Some of Benzion's Israeli critics echoed Kipling's contempt for those who 'killed Kruger with their mouths'. I was not foolish enough to suppose that I could write honestly about my own vision of the Netanyahu family in the book, but private perceptions deeply coloured my prose.

Yoni's own letters became more and more melancholy in the last years of his life. I believed that, by the time he died at Entebbe, he had reached an impasse in his own life. He had been soldiering and fighting for a decade. A youthful marriage had broken up, his brief attempts at academic life had gone nowhere. He was a man who lived and died almost without personal possessions. He seemed a cripplingly lonely figure, who had lost his way. There seemed wretchedly little laughter in his story. There was no doubt that he was a remarkable professional soldier. Few men of his age of any army in the world had seen more operational service. He strove for very high standards on the battlefield and off it. If there seemed little there to love, I could see a good deal to respect – and to pity. Greatly as I have always admired soldiers, and soldiers of Israel, the vision of a man who seemed unable to find peace anywhere save at war had to be a tragic one. That is not to suggest that Yoni was a killer, one of those special forces psychopaths of whom every army possesses a few. I suspect that he killed sadly, as he did so much else. One night after he told his friend Shlomo that he was to take command of the Sayeret Matkal, Shlomo said in exasperation, 'Why do it? If you stay alive, you're going to be a general. But if you go on like this, you're going to be killed. Why push in the queue for hell? If you wind up there, you're going to have to stay.'

The book was written, the manuscript dispatched to George Weidenfeld. I had spent a lot of money doing the research, and I waited anxiously for the acceptance cheque as I started work on *Bomber Command*. There was a pause, then some uneasy words from my editor at Weidenfelds. There was trouble about the book. First, the Netanyahus were very, very unhappy about the manuscript. They thought that it wholly misrepresented and misunderstood Yoni. Second, and much more serious, the Israeli government had made it plain that under no circumstances could the book be published in anything like its existing form, because it revealed far more than Zahal was willing to admit about military operations and about the special forces. For a start, there could be no mention even of the existence of the Sayeret Matkal. I was appalled. How could the book hang together, save around the Sayeret and its men? Without the Sayeret as a theme, I saw no story worth telling. Could I at least have my cheque, to keep the family afloat while we argued about this? Er, no, said Weidenfelds. The contract specified that the book must be 'accepted', and 'acceptable' was what it was not. Acceptable to whom? I demanded. The Israeli government had themselves initiated this project, approved all my meetings and contacts. Yes, but unfortunately the Israeli government had now changed. Shimon Peres was in opposition. Menachem Begin's government had sought the advice of Zahal, who made it plain that they strongly opposed publication. That was that.

It was the beginning of a nightmare period. The Netanyahu family organized a remarkable letter-writing campaign. Almost every single person I had interviewed wrote personally to me, to declare that I had misunderstood and underestimated Yoni as a soldier, as a scholar and as a human being. In the argument which now began, more than once it was suggested bitterly that there was so much I could not understand, because I was not a Jew – a nice irony, since this was alleged to have been one of my credentials for writing the book in the first place. To this day, I would not venture to assert that I was entirely right, and that those who knew Yoni were wrong. I have made more than my share of mistakes and misjudgements in my writing. But never in my career before or since have I been told that I wholly misinterpreted someone whom I have studied as closely as I studied Yoni. I had run up a big overdraft. I had no employer to turn to. I had no more income in the pipeline until I finished *Bomber Command*. I was desperate for the money for the book. I telephoned George Weidenfeld personally and pleaded in vain. George's relationship with Israel had been a dominant force in his life. He had no intention of quarrelling with the Jewish state about me. I would be paid only if and when a deal could be agreed for the book's publication on terms acceptable to all the interested parties.

I had always found Ehud Barak the most intelligent, the most admirable of the senior Israeli soldiers with whom I dealt. I tried to telephone him and arrange to meet. He was in the United States, on an attachment to the Israeli Embassy. I flew to Washington, where anyway I had some research to do on another project, and met him. Ehud was polite, charming as ever, but his words were steel. 'I warned you,' he said. 'I warned you. You are dealing here with the most vital interests of the state of Israel. Do yourself and everyone else a favour. Forget this book. Throw it away. Go and do something else.'

'I can't,' I said despairingly, in what with hindsight was one of the least principled and most humiliating moments of my life, 'I need the money.'

Ehud shrugged. 'There is nothing I can do. I was asked my opinion. I have given it. This book should not be published.'

In New York, I talked to my agent John Cushman, who had no part in the Yoni deal, and with the American publisher of *Bomber Command*, Jim Wade of Dial Press. The three of us met in the bar of the St Regis. Was there a chance we could defy the Israelis, go ahead and publish the book anyway, under a different imprint? Jim, the most charming and resolute of men, said unhesitatingly, 'I only wish there was. I'd love to do it. But this is a Jewish town. No publisher with a brain is going to touch a book the Israelis say drives a tank through their security. They'd injunct you – and win. The Netanyahu family will rain on the whole thing from a great height, and anyway they can legally stop you using any copyright material such as Yoni's letters, which blows most of the story away. Sorry, but that's the way it is.'

I flew back to Ireland consumed with misery and self-pity. My old friend Thomas Pakenham dismissed the second, at least. 'Only you, Max,' he said cheerfully, 'would have supposed that you could make a deal with either George Weidenfeld *or* the Israelis for a project like this, never mind both, and have a chance of staying your own man.' He was right, of course. Greed had impelled me, not only for the money, but also for a wonderful story. Now, I wanted merely to escape on almost any terms from the project and from the threat of bankruptcy.

I wish that I could now describe how truth – or my version of truth – triumphed; how I walked away from the shoddy negotiations; refused to compromise merely for cash. It was not like that. A deal was struck in the end. It always is. After weeks of tense and bad-tempered telephone calls and correspondence, I got my cheque. Weidenfelds eventually published a bowdlerized version of the book, after the manuscript had been rendered acceptable both to the Netanyahus and to the Israeli army. I did no publicity for *Yoni* on its publication, and enough had leaked out into Fleet Street about the book's sorry provenance to ensure that it was scantily reviewed. It did not become a *cause célèbre*, or indeed a *cause* anything. It was merely an ambitious young journalist's project that went disastrously wrong.

Looking back, I can honestly say that my own hostility to Israel's policy towards the Occupied Territories was born before the disaster over my book. When I was writing *Yoni*, I met many people whom I admire as much today as I did in 1977, Ehud Barak prominent among them. Those long months were not all wasted time, for the experience of researching the book taught me a great deal about the Israeli way of war, and about Israeli warriors, that have been of lasting use to me as a writer. Bibi Netanyahu, of course, became prime minister of Israel as I feared that he might, and his policies – still encouraged and promoted by his appallingly indefatigable octogenarian father – proved as disastrous as any of his early acquaintance might have expected. I have never set foot in Israel since 1977, and I feel towards the country something of the sadness and pain one cherishes towards a past lover with whom one quarrelled bitterly. I adored so much about the country, above all its courage. Yet I learned to fear its ruthlessness and absolute sense of self-interest. For all their virtues, so many of the Israelis I knew had come to believe there could be no place in their polity for charity or generosity of spirit. Little has happened since, to persuade an outsider that this has changed. Israel's policy towards the Palestinians has cost the country many of its most devoted friends in Europe and even the United States. Tragically, the nation has committed itself to a future founded upon the sword rather than upon justice. The spirit of the Netanyahus has thus far triumphed, even though Bibi was mercifully dispossessed of Israel's prime ministership in May 1999.

As is sometimes the way of things, my own career was redeemed from the brush with disaster which *Yoni* represented, by an unexpected stroke of fortune. *Bomber Command*, upon which I embarked with far less ambitious hopes and expectations than the Israeli book, was published in 1979. It became my first substantial critical success, and even sold well, too. It was awarded the Somerset Maugham Prize, and set me on the path to writing a succession of books about the Second World War, which occupied most of my life in the years that followed. To my family's heartfelt relief, we moved back from Kilkenny and settled in Northamptonshire. I ventured abroad only occasionally for newspapers and television companies, and heard no gunfire. I believed that my days of going to the wars were over. Researching books, I spent innumerable hours listening to the reminiscences of military veterans – in Britain, Germany, France, China, Korea, the United States. Perhaps the most important advantage I gained from the success of *Bomber Command* was the revival of self-confidence. I had been deeply shaken by the experience of *Yoni*. Were those bitter Israeli critics right? Was I prone so deeply to misunderstand the experience of others? Was my historical judgement about people and events fatally flawed? Over the years that followed, I wrote much about wars and warriors, and my books were kindly received, even by those who had experienced the battles I described in print. I began to believe that my love for soldiers and knowledge of their doings could enable me to interpret warfare successfully, above all for a new generation of readers who had never seen a battlefield. I thought I was now content to do this at second-hand. In future, I would research in archives and libraries, and leave others to wander battlefields. Fortune, however, had one more military experience in store for me, of a kind the wildest imagination could not have conceived before the first shots were fired.

CHAPTER THIRTEEN

Voyage to the South Atlantic

ONE FINE MORNING in April 1982, I was sitting before my typewriter at home in Northamptonshire, working on a book about the Normandy campaign. It was seven years since I had heard a shot fired in anger. I was staring sightlessly out of the window, seeking that leap of imagination essential to writing any history of such a kind. What was it like to be crouched in a bucketing landing craft approaching the coast of France on 6 June 1944? How did it feel to fight soaked in salt water and vomit? What did men say to each other in those last minutes before the battle enveloped them? The telephone rang. An old friend, Tom Bower, said, 'Isn't it amazing about the Argentine landing in the Falklands?' I don't watch television or listen to the radio when I am writing a book. The news of that extraordinary stroke by the military junta in Buenos Aires came as a thunderbolt. There had been a brisk and almost bloodless firefight, it seemed, before the tiny Royal Marine garrison surrounding the Governor's residence in Port Stanley surrendered to Argentine special forces. Then Buenos Aires assumed control of the destinies of the 1,500 residents of the Falklands, henceforward to be known as Los Malvinas.

Despite the wave of hysteria that followed at Westminster, in Whitehall and the media, most British people at first seemed inclined merely to lament a national humiliation. There was nothing inevitable about the events which followed the Argentine invasion of the Falklands, save the red faces of yet another British government overwhelmed by yet another unexpected and apparently irreversible event. One day back in 1975, I was lunching with Kenneth Baker, Edward Heath's parliamentary private secretary. I asked him how a future Tory administration could avoid a further defeat at the hands of striking coal miners. 'Very simple,' he said cleverly, 'we shan't make the mistake of taking on the miners again.' In 1982, despite Margaret Thatcher's triumph over the coal unions in the previous year, British governments were still deeply attuned to acquiescence in the process of decline. That the loss of a tiny colonial hangover 8,000 miles from Britain might now be reversed by force of arms, by fighting a war against Argentina to recover them, seemed at first fantastic, not least to me. It was Kenneth Baker, by a nice irony, who later revealed his own diary entry for 4 April 1982: 'I spoke to Max Hastings who told me "the whole expedition was madness . . . the game's not worth the candle . . . the colonial right of the party is baying for blood, and that is one of the most unpleasant scenes in British life".' In the light of what followed, I blush to be reminded of my first thoughts. Yet, in the beginning, the dispatch of the task force *did* seem an extraordinary idea. Whatever youthful jingoism my father promoted, I had long since become a committed European, profoundly sceptical about military adventurism. Thatcher was talking about fighting – going to war with horse, foot and guns in the year of our Lord 1982 – to recover some meaningless piece of real estate at the other side of the world. For God's sake. Take a pill. Lie down. The fever will pass. Flippant or not, that is how many people felt, including some at the summit of government and military command.

The Prime Minister did not lie down, nor take a pill. The fever did not pass. Instead, the carriers *Invincible* and *Hermes* were ordered to sea, and sailed with their escorts on 5 April. 3 Commando Brigade, Royal Marines, was readied to embark for the South Atlantic. Sea Harrier and Sea King squadrons were earmarked for service. The Royal Navy's two assault landing ships, those elderly veterans *Fearless* and *Intrepid*, prepared for a role no soldier or sailor could have imagined they would ever fulfil in earnest. And I sat before the television in Northamptonshire, gripped by the vision that a major British expeditionary force was mobilizing for the first time since Aden fifteen years before – without me. I was thirty-six, getting on a bit for battlefields unless one was among those rather sad middle-aged reporters incapable of anything else. I earned a good living chiefly by writing books. I had made up my mind never again to risk my neck under fire, especially since I had 'bottled out' of Saigon. Yet I liked to think that I knew as much about war corresponding as most journalists in Britain. I loved the British army more than any. If the unbelievable was to happen, if we were to fight, I had to be there. I was sure I could tell the story well. Come to that – never mind the story, to hell with my own scepticism about the cause – I wanted to be with these men on this unique post-imperial adventure. I was born several generations too late to go with Kitchener to Khartoum, with Roberts to Kabul, with Wolesley to crush Arabi Pasha. There was still time, however, to sail on a no less preposterous yet irresistibly romantic expedition, with Thatcher (by proxy at least) to the Falklands. After one of many tense conversations with the *Evening Standard*, for whom I still had an arrangement to contribute a piece a week while I was writing my book, I put down the telephone in the kitchen and said to my wife Tricia, 'I feel it's for this moment I was born.' (Promise – I really did say that.) 'I've *got* to go.'

'You should have grown out of all this by now. You say yourself you don't think there's actually going to be a war. And what about your Normandy book?'

'I can do that any time. There will never be another Falklands task force. Okay, so there's only a one-in-five chance that anything will happen. But I've *got* to take it.'

I began an increasingly feverish, round-the-clock struggle to win a passage to the South Atlantic. The *Standard* was happy for me to go as its man, but some of the paper's staff reporters were outraged to be passed over for the role by a part-timer, and protested fiercely to the editor. The Ministry of Defence grudgingly conceded a few places for correspondents to accompany the task force, to be balloted through the Newspaper Publishers' Association. Neither the *Standard*, nor half Fleet Street for that matter, was thus included. I rang Charles Douglas-Home, *The Times*'s editor, to wind up his outrage about the titles which were not represented. Charlie was outraged sure enough, and got busy winning a slot for *The Times*, but the *Standard* was no further forward. I tried Bernard Ingham, Margaret Thatcher's abrasive press secretary, pleading my experience and qualifications to join the fleet. The Royal Navy, it seemed, having loathed journalists since time immemorial, wanted to take no media at all to the South Atlantic. Only with the utmost reluctance were a few reporters allowed to sail with the *Hermes* battle group. In Northamptonshire, I was growing hysterical. 'I feel I don't want to go on living if I'm left behind on this one.' (I really said that, too.)

Most of Fleet Street's star war correspondents, however, felt differently. Several called me. 'Max, get it in your head: there isn't going to be a war. The shot just isn't on the table. You'll waste weeks of your life sailing in circles round and round the Atlantic – for nothing. If anything important looks like happening, you can do the same as the rest of us and fly out

Above: Rhodesia: the would-be hunter (right) in the bush in 1973 with a white farmer on a guinea fowl shoot.

Below: Angola 1976: some of Jonas Savimbi's men present arms for our BBC *Panorama* crew at their base near Silvaporto.

Above: The last act in Vietnam: the sort of scene which made so many of us succumb to the beauty of the country even amid the war: high-school girls in their ao dais cross a street in the hill station of Dalat, where we were filming.

Below: A shot I took on the road from Vung Tou to Saigon, thirty-six hours before the city fell. This was the last of the vast, terrible migrations of Vietnamese refugees fleeing before the communist advance.

One of my pictures in the compound of the American Embassy on the
final afternoon, waiting for evacuation: a US Marine waves back some of the
waiting crowd as a helicopter lands.

Right: The author, extremely frightened, waits his turn for a flight to the US Fleet.

Below: Safe out of Saigon: a group photograph of the correspondents who fled the city in the last days, aboard the US carrier *Okinawa*. The author is looking sideways on the right of the third standing row, one away from old BBC colleague Tom Bower in sunglasses.

Above: The Falklands, 1982: one of my own pictures of the stricken frigate *Antelope*, bleeding smoke but still afloat, shortly before the Argentine bombs aboard her exploded.

Below: Yomping – a shot taken soon after we left Teal Inlet with 45 Commando: l to r unidentified marine, Ian Bruce of the *Glasgow Herald*, Charles Laurence (*Sunday Telegraph*), self with appropriately bowed head, and Robert Fox of the BBC.

Above left: Typing a dispatch at San Carlos; standing orders obliged us to wear the somewhat ridiculous helmets during air attacks. The parachute smock was a souvenir of my 1963 debacle, the cigar the last of my precious supply.

Some of the men who gave me priceless help during the war: (*above right*) the Lt. Col. Michael Rose, commanding 22 SAS, in ski cap with a mortar team during training; (*below left*) RN Captain Jeremy Larken of *Fearless*; (*below right*) the dashing Lt.-Col. Nick Vaux, briefing his 42 Commando officers before the attack on Mount Harriet on which I went with him.

Above: Mirror images: my picture of the Argentine TV team I met a few minutes after crossing the lines during my illicit walk into Port Stanley in the last hours before the 14 June ceasefire.

Right: A shot the Argentines took, and sent to me years afterwards. I had stripped to a civilian anorak and clutched my walking stick in an effort to look as unmilitary as possible approaching the Argentine positions.

Above: Defeat: some of the thousands of Argentine prisoners being mustered in Port Stanley the day after their surrender, whose weapons I was sent to harvest for the Royal Navy's souvenir-hunters.

Below: Armchair correspondent: by 1991, as editor-in-chief of the *Daily Telegraph*, I was happy to visit the Gulf only after the shooting had stopped, on an absurdly luxurious trip to Kuwait by an aircraft of the Queen's Flight with Defence Secretary Tom King (seen here asking a question after our briefing by 1ˢᵗ Armoured Division Commander Maj.-Gen. Rupert Smith). Beside him are Chief of Defence Staff Sir David Craig, General Sir Peter de la Billière, the author, and the BBC's John Birt. I felt too old to be jealous of the war correspondents who had been doing the rough stuff. Thenceforward, this was as near to the battlefield as I wanted to get.

when the shooting starts.' Fleet Street's first team took it for granted that the game would be played as it always was: the news desk could send anybody who happened to be available from Southampton to represent the paper in transit. There would be weeks of indecisive politicking while the fleet sailed south. Then, if matters started looking serious, the big bylines could fly out to join the task force at Ascension Island. God knows why I did not take the same view, why I became obsessed with the need to be on board from the start. But obsessed I was. My luck started to change. The Royal Navy requisitioned the vast cruise liner *Canberra* to carry 3 Commando Brigade. Suddenly, there was space for another thirteen broadcast and print journalists – including me. I packed a suitcase of research material for my Normandy book, determined to have useful work to keep me busy while I bucketed about the Atlantic (though I did precious little work on *Overlord* in the months that followed). At home, we were nursing the hottest tickets in town, for *Guys and Dolls* three weeks hence. I asked Tricia not to give away mine until the last minute. I would be back to use it, when the almost inevitable diplomatic settlement came.

I opened the cupboard in which I kept warry gear accumulated over thirteen years and several continents: web equipment, fatigues, bergen rucksack, flak jacket, helmet, mess tins, waterbottles. Superstitiously I thought, 'If I turn up with this lot, somehow I know I'll never get the chance to use it.' I left behind everything save my old parachute smock, so hardly won nineteen years before, and my wonderfully comfortable shooting boots, made at Lobb's in St James's Street ten years earlier, for money I could ill afford. My feet are enormous. I knew that if we got as far as the Falklands and had to walk, fantastic as that idea seemed, there would be no chance of borrowing boots. The Ministry of Defence issued every correspondent with accreditation obviously left over from the Aden campaign of 1967, the language of which would have seemed perfectly appropriate for a journalist accompanying Kitchener up the Nile in 1898: 'The undermentioned correspondent is hereby licensed to accompany a British operational force . . .' Though the words 'to the South Atlantic' had been written in, the document's superbly anachronistic phrases bore an Arabic translation. My goodbyes were deliberately understated, because this journey seemed so likely to end in anticlimax and bathos.

I made one call which afterwards proved important, to the political editor of *The Economist*, my old friend Simon Jenkins. 'Simon, if there's a war, the story will make a wonderful book. I can write the military side, because I shall be there to see it. But I won't know anything about what's going on politically. Can we agree to write something together, with you doing the political end and me the warry bit?' Simon accepted at once, and we clinched on this remote contingency. Then I took a taxi down the familiar road through middle and southern England in glorious spring weather to the dockside at Southampton, where below the towering flank of *Canberra*, 2,500 Royal Marines and paras, a vast accumulation of stores and a little knot of my fellow-correspondents were embarking for the long, long voyage to the South Atlantic. On the evening of 9 April, Good Friday 1982, while the Royal Marine and Parachute Regiment bands vied with each other beneath the huge cranes on the quayside, *Canberra* cast off and edged away from Berth 106, a thousand or two very thoughtful men crowding her sides. 'No skylarking now, lads,' said an enormous chief petty officer, mustering the Royal Navy party aboard, 'this is serious.'

The requisition of *Canberra* – a 'STUFT' or Ship Taken Up From Trade – was a stroke of genius by the Ministry of

Defence. If the amphibious landing force had been obliged to sail in warships, the strain on so many men confined in overcrowded naval mess decks would have been unbearable. Yet that breezy day at Southampton, had we known we were to remain aboard *Canberra* for six weeks, we would have been appalled. The weary phrase we read so often, about 3 Commando Brigade 'going to war in a luxury liner', seemed irksome when many of the comforts and every hint of culinary talent had been stripped out of the ship before she embarked her military contingent. Sparks were still cascading from welders' torches. The hammers of Southampton workmen echoed across the upper decks for days at sea, as they laboured to complete new helicopter pads. Even a 40,000-ton liner becomes claustrophobic when it is home to thousands of men training, briefing, eating, sleeping and playing for weeks on end. Yet compared with the conditions in which troops have sailed to war throughout history, it was paradise. There were beds, showers, alcohol, movies, even cigars. The captain had been lording it over generations of cruise passengers for too long to be a congenial companion, but most of his officers and crew were delightful. The senior Royal Navy officer aboard, Chris Burne, was a richly comic figure who had earned a kind of immortality when commanding HMS *Coventry*, by inviting the lifebuoy sentry on the ship's stern to test 'man overboard' procedure by jumping himself. When this intelligent matelot declined, the captain sprang over the side instead. Now, 'Captain Fawlty' – as he became known to us all – was so horrified by being asked to take journalists to war in his ship that we found ourselves assigned to the Goanese stewards' quarters, on G Deck somewhere near the bilges. Somebody pointed out, however, that this was unlikely to win the Navy a good press. Within twenty-four hours we were grudgingly transferred to four-bunk passenger cabins, and then – in my lucky case – to a twin-berth cabin with Jeremy Hands of ITN. For the first few days, the atmosphere was that of a vast floating boarding school, in which we were all new boys, finding our way to classrooms and learning the prefects' names. If one had indeed been to boarding school, it was easier now to reaccustom oneself to all those male routines which involved undressing and showering in company, resisting bullying and avoiding the unwelcome attentions of the headmaster. If IVa is doing prep in Old School at five, can IIIb have the gym until four? Or rather, if Support Company is doing mortar drill on the Sun Deck at 1500 hours, can B Company have the Promenade Deck at 1430? Military life suffers from an inescapable bias towards the moods of adolescence, above all in its confiscation of privacy.

We won our sea legs without much pain, during the passage through the chops of the Channel and down the Bay of Biscay. Few men suffered from sickness thereafter. The pattern of the voyage was quickly set. We were wakened by the stamp of pounding feet, as troop after troop of Royal Marines in shorts and singlets jogged their marathons round the promenade deck, exposing tattoos of dreadful political incorrectness, and chanting as they ran, 'We-are-strong-we-are-tough-because-we-eat-our-Wheatipuffs.' The mornings passed in endless training sessions, some of which the journalists were invited to join: weapons familiarization, lectures about the Argentine army, talks on the Falklands by marines who had served there, and on Arctic warfare in which the corps specialized. We savoured the timeless humour of the NCO lecturing on the 81 mm mortar: 'This weapon, gentlemen, will definitely spoil their breakfasts.' Few of the stories we filed about *Canberra* and the amphibious force saw the light of print. Back in Britain, war still seemed remote. The headlines were all about the politics and the diplomacy. Every hour on the hour, from under a hundred cabin doors seeped the strains of 'Lillibullero', as men listened intently to BBC World Service bulletins reporting the latest twist of shuttle negotiations by the American Secretary of State. Every few days, an aircraft swooped low overhead, to parachute mail and newspapers into the sea for us. We gossiped for hours in the Crow's Nest bar which had become the officers' mess, disfigured by scaffolding to support the new helicopter landing platform on the roof. The barmen, Geoffrey and Taffy, were a delightful pair, in the grand tradition of raffish ships' stewards. They faced competition from the dining-room steward who nearly cut himself on a broken glass at dinner: 'Oooh, goodness gracious me! Danger money already!' Every night there was a movie, almost invariably a blood-curdling war film, though I managed to arrange a shipment of videos from London to vary the cultural diet. I played a lot of poker, and for the first time in my life found myself winning, because I was handling cards with a carelessness fed by possession of a wad of expenses money I had nowhere to spend, against marine officers who were cautiously using their own wallets.

Although I knew many soldiers, I had never encountered the Royal Marines. They are a special breed, intensely proud of their corps. They cherish the customs of the Royal Navy of which they are a part, though sensitive to the unfortunate truth that, by the 1980s, many naval officers would happily have signed away the marines and their share of the defence budget to buy themselves more ships. The army mocks the marines' supposed lack of brains. I remember a general shaking his head sadly and remarking, 'The trouble with the marines is that they become *absolutely hopeless* as soon as they get out of sight of the sea.' But most of the journalists on *Canberra* came to admire, and even to love, the green berets.

During every war I had reported in the past, I met the fighting men only in brief encounters on the battlefield, seldom recalling their faces, far less their names, for more than a day or two. Yet here at sea, we passed weeks among the people with whom we were to go ashore, learning about their hopes and fears, families and careers, companies and troops. There were three major units on *Canberra*: 40 and 42 Commandos, 3 Para – one of the two parachute battalions deployed to reinforce the Commando Brigade – and a leavening of gunners, engineers, doctors – the latter a pretty eccentric lot, save the superb Commander Rick Jolly, who later covered himself with glory. 45 Commando was sailing in company with us, albeit in rather less comfort, distributed among the Royal Fleet Auxiliary's LSLs – Landing Ships Logistics. The North Sea ferry *Norland* carried 2 Para. 3 Commando Brigade's headquarters had gone ahead, crowded into the assault ship *Fearless* with a vast assortment of vehicles and equipment. The amphibious force had sailed in haste, the government desperate to get the troops to sea, on to the chessboard as a piece in play. In the few short days before embarkation, the commanders had simply gathered a miscellany of everything they thought might be useful: the Commando Brigade's artillery of course; Rapier air-defence batteries; some Blowpipe anti-aircraft missiles; two troops of the Blues and Royals' Scorpion and Scimitar light armoured reconnaissance vehicles, though no one was sure whether their tracks could manage the soft going on the islands; a few dozen skis, God help us, for the marines were all ski-trained and somebody vaguely thought they might be handy; and some 'BVs' – the marines' Volvo Arctic cross-country vehicles, newish bits of kit bought on an impulse with the fag-end of last year's equipment budget. The paras had brought their BAT recoilless anti-tank weapons, even now lashed to the upper decks of *Canberra*, which those guns were never to leave. This was a force hastily scrambled together for a contingency which, even as we sailed southwards and diplomacy faltered, no one could yet believe would come. The decks were crammed with crates of toys of war labelled 'Belts, Linked; Grenades, Fragmentation; Bombs, Mortar'. Yet it still seemed incredible that they might be used in earnest.

Robin Innes-Ker, one of the Blues and Royals' troop commanders, often ate with the correspondents. The Duke of Roxburgh's younger brother, the amiable Lord Robin possessed his regiment's historic distaste for the supposedly brutish habits and homicidal inclinations of the paras and marines. One day we found him mugging up the army manual on handling of prisoners of war and burial of the dead, routines seldom in much demand at Windsor, it seemed. 'This isn't *at all* what I joined the army for,' he would say with a shudder. 'I just wanted to play polo.' I said, 'If you stop moaning and do your job halfway decently, Robin, since you lot represent this expedition's only armoured contingent, you'll come home covered in glory with a Mention in Dispatches.' Which is exactly what happened.

From the outset I enjoyed the company of Nick Vaux, who commanded 42 Commando. A short, slight figure with a reputation for past naughtiness, the colonel was a former amateur rider whose wife, a general's daughter, bred ponies at home on the edge of Dartmoor. Nick was one of those impish, understated professionals whom men find easy to follow in war. They command confidence, because they know their business with no need to show off about it, and their chief ambition is to bring back alive the men whom they lead. Officers with obvious heroic aspirations, in my experience, make those who have to follow them very nervous. The spoken or unspoken doubt is in many men's minds: 'It's all right for *him* if he wants to win a VC, but what about *us*?' Nick Vaux was greatly respected because he always cared about 'us'. The commanding officer of 2 Para inspired a different kind of interest. When

'H', as Herbert Jones was always known, began to visit us on *Canberra*, Robert Fox of the BBC and I spent a good many hours gossiping with him in the Crow's Nest, mostly about military history for which the three of us shared a passion. 'H' would staunchly defend – for instance – Haig's record in France in the First World War. He was a Roman, for all his twinkling laughter, who yearned for the opportunity to show his own steel on the battlefield. He thought well of 'the boy stood on the burning deck . . .' I will not pretend that any of us anticipated Goose Green, or what 'H' would do there, or his posthumous Victoria Cross. But none of us doubted his passionate yearning for distinction, nor his inevitable personal rivalry with Hew Pike, CO of 3 Para, a sharp, crisp, clever, equally ambitious soldier in a more conventional pattern, who was plainly destined for higher things in the army. The common strand among all these characters, indeed among every man in those ships save a few visibly uneasy civilian ships' crewmen, was that they craved the chance for action in the Falklands. Why should they not? They were professional warriors, men who had spent years training in Norway, Germany, Wiltshire, Northern Ireland, Canada, Kenya for one eventuality: battle. This did not make them cruel or bloodthirsty, still less insensitive. They simply saw in those April and May days of 1982 the glow on the southern horizon of a chance to fulfil the promise and preparation of a lifetime. When we reached Ascension Island, the COs of the infantry units discussed what was to be done if a diplomatic settlement was reached, and everyone had to sail bathetically home again. It was agreed that in such a case, the force must be landed to carry out a long and arduous exercise, to let off steam as noisily and exhaustingly as possible. It would otherwise have been not merely harsh, but actively dangerous, to send ashore at Southampton thousands of young men keyed to the highest pitch of expectation of hardship, action and – yes – violence.

In the hot, blue waters off Ascension, we rendezvoused with the *Fearless* group which had preceded us, and began a long wait at anchor, though we frequently spent the hours of darkness ploughing a circuitous course round the island because of the alleged Argentine submarine threat. For seventeen days we lingered, and picked interminably at our hopes and fears. All through the hours of daylight, helicopters clattered between the ships, shifting heavy equipment for restowage, assault-loading the amphibious force. Landing craft laden with men in shirtsleeves and lifejackets shuttled between *Canberra* and the beaches, practising embarkation and disembarkation drill. The sandy shore was as far as any correspondent got, for the powers-that-be decreed that the airfield and its secret comings and goings must be hidden from media eyes. As the days dragged by, our boredom grew. So too did our uncertainty about what lay ahead. The political stalemate between Britain and Argentina remained unbroken. The small dark cloud of war was growing, and with it our own selfish professional fears. Each day as boats and helicopters plied forth from the shore, we dreaded the coming of rivals from Britain – the seasoned correspondents for whom a Falklands war would be a glittering assignment – the John Pilgers, Don McCullins, Simon Winchesters, Colin Smiths, Jon Swains. Yet, to our bewilderment, only one media reinforcement arrived, a bulky, stolid, professional northerner from the *Yorkshire Post*. He was the replacement for the previous representative of Britain's provincial press, a young man who had insisted upon being flown home, despite all the imprecations of his colleagues. Offered the greatest opportunity of his professional career, he simply decided that he had no wish to go to war. We argued with him, we harangued him for days. We told him that he would lament turning back all his life. He remained quietly immovable, and was duly taken ashore at Ascension. I have wondered ever since whether he regretted the decision.

It seemed time to address one mundane concern. I have always been a cynic about the merits of relying upon one's employers' goodwill if anything disagreeable happens. Saigon veterans never forgot the day a *Telegraph* stringer died in his hotel, and his friend Dick West wired the paper to explain that the body would be repatriated for the cost of a first-class air fare. Parsimonious as ever, the *Telegraph*'s answering cable demanded: 'COULDN'T HE TRAVEL ECONOMY?' Now, I telexed the *Standard*'s managing editor, my old friend Jeremy Deedes: 'BEFORE I LEFT YOU WERE GETTING MY INSURANCE INCREASED TO £200,000. WITHOUT BEING MORBID, I WOULD LIKE CONFIRMATION THIS DONE, BEFORE ANY DEATH OR GLORY STUFF BECOMES IMMINENT. AT THE EARLIER LEVEL THE MANAGEMENT TALKED ABOUT, MY ENTHUSIASM FOR GOING PADDLING WOULD BE VERY SLENDER INDEED.' Reassurance was forthcoming.

My chief sentiment, the day we set sail southward from Ascension in the great flotilla of amphibious shipping, deployed tactically with frigate escorts upon our flanks, was sheer exhilaration that no more reporters had come. Some fine and experienced broadcast journalists were with the amphibious squadron or the battle fleet, my old colleague Michael Nicholson of ITN prominent among them. But among the few newspaper reporters, none possessed the advantage I did, of knowing war in the way that makes it much easier to tell the story. It was a wonderful break for me, but very foolish of the Ministry of Defence, not to allow some of Fleet Street's star war correspondents to join the task force at Ascension.

Over the past twenty years, the generation of journalists who did National Service, or even took part in the Second World War, has faded away. Most of their successors, inevitably, know next to nothing about soldiering, or about the difference between a division and a brigade, an LMG and GPMG, a staff-sergeant and a sergeant-major. This sort of thing is not mere cant or mumbo-jumbo for aficionados, it is the currency in which armies traffic. However hard a newcomer tries, it is very difficult for him to look at a battlefield, and to interpret what is happening before his eyes. How many times has a reporter said on a nightly television news bulletin: 'There was heavy fighting in Sarajevo last night'? It is not in doubt that there were noisy exchanges of artillery and small arms. But are the people letting off the guns serious soldiers carrying out serious operations of war? Or are they simply half-trained guerrillas and conscripts, pouring fire in each other's general direction? What weapons does each side have, and do they know how to use them? Do their commanders seem to have coherent plans? To report war intelligently, one needs to be able to make some shot at judging these things. It is as important for an effective war correspondent to know something about armies as for a theatre critic to have seen some plays, a political editor to have talked to a lot of politicians, and so on. Otherwise, the spectacle on the battlefield is liable to represent no more than a lot of men in camouflaged suits shooting at each other. The courage and literary skills of many of the men and women who now report from the Balkans, for instance, are not in doubt. Their military judgement often seems pretty flaky.

Aboard *Canberra*, I was always close to Robert Fox of BBC, friendly with John Shirley of the *Sunday Times* and Pat Bishop of the *Observer*. But others, especially from the tabloid papers, did not much trouble to hide their contempt for me, and perhaps I was not terribly friendly to them either. Mike Nicholson wrote a book about his own experiences long afterwards. He was sitting miserably on *Hermes* at the time, but he reported that I 'was hugely disliked by most of the Falklands press corps, and treated with some suspicion by the junior military; by the former because he was a thoroughly skilled, ruthless, incorrigible and tireless operator; by the latter, because of his connections in high military places; they referred to him either as General or Lord Hastings. He was considered an insufferably pompous, bumptious egoist, which of course he was and remains.'

Gosh. Was it really that bad? I hope not, but I quote Nicholson's words because it is sometimes helpful to admit how others see us. There is no doubt that some journalists became deeply bitter and frustrated amid the difficulties of reporting, once we landed at San Carlos. It remains hotly debated, where fault lay. We knew now that the odds favoured war. More likely than not, we were to witness what was surely Britain's last great imperial military adventure. One evening as we ploughed through the vast emptiness of the ocean in warm evening sunshine, the band of 3 Commando Brigade mustered on deck to Beat Retreat. On every corner of *Canberra's* upperworks, deeply tanned young men sat and squatted and hung from the rails, as drums and brass and wind instruments brought forth a succession of the classics of military music – there was 'Rule, Britannia', of course, 'Hearts of Oak' and that tune which haunted our voyage, 'Sailing'. Sentiment is inseparable from expeditions of war. The sunset, the glassy sea and the silent crowd of soldiers, sailors and marines amid that great ship, streaks of rust now showing on her white hull, were irresistible.

I thought of millions of people at home in Britain and around the world consumed with wonder and doubt about where we were, and what we were doing. Whatever was to come, I thanked my stars for the chance that had brought me here with these men, to share this unique experience. I wrote to Tricia and my children: 'Right now, I feel I can hear all your voices across the breakfast table in the kitchen, and a large part of me wants to be there with you. But you know also that I have a passion for adventures that I could not live without. What man in England would not give anything to be sailing with us into the South Atlantic today?'

The pace of briefing and training intensified rapidly. We were shown graphics and slides about the Argentine army, warned of the menace of their Pucara ground attack aircraft, and of course of the Mirages and Skyhawks of their air force. The civilian press 'minders' from the Ministry of Defence, always absurd figures, explained how any helicopter pilot we met ashore would convey our copy to headquarters for censorship and transmission. I never believed a word of this. In the stress of battle, what pilot would regard journalists' copy as a priority? The only way to move a story would be to ensure its transmission personally. The oldest rule of war corresponding, indeed of all journalism, is that it is useless to have the best story in the world to tell, unless one can ensure that it gets into the paper.

One morning, we were ordered to crossdeck for briefing to *Fearless*, the amphibious command ship. The trip was daunting for landlubbers. We jumped from a galley port low in *Canberra*'s side into a steeply pitching inflatable Rigid Raider, manned by a macho young marine in a wetsuit, then powered across the swell to *Fearless*, where a rope ladder hung precariously from the deck. Reaching and climbing that ladder frightened the life out of me. Once mercifully over the rail, we passed through a succession of heavy steel hatches prominently labelled CITADEL into the ship's superstructure, conscious that we had arrived in a professional naval setting quite unlike the panelled spaciousness of *Canberra*. Generators whined, brief messages echoed metallically round the ship's tannoy system. Men clattered to and fro on the steel ladders between bridge and Ops Room, officers' cabins and the huge dark caverns below, which housed the landing craft and a shrouded mass of vehicles. Staff officers edged past us in the passages, clutching sheaves of maps and signals. I thought of the immortal line of the gay war correspondent Godfrey Winn, asked how he had enjoyed his time on an aircraft carrier with the terrible Arctic convoy PQ17 in 1942: 'Admirals are heavenly, but captains make me shy.'

This was our first encounter with Commodore Mike Clapp, the amphibious force commander, and Brigadier Julian Thompson, who led 3 Commando Brigade. Clapp, a big, fair man in impeccable naval whites and Thompson, dark and slight, addressed us in turn. Ashore, we were to come to know Julian well, to sympathize with his many troubles and to respect his careful professionalism. But that morning both men were cool and visibly uneasy at this, their opening joust with the correspondents. We knew nothing then concerning the fierce arguments which had been raging about where and how 3 Brigade should land; or about the planning to avoid an opposed assault from the sea; or the tensions of the daily Satcom conversations between the fleet and task force head-quarters back at Northwood. For all Julian Thompson's con-siderable talents, it was foolish to have sent the land force under the direction of a relatively junior officer, who could not possibly be expected to grapple easily with the political dimen-sion of a campaign on which, regardless of the small scale of forces deployed, the nation's prestige rested. We had no inkling of the gravity of the Navy's fears about the difficulties ahead and the threat from the Argentine fleet, though Julian told us he had just finished making a video for screening to all ranks, entitled 'Do not Underestimate Your Enemy'. Since the Navy controlled our communications, we had hoped to be told a good deal. We could scarcely reveal any secrets. But that day we discovered little, save that Clapp and Thompson were politely wary of us. After a couple of hours aboard, we swayed precariously down the loathsome rope ladder once more, to be carried back to *Canberra*.

Very early next morning, while the ship still slept, I began my own discreet preparations for war. I knew how unfit I was, yet felt too ashamed of my flaccid white body to expose it to the derision of the marines or paras on their morning marathons. Each day thereafter until we entered the southern seas where spray lashed the decks around the clock, I ran the long circuit of the promenade deck alone and did my exercises among the lifeboats, looking out at the distant escorts in the dawn. I was thirty-six, painfully conscious of being at the outer limit of my own ability to survive on a battlefield among a force of superbly fit young men. If I had to run fast in either direction, I was determined to be as agile as I could make myself in the dwindling days left.

There was a struggle to find kit for us. Every man of the embarked force was suitably clothed and equipped, but no one had thought to provide for journalists. Unit quartermasters were cajoled and bludgeoned into finding what they could – windproofs and packs, waterbottles and mess tins, field dressings, webbing, sleeping bags, groundsheets, ration packs. There was a brief protest from one or two of the least military-minded journalists about wearing camouflage fatigues – media custom in every recent conflict had been to wear decisively civilian clothes, and to despise 'warry types' who affected combat dress. Yet the reality of what we faced stifled their reservations. We were to land in the most hostile imaginable environment, where we would be fighting damp and cold from the moment we left the ships. We needed all the specialized clothing and equipment the ships could provide, if we were to have any chance of keeping up with the men of the landing force. I checked my binoculars, cameras, boots, sweaters, and the old puttees I had preserved almost twenty years, from 10 Para – yes, the ones I was so often rebuked for failing to tie correctly, by that Glaswegian lieutenant in Cyprus. A cocky young para NCO checked me one morning in my old smock.

'What are you doing, wearing wings on your arm? Nobody's supposed to wear wings unless they've jumped.'

'I got these while you were still a gleam in the milkman's eye, sonny,' I said, and narrowly lived to tell the tale. One accessory I lacked. I mentioned it aloud, 'If I'm going to walk, I do like to carry a stick. But I suppose there's precious little chance of finding one here.' 'Don't be damn silly,' said a ship's officer. 'A cruise ship is awash with walking sticks, crutches and Zimmer frames. Get down to the medical centre and take your pick.' Then I felt as ready as I should ever be.

It was a notable aspect of our voyage that those of us sailing with the amphibious force, correspondents and soldiers alike, felt entirely divorced from the Royal Navy's carrier group, its successes and tragedies. We learned of *Conqueror*'s sinking of the *General Belgrano*, the fatal Exocet attack on *Sheffield*, the recapture of South Georgia by the SAS and a company of 42 Commando, through World Service along with the people of Britain. As we heard the superb voice reports of BBC's Brian Hanrahan and ITN's Michael Nicholson from *Invincible* and *Hermes*, hundreds of miles further south, the *Canberra* journalists grew increasingly fearful that we had been brushed aside from the serious business of the conflict. We learned of the first skirmishes between the Argentine air force and the battle fleet, and gained some sense of the imperfections of the Navy's defensive missile systems. We begged feverishly for crumbs of information about the progress of the sea war to file to our own newspapers. None were forthcoming. Day by day, this was becoming a more serious and deadly enterprise, whose outcome could only be bloody. But Julian Thompson and Mike Clapp remained in purdah on *Fearless*, visiting the troopships merely to brief their officers and men. We learned that 5 Infantry Brigade was to sail from Britain in QE2 to reinforce 3 Commando Brigade. Did that mean we must wait yet more weeks before landing? Would additional journalists be coming with them? Were we to wait forever in the wings?

I filed a piece to *The Spectator*, reflecting an urbanity I am not sure that I felt, but which still seems a fair reflection of the mood of those days. I quoted Waugh, of course: ' "Remember that the Patriots are in the right and are going to win," declared Lord Copper. "But they must win quickly. The British public has no interest in a war which drags on indecisively. A few sharp victories, some conspicuous acts of personal bravery on the Patriot side and a colourful entry into the capital. That is *The Beast* policy for the war." ' I told of the *Daily Mail* reporter requested by his office to file an interview with Miss Cindy Buxton, then resident on South Georgia, some 3,000 miles distant; of the *Observer* correspondent, a passionate anti-militarist, distressed to find that a photograph of himself stripping an automatic rifle had been sent to London for the shame of publication; of the *Sunday Times* reporter, the mercurial John Shirley, a sturdy socialist, who sulked in his cabin in a most unegalitarian fashion until promoted from the marine quarters to a cabin in keeping with his alleged officer status. I mocked the ministry 'minders' and censors.

To be fair to them, however, the root of the problem lies in the attitude of the Royal Navy. The Navy regard what is taking place in the South Atlantic entirely as a private affair between itself and the Argentinians, and absolutely no business of anyone else's. Having failed in its initial struggle to prevent reporters from accompanying the task force at all, the Navy has since dedicated itself to ensuring that it provides no information worth reporting. Each element of the fleet informs the reporters attached to it that, if they want to know what is happening, they will simply have to listen to the World Service, won't they? The Navy is not hostile to the notion that a life and death propaganda struggle is being waged alongside the naval one. It merely denies its existence.

The Royal Marines cheer us up by pointing out that the Navy is just as unhelpful to them. It is simply age-old Admiralty policy to assume that it alone knows best. Some days (Trafalgar, etc.), it has been right. Others (Jutland, *Prince of Wales* and *Repulse*, PQ17, *Hood*, etc.) it has been wrong. Mrs Thatcher, Mr Nott and those of us whose safety is entirely in the Navy's hands today simply have to hope fervently that the sailors are on one of their Trafalgar streaks.

Seldom in history can a force have been sailing towards war with such a huge amount staked upon the efficiency of untested technology. The survival of the battle fleet, the success of a landing, the prestige of the nation all seem to hinge upon a variety of exotic rockets and infernal machines never before used in war. It is not surprising that while nobody with the task force flinches from doing the job on hand, many men are disgusted by the wilder manifestations of jingoism that emerge from the British papers which reach us here.

This morning, as I write this, like every morning, a knot of intrepid war reporters will seat themselves behind the windows of the Crow's Nest bar high in *Canberra*'s superstructure, and gaze out at the fleet through binoculars, like so many aged residents peering out from the conservatory of a Bournemouth seafront hotel. It would be pleasant to suppose that by this time next week the atmosphere will remain equally fanciful. Instead, it seems more likely that we shall be face to face with an overdose of noisy and possibly bloody reality.

The Royal Navy possessed little experience of the media before the Falklands War, and made plain its distaste for the journalists *Hermes* and *Invincible* so reluctantly carried. The tabloid representatives, in particular, outraged senior sailors by jamming overloaded signal circuits with thousands of words of nonsense about 'How the Page Three girls are going to war'. For all our frustrations, the *Canberra* group of correspondents afterwards came to perceive how lucky we had been. We were able to forge friendships with the Royal Marines and paras which served us mightily well ashore. From Julian Thompson downwards, they did their utmost to help us do our job – which was to tell their story. I blush now to remember our selfish impatience in those last days before San Carlos, though the mood was shared by almost every man of the landing force. We had been at sea for almost six weeks, through sun and wind and rain and into the steep swells of the South Atlantic. We were more than ready. We were stifled by confinement on the ships, by the nail-biting vacillations of diplomacy, by our absence from the scene of the dramas which beset the carrier group all through those May days. We had exhausted the charms of the endless tannoy calls: 'Hands to Flying Stations! Hands to Flying Stations!' 'RAS parties close up! RAS parties close up!' We had had enough of the ship's 'buzzes', the rumours that swept the decks daily from the moment we sailed: the Argies had surrendered; we would land on Friday;

we would land on Tuesday; *Hermes* had been hit. I wrote home to my wife, 'If the task force pull this off and win a decisive victory with not too many casualties, Mrs Thatcher's government is probably safe for years. And I think we should be able to do it – I have great faith in the marines and the paras.'

Now, at last, our turn was come. Each correspondent was detailed for attachment to a specified unit, though it never seemed plausible that such an arrangement would survive much past the landing. I was to go ashore with 40 Commando, at San Carlos settlement. There was a final briefing in one of *Canberra*'s big saloons, given by the unit CO Malcolm Hunt. 'And now, good luck, and may your God go with you,' he concluded. Phrases like that seem perfectly appropriate on the eve of battle. Wars overflow with clichés. Many men were attending Sunday service when the tannoy interrupted brutally: 'Air raid warning yellow! Air raid warning yellow! Enemy air activity over the battle fleet. Air defence teams close up.' Then we sang 'For Those in Peril on the Sea', without anyone even for an instant thinking it trite. We filed thoughtfully back to our mess decks to gaze across at the landing ships and escorts, pitching deep into the seas around us. The wind was gusting to Force 9, sometimes obliging the lookouts even on the big ships to withdraw inside the shelter of the bridge. The great 12,000-ton bulk of *Fearless* seemed to bounce each time she struck the waves. From a distance, the old ship possessed the elegance of a cruiser's silhouette, though closer to, she looked the workhorse she was. Years before, avidly reading Monsarrat's *The Cruel Sea*, I conjured visions of long columns of ships battling grey Atlantic rollers, amid the constant fear of submarine attack. Never had any of us expected to see the sight in good earnest, nor to hear the submarine alarms which had been troubling the Navy since Ascension.

Waking in the midst of that night, I dressed and went up

to the darkened bridge. All ships were blacked out now. The officer of the watch and the helmsman gave me a nod. After peering at the emptiness outside for a moment, I crossed to the hooded screen of the radar repeater. There, crawling laboriously across the tube like so many sea slugs, were the tiny representations of ships on whose course the eyes of the world were fixed, and upon one of which I stood. I gazed fascinated at this microcosm of the D-Day armada I had been contemplating, back at home in Northamptonshire six weeks before. What would happen if the Argentine air force caught us in open water? Did I myself have the nerve any longer to cross a battlefield with men under fire? Had I pushed my luck too far, venturing on this one last war assignment, seven years after I thought I had said goodbye to it all for ever, on the passage home from Saigon? In the days before the landing, I became morbidly preoccupied with fears that I had overdrawn my capital of luck, after so many assignments on which I had never suffered a scratch. I did not confide my apprehension about what was to come, however, to any of those with whom I drank and chatted for so many hours in the Crow's Nest, nor did I hear any other man's confession. We shared intimacies about families and about our professional lives, but I heard no philosophizing about the battlefield. For the most part, our exchanges were mere diary conversation about what we were doing today, what we might find ourselves doing tomorrow.

What sort of show would the Argies put up? Michael Rose, the splendidly hawkish and fluent CO of 22 SAS, said from the beginning that he was sure they would fold, given one good push. He was openly contemptuous of more cautious spirits such as Admiral Sandy Woodward. Buoyed by his men's triumph in breaking the Iranian Embassy siege in London almost two years before, and by the mystique inseparable from the SAS, Rose could get away with frankness bordering on insubordination. Mere lieutenant-colonels, however, do not make themselves loved by speaking their minds to generals and admirals carrying the huge responsibility for a campaign. Michael might be untouchable, and was of course adored by the correspondents for his openness. The ski cap and blue anorak he normally affected in lieu of boring old uniform characterized the unique position of his unit as much as its exotic range of weaponry. The prestige of 'the Sass' soared with their successful raid on the Argentine airfield at Pebble Island. But we were conscious that he had enemies. In those last days before the landing, even Rose's imperturbability was shaken by the tragic crash in which a Sea King fell into the Atlantic, killing eighteen of his unit, including some of its ablest and most experienced men. It was a ghastly blow, which reminded every soldier and sailor at sea of the price this war looked set to exact before its ending.

And as we brooded in our cabins, packing gear, most men asked themselves how they would stand up to conditions in which our resident Falklands expert, the dashing Major Ewen Southby-Tailyour, reminded us that we could expect no shelter in any house, nor even water to drink free from sheep liver fluke, save what we carried for ourselves. God knows, I was conscious of my own limitations. I had never forgotten the humiliation I thrust upon myself in Cyprus nineteen years earlier. Would I fail likewise again? Yet I was warmed by a companionship with the fighting units, and a confidence in their abilities, such as I had never known before, on assignments where we were strangers to the battlefield soldiers, whom we briefly visited. Here, the correspondents belonged to the task force in a fashion that never obtained among the Israelis on the Golan Heights or with Lon Nol's ragtag army on Route I in Cambodia. I believed that my life was in the hands of the finest troops in the world.

Many, perhaps most, men in the task force took a sardonic view of the merits of the cause for which we were going to war. They knew they were embarked upon a throwback of history, in consequence of a huge political failure at home. I saw no Thatcher-worship in the South Atlantic, only a powerful professional commitment to doing the job, to proving that the military art, so often apparently irrelevant in eighties Britain, could still accomplish great things where the men of peace had failed. Britain, home, the government, the mortgage all appeared impossibly remote. I had often doubted the justice of Balzac's line about the essentially carefree nature of the soldier's life. But now it seemed valid. All domestic responsibilities were brushed aside amid the simple purpose – though, God knows, by no means simple task – of engaging and defeating the enemy. All that mattered was here, in these ships laden with men – some bad, some ugly, some tiresome, of course, but most good and honourable people with a sense of duty and comradeship hard to find in peacetime Britain. I had put aside my own rational doubts about this war. Now, Britain was committed. I was among men set to put my country's purposes to the test. When it was over, we could argue once more about whether the cause was just, the lives well lost. For now, I merely wanted our side to win, and cherished the opportunity to tell the story of how my companions achieved victory.

The next day, 19 May, the amphibious force was granted a miracle. Its commanders had been racking their brains about how to crossdeck 1,500 men from *Canberra* to their designated assault ships. The Sea Kings had already used up an alarming number of flying hours transferring equipment at Ascension. If now they had to move three fighting units, most of the helicopters would be maintenance cases before they ever reached the shore. Yet how else could the Commandos be transferred in mid-Atlantic? There was gloomy talk about resorting to breeches-buoys. Somebody up there was listening. On 19 May, the angry sea fell to a light swell. All day, long files of laden men shuffled through the galley areas of *Canberra* to the lower deck port, from which one by one the marines leapt heavily into the landing craft pitching beneath. Once more, I found myself full of fear about doing this simple thing, and absurdly grateful that I made it intact. Then, four or five bodies after me, a marine tried his leap – and missed. He disappeared abruptly between ship and LCU. A rush of men to the side tried to fend off the gap with rifles. 'Swim! Swim!' shouted an NCO to the struggling figure in the water, whose only chance was to clear the stern before the ships clashed again. Those of us who possessed no means to help watched in impotent horror. Then there was a second miracle of the day. Somehow, that man was dragged from the sea between those clashing walls of steel, no whit the worse for his experience, save that his kit was soaked and ruined. We bumped across the water to *Fearless* amid blasts of spray and turned into the vast flooded dock beneath her landing deck. As we crossed the ramp into the tank deck, arc lights cleared a path for us through the darkness of a mass of vehicles and equipment. We clanked up innumerable ladders and through a succession of hatches into the messdecks. I was billeted with the ship's dentist, a kindly young man who gave up his bunk so that I could make the most of what looked like our last comfortable sleep for days. Every passage, every living space, was crowded with men and kit. Marines stripped and cleaned weapons for the last time, painstakingly encased equipment and maps in polythene, tightened bergen straps, greased boots. I met Ian Jackson, the 40 Commando troop leader with whom I was to go ashore the next night. He was just twenty-two. The terrible cliché assailed me at once. He seemed ridiculously young to be commanding anything. Somebody had got hold of the latest air photographs of the Port Stanley runway, which the RAF had been attacking with Vulcans at extreme range. 'Typical bloody RAF!' said a marine, gazing without enthusiasm at the ineffective bomb craters fringing the Argentine landing zone, 'all that peacetime bullshit, then they can't do the business when it matters.' Unfair, of course, but that was how men felt.

I spent much of the next day, 20 May, on the sandbagged bridge of *Fearless* behind the lanky figure of Captain Jeremy Larken, as he conned the amphibious force through its next miracle — a heavy fog — towards San Carlos. Every man in the ships knew that this was the time of utmost risk. If the Argentine air force found us in the open sea, the Skyhawks and Mirages could do awful, perhaps fatal damage. We were protected by *Broadsword* and *Brilliant*, the only Type-22 frigates equipped with Sea Wolf, believed to be the Navy's most effective close-defence missile system. Sea Wolf was formidable, but it was not infallible, as we discovered in the days that followed. Hour after hour, as glimpses of accompanying ships came and went in the thick whiteness, we forged onward, scarcely believing our luck. At intervals, the bridge tannoy briefly reported Argentine aircraft movements, course and speed, monitored by radar and distant British observers. Would they find us? How could they *not* find us? Jeremy Larken, imperturbable and even affable in a helmet and anti-flash cape which did not flatter his bony features, proved one of the outstanding naval officers in the South Atlantic. Part of his childhood had been spent living on a canal barge, an experience about which his mother had written a charming book. A studious, literate man, he shared none of his naval colleagues' disdain for correspondents — nor, for that matter, for the land force. He simply wanted to make things work. In his concern for the problems of other units, other services, he displayed a bedside manner which some soldiers afterwards suggested that

Admiral Sandy Woodward might have studied to advantage. Woodward remained a remote figure in every sense. I never met him in the South Atlantic. But the brusqueness of his signals matched the manner of the man, according to a sardonic naval staff officer who showed me one of the admiral's more school-boyish 'brace up and take a shower' communications from *Hermes*. History will almost certainly judge that Woodward did most of the right things in the South Atlantic, above all by treating the security of his carriers as the foremost priority. But he did them in a manner which made him unloved.

On through that welcome mist we sailed, some of us ex-ulting like schoolboys as it began to seem that we should make it through to blessed darkness. There were jokes on the bridge, and some relaxation of tension. The last vital signal for the landing force came: **TOP SECRET OPERATION SUTTON CTG 317.0 19N 190230Z MAY SHIPS PASS TO EMBARKED FORCES 1. D-DAY 21 MAY 82 2. H-HOUR IS 210639Z MAY 82 3. BREAK DOWN AND ISSUE FIRST LINE AMMUNITION FORTHWITH 4. ACT IMMEDI-ATELY.** Below, small arms ammunition and grenades were being passed among the companies. 'Just remember this ship is a floating bomb,' an Ordnance officer warned a party of marines, pointing to the vast stockpiles of fused mortar rounds, grenades and shells. We queued for a last hot meal – even at these extremities of overcrowding, the food on *Fearless* was always far better than in that celebrated 'luxury liner' *Canberra*. I wrote my last letter to Tricia.

> Well, I have got my great wish . . . I should be behind the first men of the Commando who knock on the door of the little farm settlement where we are to beach tonight . . . I believed when we left England that in return for weeks of boredom on *Canberra*, we had a one in five chance of being

present at one of the great events of British post-war history. And so it has fallen out. Our greatest fear is of what the Argentine air force may be able to do after we have landed, but I think we shall be okay. There are believed to be no enemy in the area where we are going in, and it will probably be a week or two before the landing force is engaged in battle with their main forces. I am afraid it is going to be horribly uncomfortable living in trenches ashore for weeks, but in return for one of the greatest stories of my lifetime, I can stand it . . . I find the whole experience enormously moving. To go into an amphibious landing with the cream of the British forces is one of those experiences I have always dreamed of, and I think I am just young enough to get away with it, although as usual very scared. You'd laugh to see me, crouched in the corner of this tiny cabin in my smock and boots, smoking a cigar, and with a tiny tear in my eye, because this whole business is deeply emotional . . .

I snatched a couple of hours sleep in the dentist's welcome bunk, and awoke to find that the ship had stopped. I slipped through the hatches on to the upper deck, to be overwhelmed by the sight before me. There, in the darkness, lay the long, low coastline of San Carlos, the hills of the Falklands of which we had thought and dreamed for so long. The sky was icy cold, crystal clear. Not a light was showing in the ships. I thought of the teeming, floodlit activity beneath my feet; the SAS and SBS teams already waiting ashore; the naval gunfire support preparing to open fire. We blacked our faces with camouflage cream and pulled on packs. In one hand I clutched my battered typewriter; I knew that no one transmitting dispatches would bother to read handwriting. As one of the privileges of civilian status (though the day before, we had been solemnly informed that henceforward, we were subject to the Military Discipline Act), I wore tennis shoes, with my boots tied round my neck. We were bound to get wet feet wading ashore. I had no desire to walk for days thereafter in salt-sodden boots. I felt no embarrassment about being so fastidious. I knew from bitter experience that I would need to give myself all the help I could get to survive the hardships which lay ahead, even before taking the enemy into account.

One by one, we dropped from hatch to hatch through the deck levels, helped with our clumsy burdens by sailors who muttered the immemorial clichés of these moments: 'Good luck, mate.' 'Give 'em hell.' Don't laugh – I muttered clichés of my own: 'And he that hath no stomach for this fight, let him depart; his passport shall be made, and crowns for convoy put into his purse . . .' This was the greatest romantic adventure of my life. The knowledge overwhelmed fear, discomfort, doubt. A chain of red pinpoint lights hung across the darkened tank deck, to guide us into the landing craft. Each man was handed a case of mortar bombs as he embarked, to carry ashore. Correspondents were not excluded. We crouched on the steel floor of the big LCU, a company strong, slipping off our packs. Above us, the sky still seemed supernaturally clear and crisp. Then the harsh squawk of the tannoy interrupted: 'Air raid warning red! Air raid warning red!' Oh Christ, now they were going to catch us sitting. Men swore and hugged their fear as the stern gate slid down, and the dock began to flood. Then relief: false alarm. Thank God. The big diesels throbbed as we sidled astern, out of the womb of *Fearless*, and into open water. Above and behind us in the LCU's apology for a wheelhouse, we could see the dimly lit figures of the marine coxswain and guide taking us in, and glimpse other LCUs out there in the dimness. It was icy cold, though our clothing gave us protection enough. Now we were clear of the ship and its multitude of mechanical sounds, we could hear the distant 'crack-boom' of the naval bombardment, engaging the Argentine positions at Fanning Head.

Few men spoke, and when they did so it was only in whispers, as if the Argies might hear. I thought back six weeks, to that moment when I was staring out of my window in Northamptonshire, seeking to conjure in my imagination the experience of crouching in a landing craft heading for a hostile shore on 6 June 1944. This was the merest shadow of that great event, an anachronism which owed nothing to logic nor to the problems of Britain in the last fifth of the twentieth century. But it is given to few of us, in the humdrum existences that are our lot, to share a unique experience on which life, death and the prestige of one's nation have been staked. I never felt more conscious of the sorry truth, that mankind has yet to evolve any means of harnessing the spirit of young men as powerful as war. We chewed chocolate – the marines' beloved 'nutty' – and huddled to gain the warmth of the diesels behind us. We prayed that the Argentines were not waiting.

CHAPTER FOURTEEN

On the Shore

EVEN IN THE darkness, the steam of our breath was dimly visible. The stars shone bright above. A few hundred yards distant on both sides, the low hills flanking San Carlos Bay were dimly visible shapes, as we hastened towards our landing place beneath the settlement. Behind me, the Royal Marine coxswain was still intent on the helm. If only we could get ashore unopposed. If only we could create a beachhead, establish a perimeter, before the Argentines responded. I felt less afraid, more profoundly excited by the experience, than ever before in a war. Partly, this was because unlike Vietnam or Yom Kippur or even Northern Ireland, here I was an authorized appendage of an army, if not a part of it. I knew the plan. I was not blundering through the darkness of another nation's battlefield, as so often, but travelling purposefully to a known destination – though we possessed no inkling what we would find there. This was my country's war, in however bizarre a cause. And it made a difference.

There was a muffled call: 'Okay, this is it.' It was just after 4 a.m. on 21 May. We clambered stiffly to our feet, shouldering huge packs, the marines checking their weapons. The ramp went down with a clatter of chains. 'Troops out!' called a voice. We shuffled rapidly forward to the bow, and splashed through a few inches of water to the beach. Two Scorpions, two Scimitars of the Blues and Royals were there a few moments ahead of us, to provide fire support. A shaggy little band of filthy and unshaven figures formed the reception party – one of the Special Boat Service teams which had been in the hills above the bay for days. As soon as we touched the shore, a voice muttered, 'Bombs here,' and each man tossed down his case of mortar rounds. A and B companies were pushing forward on our flanks, to secure the open ground around the settlement. Charlie Company hastened towards a dim light shining outside a modest two-storey white house a few hundred yards above the beach. The dogs were yowling and barking in the farm buildings. This was the moment we had been waiting seven weeks for, since that day I told Kenneth Baker it seemed crazy to send a task force. Paul Allen, 7 Troop commander, headed for the front door with Lieutenant Paul Thurman, a marine who had served a tour with the Falklands detachment, and was engaged to the daughter of the governor, Rex Hunt. I hurried to keep pace, a couple of steps behind them. Thurman knocked on the door, while 7 Troop adopted defensive positions a few yards out in the darkness. It was opened gingerly by a face and then an exclamation: 'You're British!' It was Pat Short, the settlement manager. He had been awakened by the naval gunfire, and then his young son told him he could hear noises on the shore. 'We've been expecting you these last two or three nights,' he said. His wife Isabel put in, 'We were getting fed up with waiting for you. Every morning we've been saying "Perhaps it'll be today!" Pat, a slight, soft-spoken figure in his late thirties, rapidly confirmed that there were no Argentines in the settlement. The last enemy patrol had passed through two or three days before. After a few more words with the Shorts, we left them while the company marched on through San Carlos, home to some thirty people, shepherds and farmworkers. Marines knocked on doors one by one, to tell dressing-gowned families of our coming. In the understated manner of remote rural communities, they were friendly enough but showed little emotion.

One of the housewives, a jolly woman named Monica May, invited us in for coffee. I accepted eagerly and clumped into her little bungalow, so like a million in Britain, where we leaned against the kitchen table, blinking under the light and exchanging cheerful platitudes. 'We knew somebody would turn up sooner or later,' said Mrs May, 'but we didn't expect it to be here.' Out in the darkness, C Company had unfurled the Union flag it carried for just this moment, and raised it on the pole outside Pat Short's house. There was not enough breeze to ruffle the colours, but the gesture had been made. We were here, we were ashore, alive, intact. On the beach, vehicles and men were streaming out of the landing craft as fast as they could shuttle from the ships. On our right, 2 Para under H Jones was scaling the high ground of Sussex Mountain. 45 Commando was safely established on the other side of the bay, around the refrigeration plant at Ajax Bay. 3 Para landed very late from *Intrepid*, and eventually secured Port San Carlos after a firefight with an Argentine detachment in which two British helicopters and their crews were lost.

Dawn found me digging. 40 Commando was entrenching itself a few hundred yards south of the San Carlos settlement. When the Argentines attacked, since I would presumably expect to have a hole to hide in, it was suggested that I should help create it. In a host of ways, the correspondents in the Falklands found ourselves sharing the lot of soldiers in a manner that seldom befalls journalists. In all the years I had been going to wars, this was the first time I had been obliged to dig. I found it painfully slow going, hacking at the stony ground beneath the peat with a short entrenching tool. My fit

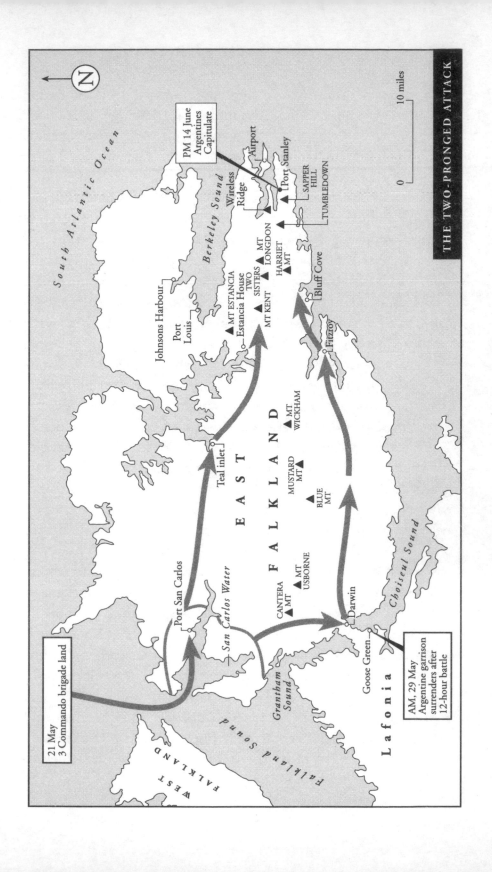

N

THE TWO-PRONGED ATTACK

0   10 miles

South Atlantic Ocean

Berkeley Sound

PM 14 June
Argentines
Capitulate

Airport
Wireless
Ridge
Port Stanley
SAPPER
HILL
TUMBLEDOWN

MT
LONGDON
MT
SISTERS
TWO
HARRIET
MT

Bluff Cove

Johnsons Harbour
Port
Louis
MT ESTANCIA
Estancia House
MT KENT

EAST

Fitzroy

Teal inlet

MT
WICKHAM

FALKLAND

MUSTARD
MT
BLUE
MT

Port San Carlos

San Carlos Water

CANTERA
MT
USBORNE

Darwin

Choiseul Sound

Grantham Sound

Goose Green

AM, 29 May
Argentine garrison
surrenders after
12-hour battle

Falkland Sound

21 May
3 Commando brigade land

Lafonia

WEST
FALKLAND

young marine companions were unimpressed. As the light grew, we enjoyed the useful stimulus of knowing that it was only a matter of time before the enemy air force came. Spades moved quicker. At last, our holes were dug. The marines deftly stretched their KIPs across them – Kits Individual Protection, cats' cradles of pegs and cords on which they laid groundsheets to form foundations for turf roofs. The worst aspect of this kind of soldiering is that every man knows that within hours or days, he will be moving on – and digging all over again. I wandered across to one of the Blowpipe anti-aircraft missile teams, busy preparing their clumsy toys. Will they work, I asked? 'At sixteen thousand quid a shot, they bloody well ought to,' said a chirpy corporal.

It was a beautiful clear, crisp morning, which the autumn sun was suffusing with a glow of warmth. Flocks of geese and ducks accustomed to undisturbed tranquillity wheeled restless across the sky. The unmistakable scent of peat smoke drifted gently down the wind. A young marine officer gazed at the hills and the sea, so like those of Scotland's Western Isles. He glanced at me. 'Just like UK, isn't it?' And of course, it was. Save for the fighting men and the ships, San Carlos could have been any of a hundred Scottish sea lochs I knew and loved so well. I walked back up to the settlement, where a party of engineers was emplacing Bren guns, while a battery of dixies prepared tea, heated by those huge old petrol pressure cookers whose roar has been beloved by the British army for generations. It was a homely sight. The settlement children waved at every passing helicopter. Sea Kings were shuttling 105 mm guns over our heads to their battery positions. Pat Short's ten-year-old-son Derek kept asking his father, 'When can I go out to the ships, Daddy?' We were surprised to hear that the settlement had not been looted, but in every other respect Short was unimpressed by the Argentines. 'They don't look a lot to me. I don't think the Brits will have to fight them too much.' Not surprisingly, he expressed his passionate hostility to any deal that would allow any Argentines to stay on the islands. 'As long as they're the hell out of it, I don't mind what's arranged.'

I met Pete Holdgate, a Royal Marine photographer. He had come to take a picture of the raising of the colours. Yes, again. He landed with orders that his first duty was to send a picture to London of the Union flag going up. In darkness, he could do nothing. The little ceremony had to be repeated. The picture flashed around the world, and into the history books. I took my own shots. Then Pete did me one of the biggest favours of my life. He took a photograph of a British correspondent, tired and still blackened with camouflage cream, draped in web equipment, helmet, cameras and binoculars, standing stick in hand on the Falkland Islands. That image was transmitted to London along with the shot of the flag-raising. It helped to make me quite famous for five minutes, and was reproduced again and again in a host of newspapers over the weeks that followed. I have cherished it ever since, of course, because it represents the war correspondent as he would like to see himself. It was a melodramatic moment, a melodramatic pose, and I have a thousand reasons to be grateful that Pete recorded it.

Tractors and trailers rattled through the settlement, as the Falklanders helped the landing force to move kit inshore from Blue Beach, which was the designation of our landing place. Everybody looked up uneasily as a measured series of detonations echoed around the anchorage. 'Incoming?' No. 'Outgoing.' Somebody shouted: 'It's just the guns bedding in.' The helicopters had already finished moving the RA batteries' 105 mm light guns to their destined positions. Once laid and camouflage-netted, they were firing a few rounds to register.

Many people, both among the landing force and the inhabitants, found it hard to believe that the tranquil hills and shoreline of San Carlos Bay were now to frame the setting for a battle, though all logic told us that it must be so. Monica May said cheerfully to a passing group of marines, 'You'll have to watch yourselves around here, because with all the goings-on in the past few weeks, we haven't been able to get the rams out to the ewes.' Everybody laughed. In the innocent sunlight of that early morning, danger seemed very remote.

The first most men knew of air attack was the roar as a low-flying Argentine aircraft tore across the anchorage, quickly drowned by the rattle, bang and whoosh of small arms, Bofors and missile fire from the ships and every man ashore holding a weapon which would bear. Wave after wave of attackers came through the day, and with each one our fears mounted for the ships in the anchorage, above all *Canberra*, the 'great white whale'. It seemed impossible that the enemy could miss that huge, bloated target, whose loss would be such a disastrous blow to the British. Attacks came and went so quickly. An aircraft was upon us and then out of range inside twenty seconds. It was difficult to tell what the Argentines were hitting. We heard of *Ardent*'s sinking only hours past the event, and about the damage to *Argonaut* and other frigates long after the bombs struck them. To every man around the anchorage, though, it was plain that the enemy's air force was striking hard. We feared they might follow up at any time with a ground assault on the beachhead. If the Argentine command possessed the slightest initiative, they could move men forward by helicopter to harass our landing, and at the very least disastrously retard unloading. It was days before we could be sure that the enemy lacked the will and competence for any such action, days during which we were full of apprehension.

From the first moment of the landing, I made a decision about my own work, which served me well through the weeks that followed. I would make no attempt to file spot news to London. First, any details of naval or military action would almost certainly be struck out by the censor. Second, wherever I was ashore or afloat, I could not hope to learn much about 'the big picture', how the battle was going. Any report the government was prepared to release about troop movements or ship sinkings would come from the Ministry of Defence, probably before we even knew about it. In the days to come, colleagues who did try to report immediate news – '45 Commando is now halted twenty miles east of San Carlos' – were almost entirely frustrated. Some wasted hours on dispatches which never reached their destinations, or were so mangled by the censors as to become meaningless. For my part, I decided I would simply report what I was seeing and hearing all around me – on the ships and on the shore. I would try to tell people at home what it was like to be fighting in the Falklands; how this remote wilderness felt and sounded to us, the interlopers; what people were saying to each other. Over the weeks that followed, I filed tens of thousands of words of description. And because my dispatches did not deal with details of specific military movements, few were much injured by the censor, save that he deleted all references to named individuals, ships or units.

More than this, I took extravagant precautions to ensure that my copy was transmitted. Amid the stress of operations, I never believed for a moment that any military channel could be expected to bother with moving press copy quickly. The only occasion of the war when I relied upon the official routeing proposed by the Ministry of Defence minders – much later, when I handed a dispatch to a helicopter pilot for passing to 3 Commando Brigade HQ – it was never seen again. From the moment we landed at San Carlos, I either gave copy to 3 Brigade's press officer, Captain Dave Nicholls – a quietly effective mountain-warfare specialist with distant blue eyes, a shaggy Old Bill moustache, and an immense fund of charm and goodwill – or somehow hitched a lift to a ship in the anchorage equipped with Marisat facilities, and personally punched a telex tape of my dispatch. There were sixteen hours of darkness every night of the Falklands War, during which all military activity ashore except patrolling had to stop. I used many of those hours to get out to the ships and file a story, not sleeping until I had seen the telex tape clatter through the machine on transmission to London.

There was one more twist, of essential importance to what happened to me in the Falklands: from the moment of the landing, we were no longer permitted to file any dispatch exclusively to our own newspapers – all copy sent from the Falklands to the Ministry of Defence was 'pooled', and passed to every news outlet, to use as they saw fit. If I had been reporting as usual only to the *Evening Standard*, stories would have reached a relatively modest London readership. As it was, from 21 May my words began to appear in almost every newspaper in Britain. I was able to reach a vastly wider audience than any reporter could normally dream of, from the *Sun* to *The Times*. I felt a surge of single-minded passion and ambition welling up within me, which persisted through all the days that followed, even amid exhaustion and frustration. I sent stories about digging trenches and cooking arctic rations, interviews with shot-down Harrier pilots and Argentine prisoners, Falkland islanders and Rapier operators, word portraits of warships in action and marines under air attack. I knew that I must simply keep writing and filing, writing and filing about everything that befell me or which I witnessed, small or large. And so I did.

That first night, I slept with 40 Commando in their positions, shivering constantly in the icy stillness. We had all been shaken by the spectacle of the air attacks. One frigate had been sunk and four damaged. 4,000 men were now ashore, but we knew we were engaged in a deadly race between the speed of the Commando Brigade's build-up, and that at which the Argentine air force could batter the fleet. *Canberra* and a string of other ships had left the anchorage, sent to sea in whatever state of unloading they had achieved, rather than allow the enemy to find them inshore again at dawn. Henceforward, only two or three storeships at a time would anchor in San Carlos, drastically slowing the Commando Brigade's offload.

We wakened on Saturday to another beautiful day. I walked over the lank grass to one of the Rapier missile batteries on a low rise above the settlement, and stood with an NCO, gazing out on the extraordinary panorama of the anchorage. 'Never really thought we'd get to this, did we?' said a ruminative Sergeant Steve Brooks. 'At base we said – "They'll turn us round at Portsmouth." At Portsmouth we said – "They'll turn us round at Ascension." At Ascension we said – "This is where we go home." But it wasn't, was it?' Men were in subdued mood after the previous day's losses. A marine officer – I think it was Malcolm Hunt – said, 'I don't want to hear anybody moaning about that frigate sinking yesterday. What matters is that by a miracle they got just about everybody out. The Navy can build themselves some new hardware. You can't have a war without losing hardware. The Navy is just having to pay in blood, sweat and tears for some of its extra air defence.'

All that day, 22 May, we waited expectantly, uneasily, for the Argentine air force to come again. It did not. The Skyhawks' home bases were shrouded in cloud. For the landing force, it was a godsend to be able to keep the helicopters and landing craft shuttling constantly to and fro, offloading the weapons and supplies to reinforce the beachhead. But it was painfully slow work. Already the strain on the marines and the paras was becoming apparent, of living and sleeping in water-logged trenches. The men's condition must deteriorate with every day that passed. The land force had been instructed before coming ashore to deploy away from civilian buildings, to avoid making the settlements enemy targets. But it quickly became obvious that 3 Commando Brigade must use every shelter it could find, to protect as many men as possible from the climate. Those in forward positions on the hillsides had to stay where they were, their feet permanently squelching in sodden peat. But many of those close to the shore, including correspondents, moved into farm buildings. For much of the remainder of my time at San Carlos, I slept in a shearing shed, and thanked God for a place to cook and dress sheltered from the weather. Dropping one's trousers to relieve nature remained an agony, however, for every day of the war unless one was visiting a ship. For hours in advance, I dreaded growing awareness that the inevitable could not be long delayed. Unclad, within seconds the cold bit into one's most vulnerable parts. It is a fundamental fact of soldiering, that on operations a man spends hours of each day doing things which in his own home occupy only a few minutes. Building a shelter, cooking and preparing food, washing, shaving – and defecating – become infinitely complex and laborious tasks on a battlefield. In every war, men spend far more time doing these things than shooting at the enemy. Journalists are normally shielded from sharing hardship for more than a few hours, before they return to their cushy hotels. Here, it was different. We lived among the men – not as harshly as those in the forward positions, to be sure; but harshly enough for a man of thirty-six to feel every day of his age, and to get as cross as any marine if we found we had got the Arctic Ratpacks with Chicken Supreme – again.

We awoke cheerfully on Sunday, because after that wonderful lull the day before, we began to tell each other that the Argentine air force had retired from the contest. I shared breakfast in the shearing shed with Bob Fox of the BBC, always my favourite colleague. As we sniffed the reassuring scent of burning paraffin wax tablets brewing our tea, I assured him that the worst could well be over, now we had established our beachhead unopposed. Almost on cue, the first waves of Skyhawks and Mirages streaked over the Bay. It was the beginning of a terrible day. Two Landing Ships Logistics, *Lancelot* and *Galahad*, were anchored close inshore, half unloaded. Two bombs hit the former, one the latter, with a succession of dull, brutal clangs that resounded across the water to us. They failed to explode, but the civilian crews abandoned ship with what seemed to some naval officers indecent haste. The bomb-disposal teams, those extraordinary heroes, faced hours of labour under impossible strain before the weapons were defused, the ships remanned. The survival of those ships at San Carlos was one of the wonders of the campaign.

Dave Nicholls managed to fix a ride for some correspondents out to the supply ship *Stromness*, equipped with Marisat. I raced up the ladders to the radio room, where I found Brian Hanrahan and Mike Nicholson – our first meeting of the campaign. Brian was talking on a live link to BBC, so I dashed back to Foxy, telling him the good news. I sat down in the wardroom to scribble a dispatch, and wait for a turn on the link, for once impelled by no great sense of haste, in the midst of a British Sunday morning. Air raid warning red. A gaggle of correspondents scurried up the ladders to the upper deck, pulling on our helmets and anti-flash hoods, to stand watching the enemy aircraft tear past, pursued by an extraordinary array of missile streaks and automatic fire. One aircraft was hit, and crashed into the sea between the two abandoned LSLs in what Bob Fox described as 'a crescent of roaring flame'.

Later that afternoon, we saw the frigate *Antelope* steam slowly past us, bleeding smoke from a hole in her side. She seemed only moderately damaged, and anchored perhaps a quarter of a mile beyond us. We did not know that she harboured an unexploded bomb. Some correspondents departed ashore. I spent most of that day on *Stromness*, revelling in the warmth, the opportunity to gossip and to file dispatches. We had to make the most of our chances to transmit, because when *Stromness* sailed, we had no means of knowing how long it might be before another ship equipped with Marisat would anchor. Darkness was falling. We were savouring the delicacies of a hot, solid Navy meal, when there was a huge detonation. *Antelope*'s bomb had exploded, even as the Disposal men were addressing it. Only one of the team was killed, but flame and smoke poured from the stricken ship. We clustered on the deck of *Stromness*, watching fascinated, horrified, as the frigate's crew abandoned ship, the rescue operation lit by searchlights, flame, flashes, silhouetted running figures, occasional secondary explosions below. None of us, I think, had ever seen a ship sink. It was a sobering experience. Later that night, Martin Cleaver of the Press Association took one of the most dramatic photographs of the campaign, shortly before poor *Antelope* was finally engulfed by fire and blast.

We awoke on Monday morning to see the tip of the bow of the stricken frigate still visible above the surface of the bay, trapped at a vertical by an air pocket. On shore, restlessness and frustration were growing. After four days and three nights living in sodden trenches, the monotony broken only by the air attacks and occasional patrolling, more and more men were demanding: when do we move? Having gained the initiative by the brilliant success of the landing, now the campaign seemed in danger of stagnation. Only those at the summit of command understood how gravely the air attacks had impeded the planned build-up of stores, how plans to leapfrog the marines and paras by helicopter across the island had been rendered void, because every Sea King and Wessex was needed merely to move equipment and supplies.

'We aren't doing a fucking thing except get attacked by fucking planes, are we?' a 40 Commando marine huddled over his GP machine-gun, a seventeen-year-old from Dunstable named Vincent Comb, complained with irrefutable accuracy.

'How long's the war going to last, Carl?' I asked young Carl Bushby, one of 40 Commando's troop leaders, as he stood giving range orders to his mortar team. 'Two weeks,' he said, laughing, 'because that's how long Sergeant Holloway says, and he's always right about these things.' The enormous Nick Holloway contemptuously dismissed anyone who complained about the weather by telling them how much nicer it was than Norway. When I said how grateful I was to have a shearing shed to sleep in, the sergeant merely sniffed. 'Buildings,' he said. 'Who wants bloody buildings? Much too dangerous with all these bombs flying about.' Yet even some marines admitted that they found the living conditions very tough. A 35-year-old sergeant-major from Perth, a charming Scot named Billy Bowie, confided, 'I'm getting on a bit to be playing boy scouts, Max. I've got to the age where I wake up every morning, look at all my kit soaked, and start worrying about rheumatism.'

That day, the Argentines did not come. Even the next, 25 May, San Carlos was left in peace – or as peaceful as anywhere could be when the noise of helicopter movements never abated through the hours of daylight. I sent dispatches about our lives beside the anchorage, interviewed officers and men of all manner of ranks and units, and surreptitiously reinforced my own commissariat by buying some tinned food at exorbitant prices from the tiny settlement shop – surreptitiously, because if everybody else discovered its existence, the place would be cleaned out in hours. We heard rumours that 2 Para was being dispatched on a raid to Goose Green, and then that the raid had been cancelled. We had no knowledge of the fierce pressure being placed upon Julian Thompson from London to start moving, but whenever I called at Brigade headquarters in the gorse below the settlement, for all Julian's charm and comfortable pipe-smoking, the strain upon him was easy to see.

On Tuesday evening, I hitched a ride out to *Fearless*. As soon as I reached the wardroom, it was plain something disastrous had happened. Men stood huddled in little knots, gravely discussing the news: 'We've lost *Coventry* and *Atlantic Conveyor*.' Separate air attacks out at sea had destroyed a Type 42 destroyer – a dedicated air-defence ship – and a vital stores carrier, laden with helicopters and tentage, both with substantial loss of life. Colonel Tom Seccombe, Julian Thompson's second-in-command, said to me tersely as I passed him in a companionway, 'There goes Thatcher's government.' Tom, like more than a few thoughtful men in the task force, believed that public opinion at home would turn savagely against the war, in the face of bad losses. It was the grimmest evening of the campaign I can remember, the moment at which, suddenly, it seemed possible we could lose. A young marine said to me, 'Gor, if it goes on like this, we'll have to get the Yanks down to help.' I said: 'Whatever happens down here, we're going to have do it on our own.' Mike Rose came into the wardroom of *Fearless*, and listened to the conversation in silence for a few minutes. Then he said, 'I don't know why everybody's looking so sorry for themselves. Nobody sent us down here with some divine right to score all the goals. This is the way it is in wars – you win some, you lose some. It's the Argentines' day today

– tomorrow it could be ours again.' I admired Mike hugely then, and I have admired him ever since, for displaying the sort of robust sense that is so easy to produce at a staff-college seminar, yet infinitely harder in the midst of a battle, and after such a dreadful day.

Mike, forever the warrior, was among those most passionately impatient for the landing force to start moving on Stanley. He was always contemptuous of Admiral Woodward, sending bombastic signals from *Hermes* miles out at sea. 'Why doesn't Woodward try the revolutionary idea of coming to have a look for himself?' he enquired caustically. More than a few officers, some of them members of the Royal Navy, were withering about the admiral's style of command, even if they grudgingly acknowledged the necessity to keep his carriers as far as possible from the Argentine air threat. Michael Rose had been convinced from the first day of the war that the Argentines were poor soldiers, who would crumble quickly if they were hit hard. 'We're deteriorating, hanging about here in trenches day after day,' he fretted. 'We've simply *got* to get on with it.' At about this time, he also made a conscious decision that it was time the role of the SAS in the war was publicly recognized. Fortunately for me, he decided that I was an appropriate conduit. I was invited into his headquarters, a tiny corrugated-roofed hut in the settlement, and painstakingly briefed about all he thought it safe to reveal of what the SAS had been doing since the task force sailed. I typed my dispatch there and then on his table, and he checked every detail before I went out to the ships to transmit it. He believed that the families back at home in Hereford, stunned by the heavy casualties following the *Sea King* crash on 19 May, needed to know that the unit's achievement was being recognized. I did nothing very clever in being given the story, but obviously it was a marvellous scoop to send under my byline. After I had filed, the inexhaustible colonel took me for a two-mile evening walk around the shoreline at his usual breakneck pace, working off some surplus steam as we picked a path through the sad debris of battle – lifejackets, ammunition boxes, ships' wreckage, empty ration packs, fragments of sailors' kit drifting on the tide against the shingle. Rose was the only man I met in the South Atlantic who never seemed to tire, and always knew what he wanted to do next.

Early next morning, stirring some brew of oatmeal with apple flakes in a mess tin over a Hexamine cooker as we waited for the next air attacks, I decided I must leave 40 Commando, who were obviously going nowhere in a hurry. I was desperate to get out to the warships. It was at sea that the critical battle was being fought, by the frigates of the Royal Navy. The time to join the landing force would come when 3 Brigade's units began to move, and that would obviously not happen for days. Down on the shoreline, by the tent that marked the headquarters of the Rigid Raider squadron, San Carlos's vital taxi service, I persuaded somebody to give me a ride out to *Fearless*. We bounced across the bay at the usual breakneck pace of Rigid Raider coxswains, and spun into the great cavern of the command ship's dock with a whoosh like a settling mallard, as the helmsman cut the big outboard. It was strange to see the assault ship's tank deck echoing and almost empty, after so many weeks packed with vehicles and stores. In the companionway outside the operations room, I pleaded in vain with several naval staff officers to let me go to one of the frigates. They were brusquely unsympathetic. 'They're much too busy out there to bother with you.' Then I saw Jeremy Larken, the captain, sympathetic and friendly as always. I told him it seemed much more important to be telling the Royal Navy's story that day, than to be sitting ashore with the land force. He thought for a moment, then nodded. 'Hang about a bit.

I'll see what we can do.' In the blessed warmth of the superstructure, I used the pause to take a fast shower, a godsend to body and soul, and to shave properly. A sailor's ship is his home. Throughout the war, it was always an odd experience to pass from the primitive, muddy bivouacs of the men ashore into a warship cabin, decorated with books and family photographs, tiny personal comforts and – in the case of Commodore Clapp's splendid sitting room on *Fearless* – even a club-fender. Revived, I went up to the bridge in time to hear Jeremy broadcast to the ship's company, so many of whom never glimpsed the battle, at their action stations far below the waterline.

'Good morning.' His calm, crisp tones echoed through the tannoy system. 'It's quite a murky day outside, but not as murky as we should like to see it. I wanted to warn both the ship's company and our visitors what a tremendous noise a bomb makes when it explodes in the water. It's liable to make the ventilation system go "splutter-putt", caulking fall from the decking and so on. I'm simply lining you up so that if you hear a very big bang, you needn't feel the world is coming to an end.'

All over the ship, men listened at their action stations, lying or crouching or sitting in their sealed steel compartments. In the wardroom of *Fearless* a scattering of spare pilots and survivors from lost ships clustered round the loudspeaker in their life jackets and respirators. The second officer of a damaged landing ship, *Lancelot* I think, tinkled tunelessly at the piano. Jeremy finished by explaining the morning deployments. '*Broadsword* is leading the band, with *Plymouth* as goalkeeper. Rapier is in good form and bright-eyed, so let's all hope for a good day.'

A yellow dinghy drifted over the last resting place of *Antelope*, which we had watched burn on Sunday. Suddenly there was a broadcast for me. 'Max Hastings to the flight deck.

Max Hastings go immediately to the flight deck.' I hurried down the long, narrow passage below the deck, where men worked and prepared equipment in a rabbit warren of crowded little offices and workshops amid the unbroken whine of generators and ventilators. The blast of cold as one left the ship's living spaces and opened the hatch to the upper deck never ceased to inflict a moment's shock. A Lynx was poised, rotors clattering. I was gestured towards it, clambered aboard, strapped in, and whirled into the air. A few minutes later, I landed aboard *Arrow*, one of the most heavily engaged frigates of the war thus far. The holes in her boats and funnel, crudely patched with hardboard, provided mute testimony to her brushes with disaster.

Very much as I expected, most men started by asking rude questions about why no reporters had been to see them before. 'What are all you buggers doing sitting on the shore? Why are we always hearing about the land force on World Service when they're doing fuck all? We're the ones who are doing the fighting.' The lesson the Royal Navy was so slow to learn in the South Atlantic is that when men are risking their lives for a cause, they passionately want to know that what they are doing is being noticed – and that means written about and broadcast to the world. From the outset, the disdain of senior officers for the media did no service to the morale of their own men. The Navy's official contempt for publicity and those who generate it ignored the nature of this struggle, of any modern war, in which every man's ear is glued to a radio, even in action.

Arrow's upperworks looked like a scene from any of a score of Pinewood Studios' Second World War dramas at sea. Helmeted and balaclaved gunners manned 20 mm Oerlikons, Brens, GP machine-guns, even rifles and LAW anti-tank rocket launchers. Their objective was simply to throw the heaviest possible weight of metal into the sky whenever enemy aircraft attacked. When the red alert sounded for an imminent air threat, *Arrow*'s captain, Paul Bootherstone, said over the tannoy, 'Remember, when they come – give 'em hell.' How could any man avoid clichés, when this situation represented one of the most familiar British clichés of all? Attempts by the film industry to remake old classics of imperial pluck such as *The Four Feathers* and *Aces High* always founder on the inability of modern actors credibly to simulate the stiff upper lips of their grandparents. Kenneth Branagh always seemed to me risible in the role of Henry V. Kenneth Branagh could not play any of the men on the upper decks of *Arrow*.

I descended into the bowels of the ship. In the engine room, just three men presided over the great gas turbines that whined to a crescendo every few minutes, as the ship adjusted position against the tide. One of the mechanics, a 22-year-old named Ashley Baldridge, with a half-grown beard and a grin that never faltered, said he never heard a thing in action unless *Arrow*'s 4.5 inch gun fired. 'The old man said "Join the Navy and see the world." He didn't say anything about fighting wars.' I asked where the waterline was. He pointed at waist level. 'So they've got a choice – they can get us with missiles or torpedoes. Down here, ignorance is bliss,' he shouted cheerfully.

The fourth red warning of the day sounded. Paul Bootherstone gave us a running commentary over the broadcast system: 'Two waves of Mirages coming in on Bearing 320. CAP is orbiting overhead. CAP is closing on them. They are now at thirty-two miles. Heads up everybody.' The gunners tautened in their positions, the Seacat launchers traversed. In the distance we could heard gunfire. 'It sounds as if Rapier has got one. Bogeys now going west at 600 knots. CAP has turned them. Second wave of hostile aircraft has now disappeared from our screen. There are no hostile aircraft within one hundred miles of the fleet. Relax to condition yellow.'

Back ashore at San Carlos, I wrote and sent a dispatch, then wandered among the marine positions, taking a few photographs of men lying over their weapons, waiting for the next Argentine attack. An hour later, I was walking back towards them when two pairs of Skyhawks swept down the bay from opposite directions. They came so low over our heads – perhaps 150 feet – that we could read the markings on the white fuselages. A succession of objects fell from their wings. Parachutes burgeoned. In strange and terrible slow motion, I and a thousand others watched the bombs descend to earth and explode among the positions below the settlement. The shockwaves of the explosions reached me two hundred yards away. They broke the windows of houses and blew one man through a doorway without scratching him. Marines ran towards the point of impact, and began dragging out buried and wounded men. Considering the accuracy of the bombing, casualties were extraordinarily light. Yet one of those killed, by a bomb which landed almost on top of him, was a soldier I had photographed in his trench barely an hour before. All war seems unreal to those taking part, and I struggled to grasp the notion of that young man, whose living image still lay unprocessed in the camera on my chest, now living no more.

Smoke was rising from Ajax Bay, where the same wave of attackers had struck the big weapons and ammunition dump, so close to Rick Jolly's marvellous field hospital in the old mutton-freezing plant. I ran down to our friends at the Rigid Raider base on the beach and begged a ride across the water. They were as keen as I was to discover what had happened. Ten fast and wet minutes later, I was scrambling ashore in the dying afternoon light, to join a lot of unhappy and angry men. Secondary explosions from the dump were rocking the air every few minutes. 'Bastards got us in the right place this time. This'll put the cat among the pigeons for getting any big attack going.' So much kit, so many weapons carried 8,000 miles and brought ashore at such cost in effort and helicopter hours were going up in smoke before our eyes. Six men were dead and twenty-one wounded. In the hospital, chaplains moved among the injured on their stretchers, as doctors checked who needed care most urgently.

Moments of farce interrupt the tragedy of all wars. A Royal Marine coxswain spotted another Raider closing the shore and waded in his wetsuit out into the shallows in the dusk, amid the tension sporadic explosions and chaos that followed the bombing, shouting as he went, 'I can see you, Ginger, you bastard! What have you done with that fucking whisky? I know you got it, I know you nicked it! I'll kill you when I get at you!' The Raider engine died. Even as the furious NCO reached out to seize the helmsman, a grim Brigadier Julian Thompson and two accompanying staff officers stepped ashore to survey the disaster for themselves. They wisely ignored the altercation in the boat, and set off up the beach with me trailing in their wake. Obviously, correspondents could not report the hits on the Brigade Maintenance Area, nor speculate in print about the consequences for an advance across the island. But one always wanted to know.

That night, struggling to type a dispatch by torchlight in a little greenhouse back at San Carlos, I found my fingers so cold I could not master the keyboard. With a sigh, I took up the Olivetti and trudged to Pat Short's house. Sorry to bother you, I said, but could I possibly write a story in the warm? He showed me into the sitting room. Equipped with a cup of coffee and savouring the wonderful fug, I sat at Pat's table tapping away. The family were gathered around the television screen, watching a video like any one of ten million households back in Britain. It was a homely scene, after the things that each of us had witnessed that day out in the Bay – the gunfire, the air attacks, the pillars of smoke rising from Ajax Bay across the water, the young man who had died only two or three hundred yards from where we sat. Yet here was this local family, apparently uncoupled from all these experiences, who had chosen to relax amid a storm of screen bombardment and Hollywood heroics – watching *Patton: Lust for Glory.*

CHAPTER FIFTEEN

Mount Kent

SINCE LONG BEFORE the landing at San Carlos, SAS patrols had been watching the Argentine positions from hiding-up points all over East Falkland. It was their reports which caused Michael Rose to adopt such a scornful view of the enemy's capabilities. 'You can tell from the way they do everything – wash, eat, post sentries, dig trenches,' he said, 'these are not serious people. One good push and they'll roll over.' Julian Thompson and even the chronically impatient Fleet head-quarters at Northwood rejected Mike's proposals for a fast drive on Stanley. 'Mike always tended to forget that we were a one-shot force,' Julian Thompson said to me afterwards. 'It wasn't like the Second World War, where if you mounted an offensive and it failed, you could try again a couple of weeks later. We *had* to get it right first time or we were done for.' This was why Julian was so reluctant to support the 28 May assault on Goose Green by 2 Para, which Bob Fox and David Norris of the *Daily Mail* accompanied at the cost of so much hardship and peril. Although the victory at Goose Green proved of value in the end, inflicting a heavy blow on Argentine morale, Thompson thought it a diversion from the vital drive on Stanley, and thus a battle fought to appease the politicians back at home. It was plain there was not enough helicopter lift to take the brigade forward by air, as the planners had assumed from the outset. Almost everybody would have to walk. On 27 May, 3 Para and 45 Commando were launched on a long, long 'yomp' across the island, which proved every bit as hard going as their commanders had feared.

But on 30 May, Mike Rose's relentless pressure for a big move was rewarded. Using 3 Brigade's limited spare Sea King and Chinook lift, it was agreed that 42 Commando would leapfrog forward to Mount Kent, forty miles east of San Carlos, within artillery range of Moody Brook, the old Royal Marine base outside Stanley. Nick Vaux's K Company would make an initial night helicopter landing. Rose himself and some SAS reinforcements would go with them. Most of the SAS's D Squadron was already established below the summit, meeting occasional Argentine patrols but no established enemy presence. The risks of moving on to Kent remained formidable, because if the Argentines counter-attacked like a serious army, the British would be dangerously exposed for some days before a full kit of support weapons and ammunition could be lifted in. More than that, the wind and cold on the mountain made it a terrible place for men to spend long days and nights in the open. By now, however, frustration and anxiety to move were gnawing almost every man in the task force. Including me. That morning, when I heard what was to happen, I went to Michael in his little hut at San Carlos, and begged him to take me to Mount Kent. He agreed. As I began to gather my kit and rations, under no delusions about how rough it would be on the mountain, my greatest fear was that other reporters might hear about my intended outing. If they made a fuss – as they would – complained to Julian Thompson, the MoD minders and so on, it would probably be decided that it was more bother than it was worth to let me go. Yet at last light that evening, I found myself in one of the three Sea Kings flying at very low level across the island guided by pilots wearing PNG, Passive Night Goggles, those vital first-generation tools for piercing darkness, which rendered the impossible narrowly feasible. We had only been in the air twenty minutes when our helicopter swung steeply on its axis, turning back towards San Carlos. 'Sorry,' bellowed the crewman to his irate passengers. 'It's no go. We've got a "white out" up ahead. Can't see a thing. We've got to go back.' After screwing up my nerves all day for this moment, the anticlimax was bitter, of being defeated by driving snow. We landed back at the settlement and dispersed in search of somewhere to sleep. 'Sorry,' Michael said. 'Better luck next time.' But would there be a 'next time' for anyone, and especially for me? All that night and next day, I skulked around San Carlos like an escaping prisoner, fearful of seeing and being interrogated by fellow journalists. But thank God, as the light faded once more, I found myself climbing into a Sea King with Michael and a knot of SAS and Royal Marines. Professional exhilaration momentarily eclipsed the fear that had been gnawing me all day.

We had only been in the air a few minutes when the rotor note changed. Surely, surely, not another abort? Michael shouted, 'It's okay, we've just got to go into Port San Carlos to refuel and pick up more bodies.' This was the rendezvous with 42 Commando. The three helicopters landed by a settlement hut, engines stopped, and we all disembarked. I walked into the hut and saw the grinning features of Nick Vaux, 42's CO. 'Hello Max,' he said, 'what brings you here?'

'Don't tell anybody, but I seem to be going with you,' I said.

Nick said cautiously, 'Not with *us*, I think.'

'No, no, I'm with Mike Rose and his lot.'

Nick looked deeply suspicious, but agreed not to throw any spanners. I slipped away into the twilight, seeking to make myself as inconspicuous as any man of my ridiculous size ever can. Suddenly a voice called, 'Hastings! What are you doing here?' It was John Shirley of the *Sunday Times*, one of 42's designated correspondents. With him were Pat Bishop of the *Observer* and Kim Sabido of IRN. They are all delightful men, the best of company in war and peace – and the last on earth I wanted to see at that moment.

'Come on, Max, what goes on?'

I shrugged. 'I was just calling by, having a chat with Nick Vaux.'

They looked deeply suspicious. 'Hastings, you're not going to Kent, are you?'

I shrugged again. 'Depends what happens.'

'*You* can't go with 42. You've nothing to do with 42.'

'I'm with Mike Rose.'

A tide of fury was rising among my colleagues. All around us in the twilight, grim-faced men were preparing weapons and equipment to board the helicopters for an intensely risky operation. It was not hard to guess what they thought of the spectacle of four journalists on the verge of coming to blows in their midst.

'You bastard, Hastings, it's not your *turn*,' said John Shirley, jumping up and down in his rage.

'If you get on that helicopter,' said Pat Bishop, 'you will have shown yourself to be the biggest shit on this island.'

At that moment, a merciful voice shouted, 'Time to go.' I turned hastily away towards the Sea King, conscious of the laser rays of fury from colleagues striking into my back. It says a lot for the other three that the evening's events never prevented us from being the best of friends afterwards, but at that moment I was grateful they were not armed. Yes, I *was* lucky to be going to Kent. Yes, I had broken the minders' rules, by abandoning 40 Commando to whom I was supposed to be attached. But I have always thought 'rules' ludicrous in a war. The job of any journalist is always the same: to get to where the story is before his rivals. 'Pack' journalism, the philosophy of 'Buggins' turn', serves only the lowest common denominator. If one pursues this policy, however, it would be foolish to expect a hand into the lifeboat from a colleague if the ship sinks.

Once we were strapped into the Sea King, marines began to toss weapons and kit between the canvas seats – mortar rounds, Blowpipes, ammunition. By the time we lifted off, we were sitting jammed among equipment above the knee. If anything went wrong, I reflected nervously, there would be no chance of getting out quick. All through that flight in the darkness, the thrill of being there with these men at this moment see-sawed with my fear. I shouted to Mike Rose beside me: 'What happens if the Argies hit the landing zone?' He shrugged cheerfully and shouted back behind a hand cupped to my ear, 'Oh well, who dares wins.' The sangfroid of those around me calmed my own terrors. Throughout the war, I ran on pure nerves, the obsessive determination to find and tell the story overcoming exhaustion, filth, hunger, cold, fear. It was only when obliged to halt for an hour, or a night, that one or all of these things renewed their inroads upon me. The company of the men among whom I found myself – Rose, Vaux, Larken, Thompson and a host of other officers, NCOs and rankers – uplifted me. Here at last, I was at war, a British war, among the sort of heroes to whose companionship I had aspired all my life, and of which I had despaired all those years ago with the Parachute Regiment. We whirled on through the South Atlantic darkness, a few feet above the peat. I was wearing my old jump smock beneath windproofs, an earnest of the unhappy past that had become a supremely fulfilling present. For the rest of my life, some journalists would mock me for the fashion in which they believed that I had sacrificed professional integrity, by submerging my identity and my role as a reporter in the purposes of the South Atlantic task force. I have harboured no regrets. The abstract concept of fighting a war for the Falkland Islands in the last years of the twentieth century seemed ludicrous to most of those engaged in it. But in the South Atlantic, my lifelong love and admiration for the British army achieved their apogee. I found myself with the chance of telling the tale of the most remarkable British military adventure since the Second World War. I cared only that my words should match the magic of the story.

The Sea King's engine changed pitch, the aircraft descended, checked, settled, engine still turning. The door was dragged open, and men began to throw out equipment to clear a path for our own exit. Clutching my bergen, I jumped down, to glimpse tracer on the skyline. There were several brief explosions. Wholly disorientated and thoroughly frightened, I scuttled for the shelter of the nearest rocks as the helicopter lifted away into the sky. Were we under attack? As the Sea King engine faded, I could still hear desultory shooting, but it seemed quite distant. I picked myself up and looked for Michael Rose. He, in turn, was looking for his own men in the darkness. Lugging as much kit as we could carry, we made our way into the shelter of a rocky gully, where a brief torch flash revealed several men in sleeping bags. SAS. The mild, imperturbable Major Cedric Delves, OC D Squadron, emerged out of the darkness. What comfort and pleasure it provided, to meet an SAS officer who was christened Cedric. 'No problem, boss,' this gentlemanly figure told Mike. 'There was an Argie patrol up there, but we've malleted one lot, and we'll sort out the others in the morning.' Apparently the SAS stick patrolling higher up the hill had been in contact with a small party of enemy, whom it had disposed of without great difficulty. The marines' K Company, luckless fellows, set off immediately to seize and hold the summit two miles distant. They were unopposed, but they had to go through the motions of a full-dress company attack in the icy darkness. I was grateful not to have to go with them. 'Better get some sleep,' said Mike. Each of us sought a crevice among the rocks. We had made it. We were close to the summit of Mount Kent, miles ahead of any other unit of the task force save SAS patrols.

Yet that night, euphoria quickly gave way to misery. I was among the privileged, because I had a sleeping bag. The marines possessed none. They had sacrificed their personal kit to carry weapons and ammunition. I have never been so cold, before or since, as I was through those hours of darkness on Kent. Repose was impossible. I shivered relentlessly, self-pity eating into my body. Why was I the only one among all these motionless human shapes who could not sleep? Why was I here? Was any story worth this? Was I just proving to myself yet again, in the words of the contemptuous young platoon commander in Cyprus nineteen years before, that I could not 'hack it'? There was nothing to do, hour after hour, save torment myself with those thoughts as I shook with cold. I buried my head in the hood of my sleeping bag, a difficult feat since I was a foot too long for it, and sought to warm my gloved hands in my groin. I yearned to pee, but dreaded the cold outside far too much to move, and clutched my aching bladder through the small hours. God, if I can get off this damnable mountain, let me never come back. God, teach me to stop myself doing things I am not capable of. Make me learn that I am not as these men around me are, and let me stay at home in my warm house in Northamptonshire instead of clinging absurdly to the coat-tails of heroes. Olympic-class self-pitiers such as the Prince of Wales and Mr John Major would have conceded the palm to me that night. 1 a.m.,

2 a.m., 3 a.m. – would dawn never come on this damnable island?

At last it did, of course. I shook the coating of ice and snow off my sleeping bag and climbed stiffly to my feet. It was a clumsy business getting on boots, which I had clutched beside me in the bag all night. I exchanged words with other men, muttering in the half-light. I felt much better when I found that they, too, had found sleep elusive. My waterbottle contained more ice than water, but after breaking into a frozen puddle, I somehow generated enough murky liquid to toss in purifying tables and brew up. Cedric Delves descended from the ridge to go into a huddle with Michael about the night's events and his patrol clash. There was a sudden alert. Argentines had been seen moving our way. Men grabbed their weapons and took up position. Nobody was sure how many or how far away, but if they had heard us arrive in the night, they could be making a serious counter-attack. I felt absurdly impotent, standing there empty-handed among men busily preparing to fight for their lives. I picked up an Argentine FN rifle and a couple of magazines – almost the only occasion in my life as a war correspondent when I have handled a weapon. I had not the slightest wish to kill anyone, but if we were going to have a battle, I was damned if I was simply going to sit and watch. Five minutes of tension followed, then: 'Okay, everybody, stand down. Panic over. It's an SBS patrol.' We ate breakfast, and even in that cutting wind my spirits rose as the light grew and the warm food seeped into me. I photographed one of the three 105 mm guns which had been landed behind us in the darkness by Chinook, its crew labouring to camouflage and dig it in. 'We're going up the hill,' said Michael. 'Want to come?' Nick Vaux was taking his Tactical HQ up to the summit, and Michael decided to go along for the ride.

The marine Blowpipe troop was kitting up for the march,

to take position on the summit. 'You can make yourself useful, Hastings,' said Nick, pointing to the heavy, clumsy shape of a Blowpipe launcher. 'Take that with you.' It never occurred to me to decline, to plead non-combatant status, when my companions had spared precious helicopter space to lift me this far with them. I heaved the brutish thing over my shoulder and joined the long file of men threading their way up the grey scree towards the summit. It was a hard morning's hike, uninterrupted by any appearance of the enemy. We were soon sweating, even in the cold, and I found myself cursing Michael Rose's light athlete's stride over the rocks. He was five or six years older than me, but superbly fit. I hated that Blowpipe with a bitter hatred, but pride impelled me to drag it on. Then, at last, after two hours climbing, we found ourselves on the summit, gazing down upon a fantastic panorama. The roofs of Port Stanley, goal of all our hopes and purposes, were a blur in the far distance. Moody Brook was much closer, its burnt-out ruins plainly visible through our glasses, some twelve miles to the south-east. I threw down my load, and stood with Nick, Michael, the artillery Forward Observation Officer Chris Romberg and assorted marines, savouring this triumphant view.

Was Moody Brook in range? Romberg reckoned his guns could reach it on supercharge. 'Come on, let's put a few rounds into them, to show we're here,' said the irrepressible Rose. The gunner hesitated.

'You know the Chinook crashed last night, and we've got very little ammunition up here?'

'Oh, what the hell,' said Mike. 'What matters is the effect on the Argentines of finding things making very loud bangs all round them.'

Nick Vaux made up his mind and nodded to Romberg, who began to call firing orders into his signaller's handset. A few moments later, there was an obedient series of booms from our rear. Then came the distant concussions, the high puffs of dirty smoke around Moody Brook.

'That's the stuff to give them,' said Michael with complacency. 'That'll make them think,'

It also made people think back at San Carlos, where our noisy little outing caused a surge of rage towards Rose from assorted staff officers. Acutely conscious of how exposed and under-supported was our position on Kent, some of them were furious that the small force on the summit had seen fit to broadcast so unmistakably to the Argentines where we were. Vaux and Rose were unbothered. The Argentines must have known perfectly well that the British were on Kent, after last night's landing. And they were right that the enemy lacked the will or the initiative to respond. We were getting there. That morning of 1 June, we glimpsed the prospect of victory. We saw the first distant vision of the end. Michael and I set off back down the mountain, leaving the marines and Nick Vaux on the summit with many icy nights ahead of them before they were to be reunited with their sleeping bags. I soon found myself lagging well behind Rose as he moved swiftly across the grey rocks, almost dancing from one to the next, while I lumbered wearily. At last, we found ourselves back at the bivouac site. I told him I had better start looking for a ride down to San Carlos to file a dispatch. 'No problem,' he said, 'you can use my Satcom.' I was amazed. In those dim distant days before portable satellite telephones became the playthings of yuppies, I was barely aware that such equipment existed. I crawled into a tiny pup tent, in which sat a grinning SAS signaller. He spoke for a moment into his handset, then passed it to me. I took it uncertainly, and found myself talking to an officer in SAS HQ at Hereford who transcribed my dictation on a connection better than I might expect from Northampton to London. When I had finished, I said, 'Could you phone my wife and tell her I'm okay?' Then, still marvelling, I crawled out into the icy sunshine, munching a compo biscuit.

This call had three consequences. First, my wife received a baffling and perversely disturbing telephone call from somebody who said, 'I can't tell you who I am or where I'm calling from, but I have just spoken to your husband. I can't tell you where he is or what he is doing, but he is all right.' Second, the Ministry of Defence was appalled to find a correspondent's dispatch arriving from the Falklands through an SAS communications link. Their revenge was to suppress it for several days, and at last to release the copy in such truncated and mangled form that it was almost unfit for publication. Third, when word leaked out in Fleet Street that I had sent a dispatch through SAS channels, fantastic rumours began to circulate, that I was in possession of privileged communications denied to all other correspondents; indeed, some people put it about that I was travelling the Falklands with my own SAS signallers in permanent attendance. Not so. It was just the one, I am afraid. But it put a great many cats among a great many pigeons, and I remain eternally grateful for Michael Rose's generosity. I wrote in a dispatch a day or two afterwards, 'Earlier this week I had the unusual privilege – indeed I think it is almost unique for a reporter – of being the guest of men of the Special Air Service on an operation – our brilliant landing on Mount Kent. No one will be surprised to hear what impressive and delightful company they are, and how utterly confident one feels of our winning this war when watching them go about their business . . .' All right, so these were trite phrases, but they came from the heart.

Many hours of waiting later, I got a Sea King ride back to San Carlos. It was dark by the time I got out to *Fearless* to discover what was going on. I was at the limits of weariness, but also in luck. 'As Julian Thompson's ashore, you can change

in the Embarked Force Commander's cabin,' said Jeremy
Larken generously. That spacious cabin below the bridge
possessed not only a bunk, but also a bath. A bath. Tom
Seccombe happened by. 'Like a cigar?' he demanded. A cigar.
I lay for hours in that bath, smoking that cigar and reading
Gibbon. I have always loved to read incongruous books on
battlefields, as have many soldiers. I like Edward Ford's story,
of spending the day waiting to be taken off the beaches of
Dunkirk as a young Grenadier officer in 1940, reading a copy
of Homer he found among the dunes. He told me that he has
wondered ever since who left it there.

I emerged to make my way to the wardroom, where another
hack or two had turned up. I was rash enough to tell them
about my bath, which did nothing to enhance my popularity.
We sat eating the usual splendid *Fearless* dinner, complete with
a bottle of wine and the ship's TV. One of the more fantastic
features of the war was that every day, the ship's video
cameraman stood on the upper decks, filming everything that
happened around him: air attacks, sinkings, helicopter movements, *Fearless*'s routine. When he had finished, he set the tape
to music. I say again – to music. Night after night through
the campaign, after the battle had finished men sat in their
messdecks watching all that had taken place replayed before
them – many who worked below decks seeing it for the first
time – with orchestral accompaniment. In the wardroom, a
young rating wearing a T-shirt with the word 'FLUNKY'
daubed across his chest waited upon us, as if to the manner
born. I went up on deck after dinner, to see beneath us the
long black hull of the patrol submarine *Onyx* alongside, no
doubt embarking special forces for some nefarious mission. I
didn't ask what, because I wouldn't have been told. After my
night on Kent, I went to sleep in a warm and wonderfully
comfortable bunk, interrupted only by the periodic hammer

clang of scuttling charges – dropped in the sea from time to time to deter putative enemy frogmen – and thinking of my poor shivering comrades of 42, still on the summit. I felt guilty, but also very grateful.

On the morning of 3 June, Dave Nicholls told Bob Fox and me that if we wanted to see the next phase of the British advance, we would be sent to join 45 Commando at Teal Inlet. They had been advancing across the island to Mount Kent the hard way – on foot, 'yomping', to use that word which has since entered the language of the nation. Dave wasn't sure whether Foxy and I would be yomping or flying, but we should assume it would be a foot job. Although in the course of the war I did a lot of walking, it was a huge advantage denied to every soldier ashore, to be able to return to San Carlos every few days to have a shower, to dry clothes and nurse feet. With no weapon to carry, I always filled my bergen with extra rations. By contrast, 3 Para found themselves for two days without even fuel for their Hexamine cookers. They had to eat cold. In that climate, it was a bitter deprivation. An old Wessex took us to Teal, where we joined 45, the Scottish Commando from Arbroath. They had been resting up after their punishing march from San Carlos, and now they were ready to move. In long files, twenty yards between each man as a precaution against air attack, we started walking across the soggy, tussocky ground. It was hard going, but Bob and I had slept for two nights in bunks. We started dry and well fed. 45's two attached correspondents, Charlie Laurence of the *Sunday Telegraph* and little Ian Bruce of the *Glasgow Herald*, had very honourably determined to stick with their unit, even while others like Bob and I were merely pursuing the story wherever and however we could find it. Laurence and Bruce had walked from San Carlos with the Commando, and now they – and especially their feet – were in a very bad way. They had little choice save to catch a ride in one of the handful of 'BVs' – Volvo tracked vehicles – which carried the unit's heavy gear and the injured.

Within the first half-day, Foxy's and my own feet were as wet and sore as those of everyone else. Every hour, we paused to 'take ten', throw off our equipment and search out some vestige of shelter from the relentless wind, behind a rock or fold in the ground. We stuffed ourselves with biscuits and chocolate as we walked, squelching past coves and beaches, crossing enchanting rivers and fast-flowing streams which made me hanker to see them again some day, with a rod in my hand. The two men in front of me were discussing – of all things – the merits of the Ford Escort. 'You can have my pounds if you do my miles,' muttered a corporal. The task force never stopped talking derisively about its pound a day overseas allowance. We began to pass stragglers, hunched miserably beside the track. 'What's wrong with you, then?' demanded the RSM sternly. The shivering figure mumbled. 'Asthma? *Asthma?*' said the RSM in contemptuous disbelief. 'Five days yomping, and you've suddenly discovered *asthma*. Right. Wait there for the vehicles.' We moved on, meeting a terminal case of blisters or a strained tendon or flu every mile or two. 'It's all guts, though, really,' said the RSM tersely, 'or rather, the lack of them.' All but a handful of the stragglers rejoined their companies before they went into action. Our company commander passed back a furious order to spread out properly, as the sky cleared and the risk of air attack increased. 'This isn't a bloody exercise on Dartmoor.' At last light, we slumped exhausted among the marsh and tussock grass. We built bivvies with a few stakes and ponchos, and cooked a delicious hot mess of stew, peas and mashed potato. Foxy was a shockingly awful cook, so after our first breakfast together at San Carlos, I always did the Delia Smith stuff – and rather enjoyed doing so. After dusk, not a torch or candle was permitted to flicker. It was not so cold as Mount Kent. I rolled up beside Bob and slept.

We were woken long before dawn. It was a miserable business lacing sodden boots, tying a soaked sleeping bag and arctic roll on to a bergen in darkness. We set off in some dejection. Canvas webbing stiffened and shrank on our shoulders. Hair hung matted on skulls after a torrential shower. The strain of stumbling across the hillsides with weapons, linked belts, grenades, was etched into each marine's face long before evening. Men talked mostly in obscene wordbites about the fucking rain, the fucking choppers that never came for them, the fucking Argies and the fucking Falklands. They talked sometimes about women and about sex, but I have always believed this to be a mere reflex of soldiers. Given a magic wand in those circumstances, most would have settled happily for a bath, a hot meal and a warm bed alone, rather than the company of the most extravagant seductress. As usual, the coming of light brought more cheer. We stopped to make porridge and brew up, and began the slow ascent towards our objective. Helicopters clattered ceaselessly above us in the mist, shuttling forward guns and artillery ammunition for the build up. We saw occasional geese, sheep, cattle. Each creek and hill possessed some lyrical local name: Rincon de los Indios, Horse Paddocks, Halfway Cove, Letterbox Hill. A Blues and Royals' Scorpion troop came powering past us. Robin Innes-Ker popped his head out of a turret. 'What do you want me to do with this bloody typewriter of yours?' he demanded. I had asked him to stow it in his vehicle back at San Carlos. Now, I begged him to hang on to it. Bob vanished into a Gazelle somewhere in the course of the afternoon, suddenly summoned back to San Carlos on the personal orders of Jeremy Moore. I was seized by suspicion and jealousy. Was he being brought back to report some great goings-on elsewhere that I would miss out on? Bob himself never discovered the reason for his summons, but for the moment he was only grateful to have been relieved from the yomp. The rest of us marched doggedly on. Somehow, I found myself feeling better and stronger that day than at almost any moment of the war. I remembered how in Cyprus, I had not even volunteered to take a turn with my 'oppo' carrying the Bren. Now, in atonement, I asked an exhausted marine if I could spell him carrying his gimpy machine-gun. I was only half-relieved when he shook his head. In all my days as a war correspondent, few soldiers have felt cause to say anything flattering to me. But long after that yomp, I met an officer of 45, who told me that his sergeant-major had passed unfavourable judgement on the physical performance of all the journalists, with one exception. He said, so I was told, 'That big bugger Hastings is fit, though.' I cherished the compliment ever after, and always hoped the story was true.

We clambered over the last wearisome boulder falls to find ourselves in a cleft of the hill which had been designated as 45's assembly area, and sat triumphantly stirring 'beef drink' over a Hexamine. Four units of 3 Commando Brigade were now in place on the northern axis of the British advance upon Port Stanley, occupying a seven-mile-wide chain of peaks confronting the Argentine main defences, between two and five miles distant. We sat discussing the vital question: would the Brigade be launched into battle tomorrow or the day after?

A Gazelle clattered in, and from it descended the familiar figure of Julian Thompson. I strolled over to him. 'Hello, Julian,' I said breezily. 'When's the battle start, then?' 'Not for a lot longer than everybody thinks,' he answered crossly. 'We've got to wait for 5 Brigade, and we need a huge amount more kit up here.' I thought fast. If no battle was imminent, there was nothing useful for any hack to do on these mountains.

'Could you give us a ride back to San Carlos?' 'If you're quick. I'm leaving in five minutes.' I ran back to Charlie Laurence and Ian Bruce.

They said, 'We'll stay here with our lot.'

'You're crazy. There isn't going to be an Eagle Scout prize for which hack has suffered most in this war. If there isn't going to be a battle, there'll be nothing to write about here. You'll just sit and freeze.'

'We'll stay with 45.'

I shook my head, pulled on webbing, grabbed my bergen and hurried back to the Gazelle. An hour later, I was in a hot shower on board *Fearless*. Both Charlie and Ian had to be casevacced soon afterwards, stricken with the consequences of exposure. Their courage and commitment to their unit were perceived by a good many people to be in striking contrast to my own sense of expediency. But I would always do the same. It was not our job as reporters, it seemed to me, simply to share the lot of the soldiers. It was our business to tell the story, wherever this was to be found. If I had to walk, I would walk. If I had to bivouac on a mountain for a story, I would do it. But not for fun, nor comradeship, nor to show willing. The only story on those mountains for seven long days after I quitted them with Julian Thompson was one of suffering and hardship, for men enduring the extremes of wet and cold while the task force struggled to make itself ready for the decisive battle for Port Stanley.

It was almost a week since the Argentine air force had made a significant strike against the San Carlos anchorage. But after all those clear, bright days following the landing, now when good weather was desperately needed to speed the build up of stores ashore, San Carlos was whipped into white horses for many of the daylight hours, the ships pitched ceaselessly and mist clogged helicopter movements. 5 Brigade, the reinforcement from Britain, had arrived with Major-General Jeremy Moore. The unhappy struggle had begun to move its men forward across the island to form the southern axis of the British advance. An attempt by the Welsh Guards to march to Goose Green was abandoned after one day, when they simply proved unable to make it. For days to come, efforts to move 5 Brigade round the island by sea, despite the air threat, was the chief preoccupation of the British command. Around the shoreline a host of little military villages had grown up, populated by men and weapons from a variety of units with their equipment and vehicles, radio masts and latrines and camouflage netting. Poor old 40 Commando, with whom I had come ashore, still languished unhappily beside the settlement, in their role as local defence and division reserve.

The grey dawn of 5 June found me on the flight deck of *Fearless*. Clusters of muttering blue and white figures emerged from the hatches to bustle about on the wet steel, unlocking helicopter rotor blades, hosing windscreens, checking systems. Great heaps of equipment were being assembled ready for loading on the ramp leading down to the tank deck. Knots of intending passengers waited just out of the wind – staff officers, reinforcements, special forces teams with bulging bergens and exotic weapons.

Standing there in the cold, dim morning, gazing out upon the featureless ridge line above the shore, I was struck for the hundredth time by the paradox of the unseen, brightly lit world beneath our feet, the great rabbit warren of messdecks, offices, workshops, engine rooms in which 600 men were toiling, eating, sleeping. The pilots clattered down the ladder from their briefing room in the superstructure. In Britain, they flew thirty hours a month. Here, they were flying ten hours a day, often in appalling weather or under fire. I had arranged to spend the morning in the air with Simon Thornewill, who

commanded one of the Sea King squadrons, to write about
what his aircraft were doing. Simon, a personable lieutenant
commander of my own age, had been one of the men who took
us at deck level across the island on that hairy ride to Mount
Kent. 'I suppose we're all pretty tired,' he admitted. 'I had to
drag a couple of chaps out the other day to give them the day
off, because it was getting dangerous.' He ran briskly through
the cockpit checks – no co-pilots to spare now, just me beside
him up front. Today, he was moving a 105 mm battery thirty
miles forward to a new site. We heard the long whine of the
engine starting up, the hastening rattle of the rotors gathering
speed, then we lifted away from the deck and the sea, in search
of the days' cargo. We flew for fifteen minutes, then the engine
beat changed as we dropped down over the guns. Clusters of
blackened faces stared up as we descended on a muddy clearing
strewn with vehicles, stores, ammunition.

'Five feet. Four. Three. There you are.' Alf Tupper, the
crewman, talked Simon down on to his load. 'Right. Now –
taking the strain. Up we go.' With more than two tons of steel
swinging on the cable beneath the Sea King's belly, we lifted
away. Simon gazed intently towards the horizon. 'Hmm. Met
man wrong again. He said it would be a bright day. But we
could do with it a bit murkier than this. We need cloud to
hide in if the Argies show up.' It was because of the Argentines
that we flew low all the way, seldom with more than fifty feet
between the dangling gun and the ground, over broken hills
and creeks, so many of which looked indistinguishable. The
strain of flying so delicately was obviously very great. Any
violent movement made the gun swing 'like a bloody pendulum', explained Simon. He was an RAF officer's son, with
the fresh-faced athletic look of a man with no particular
troubles on his mind. Although he started his naval career at
Dartmouth, he had spent most of his time flying, some of it as

a test pilot on Sea Kings and Lynxes. At home, he lived in an old coach house in Somerset with his wife, three children and a golden retriever. Here was yet another man doing a hard and dangerous job, who nonetheless carried his responsibility light as a feather – another man I liked and admired very much.

We dropped our gun, went back for another and another. After four hours in the air, we turned back to *Fearless* to refuel. The engine never stopped turning. One of the aircraft handlers pushed a mug of coffee and a corned beef sandwich through the window to Simon. A few minutes later, we were back in the air. Later that afternoon, I was ashamed suddenly to discover that we were dropping back on to the flight deck to refuel – and I had been asleep in my seat for the past hour. I clambered stiffly out. Simon was telling Chief Tupper he reckoned they could manage another four round trips before dark. When I saw him in the wardroom that night, he said brightly that they had clocked up nine and a half hours airborne, all told.

Early on the evening of 6 June, *Fearless* steamed out of San Carlos Bay for a high-speed run through the darkness, to offload the Welsh Guards in her landing craft near Bluff Cove on the south side of East Falkland. It was almost three weeks since I had been properly at sea, and I found I had lost my sealegs. Waves of nausea attacked me as the ship rhythmically pitched and heaved. I made my way to the upper deck, to escape the fug below. *Fearless* was thrashing through the night at 20 knots, her great white wake drifting far into the sea behind us in the moonlight. It was vital for her to make the round trip and get back to the relative safety of San Carlos before first light exposed her to the enemy's air force. She was a clumsy old thing, destined for the breakers if the South Atlantic crisis had not intervened. Yet I felt a great affection and gratitude for her solid strength, the warmth and comfort of her welcome, and the remarkable capabilities of the dock and flight deck. I sat alone at the back of the superstructure for as long as I could stick the cold, watching the smoke stream past from the funnel, listening to the ceaseless throb and whine of machinery from below.

Two hours later, I was standing by the stern rail, watching 3,000 tons of water pour in to flood the dock. The stern came down, and the big LCUs crammed with Welsh Guardsmen backed away into the night headed for Bluff Cove, guided by the doughty Ewen Southby-Tailyour. We had no inkling of the travails which lay before the Guardsmen after their landing – we merely thought them lucky men to be convoyed so swiftly to their forward positions, rather than having to march across the island like 3 Brigade. I found a bunk somewhere in the bowels of the ship and slept through our return passage to San Carlos, waking in time for breakfast and a passage to the shore.

Those days were punctuated by fierce, bitter rows with the Ministry of Defence press minders on *Fearless* and elsewhere around the anchorage. All copy had to be signed off by one of them before it could be dispatched. It was a permanent source of friction, to return filthy and exhausted to the ships, desperate to file, and then have to search out a minder – which often involved hours of waiting for lifts between ships, persuading him to abandon his dinner or his bed in order to do the necessary. Most correspondents fought the minders, but perhaps I was more combative than most. I sent a stream of service messages to the *Evening Standard*, asking for the paper's support in London to have these useless mouths thrown overboard or at least out of our way. Dave Nicholls, the Royal Marine PR, was never less than totally helpful. The civilians from the MoD, by contrast, possessed no useful information or authority to help us, only considerable powers to make difficulties. One of my enraged signals provoked a minder to send a message to his London lawyers, asking them to explore the possibility of suing me for libel.

I have wasted few words in this narrative on all the hours we spent in the South Atlantic waiting – waiting for a Rigid Raider, waiting for a Marisat ship, waiting for a chopper, waiting for a line to London, waiting for an operation to start. Those are the unchanging realities of war. But when we found ourselves waiting for a warm, dry, well-rested, overfed minder, most of us exploded sooner or later. For once, it was not a mere conceit of journalists to believe that all Britain was hanging upon every word we broadcast or telexed. It was a reality which none of us forgot for a moment as we struggled manically to compile our dispatches and transmit them to London. I alone was writing an average of at least a thousand words a day.

The lack of urgency among the minders and the hostility to the media among a few task force officers was highlighted by the contrasting behaviour of the vast majority of men on the Falklands. As the days went by, I became more and more moved by the simple fact that we lived in a world in which everyone was seeking to help and support each other. It is an extraordinary experience to find oneself among thousands of people united in pursuit of a common purpose. Instead of peacetime Britain, with the competition and pettiness and selfishness which are fundamental to most of our civilian lives, here every hour men were striving to do things for each other – often, I found, to do them even for me. Wherever one went, there were offers of food, transport, a poncho, a sleeping bag, a bunk, a 'wet', a bar of 'nutty'. Hitching a ride in an LCU from the shore to a Marisat ship one icy morning, a cheery face emerged from a hatch and a Royal Marine said, 'How about some bacon and eggs, then?' He was not cooking breakfast for himself. He simply saw that I looked tired and hungry – as I usually was. I almost cried with gratitude for his kindness. And I did cry, very privately, a few days later when he and the rest of that crew were lost as their craft was strafed and sunk by Argentine aircraft on passage to Bluff Cove.

A feminist historian recently published an exceptionally foolish book, in which she suggests that men are attracted to war by the opportunity to kill people. In truth, however, insofar as some men do enjoy some conflicts, it is almost invariably because of the experience of common purpose and shared sacrifice, a comradeship unique to the circumstances of conflict. Many men find a profound appeal in the common hazard of war, not the killing. I have never forgotten a conversation with a veteran of the 1944 Normandy campaign, Andrew Wilson, who fought as a young tank officer. 'I experienced a love between men,' he said, 'which is unattainable in Anglo-Saxon society in peacetime.' He perfectly expressed the sentiments of millions of soldiers, who have found a consolation on the battlefield which is almost incomprehensible to a generation that has never known it. I wrote a piece for *The Spectator* in which I avowed my feelings about my own relationship with the task force:

> My generation of journalists . . . has described war in Indo-china and the Middle East, India and Africa if not with dispassion, at least with the disinterest of neutrals. All of us had our sympathies, and often quarrelled bitterly about them in the bars of Saigon and Tel Aviv. But the few reporters who threw in their lot wholeheartedly with either Hanoi or MACV, Jerusalem or Cairo earned at best our suspicion, at worst our contempt. I felt passionately moved by the Israeli predicament during Yom Kippur in 1973, but it was never

my war or my cause. Secure in my consciousness was the knowledge that even if the Syrian armour broke through to the Bnot Ya'akov Bridge, there would have been crumpets still for tea at home in Northamptonshire.

Yet this time, it is different. I am one of the very small number of accredited correspondents reporting a British war, that has already proved far more bitterly bloody than any of us dared to fear when we sailed from Southampton. We have watched British ships burn to the waterline and British marines and paratroopers killed by Argentine bombs and shells. Now I understand perfectly the predicament of my father's generation of war correspondents, for we have inherited it.

I would imagine there are a good many voices in London today, arguing that our reporting has been much too uncritical and indeed jingoistic. It is the reverse of everything our generation has been taught to believe that it should be doing, the nemesis of the *Insight* tradition. We have produced no revelations, very few scoops, virtually no criticism of the direction of the campaign. We have simply reported from among the ranks of the landing force, with much admiration, the manner in which the pilots and marines and paratroopers have been going about their business. Oh, that Mr Pilger might see the collected South Atlantic hacks today, blackened with cam cream and draped in bergens and web equipment – we look the very image of our role, pawns in the last fling of British imperialism. And, I have to say, secretly rather proud of it. Most of us have found great satisfaction in being able to thrust ourselves, for once in our professional lives, wholeheartedly into the service of a cause without bothering very much about moral or political dilemmas. For better or worse, we are part of British expeditionary forces 8,000 miles from home, fighting under considerable

difficulties to evict the Argentines from a cluster of islands
which feel so ridiculously British that it is hard to believe
we are not on Dartmoor, or in Sutherland or Pembrokeshire.

I have quoted that piece at length, because it subsequently
provided a focus for my critics. A number of Falklands colleagues, including some distinguished ones, said that I abused
the word 'we' in what I wrote, that I spoke for no one save
myself. Fair enough. Looking back through all my transmitted
dispatches seventeen years on, however, I do not think I told
any lies, save that sometimes I made the task force sound more
sanguine than it felt. I gave strong hints about the shortcomings and unpopularity of some senior officers, and indeed
earned the lasting enmity of Admiral Woodward by reporting
that 'however great the nation's appetite for heroes, there is no
conviction here that a new Nelson has been born'. I see no
cause today to recant the view I took in my 1982 dispatches,
that 'despite having our share of scarlet-faced majors at base
whose professional blunderings are part of every war, when
gloomy men mutter about how much is being done wrong
here, it is possible to argue with perfect sincerity that what is
remarkable is how much is being done right'. There is a school
of modern journalism, which holds that a reporter is failing in
his duty, if he speaks well of those in charge of anything. Eight
years later in the Gulf War, Robert Fisk's withering denunciations of alleged American incompetence for the *Independent*
commanded far more admiration in Fleet Street than the robust
commentaries of John Keegan, who declared in the *Daily
Telegraph* from the first day that the Coalition would win an
easy and crushing victory over Iraq. Yet it was Keegan whose
judgement was wholly vindicated by events. In the South
Atlantic, because of our intimacy with the task force, the
correspondents knew the story inside out, as do few journalists

in few modern wars. Very little of what I wrote in 1982 has been disproved by time and later evidence. Of course, many holes in our knowledge have been filled in. But if our admiration for the British performance dismayed some colleagues at home, it has been vindicated by history thus far, however fatuous the cause for which so many men on both sides were obliged to die. Our task would have become far more difficult and contentious, however, had we found ourselves confronted by the spectacle of serious British military incompetence or looming defeat.

At San Carlos, when there was nothing else to write about as we waited for the British offensive to begin, I interviewed anyone I could find willing to talk, not least the growing crowd of Argentine prisoners stowed away on board *Norland*, most taken at Goose Green. On the way south before the war, I remembered reading comments in *The Times* by V. S. Naipaul, who had spent some weeks in Argentina a short while before. Naipaul talked about the extraordinary gulf of perception and understanding between Britain and Argentina. The Argentines, he said, were forever in retreat from reality if it didn't suit them. If diplomacy failed and there was a war, he predicted, many of their people would turn around in pained astonishment and disbelief and say, 'Why on the earth did you take us so seriously? You overreacted. We never meant harm.' Naipaul said of the Argentines, 'Their gift is for fantasy.' Even when that piece was published, before the first shots were fired, I thought his remarks exceptionally shrewd and convincing. I found them all the more so now, when I talked to Argentine prisoners who spoke English. Their words of bemusement, of good intentions betrayed, matched Naipaul's expectations almost verbatim.

On the night of 8 June, I came aboard *Fearless* to learn of the devastating air attack that afternoon on the Landing Ship

Galahad at Fitzroy. Fifty-one soldiers and crew had died, scores more were wounded. *Fearless* was alerted to receive survivors. Jeremy Larken broadcast to the ship's company. 'This evening we shall be taking on board men who have been through a terrible experience. It is going to be very inconvenient for some of you, because you will have to give up your messdecks to them. But I want you to treat every man who comes into this ship not only as well as you would treat your own messmate, but better.' That night, Bob Fox and I made our way appalled among the blackened and wounded men below, retrieved from *Galahad*. I was amazed suddenly to be addressed by one of the scarecrows, unrecognizable beneath his filth and oil and rags. 'Hello, Max.' I peered, bewildered, into his face. 'Johnny Strutt.' This was the charming, impeccable 22-year-old lieutenant with whom I had chatted in the wardroom among a cluster of other Welsh Guards officers as we sailed south to disembark them in the LCUs off Bluff Cove two or three nights earlier. I could not believe what I was now seeing. In reality, fortunately, Johnny was not badly wounded, but many others were. I spoke to one terribly injured man, who mumbled through a mask of pain and bandages, 'I'm just glad to be alive.' Would this deadly business never end? We must get on and finish it.

CHAPTER SIXTEEN

Walking to Stanley

ON THE MORNING of 10 June, Robert Fox and I were warned that it was time to rejoin 3 Commando Brigade. The first phase of the attack on the hills covering Port Stanley was due to start the next night, the 11th, with simultaneous assaults on Mount Harriet by 42 Commando, on Mount Longdon by 3 Para, and on Two Sisters by 45 Commando. The weather, which had been vile for days, changed abruptly as we crossed the island by Wessex. We left behind the mist and rain of San Carlos, to meet bright sunshine shortly before we landed at Estancia House, HQ of 3 Para. A cheerful Hew Pike greeted us, and offered a guided tour of his deep dugout, prominently labelled 'Rumour Control'. In the days his battalion had been bivouacked, Hew had emplaced himself beneath several feet of earth on First World War lines. Within, his hole was festooned with union jacks, portraits of the Royal Family, and even a headed letter from Downing Street, thanking 3 Para for a message of support. Outside, his men had constructed an elaborate earth model of their objective, Mount Longdon. 3 Para were in high spirits, despite their weeks of rough living. They were confident they could crack the Argentines without too much bother. I photographed the happy scene, and took a snap of two grinning paras who walked in clutching a brace of geese they had been shooting – a favourite squaddies' sport. Months afterwards, I received a tragic letter from one of those men's mothers. She asked for a copy of the picture, because it was the last shot of her son alive before he was killed the next night, one of nineteen of Hew's men who died in his battalion's struggle for Longdon, the most costly land battle of the war. Now, I saw Hew gazing at my feet in what I can only describe as a hungry fashion.

'Where did you get those boots, Max?'

'I had them made for me in St James's ten years ago.'

'Comfortable, are they?'

'They're about the only part of me that is working absolutely perfectly.'

'Nothing like them out on the ships, is there? Practically every boot in the battalion including mine is falling to pieces.'

'Sorry, Hew, not a chance.'

'Well if anything unpleasant happens to you on this expedition, Hastings, I know which bit of you I shall be going for.'

A BV gave Foxy and me a ride up the hill to Julian Thompson's headquarters. He greeted us amicably, but flatly declined to let us attend his Brigade briefing for the battle. The journalists as a group were at that moment regarded with deep suspicion, even animosity, in some military circles. Two reporters in an imbecile moment at Teal Inlet had telephoned colleagues at Estancia House for a friendly chat on the local civilian landline about the British plan. There was uproar when this was discovered. Even when it was confirmed that the line had been cut well short of Stanley, the fact that journalists were capable of such folly said enough for most officers. This incident came after the BBC's defence correspondent in London announced over the air on 27 May that 2 Para was on its way to Goose Green. Even though no Falklands-based journalist had been involved – this shameful indiscretion was thought to have resulted from a political leak in London – at San Carlos rage towards the media was unbounded. The reporters, it was felt, had shown that they simply could not be trusted with operational information. For the rest of the war, some units would have nothing to do with any of us. I could not blame them. Today, I sometimes hear journalists argue that the media should reject censorship of any kind, when reporting wars. Yet when one's own nation is engaged, is it conceivable that any sane member of the media should want – never mind be allowed – to broadcast to the world information which could cost lives? And is it credible that journalists can be trusted to judge for ourselves what is, or is not, safe to publish? Whatever the follies of censorship in the Falklands, and there were plenty, none of the sensible journalists on the islands doubted its necessity.

We camped that night on the hillside beside Brigade HQ, and awoke to find our ponchos as well as the tussock grass lightly dusted with snow. We were contemplating the stillness with some complacency when a Sea King loaded with stores dropped in a hundred yards away, blowing our possessions in all directions across the countryside. It was the morning of Friday 11 June. Bob and I shouldered our bergens and climbed a few hundred yards across the hill to the positions of 45 Commando, whose sentries toyed with the notion of shooting us, given our ignorance of the password. But they let us through to the headquarters of Andrew Whitehead, the unit CO, a formidably tough character who showed little enthusiasm for our company. He was one of those who felt that journalists had already caused enough trouble for one war. He was about to brief his men for the battle and peremptorily ordered Foxy and me to lose ourselves. No journalists were to listen in. I was bitterly disappointed. Neither Bob nor I had any part in the telephone indiscretion at Teal Inlet, or indeed in any other security lapse. I thought we had worked our passage with 45 during the two-day yomp to the mountains. 'Oh, bugger them,' I said to Bob. 'I'm going to find 42. Nick Vaux will take me.' Bob decided to stay put.

I was lucky. Soon after, I was able to hitch a ride in a passing Wessex to the positions of 42 Commando, only ten minutes' flying time over the hill, on a barren ridge swept by unremitting wind. I trembled to think what they must have endured through the days and nights past. Sure enough, Nick greeted me kindly. Kim Sabido of IRN was already attached to the unit, but the good colonel was perfectly willing to take me, too, across the valley to Mount Harriet. Nick wrote long afterwards about the arrival of 'the gaunt frame of Max Hastings, looking as warlike and weather-beaten as the rest. Knowing his knack of judging where the most exciting action would be, I was uncertain whether to be flattered or frightened by his presence. But he seemed to have brought us luck on Mount Kent, where he and I had last seen each other.'

I settled myself to brew up, then watched Nick brief his officers for the attack. 'A numbingly cold, grey, cheerless occasion,' he wrote later. 'I was acutely conscious that I must convince these exhausted, anxious professionals that we had a sound and workable plan.' A trim, charmingly gnomic figure in camouflage windproofs and green beret, the colonel stood before an earthen model of Harriet, white-taped to mark our route. His officers sat on the rocks, huddled against the cold that bit into any man who remained still for long, blowing their mittened fingers as they listened. 'This is the decisive battle of the war,' said Nick soberly. 'Surprise and absolute silence are vital. If necessary, you must go through that old business of making every man jump up and down before he starts, to check nothing rattles. Persistent coughers must be left behind. If you find yourself in a minefield, remember you *must* go on. Men must *not* stop for their oppos, however great the temptation. They must go through and finish the attack, or it will cost more lives in the end. I won't conceal from you that the enemy is well dug in, in very strong positions. But I believe that once we get in among them, they will crack pretty quickly. We want to end up with Argies running back across those hills all the way to Port Stanley, to show the others what's coming to them.'

I stuffed away my notebook, in which I had been scribbling down Nick's words. The Commando's officers got to their feet and broke up into little clusters, each of the specialists sorting out last-minute details of signals, ammunition, resupply, casualty evacuation, prisoner handling. Then a Gazelle ferried them back to their company positions among the ridges. They had been living on the hill, often short of rations and Hexamine fuel, since the night I accompanied them to their first landing on Kent. Purifying tablets had done little to shield them from 'Galtieri's revenge', the chronic diarrhoea that resulted from drinking puddle water. They had been unshaven and scarcely washed for days. They looked battered, worn, tired – and utterly committed to the job they had to do.

We stood and waited as the last hours of daylight ebbed away. It was too cold to read or even to sit. We stamped our feet and chatted, drank tea and gazed towards that strange alien country which seemed the other side of the moon – the positions of the enemy against which we would march come nightfall. Through binos we could easily observe them on the opposite face some two miles distant. I brooded long and hard. I did not like what I saw. All through the long approach march across the valley, we would be within easy sight and range of the enemy, if they were watchful and professional. Engineers had marked paths through the Argentine minefields during many hours of nerve-stretching night patrols – how much I admired the men who had done that job. But once the Argentines detected our coming, how could they fail to bring down devastating fire upon us? That very afternoon, an enemy shell landed on 42's mortar line, killing one man and wounding several others before the battle even began. Argentine fire interrupted the silence at intervals through the afternoon with occasional airbursts, or pitched into untenanted ground below us – the ground we would have to cross come darkness. I was always at my worst when I had time to be afraid. In those hours, I worked myself up into a fever of fright. My lowest point came when Kim Sabido suddenly said to the colonel, 'Please Nick, may I go with L Company?' L, commanded by David Wheen, was a point rifle company. I was stunned by Kim's proposal. He was seeking to put himself in one of the most dangerous places in the battle. Did pride oblige me to ask to go with him? It was another moment such as that in the Reuters' office in Saigon, seven years earlier. I knew that I did not possess the bottle. I could ease my conscience by reflecting with the low cunning of experience that Kim would get no better story with a rifle company than I, five hundred yards back with Nick Vaux. As long as one could see – and God knows, we should all be able to do that – Kim would be unable to gain any unique scoop. Nick, who was as impressed by Kim's courage as I was, let him go with L. Kim got a fine yarn, but won much less kudos than he deserved for his courage in all the excitements of the days that followed. His decision to go with some of the first men up Harriet was the bravest act by a journalist in the war.

In all this tale, incidentally, television is scarcely mentioned. The reason is simple. The television reporters and cameramen did some wonderful work while the war was being fought afloat. But once it became a land campaign, they could record amazingly little. Most of the fighting took place at night, when their cameras were useless. And whatever expedients radio or press reporters like Bob Fox, Kim Sabido or I could adopt to get around the island, no man could yomp more than a few hundred yards carrying a television camera. This is one of the few wars in living memory of which no good action footage of the land fighting exists, not because the TV teams were not brave or dedicated, but because the logistical difficulties defeated them. Even when they did manage to take pictures – for instance by getting to Bluff Cove after the disastrous Argentine attack, or through the air battles at San Carlos – it was weeks before their film reached Britain by sea. No means existed in the South Atlantic for the electronic transmission of pictures because – as every journalist then supposed, and most of us still believe to this day – it suited the powers-that-be better that way, whatever the technical excuses. And, to be frank, it was a state of affairs which also suited a print reporter like myself. In this, as in almost every other respect, the Falklands was an extraordinarily old-fashioned war, probably the last of its kind the world will ever see. Just this once more, in a media now dominated by television, the wordsmiths commanded the battlefield. Our tales of the war reached a vastly more attentive audience at home than we could ever have achieved if television possessed live links. All the luck was with the likes of me.

We moved off towards Harriet in twilight, in the usual long files, which stretched far ahead and far behind. We were grateful to be marching at last, to make the deadly cold more bearable, but we knew there were four miles of open ground to cover to the start line. I thought of thousands of other men beyond our sight who were setting forth even as we were setting forth, advancing towards Two Sisters and Longdon: the gunners waiting by their pieces; the naval gunfire support ships deploying on station far out at sea; the staffs, poised tense and apprehensive by their sets and maps miles behind us – and in turn the British people waiting and watching far beyond them, 8,000 miles northward. As the darkness deepened, unexplained checks and halts to our progress lengthened. I was shivering constantly. Whenever we stopped, I adopted the wholly unmilitary resort of pulling myself into my sleeping bag. I knew that only by husbanding my strength ruthlessly, in a manner forbidden to any Royal Marine, would I get through the night.

As we marched our sodden feet turned to ice in our boots, and we cursed every delay because it brought shivering rather than rest. Then the Argentine star shells began to go up, lighting everything around us in their neon glare. We stood rock still until each brilliant glow faded. Surely, surely, the enemy must now be able to see us. Or hear us. A marine of L Company had already let off his rifle by accident, provoking the rage of Nick Vaux, indeed of the whole Commando. Yet there was no sign of automatic fire from the Argentine positions. And now, as we advanced, our own guns began to pound the objective through the darkness. The very title 'Naval Gunfire Support Officer' sounded fantastic, in the last twenty years of the twentieth century. Yet here was our NGSO Nigel Bedford, speaking coolly and matter-of-factly to the frigate *Yarmouth* almost ten miles offshore, every radio request provoking flickers of light on the horizon, followed seconds later by a series of devastating detonations amid a green glow, as *Yarmouth*'s 4.5 inch rounds landed in front of us on Harriet. Our supporting 105 mm battery provided accompaniment from the rear, salvos fizzing over in such leisurely sounding fashion that we almost expected to see the shells. Even in the darkness, flushes of dirty smoke were sometimes visible as they exploded. How could men survive up there on the objective?

A murmur ran down the column: 'Keep on the track of the

man in front. From here on, this is the only swept path through the minefield.' Perhaps there were men who did not tread daintily then, professionals who did not think about mines, but I was not among them. I placed my huge boots one by one upon the peat with a care my mother must have wished I had displayed twenty years earlier towards her herbaceous borders. I laughed nervously as Nick Vaux intervened sharply in an exchange on the radio net about a company falling behind schedule. It was not funny. L Company had strayed off the marked path through the minefield. Support Company was having trouble making contact with the Welsh Guards, who were supposed to be on 42's flank. Then a full scale firework display broke out on the horizon, as 45 Commando began its assault on Two Sisters, and 42's J Company opened up diversionary fire with full accompaniment of Milan missiles, mortars, and 'Sixty-Sixes' – hand-held anti-tank weapons. At last, the Argentine machine-guns opened up – to Nick's huge relief, firing towards J rather than K and L, who were now poised to deliver the main attack. They had half a mile to climb, after a long, circuitous approach to take Harriet from the rear. Every hundred metres, K's commander Peter Babbington murmured into the radio 'Nothing to report.' It seemed a miracle when he muttered, 'Seven hundred metres,' still without meeting fire. Then, suddenly, he called, 'One-nine. Contact. Wait. Out.' K had opened fire as soon as they spotted Argentines, waiting no longer upon the vigilance of the enemy infantry. We could see only a chaos of tracer and explosions. As usual throughout the war, fortunately, the Argentines were firing high. My own fear had ebbed away, for we were not threatened. It was the rifle companies who were engaged at close quarters, with Nick listening intently on his command net: 'One-Nine. Three. Go left. They're bugging out behind you! Use grenades. Use eighty-fours . . .'

'Sharkey. We're pinned down, for Christ's sake get a gun group here . . .'

'. . . I've lost a section commander! One of my corporals is down . . .'

The gunners were still bringing down artillery support with brilliant accuracy a few yards ahead of the assaulting marines – over a thousand shells or mortar bombs fell on the objective that night. Our attention was diverted for a moment by a small white light, moving slowly out to sea from the direction of Port Stanley. Nick said later that some of his Tac realized it was an Exocet. I did not. I merely watched with detached curiosity until there was a huge distant explosion, silhouetting the shape of a warship. The destroyer *Glamorgan*, providing fire support for 45 Commando, had been hit. At the time, deeply sobered, we believed she was sunk. In reality she somehow survived, badly wounded.

I lost track of time, but as word passed across the net about one objective after another being taken, we felt a growing exultation. It was working. With astonishingly few losses, Nick's plan had succeeded triumphantly. We began to meet prisoners being escorted down the hill, and casualties both British and Argentine. In a gully the doctor was treating wounded men by the light of a pen torch. Snow flurries dusted abandoned weapons and equipment as we passed. The first glimmers of light came, and I was climbing behind Nick Vaux and his command group into the jumble of crags which form the summit of Harriet. 'Colonel,' said a beaming Peter Bab-bington of K Company, 'I reckon we've done it . . .' Bodies and equipment, waterbottles and mess tins lay everywhere among the rocks blackened by the explosion of so many shells. Argentine 120 mm mortars and piles of bombs lay stacked, unused. 'I think we could do something with those, don't you, Mike?' said Nick to the commander of his Support Company.

'We don't have to worry about safety rules in the middle of a war.' Less agreeably, the air was polluted by the heavy stench of human excrement. The marines agreed it was a measure of the indiscipline of the enemy, that they had not bothered at all about digging latrines, but for weeks merely relieved themselves wherever they felt inclined, in the midst of their own positions.

We could still hear firing over the hill. A few wildly aimed Argentine shells were landing well short of us. Our own guns had fallen silent, after eight hours of battle. Suddenly the snow died, the early mist lifted, and we were presented with a brilliantly crisp, sunlit vision of the entire battlefield laid out before us among the rockfalls and crags and valleys. I took a photograph of a hooded marine lying with his rifle looking out towards distant Tumbledown, which later became one of the famous images of the war.

The flavour of victory, of survival, was intoxicating. 42's success, against a position the British command had expected to prove the hardest of the night to crack, had been achieved at a cost of only two killed and twenty-four wounded – almost half of whom were the unit's junior leaders. Below us, the marines were marshalling some 300 prisoners. In the distance, perhaps half a mile on, we could see clusters of ants running, running for the safety of the horizon – Argentine fugitives. The balaclava-muffled Major David Brown, our attached Battery Commander, peered through his binoculars. 'Five rounds, for effect,' he said into his handset. We heard the long sigh of the shells' passage, then saw the distant smoke plumes fall just short. Two or three seconds later, we heard the concussions. The ants ran faster. 'Height 400, one round for effect,' said the BC. There was an explosion in the midst of the ants, who scattered and ran on. 'Up 50,' said the BC. Another salvo burst among the ants. In my bourgeois way, I asked the cost of a

105 mm shell. About £250, said the major. That seemed to work out at around £5,000 an Argentine so far. What an expensive business war is. And sometimes, a very cold-blooded one. I voiced the thought aloud.

'Yes,' said Corporal Brian Evans, 'but it's a satisfying pursuit, isn't it?'

The surviving ants disappeared over the distant ridgeline. This sort of conversation, this sort of experience, was only understandable when all those concerned had just spent a night in fear for their lives beneath the enemy's guns, when the thrill of victory was fresh, when every man in the little group gazing through their binoculars knew that more hardship, more chances of death or defeat for themselves, still lay ahead. The marines who had taken Harriet so brilliantly stood or sat red-rimmed, hollow-eyed with tiredness, faces blackened with cam cream, still draped in linked-belt ammunition, grenades, in a few cases field dressings. Their boots rested in the slush beneath their feet – those poor, battered, sodden, wretched feet which caused so many men such grief in those days. It remained a mystery to us all how the Argentines had allowed Nick's rifle companies to get so close, when the defenders possessed plenty of night-vision equipment, of a quality the British could not match. The truth, we were increasingly aware, was that the Argentines were not soldiers of remotely the same quality as the Royal Marines and the Parachute Regiment.

Andrew Whitehead said after his Commando took Two Sisters, 'With fifty Royals, I could have died of old age holding this place.' And of course, he was right. The Falklands War flattered the British army, because the Argentine ground force never showed the will or competence to punish mistakes, exploit vulnerabilities, seize tactical chances, in the fashion that any first-division enemy would have done. That did not detract from the exhilaration of seeing the British forces do their business supremely well. It merely seemed tragic that so many men on both sides had to die, before the dispirited Argentine conscripts could throw down their arms.

I clambered down the hill to start looking for a ride to San Carlos and a Marisat link. In a small quarry, prisoners were being mustered, dazed and bewildered and visibly terrified for their lives. When the padre, Albert Heppenstall, appeared in his dog collar, some began to weep in the belief that he intended to give them the last rites before they were shot. They squatted, shielding themselves from the icy cold in blankets. Only the occasional dirty puff of incoming shell smoke on the road far below in the valley showed that the Argentines were continuing the war. At last I found a Wessex headed for San Carlos which would take me. I scribbled relentlessly as we flew, and kept scribbling back on *Fearless*. After a long delay hanging about in the ship's dock, I persuaded a passing Rigid Raider to take me across the anchorage to the only available Marisat ship. I punched the long telex tape of my story, handed it to the operator for transmission, then slept at last. It was 12 June.

When I awoke, beyond excitement about the success of all the night's operations, there was dismay about 3 Para's relatively heavy casualties, and apprehension about the battles to come. The next range of mountains must be taken, from Tumbledown to Wireless Ridge. Would the Argentines fight harder, as we closed on Stanley? Might they even keep fighting after the fall of the town, maintaining air attacks indefinitely against our ships? Everyone knew that the physical condition of the men of the landing force on the hills was deteriorating. They had done brilliantly well the previous night. But once again, there was no shelter in which they could now recuperate. They could only lie out in the snow and slush and relentless wind, waiting to do it all again. Time was not on our side. The pressure to finish the war before the United Nations imposed an arbitrary truce, or the task force succumbed to the terrible conditions, was very great. All that day, guns and ammunition were being shuttled, stores taken forward, in the relentless rush to get ready for the next phase, which should take the British to the brink of Stanley.

On the morning of 13 June, I flew by Gazelle to Julian Thompson's Brigade headquarters, a cluster of tents and sangars on a hillside a mile or so behind his fighting units, close to the track between Estancia and Stanley. Julian looked tired and strained, as well he might. Jeremy Moore was visiting, and the two men sat side by side on a rock, talking earnestly. Amazingly, there was a delivery of post for everybody, including correspondents. Even more astonishing, there was a package for me. Somewhere in my dispatches, I had complained about the absence of cigars on East Falkland. A kindly cigar merchant in London had posted me a box of Havanas and a half bottle of brandy. I lit up without delay. I would have kissed my benefactor if he had appeared at that moment.

A red air raid warning was alleged to be in force, but no one was taking it very seriously. Suddenly, there were jets overhead and somebody shouted, 'Get down! Here they come!' Two olive-green Skyhawks were screaming towards us. I threw myself on the ground in the Brigade air tent, among a cluster of men doing likewise. There was a succession of explosions, as 1,000 lb parachute-retarded bombs fell among us with remarkable accuracy. I lay muttering and cursing incessantly, as always when I am terrified. The Skyhawks made just two passes, then swung away over the hill. We climbed cautiously to our feet. The tents were shredded by shrapnel, vehicles and equipment all around us scarred and holed. I paced the distance to the nearest bomb crater from where we lay – 33 yards. The tail fin lay in the peat. No single incident in my life has done more to persuade me of the limitations of air power than the fact that one could lie 33 yards from the explosion of a thousand-pounder without one of us being scratched. Julian Thompson was raging. 'Where was Blowpipe?' he demanded. 'Where was bloody Blowpipe?' 'Sorry, sir,' said a crestfallen NCO. Julian exploded: 'It's like trying to shoot pheasants with a drainpipe!' We had all been thoroughly shaken, yet found ourselves curiously excited by the sensation of having survived the experience unscathed.

When something like normality had been restored, I was given my marching orders. I was to join 2 Para for their assault that night on Wireless Ridge, while the Scots Guards attacked Tumbledown. The following morning, I was to shift to 3 Para, for what everyone fervently hoped would be the last push of the war, another night attack into the approaches of Port Stanley. I gathered kit and rations. I was to be flown to 2 Para's staging area with Major Pat Butler, commander of 3 Para's Patrol Company, who was to be his battalion's liaison officer for the battle. Around noon, a Gazelle took us the few miles across the hills to the featureless expanse of grass and peat where 2 Para was ensconced, preparing for their battle. The battalion had been visited by Skyhawks that morning, from the same wave which bombed Brigade HQ. While they had suffered no casualties, their preparations for the night's operation had been set back. I was not amused when Pat Butler told me that I was to accompany him with the colonel's Tac HQ for the battle. I had earlier decided that I would watch my next action from a rather more distant seat. Tac HQ, immediately behind the forward rifle companies, was not what I had in mind at all. H Jones and half his Tac had been killed or wounded at Goose Green. But David Chaundler, who had been parachuted into the sea from Britain to take over 2 Para after

H's death, showed no enthusiasm for my company. I had had nothing to do with the battalion so far in the war, and its officers obviously regretted that they had not been sent a familiar face such as David Norris of the *Daily Mail* or Bob Fox, who had distinguished himself with them at Goose Green, and indeed was awarded a well-earned MBE for his role. Nobody showed much enthusiasm for talking to me that afternoon, far less for allowing me to attend briefings for the attack. I brewed up in the only friendly company I could find, that of Captain Roger Field of the Blues and Royals, with whom I gossiped the daylight uneasily away. He was 'spare officer' with the Scorpion troop supporting the attack – and in one of the troop's vehicles, good old Robin Innes-Ker was still carrying my typewriter.

'How's it going then?' demanded a cheery young para corporal.

'I've got a very nasty cold,' I said grumpily, 'and I shall very happy indeed if that's the worst I've got by this time tomorrow.'

Yet as men began to gather their equipment at dusk, Major Chris Keeble said, 'You're coming with me.' As second-in-command, the affable Chris would run the battalion's main HQ, with Support Company behind all the rifle groups. His position would be as safe as that of any man in the battle, if no warmer – as darkness descended, with every hour the wind and cold seemed to tighten their grip. I never spoke again to Pat Butler, but I suspect he believed that I had deliberately contrived to avoid going into battle with Chaundler's Tac. Not so – if the colonel had wanted me, I would have felt reluctantly obliged to go with him. But I was vastly, profoundly, relieved that he did not.

Once again, we were trudging across the peat, feet soaked and chilled, bergens and web equipment straining on our shoulders, jumping clumsily and vainly to avoid the deeper waterlogged holes. I still clutched the walking stick that had been my faithful support on every hike since the day of the landing. We must have advanced for some two hours, into deep darkness in which even the most agile man blundered and tripped and cursed at frequent intervals, before we crossed the start line. Quietly murmured orders sent the companies of shaggy and blackened men forward one by one on a southerly axis: 'D Company'; 'Tac One'; 'Mortar platoon', and so on. Now our guns had started to soften up the enemy positions ahead of us. Two batteries of artillery, the mortars of 3 Para as well as 2, together with naval gunfire support, were deluging, saturating the Argentine lines before the rifle companies closed with them. The only enemy response was a flurry of parachute flares. Chris Keeble established main HQ in a ruined stone sheep pen, and settled himself by the radio for a long night, astonishingly full of energy and excitement for a man who had been through so much for so many weeks, not least the temporary command of the battalion when 'H' was killed. He gave me a running commentary as we stood side by side, watching the gun flashes and the tracer, the rising crescendo of violence before us.

'This is what we call a "silent-noisy" attack – silent from the rifle companies for a bit, anyway. Right, there goes the Sustained Fire MG support' – a terrific barrage of tracer from close to our own position – 'rifle companies going in' – small arms fire ahead, punctuated by heavier metal from the Blues and Royals troop, firing 76 mm shells and 30 mm cannon, saturating the Argentines with fire, to which they responded only feebly. 'I wish we'd had this sort of back-up at Goose Green,' said Chris. Phil Neame, D company commander, called urgently for more fire on the objective as his men prepared to make their final assault. A few minutes later, he was reporting that they had seized empty bunkers. 'Looks like the Argies have legged it,' said Keeble. That afternoon, there had been an enemy company in those positions. There was no doubt the artillery barrage had been decisively successful in breaking the spirit of the defenders even before 2 Para's rifle companies closed with them. But now we began to worry about incoming shellfire, dropping into the peat behind us, as well as among the rifle companies. 'Got to find the buggers who are doing that,' said Keeble, speaking urgently into the set. To the exasperation of all the British attackers that night, most Argentine guns were firing from the midst of Port Stanley, where it was unthinkable to launch counter-battery salvos. The skyline was lit by a series of spectacular flashes. We heard an aircraft high above us. 'All these bloody shells, and now bombs,' said Chris. 'What next?' I suddenly realized that I was too tired even to be much alarmed. Anyway the rifle companies were still advancing along the ridge, reporting 'Argies legging it' in all directions. The detail of the night's events began to blur into a receding haze of gunfire, small arms and radio babble. I found I was dropping into sleep, even as I leaned against the stone wall of the sheep pen. Oblivious of care or responsibility, I lay down almost where I had been standing, and fell asleep.

I woke to find my sleeping bag and equipment encrusted in snow, like all the litter of bergens and ponchos and sleeping men in the sheepfold. It was the morning of Monday 14 June. The inexhaustible Chris Keeble was still on the handset. Dawn was breaking. I had been unconscious for three blissful hours, and I felt fantastically revived. Chris said accusingly: 'You went to sleep in the middle of our battle.' Like some serious partygoer who has stayed to the end, he regaled me with tales of the fun I had missed: there was heavy Argentine machine-gun fire in the last stages of the attack, but all companies had long since 'gone firm' on their captured positions. They were exultant, to have achieved success at very small cost – three men killed, eleven wounded. Could I go forward, I asked Chris? Of course, he said, detailing a soldier of the defence platoon to guide me, a man who had crossed the ground during the night. Desultory Argentine shells were still landing on empty peat two or three hundred yards to our right, and we could hear heavy firing of all calibres further south, where the Scots Guards were in action on Mount Tumbledown. The paras had repulsed a half-hearted Argentine counter-attack from Moody Brook, in about platoon strength. We strode away across the frozen grass, my guide chattering busily about men he knew who had been hit during the night, and the amazing helicopter pilot John Greenhalgh, who flew his Gazelle without benefit of night vision aids, to bring up ammunition and recover wounded in the midst of the battle.

We began to pass abandoned enemy positions, strewn with weapons and ammunition, clothing and food. 'Not short of much, was they?' said the para laconically. 'So much for the Navy's blockade.' We reached A Company, a few hundred yards' frontage of cheerful scarecrows surrounded by arms and equipment, their positions dotted with flickering flames from the little Hexamines on which they were brewing hot chocolate and porridge. A cluster of bedraggled prisoners sat hunched nearby, awaiting evacuation. I walked over to the parked Scorpions and Scimitars, where Robin Innes-Ker was enthusing about his troop's part in the battle. 'Did you see us? It was tremendous. We fired a hundred and fifty rounds. Once we saw somebody light a cigarette in the Argie line and that was it.' Everybody agreed that the night had been a huge success, not least because those doing the talking were still alive. On the passage south, Robin had sometimes seemed less keen on the whole venture than some of his more homicidal comrades. Now, he had entered into the spirit of the thing.

I retrieved my typewriter from his Scorpion, and sat down in an abandoned Argentine bivouac – a poncho flapping uneasily above a peat hag – to type a dispatch about 2 Para. 'Their morale is sky high,' I wrote. 'Their certainty that they have won and that the enemy is collapsing is absolute. They are very cold, very dirty, but in their mood this morning, they could march to London.' A forward gunnery observation officer came and sat beside me, asking – as every soldier asked every correspondent throughout the campaign – if I knew what was going on. I admitted my ignorance of everything save my own orders to join 3 Para that day, for what everybody hoped would be the last battle.

A cheeky eighteen-year-old private soldier from Nottingham named Bernie Bernard came and put his head under the poncho. 'Give us a cigar,' he said. I was not cheeky enough to refuse – I tossed him one, which fell into a rock crevice. He dismissed my apologies. 'If I can find my way up here in the dark and get through Goose Green,' he said, 'I can find a fucking cigar.' He lit it. 'Go on – tell them which unit did it. We did pretty good, didn't we? You get paid extra for doing this? Why does the BBC always tell everybody where we're going to attack? How many more days, do you reckon?'

Suddenly, we heard men calling to each through the latest snow shower, 'They're running away! It's on the radio! The Argies are running everywhere! Victory!' Dare Farrar-Hockley, the company commander, shouted to his platoons to be ready to move in five minutes. I pulled my dispatch from the typewriter, ran over the ridge to where I had heard a Gazelle engine idling, and thrust it into the pilot's hands, addressed optimistically to Brigade headquarters. Then I went back to gather up my own equipment.

'Do you want a lift?' came a shout from a Scimitar. It was Roger Field. I climbed clumsily up on to the hull of his beast, and clung fervently to a smoke projector as we bucketed across the hillside, shortcutting the files of paras. We halted for a few moments by one of the enemy positions captured during the night. The crew picked up a few souvenirs, and we speculated sadly about the identity of a corpse covered with a poncho, its feet encased in British-issue rubber boots. We clattered downhill until we reached the lip of the ridge. Approaching the skyline, we could see soldiers lying, standing, crouching along it, fascinated by the vision below. I thanked Roger, jumped down, and walked to join them. A few hundred feet below us lay the wreckage of a cluster of large buildings at the head of an estuary – Moody Brook, the old marine base I had last glimpsed from the summit of Mount Kent. Two or three miles down a concrete road eastward, white and innocent in the sudden sunshine, stood the little houses and churches of Port Stanley. In a few minutes this place, the climax of months of ambition, as distant as the far side of the moon at breakfast, had been transformed into a prize lying open for the taking. The soldiers, who had scarcely slept for three nights, began to chatter like schoolboys. David Chaundler started giving orders. '. . . I'm not having anybody going down that road unless the high ground is covered, so I'm getting B Company up there. The Blues and Royals will stay here and provide a firebase . . .' The first men of B were already threading their way through Moody Brook, and up the opposite hillside. The Scorpions and Scimitars deployed along the ridge, so that their fire could cover the road for miles. A Company was to march straight up the road. I trotted after Dare Farrar-Hockley.

By now, fierce and selfish ambitions were crowding into my mind. There was a chance, just a chance, that we could be first into Stanley. It would be the greatest scoop of my professional life. But what might other units be doing, on the far side of town where we could still hear firing? I did my best to wind up Dare to the risk that 45 Commando might already be approaching Stanley, that if negotiations started, our advance would be stopped in its tracks. He sent forward word to quicken the pace. With a signaller and me trailing in his wake, the major hastened up the files of the leading platoon to take up position among the point section, each man praying for the radio to remain mute. And yes, just in case you remember well enough my sorry tale of Cyprus in 1963, this Dare Farrar-Hockley was indeed the son of General Sir Anthony, the man who had commanded my miserable drop into Morphu almost thirty years before. I was conscious of the strange symmetry of the connection.

We passed a building burning opposite the seaplane jetty; abandoned vehicles; loose ammunition littering the road like sweet papers in Hyde Park. Then we were among the first demure little bungalows of the Stanley seafront. 'We've got to stop, sir, and wait for the CO!' shouted a signaller. There was a groan, then reluctant acquiescence. I was close to frenzy, fear and tiredness forgotten, with every step that we neared the town. An NCO said, 'I think I can see a Panhard moving up front.' For a moment, the men dropped into a crouch and took up tactical positions by the roadside, peering for a sight of the threatened armoured car. I cocked the Sterling I had picked up somewhere. A man with a Sixty-Six doubled forward, ready to deal with the Panhard. Nothing happened, save that a trawler began to move out across the harbour, showing a white flag. Through my binoculars, I gazed across the bay at dozens of men on the opposite hillside perhaps a mile away, idly watching our progress. We later found that these were SAS, who had taken part in a private battle of Michael Rose's the night before.

There was more excited chatter around the signallers. 'The Argies have surrendered! No one to fire except in self-defence.'

Everyone relaxed and uncocked weapons. Up the road behind us strode a knot of officers led by the colonel. 'Get in behind the colonel's party, A Company,' ordered Dare urgently. 'Nobody but A is to get in behind the colonel,' Every man who had not lost his red beret was wearing it now, passionately conscious that a unique opportunity for glory was within their reach. We marched perhaps two hundred yards further before a new message was brought to Colonel Chaundler. No British soldier was to advance beyond the racecourse, pending negotiations with the Argentines. There was a bitter murmur of disappointment. Where was the racecourse? Beside us now. There was a brief chorus about Nelson's blind eye, quickly stifled. The colonel ordered A Company to turn aside on to the green turf. Suddenly the tiredness of the men seeped through. They clattered on to the little wooden grandstand and sat down, still draped in weapons and machine-gun belts, to cheer one of their number as he clambered out on to the roof and, after some technical difficulty, tore down the Argentine flag on the little flagpole, and raised that of 2 Para. At their urging, I took a group photograph of this memorable gathering of desperadoes on the stepped benches, though my poor Nikon was giving up the ghost that morning, after the terrible battering it had received in the past weeks. Then, inevitably, men began to brew up and distribute a few cases of Argentine cigarettes they found in the starter's hut, first booty of the battle.

I wandered down to the road. It stretched empty, the cathedral clearly visible perhaps half a mile ahead. It was a peerless opportunity. I thought, very consciously: if I can walk down that road and live, I can bore everybody to death for the next twenty years talking about it. Pulling off my web equipment and camouflaged jacket and ditching the redundant Sterling, I handed them all up to Roger Field in his Scimitar, now parked in the middle of the road and adorned with a large Union Jack. I could do nothing about my face, still thickly coated in camouflage cream. I said nothing to anyone about my intentions. Then, in a blue civilian anorak and clutching my walking stick with the deliberate notion of appearing as harmless as possible, I set off towards the town. 'And where do you think you're going?' demanded the NCO in charge of the picket on the road, in the traditional voice of NCOs confronted with prospective criminals. 'I am a civilian,' I said firmly, and walked on unhindered.

Just round the bend in the road stood a large building fronted with a conservatory. This, I suddenly realized from memories of photographs, was Government House, where the first shots of the war had been fired. Its approaches were studded with Argentine bunkers. There was no sign of life. Feeling both very afraid and very foolish, I stopped, grinned towards them, raised my hands in the air – one clutching a dirty white handkerchief – and waited to see what happened. Nothing moved. Still grinning and nodding at any possible spectres within, I turned back on to the road and strode towards the Cathedral. A group of Argentine soldiers appeared. I walked up to them as they gazed curiously rather than threateningly towards me. 'Good morning,' I said with a bonhomie I did not feel. They did nothing. Then I saw a group of obviously civilian figures emerging from a large, official-looking building perhaps a hundred yards ahead. I shouted to them, 'Are you British?' They shouted back, 'Yes.' Fear ebbed away. I walked to meet them. They were kelpers – Falkland islanders – who had just emerged from the Argentine admin-istration offices. We spoke for a few moments, then they pointed me towards the Argentine colonel on the steps of the building. I introduced myself to him untruthfully as the correspondent of *The Times*, because it seemed the only English newspaper he might have heard of. We talked civilly enough for a few minutes. 'Will you surrender West and East Falkland?' I asked. 'I think so,' he said. 'But it is best to wait until your general meets General Menendez.' Could I go and talk to the British civilians, I asked? Of course, he said.

As I walked down the street, I met a succession of Falklanders. 'By God, you are welcome,' said Monsignor Daniel Spraggon, Stanley's Catholic priest, wreathed in smiles. He asked where the army was. I told him 2 Para was only a few hundred yards behind me. 'It's bloody marvellous as far as I am concerned,' said Ian Stewart, local manager of Cable and Wireless. Only four or five houses had been damaged, and three civilians killed during the battle, he said. The Argentine guns had been firing on 2 Para from the heart of Stanley the previous night. I walked on, towards that legendary Stanley hostelry The Upland Goose. A few yards down the road, I met an Argentine TV camera crew, who filmed me and then begged me to take their photograph. Years later, they sent me a photo they took that morning. I look an unconvincing representative of any victorious army, with my blackened face and filthy clothes, leaning theatrically on my walking stick. But that picture was taken at the moment at which I became sure I would live, that I would get my great story. I passed file after file of Argentine soldiers. They looked cowed, drained of hostility. Yet I did not dare to photograph them or their wounded, straggling between comrades. Officers peered curiously at me from their Mercedes vehicles. Then, at last, there it was: The Upland Goose. I walked in. 'I'm from the task force,' I said. For the first and probably last time in my life, the twenty or so people gathered inside clapped me to the bar in their joy. 'We never doubted for a moment that the British would come,' said Desmond King, the proprietor. 'We have just been waiting for the moment. Would you like a drink?' I said a whisky would be a work of genius, and emptied it in a moment.

'How about another?'

'Can you spare it?'

'We've got cases and cases in the cellar.'

At that moment, I began to suspect that the Argentines had not been entirely brutal occupiers. British troops in similar circumstances would have emptied the pub in a week.

I did not know that Jeremy Moore had issued explicit orders that no one, least of all correspondents, should enter the town. I had narrowly slipped in past his prohibition, and got my story. Now, I had to fulfil the second vital part of a reporter's job and transmit it. I walked unhindered back through the little town with all the haste I could muster, past Government House once more to the British lines. The first person I met, by the war memorial on the sea, was Julian Thompson. I told my tale, and pleaded for a helicopter to San Carlos. I could have embraced him when he nodded assent. He told a staff officer to fix it. I waited an interminable hour for that chopper. My hopes soared when a Gazelle landed, but when I dashed up to the pilot, he shook his head decisively. He had other business. A cluster of other correspondents, who had arrived with Julian, pressed scribbled stories into my hand when they knew I was heading for a Marisat. At last a Wessex pitched in. Half an hour later, I was on *Fearless*. I was told that the duty minder was on the Marisat ship, the RFA tanker *Olna*. Another half-hour later, I clambered up the rope ladder against *Olna*'s side, and ran like a madman to the radio room.

The minder on the spot put up his hand. 'Don't waste your time,' he said. 'London has imposed a complete blackout on all media transmissions, so that Mrs Thatcher can tell the House of Commons the news first.' It was a ruthless abuse of the government's powers of censorship, when Argentine radio was

THE STANDARD

Tuesday, June 15, 1982. 15p.

Incorporating the Evening News

CITY PRICES

MAX HASTINGS leads the way...

THE FIRST MAN INTO STANLEY

MAX HASTINGS in action again. . . . "I shouted: 'Are you British?' They shouted back 'Yes.'"

VICTORY

'God save the Queen'

by Frank Draper in London and Keith Durkanti in Buenos Aires

ARGENTINIAN forces on both East and West Falklands surrendered to the British land forces commander Major-General Jeremy Moore at 3 p.m. London time.

The dramatic news was contained in a message from the General to Prime Minister Mrs Thatcher today.

The message said: "In Port Stanley at 9 p.m. Falkland time, June 14, Major-General Moore accepted the surrender of all Argentinian armed forces in East and West Falklands.

The General's message continued "Arrangements are in hand to separate the men by units or sub-units and return them to Argentina and gather or place arms and ammunition will mark and make safe their munitions.

Falklands are now once under the Government desired by their inhabitants.

God save the Queen."

Talks between Jeremy Moore and Menendez is all presented through the night to arrange the formal surrender after it was put into the white flag following a brilliant and concerted dash by British parachute and infantry on the Capital.

Menendez stated terms that would not distinguish the Argentinian Army, but the British Commander was persuaded that there we are not in which Argentina forces ...

Continued Page 2, Col 4

Our day of victory...

Maggie's latest now jubilant crowds had the Prime Minister in Downing Street. Page Three.

Our home and a free standards price and can't wait to go back. Page Five.

When... crew she'd won Max Hastings on the troops reaction and the lessons we have learnt Page Seven.

THE STANDARD'S Max Hastings has led Fleet Street with his brilliant reports from the Falklands. He did it again when he was the first man into conquered Port Stanley. This is his historic dispatch.

BRITISH forces are in Port Stanley. At 2.45 p.m. British time today, men of the Parachute Regiment halted on the outskirts at the end of their magnificent drive on the capital pending negotiations.

There, we sat on the racecourse until, after about 20 minutes I was looking at the road ahead and there seemed to be no movement. I thought well I'm a civilian

so why shouldn't I go and see what's going on because there didn't seem to be much resistance.

So I stripped off all my combat clothes and I began to walk up the road with my hands in the air and my handkerchief in my hand and after about a couple of hundred yards I passed Government House which was very strongly bunkered but it appeared to be intact.

I sort of grinned at them in the hope that if there were any Argentinian soldiers manning the position they wouldn't shoot at me

Nobody took any notice so I walked on and after a few minutes I saw a group of people all looking like civilians a hundred yards ahead and I shouted at them.

I shouted "Are you British?" and they shouted back. "Yes, are you?" I said "Yes.

They were a group of civilians who had just come out of the civil administration building where they had been told that it looked as if there was going to be a ceasefire.

We chatted for a few moments and then I walked up to the building and I talked to the senior Argentinian colonel who was standing on the steps. He didn't show any evident hostility.

They were obviously pretty depressed. They looked like men who had just lost a war but I talked to them for a few moments and I said: "Are you prepared

Continued Page 2, Col 1

already broadcasting reports of a ceasefire. I was hysterical. I ranted and raved, to no avail. Kim Sabido was waiting to broadcast, in a similar state of frustration. When he heard my story, he got me to recount it to him on tape, for transmission to London when the line was reopened. Then I fell asleep.

Three hours later, I was shaken back into life. 'Thatcher's done her thing. The ban's been lifted,' said a sympathetic sailor. I had long ago punched my telex tape. I watched, delirious, as it was fed into the machine. Kim Sabido transmitted his interview with me for radio broadcast. I gave the other correspondents' dispatches to the radio operator, then walked away in a state of euphoria to find a shower and a ride back to *Fearless*. I knew that I had sent the greatest story I should ever know. 'British forces are in Port Stanley,' I began. 'At 5.45 p.m. British time today, as men of the Parachute Regiment halted on the outskirts at the end of their magnificent drive on the capital pending negotiations, I walked through the Argentine lines with my hands in the air, and met the first of the town's civilian population . . .' The *Evening Standard*'s front page banner headline on 15 June, crowning my dispatch, read: THE FIRST MAN INTO STANLEY. It was the happiest moment of my career.

Postscript

WHAT FOLLOWED WAS anticlimax, of course. It always is. There was a lot of clearing up to be done. On 15 June, I flew with a party of SBS and Michael Nicholson to Pebble Island, to report the Argentine surrender there. Back in Port Stanley, the army was struggling to round up and disarm 11,000 Argentine prisoners. I received an urgent summons to report on board *Fearless*. A Sea King was sent to fetch me. Ascending to the familiar bridge, I found Jeremy Larken. 'Well, Max,' he said, 'we've done quite a bit for you in this war. Now it's your turn to do something for us. Every soldier and marine on the islands is busy collecting souvenirs. Yet I've got several hundred men on this ship who've done just as much towards winning the war, but can't go ashore. I want to see you back on this ship tonight, with as many pistols and bayonets as you can collect.' I spent a surreal afternoon up at the airstrip, filling sack after sack with personal weapons, as dejected Argentine soldiers filed past, throwing them down in heaps. A Sea King eventually took my booty back to *Fearless*. I was happy to have paid a small part of my debt to the fine old ship and her company. Months later, I asked Jeremy what happened to all the hardware. He looked a touch embarrassed. 'Well, we were duly grateful, and handed all the stuff round. But then, when we rounded the Bay of Biscay into the Channel, sanity returned. We realized we couldn't land six hundred triumphant sailors at Portsmouth armed to the teeth. We collected the whole lot up again, and gave them the float test.'

I went to visit dear Nick Vaux at his headquarters a mile or so outside Stanley, and we exchanged memories of Mount Harriet. He was furious that the censor in London had removed all mention of 42 Commando from my dispatch, while allowing the parachute battalions to be identified. I commiserated appropriately. 'I've only one small regret, Nick,' I said sadly, 'it's all over, and I always meant to try firing a Sixty-Six.' Letting off shoulder-fired anti-tank weapons is seldom part of the recreation programme in peacetime armies. 'Mr Chisnall!' Nick called to 42's splendid regimental sergeant-major. 'Take Mr Hastings outside, and let him fire a Sixty-Six!' And so I did. Heaven knows what the geese thought.

Robin Innes-Ker of the Blues and Royals sidled up to me in Stanley. 'Tell me, Max – can you ever add personal messages to your dispatches?' Well yes, now that the war was over, one could. Did he want me to pass passionate greetings to some girlfriend? 'Er, no, actually. But could you ask somebody to ring Windsor 4543 and tell them on no account to rough off my polo ponies?'

Less happily, there was a parachute drop of several weeks' British newspapers, which were avidly read by the correspondents in the Upland Goose. There was dismay about the amount of space my dispatches had received in almost every title, as a result of the pool system. It was now that the charge was first made by some reporters in the bar, that I had conspired with allies in the marines to suppress their copy. I don't remember whether in truth I replied with a four-letter shrug, as Mike Nicholson alleges, but I hope I said something equally contemptuous. A little Glaswegian who had dined well

rushed forward wielding a bayonet. He was led away by his
mates. The *Yorkshire Post* man, though sympathetic to my
assailant's objectives, said regretfully: 'This is neither the time
nor the place to kill Max Hastings.' I understood how that
Glaswegian felt. He had been an eyewitness of the greatest
story he would cover in his life, suffered endless frustrations
and privations and, at the end of it all, gained less attention
than some great tall streak of an Englishman whom he thought
a stuck-up middle-class woofter. I was much crosser when I
got back to England, and found that one tabloid reporter had
put into print the suggestion that I had suppressed his copy. I
ran around muttering about suing him until my agent, sensible
Michael Sissons, said, 'Look, Max. You are not a popular figure
among some of your colleagues just now. A great many people
are very jealous. A lot of mud is going to be thrown. If
it deserves to stick, it will. If it doesn't, then it will all
fade away. The only sure thing, however, is that if you start
suing people, you will find yourself in a blaze of the wrong
sort of publicity that will smoulder for years.' I have never
grudged Michael his ten per cent, since he provided that
excellent piece of advice, and generally hosed me down over
lunch at Wilton's.

I suppose I should also quote Mike Nicholson's remarks
again.

Max was accused of many things in the Falklands, including
deliberately destroying other reporters' copy, which was
absurd. He had no need to; there was no competition, at
least among the newspapermen, and there were many reasons
why. He was not inclined to cooperate or to share stories and
worked harder and stayed awake longer than most. He also
made full and blatant use of his family and class connections,
he of Charterhouse and Oxford, son of Anne Scott-James and

Macdonald Hastings. Max was an officer in style and in breeding. Given the pedigree, we would have done the same!

Anyone who has read this book from the beginning will laugh heartily at a good deal of this. I learned at a very early stage in my life how sorely deficient I was in officerlike qualities. It is absolutely true, however, that I have always despised 'pack journalism', and the convention among some reporters of sharing a story around the bar, to make sure everybody gets his turn.

In the years that followed the war, the creation of academic and Whitehall reports about the media in the Falklands became a minor industry. The amount of attention devoted to our affairs seemed absurd then, and more so now. It was the war that mattered, not the coverage of it. But several media studies noted that, far from Hastings being the favourite son of the task force commanders, many senior naval and military figures would have nothing to do with me. This was true – my luck and access to action depended on the support and goodwill of a relatively small number of officers.

I consoled myself for the bickering and recriminations with a letter from my old friend John Keegan, which landed in Stanley with a parachute mail drop one day. 'Now you can do anything you like with the rest of your life,' he wrote. Kind words from John meant much to me, for I admired him so much. I flew home in the first Hercules transport to land at Stanley airport when the craters in the runway had been filled. The flight was a 28-hour marathon of air-to-air refuelling. Some marines tried to persuade me that we should share a glorious return voyage on *Canberra*, culminating in a great welcome at Southampton, but I felt able to resist that temptation, even if the cooks who had fed us on the way south were thrown aboard before we sailed home. I had had enough. Back in London, my club gave a dinner for me which I specially appreciated because of its Boot of *The Beast* overtones, but I resisted invitations to attend victory parades, reunions, or later to revisit the Falkland Islands. One should live forwards, not backwards. Perversely, perhaps, I am one of those who has felt ever since 1982 that it was right to fight the war to show that Britain was still capable of resisting aggression, but wrong not to negotiate a settlement with Argentina on sovereignty – as we should have done long before now. No big feature film has ever been made about the Falklands War, because the imperialists won and no Americans took part. I have always suspected that Hollywood would have shown an eager interest if, instead, the Argentines had driven us into the sea.

My wife and children were rather bemused by all the fuss that surrounded the war, and my role in it. My father, on the other hand, was in seventh heaven. He had been very ill while I was away, which he insisted should be concealed from me. I returned to find him surrounded by newspapers carrying my dispatches. He said, 'I just wanted to see you once again. I'm so glad I've lived to see you come back from this. Now I can die happy.' It meant everything to both of us that after all the vicissitudes of my young life, my career, my war reporting, we could both feel that I had travelled a small distance towards living up to the family reputation. He died four months later.

I took my battered old boots back to Lobb's in St James's Street, explained that they had been knocked about a bit on a walk across the Falklands, and asked if they could be mended. Absolutely, said the impassive Lobb's, most resplendent of shoemakers to the plutocracy – for me, only £500. I am afraid those boots have never been stitched together again, and now they never will be.

An old friend and rival, Simon Winchester, who had spent most of the war in prison in Argentina, said with his mischievous grin, 'I like to think, Hastings, that if I or one or two others we both know had been down there, we'd have given you a run for your money.' And of course, they would have done. In the same vein a friend said, 'Max, you must never go war corresponding any more, because you will never again be so lucky.' He was right. I was anyway growing too slow and frightened to run about on battlefields.

To my delight, of those who helped me most in the South Atlantic, Jeremy Larken became an admiral, Michael Rose, Julian Thompson and Nick Vaux all became generals. Some would say that it was miraculous they got promotion at all, after being so nice to me. A few years after the war, Nick put the wrong cartridge in his gun out pheasant shooting. The ensuing explosion blew off several of his fingers. Nick likes to tell the story of how an old beater emerged from the wood and exclaimed, 'Oh, General Nick! General Nick! Think of all those people all over the world trying to kill you all those years, and now you go and shoot yourself on your own shoot!'

In the first chapter of this book, I mentioned the miserable experience of one of my great-uncles in the First World War which killed him. Ten years after the Falklands, at a time when many of those of who had taken part were holding jolly reunions, I met a man I had known as a very young officer in the South Atlantic, who lost a foot on a mine in the last days. Naively, I supposed that far worse things could happen to anybody, that losing a foot represented a relatively minor disability. Yet when I met him, I quickly understood that the cost to his body had been far less grave than the cost to his mind. That young man's wound, which ended his military career, crippled his life and hopes for years which followed. The experience of the Falklands cast a shadow over him which remained unrelieved a decade afterwards. I came back from that encounter deeply sobered by the reminder that, if the voyage to the South Atlantic had been the greatest adventure of our lives for me and many others, there were also those for whom this war, like any war, imposed a terrible and permanent price.

I admire old colleagues and rivals who remain indefatigably warry. Robert Fox spends every hour he can contrive on Balkan battlefields, though, as he often reminds me, his birthdate fell some months before mine. I am happy now to write books about these things, and indeed Simon Jenkins and I fulfilled the promise of our hasty conversation before the task force sailed, and wrote a book about the Falklands War which became a bestseller.

As the Gulf War ended in February 1991, the Defence Secretary Tom King invited me, as editor-in-chief of the *Daily Telegraph*, to join him on a visit to the British First Armoured Division in Kuwait, along with three other editors. We flew out in pampered comfort on an aircraft of the Queen's Flight, were briefed by General Peter de la Billière, Rupert Smith and other senior officers, and toured the major units in the desert by Hercules and helicopter. There in the sands I met the *Daily Telegraph*'s own correspondent, my old friend Robert Fox, in camouflage fatigues and a suntan, looking thoroughly warry amid a leaguer of Challenger tanks. I felt a brief and tiny pang of nostalgia. Then I succumbed to gratitude that by nightfall, we should be back in air-conditioned luxury at our hotel in Riyad. I welcomed our privileged insight into the war and the British role in it, but I was content to have arrived on the battlefield after the shooting had stopped.

One sequel to this story gave me deep pleasure. On 16 February 1992, there was a great dinner in Guildhall, to celebrate the 50th anniversary of the foundation of the Parachute Regiment. I was invited, and found myself among a host of old soldiers who had done great things in faraway places over the preceding half century. Wearing my lonely Falklands Campaign Medal, I felt suitably humbled among men whose breasts glittered with gongs. The only sadness of the evening for all those veterans was the absence of the regiment's colonel-in-chief, the Prince of Wales, who had chosen instead to go off to an environmental conference, perhaps finding trees more congenial than warriors. That dinner was a marvellous occasion nonetheless, with much talk of past campaigns and legendary battles. These were men who had done much service, and I felt proud to be at their table. Suddenly, there among hundreds of names on the guest list I glimpsed that of Adrian Lee, the former colonel of 10 Para whom I had not seen since the emotional December night at White City in 1963 when I quit his battalion. I went to offer an apology for letting him down, thirty years overdue. He was as charming as ever, and assured me of forgiveness.

By a twist of fate, some years later, to my astonishment I received a letter from one of his successors, asking if I would consider becoming honorary colonel of the battalion. I was very moved, but it would have been unthinkable to accept. 'I fear,' I wrote back, 'that those members of 10 Para who knew me all those years ago would find the idea preposterous . . . So, while I am deeply touched by your suggestion, and I shall always have the warmest affection and admiration for the Parachute Regiment in general, and for 10 Para in particular, I think that for me to assume the role of honorary colonel would expose the battalion to a good deal of laughter which it doesn't need.' Yet how pleased, how very pleased, I was to have been asked. The Guildhall dinner and that invitation, though I declined it, laid many ghosts.

Less than four years after the Falklands War I became a newspaper editor, that last resort of executives and scoundrels. I have been one ever since. The company of soldiers still gives me boundless pleasure. The sight and sound of a military band always bring a lump to my throat. I do not think I shall go to the wars again, however. There are lots more things I want to do, places to see, books to write, people to meet, fish to catch, but I have heard enough gunfire. Does it sound very wicked to confess what a wonderful time I had, and how dearly I cherish the memories of those days, of the places and the men? The chief privilege was that of meeting so many fine people doing remarkable things in extraordinary places, albeit sometimes terrible ones. It is the good fortune of our generation that this country has not in our lifetimes faced a war of national survival. I and my kind have always been reporting conflicts far from our own homes which, even when they involved Britain, did not put its existence or its fabric in peril. This is a luxury denied to war-torn societies all over the world.

'Ah, horrific war,' wrote Winston Churchill as a correspondent in South Africa in 1900, 'amazing medley of the glorious and the squalid, the pitiful and the sublime, if modern men of light and leading saw your face closer, simple folk would see it hardly ever.'

I have learned one important lesson. When I was young, I valued and yearned above all things for courage, the *dono di coraggio*. Yet now I understand that physical courage comes to many young men more easily than some people recognize. This does not mean warriors do not earn their medals, only that it is less difficult than I used to suppose for the young to behave bravely on a battlefield, if they are well trained, well led and among good companions. Moral courage is much harder, more elusive and more important. Because mercifully few people have any personal military experience today, I am often asked what war is like. Men, especially, are prone to question themselves about how they would behave if put to the test, as were our parents and grandparents. The answer to that one is always the same: you would do better than you think. Most people do.

388

Index

Ranks are given as held at the time mentioned in the text.